The Bush Betrayal

ALSO BY JAMES BOVARD

AND AVAILABLE FROM PALGRAVE MACMILLAN

The Fair Trade Fraud (1991)

Lost Rights: The Destruction of American Liberty (1994)

Freedom in Chains (1999)

"Feeling Your Pain": The Explosion and Abuse of Government Power in the Clinton-Gore Years (2000)

Terrorism and Tyranny: Trampling Freedom, Justice, and Peace to Rid the World of Evil (2003)

ALSO BY JAMES BOVARD

Farm Fiasco (1989)

Shakedown (1995)

The Bush Betrayal

James Bovard

First published 2004 by
PALGRAVE MACMILLAN™
175 Fifth Avenue, New York, N.Y. 10010 and
Houndmills, Basingstoke, Hampshire, England RG21 6XS.
Companies and representatives throughout the world.

PALGRAVE MACMILLAN is the global academic imprint of the Palgrave Macmillan
division of St. Martin's Press, LLC and of Palgrave Macmillan Ltd. Macmillan® is a
registered trademark in the United States, United Kingdom and other countries. Palgrave
is a registered trademark in the European Union and other countries.

ISBN 1-4039-6727-X hardback

Cataloging-in-Publication Data is available from the Library of Congress.

A catalogue record for this book is available from the British Library.

Design by Letra Libre.

First edition: August 2004
10 9 8 7 6 5 4 3 2 1

Printed in the United States of America.

Contents

CHAPTER ONE

Introduction

As we defend liberty and justice abroad, we must always honor those values here at home.

—*George W. Bush, October 28, 2003*[1]

George W. Bush came to the presidency promising prosperity, peace, and humility. Instead, Bush has spawned record federal budget deficits, launched an unnecessary war, and made America the most hated nation in the world. Bush is expanding federal power and stretching prerogatives in almost every area that captures his fancy. Though Bush continually invokes freedom to sanctify himself and his policies, *Bush freedom* is based on boundless trust in the righteousness of the rulers and all their actions.

Truth is a lagging indicator in politics. A president's promises and speeches receive far more publicity than subsequent reports and revelations about how his cherished programs crash and burn. This book does not aim to analyze all Bush policies. Instead, it examines an array of his domestic and foreign actions that vivify the damage Bush is inflicting and the danger he poses both to America and the world.

Bush governs like an elective monarch, entitled to reverence and deference on all issues. Secret Service agents ensure that Bush rarely views opponents of his reign, carefully quarantining protesters in "free speech zones" far from public view. The FBI has formally requested that local police monitor antiwar groups and send information on demonstrators to FBI-led terrorism task forces. Thanks to the campaign finance act Bush signed, Americans have also lost much of their freedom to criticize their rulers—at least in the 60 days before an election.

After 9/11, privacy is a luxury Americans supposedly can no longer afford. The administration has left no stone unturned, giving itself powers to sweep up people's e-mail with the FBI's Carnivore system, unleash FBI agents to conduct surveillance almost anywhere, allow G-men to secretly search people's homes, bankroll Pentagon research on creating hundreds of millions of dossiers on Americans, expand the military's role in domestic surveillance, and vacuum up personal data to create a federal "color code" for every air traveler. The administration is defining freedom down, pretending that protection from federal prying is no longer relevant to liberty. Americans are supposed to accept that freedom from terrorism is the ultimate freedom—and nothing else matters any more.

Bush is dropping an iron curtain around the federal government. The Bush administration is hollowing out the Freedom of Information Act, making it more difficult for citizens to discover government actions and abuses. Bush invoked executive privilege to block a congressional investigation into the FBI's role in mass murder in Boston and in framing innocent men for those murders. The Supreme Court tacitly endorsed the Bush doctrine that the feds may carry out mass secret arrests and suppress all information about the roundup (including names of those detained, charges, and details on prison beatings).

Bush is wrapping himself in a flag drenched with the blood of Americans who died due to the failure of the federal government he commanded. The Bush reelection campaign is running television ads showing an American flag flying in front of the ruins of the World Trade Center towers and a flag-draped corpse being carried out of Ground Zero by firefighters. The Republicans will hold their national convention in New York days before the third anniversary of the terrorist attacks. Bush exploits the 9/11 dead while he stonewalls the 9/11 commission. The Bush reelection team seems convinced that Bush's actions on that day entitle Bush to rule Americans for four more years.

KING OF ALL BOONDOGGLES

Americans will be forced to pay trillions of dollars in higher taxes in the coming decades to finance George Bush's 2004 reelection campaign. Bush browbeat Congress into enacting the biggest expansion of the welfare state since Lyndon Johnson's Great Society. The White House blatantly deceived Congress about the cost of the new Medicare prescription drug entitlement, withholding key information that would have guaranteed the defeat of Bush's giveaway. The administration launched a federally financed ad campaign showing a crowd cheering Bush as he signed the new law; federal auditors ruled that the ads were illegal propaganda. The new drug benefit will expedite Medicare's bankruptcy and do nothing to improve medical care for most seniors.

Vote-buying is the prime motive of many Bush policies. Bush signed the most exorbitant farm bill in history in 2002, bilking taxpayers for $180 billion to rain benefits on millionaire landowners and other deserving mendicants. Bush repeatedly bragged that his farm bill was "generous"—as if Washington politicians have *carte blanche* to redistribute Americans' paychecks to any group they choose. Bush imposed high tariffs on steel imports, wantonly destroying thousands of American manufacturing jobs simply because he wanted to try to snare the endorsement of the United Steel Workers and to boost his reelection chances.

After 9/11, almost every expansion of government became a coup for homeland security. When Bush announced plans to bloat the AmeriCorps "paid volunteer" program, he declared: "One way to defeat terrorism is to show the world the true values of America through the gathering momentum of a million acts of responsibility and decency and service."[2] While Bush portrays AmeriCorps recruits as heroes, AmeriCorps members busy themselves putting on puppet shows to persuade three-year-olds of the value of smoke alarms, hoeing corn at tourist farms, and sanctimoniously picking up litter in bad neighborhoods. Bush summoned every citizen to give four thousand hours of "service." After dubious federal statistics showed a marginal rise in volunteering, Bush hyped the uptick as proof that his leadership is morally rejuvenating America.[3]

The Transportation Security Administration and its 45,000 member airport occupation army is one of the Bush administration's biggest shams. Despite more than $10 billion spent since 9/11, airport screeners are not any more competent than they were in 1987. Yet, as long as TSA brags about seizing millions of pointy objects each year from grandmothers and other scofflaws, Americans are supposed to believe that the endless delays are worthwhile. TSA is punishing critics, slapping fines of up to $1,500 on airline passengers guilty of showing the wrong "attitude" as they pass through TSA checkpoint gauntlets.

Some of Bush's cherished reforms consist of little more than finding new names for old boondoggles. Bush sharply boosted foreign aid and created a new program, the Millennium Challenge Account. Bush denounces traditional foreign aid for bankrolling corruption, and insists that his program rewards governments for being honest. Even though the aid still goes to many of the same Third World politician-looters, the new program's lofty rhetoric automatically converts the money into a force for goodness.

Political cosmetics pervade many Bush policies. The No Child Left Behind Act is perhaps Bush's biggest domestic fraud. The act was falsely sold as giving freedom to local school officials. In reality, it empowers the feds to effectively judge and punish local schools for not fulfilling arbitrary guidelines. Many states are "dumbing down" academic standards, using bureaucratic racketeering to avoid harsh federal sanctions. Though the No Child Left Behind Act promised to permit children to escape "persistently dangerous" schools, most states defined that term to claim that all their schools were safe. As long as people believe Bush cares about children, it doesn't matter that his education policy is a charade.

While Bush hypes himself as a "compassionate conservative," his drug policy relies on wrath and harsh punishment (except for special cases like his niece Noelle Bush and talk show host Rush Limbaugh). John Walters, Bush's drug czar, demonized drug users in federally funded TV ads, portraying people who buy drugs as terrorist financiers threatening America with complete destruction. Federal drug warriors have arrested cancer patients who smoke marijuana to control their chemo-induced nausea, busted doctors who give suffering patients more pain killers than the DEA approves, and carried out high-profile crackdowns on targets ranging from hemp food makers to comedian Tommy Chong (busted for bong trafficking).

TERRORIZING IN THE NAME OF ANTITERRORISM

Bush appears determined to force Americans to pay almost any price so that he can be a world savior. He declared in December 2003: "I believe we have a responsibility to promote freedom [abroad] that is as solemn as the responsibility is to protecting the American people, because the two go hand in hand."[4] But the Constitution does not grant the president the prerogative to dispose of the lives of American soldiers any place in the world he longs to do a good deed. Though Bush is adept at destroying freedom in America, he has yet to demonstrate any ability to create it in foreign lands.

Bush greatly exaggerates the benefits of his conquests. After the Afghan war, Bush repeatedly told Americans that they had liberated Afghan women and that Afghan girls were now going to school. Yet, women are still heavily oppressed in most of Afghanistan and most Afghan girls still do not attend schools. While Bush portrays Afghanistan as a liberated new democracy, most Afghans are brutalized either by warlords or the resurgent Taliban. But the Bush White House rarely allows cold facts to impede a warm and touching story line.

For Bush, the right to rule apparently includes the right to lie. In his 2004 State of the Union address, Bush proclaimed that, as a result of actions such as the U.S. invasion of Iraq, "No one can now doubt the word of America." A year earlier, in his 2003 State of the Union address, Bush rattled off a long list of biological and chemical weapons that he claimed he knew that Iraq possessed. No such weapons have been found. Bush has never shown a speck of contrition for his false prewar statements. Instead, he acts like a clumsy magician who assumes his audience is too feebleminded to recognize the elaborate trick that fell to pieces in front of their eyes.

The war in Iraq is the most visible debacle of the Bush war on terrorism. The president pirouetted in a flight suit on the deck of the USS *Abraham Lincoln* on May 1, 2003, in front of a giant banner proclaiming, "MISSION AC-COMPLISHED." But Iraq subsequently became far more treacherous. On July 2, when asked about Iraqi attacks on American forces, Bush issued a taunt: "Bring 'em on!" In the subsequent months, more than 600 American soldiers were killed and thousands were wounded and maimed as Iraqis took up the Bush challenge. While Bush continually brags of how the United States "liberated" 25 million Iraqis, the U.S. military government vigorously suppresses television stations and shuts down newspapers that criticize American forces or U.S. policy. While Bush rhapsodizes about winning Iraqi hearts and minds, U.S. troops carry out crackdowns with names such as Operation Iron Hammer, conduct thousands of no-knock raids in people's homes searching for weapons, routinely demolish the houses of suspected resistance fighters, imprison people solely for being relatives of insurgents, and kill hundreds of innocent civilians. Bush-style benevolence was best captured by U.S. Army Lt. Colonel Nathan Sassaman, commanding a battalion that enclosed an entire Iraqi town with barbed wire, when he observed: "With a heavy dose of fear and violence, and a lot of money for projects, I think we can convince these people that we are here to help them."[5]

Bush proudly declared last year: "No President has ever done more for human rights than I have."[6] In reality, Bush has done more to formally subvert rights than any American president of the modern era. Bush claimed the right to label people as enemy combatants and thereby nullify all of their legal rights. Once detainees had no rights, torturing them apparently became permissible—at least in the eyes of some Justice Department and Pentagon officials. The Bush administration ignored warning after warning of the gross abuses that were being committed against detainees in Afghanistan, Cuba, and Iraq. After the torture photos from the Abu Ghraib prison became public in April 2004, Bush repeatedly falsely claimed that the abuses were the result of a few wayward soldiers. In speeches in his reelection campaign, Bush continued to brag about ending Saddam's torture.

Foreign military "victories" have done nothing to increase the competence of homeland security. Even though federal agencies' failure to combine terrorist watch lists helped allow two known Al Qaeda members to enter the United States before the 9/11 hijackings, the federal government still does not have a single, up-to-date terrorist watch list. The General Accounting Office concluded in late 2003 that the feds are still doing a lousy job of pursuing terrorist finances, despite a vast increase in the financial surveillance of average Americans. A federal commission on terrorist threats reported in December 2003 that federal, state, and local government agencies are still doing a very poor job of sharing key information about terrorist threats. And some of the information that the feds do send along—such as the FBI warning that people carrying world almanacs could be terrorist plotters—aids only late-night television comics.

Bush's foreign policies are creating more terrorists than he is vanquishing. There are far more terrorist attacks in the Middle East now than before the United States invaded Iraq. Rep. Jane Harman (D-Calif.), the senior Democrat on the House Intelligence Committee, declared in early 2004 that "Al Qaeda remains as dangerous as it was before September 11."[7] British intelligence experts warn that Al Qaeda is a greater threat than before. Bush's interventionist policies and meddling are spurring intense animosity throughout the Arab and Muslim world. And there is no evidence that the Bush administration is competent to protect Americans from all the new enemies its policies are breeding.

REPEALING 1776

President George W. Bush, Attorney General John Ashcroft, and other administration officials continually remind Americans that everything changed after 9/11. But does that include the Constitution? Are the myths of 9/11 undermining the truths of 1776?

The Founding Fathers taught Americans that power is dangerous regardless of who wields it. Bush would have people believe that, after 9/11, America will perish if the president lacks boundless power. The Founding Fathers saw individual rights as bulwarks against government abuses. Bush acts as if individual rights are barriers to public safety. The Founding Fathers sought to deter tyranny with checks and balances within the federal government. Bush acts as if the only legitimate check on his power is people's chance to cast a ballot once every four years. Bush perennially talks as if tax cuts are the only protection people need against Big Government.

The Bush presidency is continuing and accelerating many of the noxious trends of the Clinton era, most of which started long before William Jefferson Clinton became president. Many of the abuses of the last few years would likely have occurred regardless of who was elected president in 2000. However, the glorification of Bush after 9/11 would not have reached such extremes without the slavish efforts of many Republican congressmen and much of the conservative news media. The president's rarely challenged power grabs revealed the cravenness of many of Washington's avowed champions of freedom.

Though this book focuses primarily on the blunders and deceits of Bush and his team, Democratic members of Congress are either complicit in or acquiescent to most of Bush's abuses. Most of the budget disputes in Washington involve how to waste tax dollars, not whether tax dollars should be wasted. Some Democrats did yeoman work—such as Sen. Robert Byrd (D-W.Va.) in opposing the war on Iraq, Sen. Russell Feingold (D-Wis.) in opposing the Patriot Act, and Rep. John Conyers (D-Mich.) in opposing Ashcroft. Yet Democratic members of Congress as a group have been less vigilant and courageous in opposing misgovernment than were Republicans during the first Clinton administration.

Regardless of who wins in November 2004, Americans must recognize the damage the federal government is inflicting on their rights, liberty, and safety. Even if Bush wins reelection, the more Americans who recognize the failures and frauds of his first term, the more difficult it will be for Bush to perpetrate new abuses in his second term. Americans must understand the Bush Betrayal if they are ever to rein in the government.

CHAPTER TWO

9/11

Canonization and Coverup

President Bush hailed the country's response to 9/11 in his State of the Union address on January 29, 2002: "It was as if our entire country looked into a mirror and saw our better selves. For too long, our culture has said, 'If it feels good, do it.' Now, America is embracing a new ethic and a new creed: 'Let's roll.' . . . We have glimpsed what a new culture of responsibility could look like. We've been offered a unique opportunity, and we must not let this moment pass."[1]

Bush portrayed 9/11 as a national moral rebirth—as if the trauma of 9/11 redeemed America's soul. The Bush administration's canonization and exploitation of 9/11 have been the central events of Bush's presidency.

There is an old Washington saying that the coverup is worse than the crime. This may not be the case when criminal negligence and incompetence left thousands of Americans dead.

Bush is not to be condemned simply because the federal government failed to stop the 9/11 hijack conspiracy. The government's antiterrorism efforts have failed many times in the past, from floundering in Beirut in 1983 to the bombing of Pan Am Flight 103 in 1988, to the first World Trade Center bombing in 1993 and the wrecking of American embassies in Africa in 1998. The 9/11 attacks might have occurred if Clinton or Gore had been president.

What made 9/11 different was the concerted effort by the Bush administration to turn 9/11 into a moral Dunkirk. Bush exploited people's grief and fear to add new fetters to American citizens, to empower federal agents to intrude further into private lives, and to seek to change the permanent balance of power between the federal government and American citizens.

"STEADY LEADERSHIP IN TIMES OF CHANGE"

The above slogan is being used in a television commercial for the Bush reelection campaign, which shows an American flag in front of the wreckage of the World Trade Center. When the ad spurred controversy, Bush reelection campaign chairman Marc Racicot declared: "Recalling this moment is about the president's record of service during a very, very difficult moment."[2] Bush reelection campaign manager Ken Mehlman declared that 9/11 was "the defining moment. . . . It's critical to who this president is."[3] White House spokesman Scott McClellan said: "September 11 changed the equation in our public policy. The president's steady leadership is vital to how we wage war on terrorism."[4]

Since Bush is campaigning for reelection in large part on his conduct on that day and in the subsequent months, his conduct demands evaluation. Bush, like every other American, is fallible. The fact that his reactions on 9/11 were not as heroic as New York City mayor Rudolph Giuliani's is not a capital offense on Bush's part. The fact that his judgment might not have been as cool as Dwight Eisenhower's on D-Day in 1944 is not sufficient to indict him. The fact that the speeches he gave were far inferior to what President Reagan would have done is neither a surprise nor necessarily damning. It was a day of shocks and many people panicked.

Three months after the attacks, Bush described the day's events to a town hall meeting in Florida: "I was sitting outside the classroom, waiting to go in, and I saw an airplane hit the tower—the TV was obviously on. And I used to fly myself, and I said, 'Well, there's one terrible pilot.'" But there was no TV footage of the first plane hitting the tower that morning. Amateur film footage of the first plane hitting the tower was not broadcast until late that day.[5]

Despite the crash of a large jetliner into the World Trade Center, Bush continued with his publicity event for his No Child Left Behind legislative proposal at an elementary school in Sarasota, Florida. Bush got ensconced in a small desk and listened as a second-grade teacher read out loud to the kids.

At 9:08 A.M., White House Chief of Staff Andrew Card walked up to the president and whispered: "A second plane hit the second tower. America is under attack." Bush's response, captured on television cameras filming the event, was classic deer-in-the-headlights.

Chief of staff Card said in 2002 that after he notified Bush, "not that many seconds later, the president excused himself from the classroom, and we gathered in the holding room and talked about the situation." However, as a *Wall Street Journal* analysis noted, "Uncut videotape of the classroom visit obtained from the local cable-TV station director who shot it, and interviews with the teacher and principal, show that Mr. Bush remained in the classroom not for mere seconds, but for at least seven additional minutes. He followed along for five minutes as children read aloud a story about a pet goat. Then he stayed for at least another two minutes, asking the children questions."[6] Presidential spokesman Dan Bartlett explained that "as the president's staff was trying to learn more about the plane crashes, there was no need to talk to Mr. Bush or pull him away." Bartlett noted that Bush's "instinct was not to frighten the children by rushing out of the room."[7]

During the time Bush sat listening to the goat story, people were burning to death in New York, while others were leaping to death from the top floors of the trade center. Bush made a brief, stumbling statement around 9:30 A.M. before leaving the scene.

Bush later proudly declared that, on the morning of 9/11, "one of the first acts I did was to put our military on alert."[8] However, Bush had no role in raising the military alert level that day. Instead, the head of the Joint Chiefs of Staff, Richard Myers, gave the order at the Pentagon with no input from Bush.[9]

Bush returned to Air Force One, which was quickly airborne on the way to Washington. However, once aloft, Bush talked to Vice President Cheney, who told him that they had received information that terrorists might be targeting the president's jet. White House press secretary Ari Fleischer announced on the following day that Bush avoided Washington for most of that day "because the information that we had was real and credible about Air Force One." White House officials later conceded that there had been no such threat; instead, it was the result of misunderstanding in a White House bunker.

White House senior advisor Karl Rove said that the president delayed returning to Washington because of reports of "three or four or five planes still outstanding" and unaccounted for as of 4 P.M. on September 11. But the Federal Aviation Administration notified the White House at 12:16 P.M. that there were no hijacked planes left in the air. A *Wall Street Journal* analysis noted that Bush "received a briefing before 1 P.M. while at an Air Force base in Barksdale, La., during which he was told that the skies were clear of any potentially hijacked planes."[10]

Bush gave a brief statement at 12:30 P.M., declaring, "Freedom, itself, was attacked this morning by a faceless coward, and freedom will be defended."[11] The "faceless coward" invocation recycled the obligatory terrorist denunciations from previous decades. *Washington Post* editor Bob Woodward, whom the Bush administration chose as the president's biographer, noted, "The president's eyes were red-rimmed when he walked in. His performance was not reassuring. He spoke haltingly, mispronouncing several words as he looked down at his notes."[12] Woodward did not specify whether Bush's eyes were red from the strain of having read too many briefing papers.

Instead of returning to Washington, Bush flew to another military base—this one in Nebraska. After Bush finally returned to the White House, he gave a televised address at 8:30 P.M. and announced that "immediately following the first attack, I implemented our government's emergency-response plans." However, Bush had nothing to do with launching such plans; instead, the Interagency Domestic Terrorism Concept of Operations Plan was activated by FBI officials. A former Bush White House official commented that Bush "was actually not involved in making decisions on 9/11 about emergency plans until he formally signed a disaster declaration" three days later, on September 14.[13]

Bush also declared in his speech: "America was targeted for attack because we're the brightest beacon for freedom and opportunity in the world." Bush announced to the world the motives of the hijackers—even before the federal government knew their identities. Bush concluded: "We go forward to defend freedom and all that is good and just in our world."[14]

THE WINDOW OF GULLIBILITY

From the first days after 9/11, the Bush administration sought to create a mythology that would spur reverence for both the president and the government. And the key to boosting respect was to suppress the truth. In the days after 9/11, Bush and his top officials repeatedly denied that the government had received prior warnings of a terrorist attack. If Americans had learned in mid-September 2001 how badly federal agencies failed across the board, the subsequent years would have been far less Leviathan-friendly.

Bush and other top officials helped sway people to rally around the government after the biggest intelligence debacle since Pearl Harbor. A poll taken in October 2001 found that the number of people feeling "very favorable" toward the government in Washington had quadrupled since before 9/11 (from 9 percent to 36 percent). The same poll showed the number of people who viewed the federal government "somewhat or very unfavorably" plunged by almost two-thirds, falling from 45 percent pre-9/11 to 16 percent after the catastrophe.[15]

The surge in trust boosted people's opinion of almost every government agency. A Gallup Poll shortly after the attacks found that, compared to one year earlier, the number of people who favorably viewed the IRS rose from 44 percent to 63 percent.[16] The number who approved of the Securities and Exchange Commission spurted 18 points, from 53 percent to 71 percent. The only federal agency with a significant fall in approval was the Federal Aviation Administration, declining from 58 percent to 54 percent. This raises the question: How many planes would have had to be hijacked before public faith in the FAA fell below 50 percent? *American Demographics* magazine summed up the pro-government poll results: "Today, love of country seems to have expanded into love of government."[17]

Many commentators exulted in how the crisis put Bush on a pedestal. R. W. Apple, the dean of the *New York Times'* Washington bureau, hailed 9/11's impact on Bush: "You could almost see him growing into the clothes of the presidency."[18] American University professor Allan Lichtman said: "It's absolutely transformed the presidency, because Bush has found purpose and meaning in what was a drifting presidency before Sept. 11."[19] The *Christian Science Monitor* proclaimed, "There's nothing like a national crisis—preferably war—to forge presidential greatness."[20]

A Gannett News Service article, headlined "God, Government Both Offer Comfort in These Times of Stress," noted: "What may have been dealt a death blow on Sept. 11 was the politics of cynicism. The government, for all its mistakes leading up to Sept. 11, is no longer such a repository of public derision."[21] The new spirit quickly captured Hollywood. The *New York Times* reported, "Not since World War II has there been such a patriotic fervor in Hollywood. . . . Scripts that denigrate the government, the Army or the C.I.A. are unlikely to see the light of day."[22]

The Bush administration applauded the rush to revere government. Vice President Cheney commented in October: "One of the things that's changed so much since Sept. 11 is the extent to which people do trust the government—big shift—and value it, and have high expectations for what we do."[23] First Lady Laura Bush announced at the National Press Club: "The cynicism and distrust with which people viewed government is replaced with a spirit of appreciation and respect for public servants, and that is healthy for our democracy."[24]

The president's team relished Bush's glory. When Bush went to New York City to throw out the first ball of Game 3 of the 2001 World Series, the crowd went wild. Biographer Bob Woodward noted, "Watching from owner George Steinbrenner's box, Karl Rove thought, It's like being at a Nazi rally."[25]

As public confidence in government soared, the Bush administration and Congress raced to capitalize on the window of gullibility. The less people knew about government incompetence, the more easily people were conned into believing that additional government power would make them safe. The Bush administration strong-armed Congress to speedily enact the Patriot Act without any substantive hearings or examination of the records of federal agencies whom the act awarded new power.

9/11 PIETY

Three days after the attacks, Bush announced in a memorial service at Washington's National Cathedral: "Our responsibility to history is already clear: To answer these attacks and rid the world of evil."[26] Though many people shrugged off the statement as irrelevant bombast, it was a clue to how much power Bush would seek and how much righteousness he would show in the coming years.

In remarks at FBI headquarters on September 25, 2001, Bush declared: "The people who did this act on America and who may be planning further acts are evil people. They don't represent an ideology. They don't represent a legitimate political group of people. They're flat evil. That's all they can think about, is evil. And as a nation of good folks, we're going to hunt them down."[27] Bush's paradigm quickly became the conventional wisdom of the post-9/11 world order.

By committing the government to a "crusade" against evil, Bush effectively transformed the government into the ultimate force for good.[28] All of the federal government's past failures became irrelevant. The simple solution was to increase the power of good—i.e., government—to vanquish evil.

The official story on 9/11 was quickly choreographed to have a happy ending—at least for Bush and the reputation of the federal government. Not a single high-ranking federal official was fired or punished for the failures of 9/11. In the weeks after 9/11, Bush visited the headquarters of the CIA and FBI to show his support. Bush gushed praise for Transportation Secretary Norman Mineta despite the failure to take measures that would have stopped the hijackers.

Bush turned 9/11 into a moral allegory. He continually invoked the story of Flight 93 to persuade Americans of the need to reform their lives:

I think the most telling event on September 11th, and one that I hope a lot of people remember, is what happened on Flight 93. Basically, what I'm saying is, it's important to serve something greater than yourself in life. It's important to serve a call greater than yourself and a cause greater than yourself. Flight 93, we had average citizens flying across the country, and they realized their plane was fixing to be used as a weapon on the Nation's Capital. They called their loved ones on the phone. They said a prayer and told them they loved them, said a prayer, and they drove the plane in the ground to serve something greater than themselves. That's the American spirit I know. That's that sense of sacrifice that makes this country so strong.[29]

Everyone not comatose during all of 2002 likely heard Bush's spiel. On March 18, 2002, Bush declared that Flight 93 would help launch a new "period of personal responsibility."[30] In Knoxville on April 8, 2002, Bush declared, "Flight 93 told me a lot about America. . . . It is that spirit that is alive and well in America, and it's that spirit that makes me so optimistic about the future of this great country."[31] At an April 29, 2002, California political fundraiser, Bush invoked Flight 93 as proof of the "new culture" of "serving something greater than yourself in life" and claimed that "Out of the evil done to America is going to come incredible good" because "we are such a good nation."[32] The next day at another fundraiser, Bush declared that "Flight 93 really, in many ways, epitomized the best of America."[33] At yet another Republican fundraiser, this one in Florida on June 21, 2002, Bush declared that Flight 93 was "the most compelling story, of course, in my judgment, after 9/11 or during 9/11."[34] And on September 17, 2002, at a school in Nashville, Bush expanded his parable to include the love of freedom: "It's a lesson of people loving freedom so much and loving their country so much, that they're willing to drive a plane into the ground to save other people's lives."[35] Yet, at the least, there was never any evidence that Flight 93 passengers chose to commit suicide (as opposed to fighting to capture control of the plane from the hijackers).

Bush's obsessive focus on Flight 93 shifted public attention to heroic citizens and away from incompetent bureaucrats. But Bush had no excuse not to know that his Flight 93 allegory was a sham. FBI director Robert Mueller told a closed congressional hearing in 2002 that Flight 93 crashed a few minutes after one of the hijackers "advised [Ziad] Jarrah [the hijacker piloting the plane] to crash the plane and end the passengers' attempt to retake the airplane."[36] An Associated Press report noted that the FBI's interpretation, "based on the government's analysis of cockpit recordings, discounts the popular perception of passengers grappling with terrorists to seize the plane's controls." No one did more to popularize the false version of events than Bush.

The FBI director's conclusion was not made public until the report of the joint congressional intelligence committees was released in late July 2003.

The FBI has refused to release the tapes of the cockpit recorder that would include the last travails on the flight. The final three minutes of the flight recorder have mysteriously vanished.[37] The government has the black box with key information about the crash but claims that it must avoid disclosing its contents because of national security. (The Justice Department initially claimed that it must keep the black box secret to save the information for revelation at the trial of Zaccarias Moussaoui, the alleged twentieth hijacker.) Some people have speculated that a U.S. jet shot down the plane after the people on board captured control from the hijackers.[38] Vice President Richard Cheney gave orders to shoot down Flight 93 at a time when it was 80 miles—barely 15 minutes—from Washington.[39] According to the Bush administration, the plane crashed before it could be shot down.

STIFFING CONGRESS

In June 2002, the House and Senate intelligence committees began joint hearings into law enforcement and intelligence failures leading to 9/11. The Bush administration fought the committees every step of the way—denying requests, stalling responses, and undermining their work whenever possible. Despite the stonewall, the committees still uncovered a vast array of evidence of failures by the FBI, CIA, the National Security Agency, and other agencies that culminated in the terrorists' success.[40]

The 858-page report of the congressional joint intelligence committees was finished in late 2002, but the Bush administration raised one objection after another before permitting it to be published. The report finally came out in late July 2003. Former Sen. Max Cleland (D-Ga.) commented, "The reason this report was delayed for so long—deliberately opposed at first, then slow-walked after it was created—is that the administration wanted to get the war in Iraq in and over . . . before [the report] came out."[41]

The report included an appendix detailing the Bush administration's efforts to thwart the investigation after it had promised the congressional investigators "complete and unprecedented" access and that federal agencies would "'bend over backwards' and 'be forward leaning' in response to requests for information made in the course of the Inquiry."[42]

No such luck.

Two of the 19 hijackers rented rooms in the home of an FBI informant in San Diego in the months before 9/11.[43] The joint inquiry sought to interview the informant "to resolve some of the inconsistencies in the informant's reporting and to better evaluate how effectively the FBI utilized the informant."[44] The Bush administration refused to permit the informant to be interviewed and also refused to disclose his whereabouts, thereby preventing Congress from subpoenaing him. The FBI agreed to permit the joint inquiry to submit written questions to its informant, but the informant refused to answer the questions.

Several officials with the CIA or other intelligence agencies who testified to the joint inquiry complained of insufficient counterterrorism budgets. The Bush administration refused to disclose whether the Office of Management and Budget—the White House's budget arm—had increased or decreased the budget requests of intelligence agencies.

The Bush administration refused to permit the joint inquiry to interview CIA director George Tenet. The CIA and other intelligence agencies "insisted that agency representatives be present to monitor all interviews of their personnel—present or former." Both the CIA and the National Security Agency refused to permit congressional investigators to make copies of their documents. The National Security Agency refused to provide more than a smattering of information on how it planned to "cope with changing technology and requirements, and how it is equipped to manage the allocation of scarce resources for research and development in the counterterrorism area." Despite the NSA's failures to translate key intercepted messages in a timely fashion before 9/11, the NSA believed that Congress had no right to know how the agency was planning (or neglecting to plan) to meet future challenges.

The Bush administration was passionately devoted to keeping secret the President's Daily Brief (PDB) of August 6, 2001. National Security Adviser Condoleeza Rice and others perennially portrayed this as simply a "historical" review of evidence of terrorist threats. The administration refused to even permit CIA personnel to discuss with congressional investigators "the simple process by which the PDB is prepared."

The Bush administration doggedly fought congressional investigators to prevent them from learning when Bush received specific warning information about terrorist plots. It was as if anything that would potentially undermine faith and trust in George W. Bush presumptively violated national security.

ANOTHER COMMISSION,
ANOTHER RATION OF TRUTH

Because the Bush administration was stonewalling the congressional investigation, 9/11 widows and other activists began pushing in mid-to-late 2002 for
an independent commission that could more vigorously and thoroughly investigate 9/11. The Bush administration and its Republican allies fought proposals for such a commission as long and as hard as possible but finally
relented in October 2002. The president managed to get severe restrictions
placed on the commission, reserving the right to appoint the commission's
chairman and weakening its subpoena power.

On Thanksgiving Eve, 2002, Bush announced his choice for chairman of
the National Commission on Terrorist Attacks on the United States—former
Secretary of State Henry Kissinger. Many people were shocked at the selection,
since Kissinger was notorious for stiffing and misleading congressional and
other investigations when he worked in the Nixon and Ford administrations.
Kissinger forfeited the chairmanship after he was pressured to reveal his list of
foreign government clients.

The commission finally got rolling in 2003. It issued a number of subpoenas to the Federal Aviation Administration and other agencies. The agencies fought to avoid responding but eventually divulged some of their precious
internal data.

Some of the commission's early work looked feckless. Aviation consultant
Michael Boyd flayed the 9/11 commission for its January 2004 hearings on aviation security. Boyd noted that the commission included five former members
of Congress—all of whom had been or should have been privy to information
on the failures of airport security prior to 9/11. Boyd noted the commission included "four members who are senior partners or officials at some of Washington's most powerful—and connected—law firms. These are people who trade
in 'who-has-access-to-who' inside the Beltway. And that means they're not
likely to take any hard aim at any current or former federal officials." The commission was further compromised because three of its members "work for law
firms that represent the airlines whose airplanes were hi-jacked on 9/11."[45]

Boyd noted that while the commission treated former FAA chief Jane Gar-
vey very courteously, they largely ignored Bogdan Dzakovic, a former leader
of an FAA elite team that carried out covert tests of airport security. In early
2002, Dzakovic publicly revealed that the FAA had long ignored his team's
blunt warnings about the pathetic state of airport security. Boyd noted that the

commission "treated this man as if he were a copier salesman that entered the room by mistake. Here's a hero that has had his career destroyed simply by being an honest whistleblower trying to protect the public."[46]

HITTING THE PAVLOV BUTTON

The more Bush was praised after 9/11, the more swollen his ego became. Bush eventually became convinced that he had been a great leader on that day.

In March 2004, the Bush reelection campaign launched television ads using 9/11 images to rally support for the president. One advertisement, entitled "Safer, Stronger," showed firemen carrying a flag-draped corpse from the rubble at Ground Zero. A second ad, featuring the motto "Tested," began with a statement from the president—"I'm George Bush and I approve this message." An announcer then informed viewers: "The last few years have tested America in many ways. Some challenges we've seen before. And some were like no others. But America rose to the challenge. . . . Freedom, faith, families, and sacrifice. President Bush. Steady leadership in times of change."[47]

The commercials provoked harsh criticism from 9/11 widows, widowers, and other family survivors. At the same time Bush exploited the flag-draped corpse from 9/11, he continued prohibiting any pictures of flag-draped coffins of American servicemen and women either leaving Iraq or arriving back in the United States at Dover Air Force Base.

Republican operatives wasted no time smearing the critics. Conservative talk show host Rush Limbaugh (back on the air after drug rehab) accused family members who complained about the Bush reelection ads of being tools of the Democratic party:

> I couldn't believe that the Democratic Party would sink this low, to exploit and capitalize on the misery and loss of families. But they did it. They found a way. In fact, they found some family members—and I'm going to say this—they found some family members who seemed to have more concern over who the president of this country is than over the sanctity of the loss of their own family members. It is beyond the pale. . . . You know, these people are poisoned. They have literally been poisoned by their hate. They have been poisoned by their rage. It is unbelievable, the depths to which they will sink. . . . These were prepared by Democratic campaign consultants. . . . I do not know this kind of hatred; I don't know this kind of venom.[48]

One of the people Limbaugh maligned was Kristen Breitweiser, a true American patriot who has fought doggedly to learn the truth and who now finds herself dragged in the mud behind a would-be bandwagon for Bush. Breitweiser, a 33-year-old mother of two young children, responded: "I am not a Democrat. I voted for President Bush. So did my husband who was killed on 9/11. . . . Sadly, President Bush has been our biggest adversary in trying to find out what happened on 9/11. And, after voting for him in the last election, I am gravely disappointed in his behavior in fighting this commission and their noble efforts to explain why we as a nation were so vulnerable to terrorism on 9/11."[49] For 18 months, Breitweiser had been publicly saying the types of things that Limbaugh denigrated. Breitweiser has shown far more courage than the vast majority of members of Congress and far more dedication to finding the truth than the mass of the Washington press corps.

Bush responded to the controversy over the ads by declaring that he "will continue to speak about the effects of 9/11 on our country and my presidency. I have an obligation to those who died. I have an obligation to those who were heroic in their attempts to rescue [people injured that day]. And I won't forget that obligation." Yet, Bush's obligation to the dead apparently does not include disclosing what the government knew before the attack and why the government failed to stop the hijackers. Bush added: "How this administration handled that day, as well as the war on terror, is worthy of discussion. And I look forward to discussing that with the American people."[50]

The reelection ads show how the Bush administration views the public. All that is supposedly necessary is for Americans to see a few flickering images of the devastation of that day, and once again recognize Bush as the great leader who saved America after 9/11. The Pavlov button is expected to convert Bush from a mediocre, floundering president to the Great Righteous Avenger.

WARNING? WHAT WARNING?

Bush's attempt to exploit 9/11 received a rough jolt from his former chief counterterrorism official, Richard Clarke. Clarke laid out to the 9/11 commission the details of how the administration failed to take Al Qaeda as an urgent threat. Bush responded to the controversy on March 23, 2004: "Had my administration had any information that terrorists were going to attack New York City on September the 11th, we would have acted."[51] Supposedly, unless Bush had a warning that the terrorists intended to attack precisely on September 11, then none of the warnings of growing terrorist threats and suspicious activities and foreign intelligence alerts about Al Qaeda plots against America counted.

As the 9/11 commission neared completion of its work, it ratcheted up the pressure. The Bush administration fought to block efforts to have Condi Rice testify but finally relented. The commissioners were intensely interested in the August 6, 2001, President's Daily Brief (PDB). Rice, testifying under oath, stressed that "this was a historical memo. . . . It was not based on new threat information."[52]

A redacted version of the memo was finally released on the evening of Saturday, April 10, 2004—two days after Rice finished testifying. The memo warned, "Al-Qa'ida members—including some who are US citizens—have resided in or traveled to the US for years, and the group apparently maintains a support structure that could aid attacks." The memo mentioned Bin Laden's call in televised interviews to "bring the fighting to America" and quoted an Egyptian Islamic Jihad source warning that "Bin Ladin was planning to exploit the operative's access to the US to mount a terrorist strike." The memo mentioned a 1998 report that "a Bin Ladin cell in New York was recruiting Muslim-American youth for attacks." The memo conceded that the CIA has "not been able to corroborate some of the more sensational threat reporting, such as that from a . . . [redacted portion] . . . service in 1998 saying that Bin Ladin wanted to hijack a US aircraft to gain the release of 'Blind Shaykh' 'Umar 'Abd al-Rahman and other US-held extremists. Nevertheless, FBI information since that time indicates patterns of suspicious activity in this country consistent with preparations for hijackings or other types of attacks, including recent surveillance of federal buildings in New York." The memo also noted "a call to our Embassy in the UAE [United Arab Emirates] in May saying that a group of Bin Ladin supporters was in the US planning attacks with explosives."[53]

On the day after the memo was released, Bush commented to reporters: "There was nothing in there that said, you know, 'There is an imminent attack. That wasn't what the report said. The report was kind of a history of Osama's [bin Laden's] intentions." Bush stressed that the document has "nothing about an attack on America. It talked about intentions, about somebody who hated America—well, we knew that."[54] Bush may have missed the title of the PDB—"Bin Ladin Determined To Strike in US." A reporter asked about the brief's warning of Al Qaeda hijacking plans. Bush replied, "It was not a hijacking of an airplane to fly into a building, it was hijacking of airplanes in order to free somebody that was being held as a prisoner in the United States."[55] Bush did not explain why terrorist hijackings are benign.

Bush repeatedly insisted that he was the person who asked for the August 6 memo on Al Qaeda. *Slate's* Fred Kaplan concluded that "this story is almost certainly untrue. On March 19 of this year, Tenet told the 9/11 commission that the PDB had been prepared, as usual, at a CIA analyst's initiative. He later retracted that testimony, saying the president had asked for the briefing."[56] The *Washington Post* reported, "According to senior intelligence officials familiar with the document, work on it began at the end of July, at the initiative of the CIA analyst."[57]

In her testimony to the 9/11 commission, Rice claimed that after Bush received the August 6 PDB, Bush "had us at battle stations during this period of time."[58] But, according to a former Bush aide, the government's response was casual: "In a pre-9/11 world, it was like, 'Check it out and see what you find and get back to us after Labor Day. It wasn't just the president who was on vacation. It was the whole government. It was the Bureau [the FBI] and the Agency [the CIA], too."[59] President Bush, in a 2003 interview, described his attitude prior to 9/11: "I didn't feel a sense of urgency about al Qaeda. It was not my focus; it was not the focus of my team."[60]

The PDB should have set off alarm bells because of memos and articles Bush received from the CIA in April and May 2001 with titles like "Bin Ladin planning multiple operations," "Bin Ladin public profile may presage attack," and "Bin Ladin network's plans advancing." The 9/11 commission reported that the CIA "consistently described the upcoming attacks as occurring on a catastrophic level, indicating that they would cause the world to be in turmoil, consisting of possible multiple—but not necessarily simultaneous—attacks."[61] The *New York Times* summarized the commission's staff reports: "Al Qaeda and its leader, Mr. bin Laden, did not blindside the United States, but were a threat recognized and discussed regularly at the highest levels of government for nearly five years before the attacks, in thousands of reports, often accompanied by urgent warnings from lower-level experts."[62]

At his April 13, 2004, press conference, Bush vindicated his actions prior to 9/11 by invoking the number of briefings he received: "I was dealing with terrorism a lot as the president when George Tenet came in to brief me. I wanted Tenet in the Oval Office all the time." But Tenet told the 9/11 commission that he did not brief Bush a single time in August 2001. One of Tenet's aides later called reporters to say that Tenet had forgotten two briefings he gave Bush—one on August 17 and the other on August 31.[63]

Bush declared on April 13, 2004: "There was nobody in our government, at least, and I don't think in the prior government, that could envision flying airplanes into buildings on such a massive scale." But the 9/11 commission reported a few days later: "For the previous few years, the CIA had issued several warnings that terrorists might fly commercial airplanes into buildings or cities."[64] The Pentagon briefly considered in the summer of 2001 conducting a training exercise involving "a scenario in which a hijacked foreign commercial airliner flew into the Pentagon" but rejected the exercise as "too unrealistic."[65] In July 2001, when Bush visited Genoa, Italy, for a G–7 summit, the Italian government closed the airspace and "mounted antiaircraft batteries based on information that Islamic extremists were planning to use an airplane to kill President Bush."[66]

The 9/11 commission lobbied long and hard for Bush to testify before it. Bush finally agreed to speak to the commissioners—as long as there was no tape or transcript of his comments, as long as the meeting was in the White House, as long as he could have aides with him, and as long as Vice President Dick Cheney could be by his side. The White House initially stressed that Bush could spare only an hour to answer the commission's questions but eventually relented.

At his April 13 press conference, Bush was asked, "Why are you and the vice president insisting on appearing together before the 9–11 commission?" Bush replied, "Because the 9–11 commission wants to ask us questions, that's why we're meeting. And I look forward to meeting with them and answering their questions." The journalist clarified: "I was asking why you're appearing together, rather than separately, which was their request." Bush clarified: "Because it's a good chance for both of us to answer questions that the 9–11 commission is looking forward to asking us. And I'm looking forward to answering them."

After meeting with the commissioners for several hours on April 29, Bush cheerfully announced in the Rose Garden, "We answered all their questions. . . . I think it was important for them to see our body language, as well, how we work together."[67] But the commissioners were presumably seeking historical evidence, not scoping out prospects in a singles bar or viewing the president and vice president like a marriage counselor would study a troubled couple. Bush also declared: "There was a lot of interest about how to better protect America. In other words, they're very interested in the recommendations that they're going to lay out."[68] Bush's light-hearted manner after the meeting indicated that the commissioners had likely genuflected to the man and the office. Some of the commissioners characterized the meeting with Bush as "jovial."[69] Shaun Waterman, the national security editor for United Press International, noted that "the commission has generally chosen to pull its punches, avoiding confrontation wherever possible."[70]

Some of the commissioners did not seem hell-bent on digging as hard and as long as necessary to get the truth. Two of the Democratic members left the White House meeting early because they had prior engagements. Vice Chairman Lee Hamilton left because he was booked to "introduce the Canadian prime minister at a luncheon, and former Nebraska senator Bob Kerrey left to meet with Sen. Pete V. Domenici (R-N.M.) on funding issues related to New School University, where Kerrey serves as president."[71] The commissioners' early exits vivified their willingness to pay any price and make any sacrifice to find the truth about 9/11.

ASHCROFT: GOVERNMENT AS VICTIM

"The simple fact of September 11th is this: We did not know an attack was coming because for nearly a decade our government had blinded itself to its enemies."[72] So revealed John Ashcroft to the 9/11 commission on April 13. Ashcroft's comment is true only if stupidity is considered a form of blindness. The commissioners sought information on federal failures leading to 9/11. Ashcroft turned the session on its head, portraying the government as a victim and seeking to induce guilt far and wide about the mistreatment of G-men.

Ashcroft declared, "The single greatest structural cause for the September 11th problem was the wall that segregated or separated criminal investigators and intelligence agents. Government erected this wall, government buttressed this wall and before September 11th government was blinded by this wall."[73] From Ashcroft's view, the wall's guilt practically made all other government failings irrelevant. President Bush also implicitly invoked the wall to explain pre-9/11 failings: "We were kind of stovepiped, I guess is a way to describe it. There was, you know, kind of departments that at times didn't communicate—because of law, in the FBI's case."[74]

The 1978 Foreign Intelligence Surveillance Act (FISA) authorized wiretaps, searches, and other intrusions against suspected foreign intelligence agents based on much lower standards than normally required by the Constitution and federal courts. FISA search warrants are granted by the Foreign Intelligence Surveillance Court, a docile collection of judges who meet in a secure room in the Justice Department headquarters. To prevent prosecutors from relying on FISA search warrants to carry out routine surveillance of Americans, the act restricted the cooperation of FBI agents and prosecutors.

Ashcroft claimed that the wall "specifically impeded the investigation of Zacarias Moussaoui." Moussaoui had links to Al Qaeda and was acting very suspiciously when he was arrested in mid-August 2001. On August 18, Minneapolis FBI agents sent a 26-page memo to FBI headquarters warning that Moussaoui was acting "with others yet unknown" in a hijack conspiracy. Three days later, Minneapolis agents notified headquarters: "If [Moussaoui] seizes an aircraft flying from Heathrow to New York City, it will have the fuel on board to reach D.C." Some of the information got passed on to the CIA, which alerted its overseas stations that Moussaoui was a "suspect airline suicide hijacker" who might be "involved in a larger plot to target airlines traveling from Europe to the United States."[75]

FBI agents in Minneapolis could have easily gotten a regular search warrant from a federal judge—if they had not been hogtied by FBI headquarters. Ashcroft told the 9/11 commission that FBI agents "sought approval for a criminal search warrant to search his computer. The warrant was rejected because FBI officials feared breaching the wall." Actually, FBI agents in Minneapolis asked FBI headquarters for permission to request a search warrant from a federal judge in Minnesota (which would not have involved "the wall"). FBI headquarters refused permission, instead insisting that the Minnesota agents file a FISA search request—which had to be handled by the experts at FBI headquarters. FBI headquarters agents incorrectly insisted that FISA required Minneapolis agents to prove that Moussaoui was linked to a foreign power before a search warrant could be issued. Because a French intelligence agency indicated Moussaoui might be linked to the Chechen resistance, FBI headquarters insisted that Minneapolis agents find evidence connecting the Chechens to a recognized terrorist organization. The congressional Joint Intelligence Committee report on pre-9/11 failures noted that "because of this misunderstanding, Minneapolis [FBI agents] spent the better part of three weeks trying to connect the Chechen group to al Qaeda."[76] The Senate Judiciary Committee concluded in a 2003 report that "it is difficult to understand how the agents whose job included such a heavy FISA component could not have understood" the FISA law.[77]

The FBI headquarters' mindless blocking of the Moussaoui search warrant may have cost thousands of American lives. A 9/11 commission staff report concluded: "A maximum U.S. effort to investigate Moussaoui could conceivably have unearthed his connections to the Hamburg cell [of 9/11 hijackers]. . . . The publicity about the threat also might have disrupted the plot."[78] Commission Chairman Thomas Kean commented: "Everything had to go right for [the hijackers]. Had they felt that one of them had been discovered, there is evidence it would have been delayed."[79]

Yet, in Ashcroft's view, the FBI's failures on Moussaoui are irrelevant because the agency did not have unlimited surveillance power. Ashcroft personally attacked 9/11 commissioner Jamie Gorelick for a memo she wrote in 1995 setting guidance on "the wall." To aid his assault, the Justice Department de-classified a confidential memo (written by Gorelick in 1995) for Aschcroft to unveil at the hearing. A few weeks later, the Justice Department declassified other Clinton administration memos. And, though Ashcroft now blames "the wall," the *New York Times* reported that, prior to the terrorist attacks, "Ashcroft had resisted signing emergency warrants that would have allowed eavesdropping in terrorism investigations, apparently because he had only a rudimentary knowledge of how the warrant process worked," according to 9/11 commission officials.[80]

The FBI's terrorist surveillance efforts were a train wreck long before 9/11—and not because of any wall. The 9/11 commission staff reported:

> Many agents also told us that the process for getting FISA packages approved at FBI Headquarters and the Department of Justice was incredibly lengthy and inefficient. Several FBI agents added that, prior to 9/11, FISA-derived intelligence information was not fully exploited but was *collected primarily to justify continuing the surveillance.* . . . The FBI did not have a sufficient number of translators proficient in Arabic and other languages useful in counterterrorism investigations, resulting in a significant backlog of untranslated FISA intercepts by early 2001.[81]

Though the FBI's budget has soared since 2001, the FISA wiretap process is still a bureaucratic quagmire. The FBI and Justice Department's procedure for approving such wiretaps "continues to be long and slow." The numbers of requested wiretaps "are overwhelming the ability of the system to process them" and causing "bottlenecks," according to an April 2004 report by the 9/11 commission.[82]

Ashcroft explained to the commissioners: "Under FISA, you can't have an order without first seeing the federal judge. Or unless it's an emergency order, and then it has to be brought before a judge within 72 hours. So there's a lot of safeguards here."[83] But many of the searches are carried out on Ashcroft's command and are only retroactively approved by the most pliant court in America. Ashcroft personally issued over 170 emergency domestic spying warrants in 2002—permitting agents to carry out wiretaps and search homes and offices for up to 72 hours before the feds requested a search warrant from the Foreign Intelligence Surveillance Court. Ashcroft is using such powers almost a hundred times as often as attorney generals did before 9/11.[84] And there is practically no "safeguard," since the lapdog Foreign Intelligence Surveillance Court has approved almost every one of the 15,000 search requests the feds have submitted since 1978.

Ashcroft also informed the commissioners that "another limitation government placed on our ability to connect the dots of the terrorist threat prior to September 11 . . . was the lack of support for information technology at the FBI." Ashcroft asserted, "The FBI's information infrastructure had been starved. And by September 11, it was collapsing from budgetary neglect." Ashcroft revealed the damning proof: "Over eight years, the bureau was denied nearly $800 million of its information technology funding requests."[85]

Ashcroft was correct that the FBI's computer system was pathetic. Agents had ancient machines that were often incapable of sending e-mail. The FBI had 42 separate databases and it was often impossible to conduct searches on more than one database at a time. Many FBI agents simply gave up trying to use office computers and relied on their children's PCs at home to do some of their work.

Ashcroft has a perverse notion of budgetary neglect. Congress gave the FBI almost $2 billion in the eight years before 9/11 for computer modernization projects. The FBI squandered almost all the money or simply shifted it to pay for priorities favored by FBI director Louis Freeh. Rob Nabors, a Republican staffer with the House Appropriations Committee, commented that Freeh "wanted more cops on the beat, and he was robbing from the equipment side to pay for people."[86] Law enforcement officials told the *Los Angeles Times* that Freeh "allowed the FBI to raid its computer budget repeatedly, taking money intended by Congress for systems and infrastructure upgrades and using it instead to fund shortfalls in staffing and international offices. The diverted money, much of it designated for vital computer upgrades, totaled $60 million in 2000, with millions more in other years, according to a former senior official at the Justice Department."[87]

The FBI also suffers from an almost primitive aversion to using any form of writing as a means to store and transmit knowledge. Bush's counterterrorism czar, Richard Clarke, complained that the National Security Council "never received anything in writing from the FBI whatsoever." FBI officials were "comfortable relying on their individual professional judgment regarding the terrorist threat and did not value a formal written assessment that uses a structured methodology," the 9/11 commission reported.[88]

The FBI failed to stop the hijackers in part because some agents seemed more afraid of defense lawyers than of terrorists. "Agents investigated their individual cases with the knowledge that any case information recorded on paper and stored in case files was potentially discoverable in court. . . . Analysts were discouraged from producing written assessments which could be discoverable and used to attack the prosecution's case at trial,"[89] the 9/11 commission reported.

Government incompetence was a far greater cause of 9/11 than were restrictions on government surveillance. The FBI tripled the number of intelligence analysts on its payrolls in the 1990s. But an internal review found that two-thirds of the analysts were unqualified "to perform analytical duties."[90] Despite the warning that Al Qaeda had agents in the United States and aimed to attack, the FBI had only two analysts looking at Osama bin Ladin threat information. "The FBI had never completed an assessment of the overall terrorist threat to the U.S. homeland," the 9/11 commission reported.[91]

Ashcroft talks as if fighting terrorism was always one of his top priorities. Yet in May 2001, the Justice Department, the 9/11 commission reported, "issued guidance for developing the fiscal year 2003 budget that made reducing the incidence of gun violence and reducing the trafficking of illegal drugs priority objectives. [FBI counterterrorism chief Dale] Watson told us that he almost fell out of his chair when he saw the memo, because it made no mention of counterterrorism."[92] On September 10, 2001, Ashcroft rejected a request by the FBI to add $58 million to its counterterrorism budget. When asked about these actions by a 9/11 commissioner, Ashcroft replied: "I would just indicate in the budgeting process that the label of counterterrorism should not be controlling when assessing whether or not items were important to the development of a defense for national security interests vis-à-vis counterterrorism, counterintelligence or other things that challenged the United States."[93] Ashcroft caught no guff for redefining the English language.

Ashcroft apparently had scant interest in the terrorist threat before 9/11. FBI acting chief Thomas Pickard informed the 9/11 commission staff that, though he briefed Ashcroft once a week, "after two such briefings the Attorney General told him he did not want to hear this information [on the danger of terrorist attacks] anymore."[94] (Ashcroft denied making this statement to Pickard.) The *New York Times* reported that a 9/11 report would "quote from internal memorandums by Pickard in summer 2001, in which Mr. Pickard described his frustration with Mr. Ashcroft and what he saw as the attorney general's lack of interest in the issue of how the bureau was investigating terrorism suspects in the United States."[95] The initial staff report issued that week ducked that issue, perhaps in part because of the "aggressive, last-minute effort" the Justice Department launched "to persuade the commission to rewrite the parts of the report dealing with Mr. Ashcroft, describing them as one-sided and unfair to him."[96]

When asked about his pre-9/11 response to threats, Ashcroft declared: "Well, I think it's pretty clear that I was pulsing the FBI. I asked them regularly in my briefings with them if there were any evidence regarding threats domestically and the kind of conduct by the FBI was the kind of thing that I would have expected them to be involved in as a result of that kind of request on my part."[97] Ashcroft's idea of "pulsing" apparently did not extend beyond a simple inquiry—as if merely asking a question was the equivalent of waving a magic wand over the bureaucracy.

At the request of Condi Rice, Ashcroft was briefed by the CIA on July 5 about the surge of information about an imminent terrorist attack. Ashcroft was not on the short list of people Bush approved to receive the August 6, 2001, President's Daily Brief (PDB). But on the following day, Ashcroft was among those who were sent a Senior Executive Intelligence Brief. The version Ashcroft received had the same headline as the PDB: "Terrorism: Bin Laden Determined to Strike in the United States."

Commissioner Jamie Gorelick asked if he recalled seeing that brief, and Ashcroft replied: "I do not remember seeing that. I was in—I believe I was in Chicago speaking at the American Bar Association meeting, I believe, at the time. So I do not have a recollection of seeing that." Gorelick asked whether his staff subsequently brought the memo to his attention. Ashcroft replied, "These items had been briefed to me."[98] Yet, a few days before the commission hearing, Ashcroft's chief spokesman, Mark Corallo, had adamantly declared that Ashcroft "was not briefed that there was any threat to the United States."[99] If Ashcroft was briefed, it did not spur him to read the page-and-a-half memo. The fact that Ashcroft apparently ignored an ominous warning a month before 9/11 did nothing to stifle his subsequent righteousness, even though, as attorney general, Ashcroft was responsible for the FBI and its failures from late January through September 2001.

At the end of his prepared statement to the 9/11 commission, Ashcroft shifted into his Chief National Therapist mode: "I am aware that the issues I have raised this afternoon involve at times painful introspection for this commission and for the nation." Ashcroft sought to portray his attacks on Gorelick and on anyone who ever denied an FBI budget request as fodder for reflection—instead of simply spin to dominate news coverage and divert attention from his own failings before 9/11. Ashcroft closed by assuring the commissioners and the world: "I have spoken out today not to add to the nation's considerable stock of pain, but to heal our wounds."[100] And the surest way to heal America's wounds is to smear anyone who wants to limit government power.

CONCLUSION

After 9/11, Bush and many federal agency chieftains used a "silver platter" standard to absolve themselves. Americans were supposed to accept that unless the Bush administration received all the information regarding the 9/11 plot—including hijackers' identities, flight schedules, and perhaps seat assignments—then the government cannot possibly be considered negligent. One of the most brazen examples involved the CIA. The German intelligence service provided the CIA with the first name and phone number of Marwan al-Shehhi, an Al Qaeda member who was behind the controls of the jetliner that smashed into the Pentagon on 9/11. German experts alerted the CIA in 1999 that Marwan had contacted a suspected Al Qaeda cell in Hamburg. But the CIA never bothered to track the guy down. When CIA chief Tenet was asked about this failure to follow-through at a congressional hearing in February 2004, Tenet explained: "The Germans gave us a name, Marwan—that's it—and a phone number. They didn't give us a first and a last name until after 9/11, with then additional data."[101] The CIA's budget is classified. Yet, regardless of how many billions of dollars the agency receives, its wizards apparently cannot be expected to show the initiative routinely demonstrated by an hourly-wage employee sitting in a call center in Omaha, Nebraska, tracking down late credit card payments.

Bush's glorification of government put Americans at risk. By choosing to sanctify the government after 9/11, Bush effectively assured that necessary improvements would either be delayed or never occur. The more that Bush, Ashcroft, and others are permitted to exonerate the federal government's actions and negligence before 9/11, the less likely that fundamental reforms will be made to prevent more devastating terrorist attacks. The more the government is exalted, the less likely national security will be improved.

Bush's exploitation of 9/11 for his reelection campaign may explain why his administration fights so doggedly to suppress the truth of what happened that day. The more Americans know about 9/11, the less likely they are to revere Bush and the federal government. Only with an aura of piety around 9/11 can Bush turn one of his greatest failures into a reason to support him.

Post-9/11 America shows what happens when a nation worships its leader and permits him to tell one lie after another, distorting facts and manipulating the public's emotions. If Bush had not been treated so respectfully after 9/11, he may not have been able to so easily lead the nation to war against Iraq. If Bush had not been permitted to exploit government failure, he would not have been able to make government far more powerful.

The myths of 9/11 continue to threaten American safety. Until the government opens its files and reveals what happened that day and in the months and years leading up to and following that debacle, no American can safely trust government utterances on terrorism. There will be some details that cannot be revealed. But the standard for disclosure should be national security, and not the president's reelection campaign.

September 11 is an acid test for Bush secrecy policies. When it is convenient for the president—when it serves his interests—information is speedily disclosed. While Bush battled for almost two years to prevent either Congress or the 9/11 commission from seeing the President's Daily Brief from August 6, 2001, hand-picked Bush biographer Bob Woodward was shown copies of other President's Daily Briefs.[102] Similarly, Attorney General Ashcroft's declassification of Clinton administration memos was a political machination masquerading as public service.

The Bush administration has never disclosed anything embarrassing about 9/11 except under severe duress. It is as if "honesty in government" is now subsumed by the need for "reverence of government"—as if information existed solely to help the government maximize public docility.

September 11 happened in part because Americans naively trusted their government to protect them. To conclude from 9/11 that the government should be more sacrosanct is among the worst possible lessons that could be drawn.

CHAPTER THREE

A War on Dissent?

I love coming outside the nation's capital because it gives me a chance to see Americans line the road, saluting the institution of the presidency as I drive by.

—*George W. Bush, April 11, 2001*[1]

On December 6, 2001, Attorney General John Ashcroft informed the Senate Judiciary Committee: "To those who scare peace-loving people with phantoms of lost liberty . . . your tactics only aid terrorists for they erode our national unity and . . . give ammunition to America's enemies."[2] Some commentators suspected that Ashcroft's statement, which was vetted beforehand by top lawyers at the Justice Department, signaled that the Bush administration would take a far more hostile view toward critics than did recent presidents.

The Secret Service has done all it could to vindicate such fears. When Bush came to the Pittsburgh area on Labor Day 2002, Bill Neel, a 65-year-old retired steel worker, was there to greet him with a sign proclaiming, "The Bush family must surely love the poor—they made so many of us."[3] The local police, at the Secret Service's behest, set up a "designated free-speech zone" on a baseball field surrounded by a chain-link fence a third of a mile from the location of Bush's speech. The police cleared the motorcade path of all critical signs, though folks with pro-Bush signs were permitted to line the president's way. Neel refused to go to the designated area and was arrested for disorderly conduct; the police also confiscated his sign. Neel compared the fenced-off area to a "concentration camp."[4]

At Neel's trial, police detective John Ianachione testified that the Secret Service told local police to confine "people that were there making a statement pretty much against the president and his views" in a "free speech area."[5] Paul Wolf, one of the top officials in the Allegheny County Police Department, commented that Secret Service agents "come in and do a site survey, and say, 'Here's a place where the people can be, and we'd like to have any protesters be put in a place that is able to be secured.'"[6] Pennsylvania district judge Shirley Rowe Trkula threw out the disorderly conduct charge against Neel, declaring, "I believe this is America. Whatever happened to 'I don't agree with you, but I'll defend to the death your right to say it'?"[7]

Similar suppressions occurred during Bush visits to Florida. A *St. Petersburg Times* editorial noted: "At a Bush rally at Legends Field in 2001, three demonstrators—two of whom were grandmothers—were arrested for holding up small handwritten protest signs outside the designated zone. And last year, seven protesters were arrested when Bush came to a rally at the USF Sun Dome. They had refused to be cordoned off into a protest zone hundreds of yards from the entrance to the Dome."[8] One of the arrested protesters was a 62-year-old man holding up a sign, "War is good business. Invest your sons." The seven were charged with trespassing, "obstructing without violence," and disorderly conduct.

When Bush visited St. Louis on January 22, 2003, 150 people carrying signs were shunted far away from the main action. Denise Lieberman of the American Civil Liberties Union of Eastern Missouri commented: "No one could see them from the street. In addition, the media were not allowed to talk to them. The police would not allow any media inside the protest area and wouldn't allow any of the protesters out of the protest zone to talk to the media."[9] When Bush stopped by a Boeing plant to talk to workers, Christine Mains, accompanied by her five-year-old daughter, disobeyed orders to move to a small protest area far from the action. Police arrested Mains and took her and her crying daughter away in separate squad cars.[10]

Police in Phoenix were considerably rougher on protesters during a Bush visit to that city. The ACLU reported:

> On Sept. 27, 2002, President Bush came to the downtown Civic Center for a fundraising dinner for two local candidates. A coalition of groups opposed to a variety of the president's policies, consisting of approximately 1,500 people, negotiated with the local police for a demonstration permit. Phoenix police advised the protesters that the president had requested a federal protection zone. These protesters were required to stand across the street from the Civic Cen-

ter. People carrying signs supporting the president's policies and spectators not visibly expressing any views were allowed to stand closer. Eleanor Eisenberg, director of the local ACLU, was present as a legal observer. When mounted police in riot gear charged into the crowd without warning, Eisenberg, who was across the street taking photos, was arrested and charged with disorderly conduct. The charges were later dropped.[11]

On October 24, 2002, President Bush flew to Columbia, South Carolina, for an airport speech for Republican congressional candidates. Bush told an adoring crowd: "There's an enemy out there that hates America because of what we love. We love freedom. We love the fact that people can worship freely in America. We love our free press. We love every aspect of our freedom, and we're not changing."[12]

The Secret Service made the airport area safe for freedom-loving rhetoric by vigorously suppressing dissent before Bush arrived. Brett Bursey, 54 years old, was arrested for holding a "No War for Oil" sign too near the hangar where Bush would be speaking. Local police, acting under Secret Service orders, purportedly established a "free speech zone" far from the airport hangar. Bursey was standing amidst hundreds of people carrying signs praising the president or his policies. Police told Bursey to remove himself to the "free speech zone."

After moving twice, Bursey refused to move again and was arrested. Bursey said that he asked the policeman if "it was the content of my sign, and he said, 'Yes, sir, it's the content of your sign that's the problem.'"[13] Bursey stated that he had already moved 200 yards from where Bush was supposed to speak. Bursey complained: "The problem was, the restricted area kept moving. It was wherever I happened to be standing."[14] Bursey later commented: "They put the cuffs on me. Behind my back. In a paddy wagon. And they moved me behind the hangar where I could see Air Force One. That was really bizarre. Bush gets off the plane. And I can see the whole tableau through the bars in the paddy wagon. He goes inside the hangar and gives this speech where he says they hate us because we're so free, and here I am handcuffed in the back of a paddy wagon, thinking, 'No, Mr. Bush, they don't hate us because we're free. They hate us because we're hypocrites.'"[15]

Bursey was charged with trespassing. Five months later, the charge was dropped because South Carolina law prohibits arresting people for trespassing on public property (as a result of a state Supreme Court decision involving a 1969 Bursey arrest). But the Justice Department—in the person of U.S. attorney Strom Thurmond, Jr.—quickly jumped in, charging Bursey with violating a rarely enforced federal law regarding "entering a restricted area around the president of the United States."

Federal magistrate Bristow Marchant denied Bursey's request for a jury trial because his violation was categorized as a "petty offense"[16]—even though the issue is at the heart of American freedom. Some observers believed that the feds aimed to set a precedent in a conservative state such as South Carolina that could be used against protesters nationwide.

During his trial before the magistrate, Bursey's lawyers sought the Secret Service documents that they believed would lay out the official policies on restricting critical speech at presidential visits. The Bush administration sought to block all access, but Marchant ruled in September that the lawyers could have limited access to some documents. Bursey sought to subpoena Attorney General John Ashcroft and Bush political advisor Karl Rove to testify. Bursey's lawyer Lewis Pitts declared: "We intend to find out from Mr. Ashcroft why and how the decision to prosecute Mr. Bursey was reached."[17] The magistrate refused to issue the subpoenas.

Secret Service agents testified that because Bursey's sign was attached to a wooden stick, it could be used as a weapon. But testimony showed that the area where Bursey stood had plenty of "signs backing GOP candidates staked in the ground."[18]

Secret Service agent Holly Abel testified at the trial that Bursey was told to move to the demonstration area but refused to cooperate.[19] Bursey and other protesters testified that, though they were directed to go to the "protest zone," no such zone had been designated. Instead, the protest zone was simply "go farther away."

Gerald Rudolph, a protester who was next to Bursey that day, testified that a policeman "actually didn't tell me to leave, he told me I couldn't be there with a sign. . . . They said, 'Arrest them.' We were both holding signs. I gave up my sign at that point, and they left me alone and they arrested Bursey." In an earlier sworn statement to the court, Rudolph attested: "The Secret Service agent directed the police to arrest me unless I put down my sign. Once I discarded my sign, I was allowed to remain in the area." Rudolph commented that the Secret Service's suppression was especially important because "citizens have very few occasions to be in a position to directly communicate their views to the President or an audience he has gathered."[20]

Bursey testified that it was the reaction of a third protester that made him determined to stand his ground: "Virginia Sanders, who was standing with me at the time of the arrest, was crying. The fact that she was scared of her own government was the tipping point in my decision to take a stand for free speech."

The Justice Department asserted in a formal brief that no court should have the power to "second-guess the Secret Service and law enforcement on security decisions"[21]—thus potentially entitling the feds to shut down all future protests in the president's vicinity. Marchant did not buy that argument. Assistant U.S. Attorney John Barton explained the government's view: "I don't think there can be any debate or any—it really cannot be contested that [Bursey] was told by a United States Secret Service agent, 'I'm from the United States Secret Service, you are in a restricted area.' What more does he need to know?" Bursey retorted: "I didn't feel that I should acquiesce to what I took to be an unlawful order."[22]

Magistrate Marchant issued an opinion that should qualify him for Bush's short list of nominees for the next opening on the Supreme Court. The decision largely turned on the absence of a ticket. Marchant stressed: "The event was restricted to ticket holders only. . . . The evidence clearly establishes that the Defendant was not a ticket holder for the event, nor was he there to attend the event. Hence, it was a violation of the regulations governing ingress or egress thereto for the Defendant to have remained in the restricted area." Marchant's decision did not specify the ticket price for free speech.

Marchant denied that there was no free speech zone. His ruling noted: "The site agent for the President's visit testified that the restricted area consisted of an area about 100 yards up from the hangar to the parking lot, to the right of the hangar down Airport Boulevard to the intersection of Airport Boulevard with the main highway (Hwy. 302), and to the left of the hangar down Airport Boulevard for about 100 yards to the next intersection." Apparently, since the "free speech zone" was still in the state of South Carolina, the government did not violate anyone's rights. The allegedly designated protest zone would have made the protesters invisible—which apparently meshed with Marchant's understanding of the First Amendment.

The Secret Service had raised a new issue at the trial—asserting that Bursey was standing by the road where Bush's limousine would need to slow down to make a U-turn. Marchant wrote that "in this age of suicide bombers, the Secret Service's concerns about allowing someone to stand near where the president's vehicle is expected to drive by slowly is manifestly understandable."[23] Though this could be a legitimate concern, Bursey was presumably not standing in the Designated Suicide Bomber Spot until cops shooshed him away from his original location.

Marchant declared that he saw no evidence of selective prosecution—and yet he had impeded Bursey's lawyers from presenting evidence showing the nationwide pattern of Secret Service–spawned crackdowns on demonstrators.

Marchant also pointedly questioned why the Justice Department bothered to prosecute Bursey[24] and said that he felt that Bursey was taking a "principled stand" for freedom of speech and meant no harm to the president. Instead of hitting Bursey with the maximum of six months in jail and a $5,000 fine, Marchant only fined him $500.

Bursey asserted after the verdict that his case "will help determine if free speech in America can be zoned to protect the political interests of whoever is in charge of our government."[25] Bursey also declared that the Secret Service "sanitized" zones "concerns me because people watching television all around the world think that all Americans love George Bush and his policies. And what concerns me more is that George Bush may think the American people love him."[26] Bursey is appealing the conviction.

The Bursey prosecution spurred a dozen members of Congress, including Rep. Ron Paul (R-Tex.) and Rep. Barney Frank (D-Mass.), to write to President Bush to protest the administration's crackdown on demonstrators:

> As we read the First Amendment to the Constitution, the United States is a "free speech zone." In the United States, free speech is the rule, not the exception, and citizens' rights to express it do not depend on their doing it in a way that the president finds politically amenable. . . . We ask that you make it clear that we have no interest as a government in "zoning" constitutional freedoms, and that being politically annoying to the president of the United States is not a criminal offense. This [Bursey] prosecution smacks of the use of the Sedition Acts two hundred years ago to protect the president from political discomfort. It was wrong then and it is wrong now.[27]

The feds offer some bizarre rationales for hog-tying protesters. Secret Service agent Brian Marr explained to National Public Radio: "These individuals may be so involved with trying to shout their support or nonsupport that inadvertently they may walk out into the motorcade route and be injured. And that is really the reason why we set these places up, so we can make sure that they have the right of free speech, but, too, we want to be sure that they are able to go home at the end of the evening and not be injured in any way."[28]

Except for having their constitutional rights shredded. Somehow, after George Bush became president, people became so stupid that federal agents have to cage them to prevent them from walking out in front of speeding vehicles. Or perhaps the Secret Service assumes that becoming a political protester automatically turns people into imbeciles who must be protected against themselves.

The American Civil Liberties Union, along with several other organizations, is suing the Secret Service for suppressing protesters at Bush events in Arizona, California, Connecticut, Michigan, New Jersey, New Mexico, Texas, and elsewhere. The ACLU's Witold Walczak commented that the protesters "didn't pose a security threat; they posed a political threat."[29]

The Secret Service is duty bound to protect the president. But it is ludicrous to presume that would-be terrorists are lunkheaded enough to carry an anti-Bush sign when carrying a pro-Bush sign provides closer access to the president. And even a policy of removing all people carrying signs—as has happened in some demonstrations—is pointless, since potential attackers would simply avoid carrying signs. Rather than protecting the president's safety, the Secret Service aims to suppress *Lèse Majesté*—any affront to the dignity of the supreme ruler.

The Bush administration's anti-protester bias proved embarrassing for two American allies with long traditions of raucous free speech. Bush visited Australia in October 2003. *Sydney Morning Herald* columnist Mark Riley observed, "The basic right of freedom of speech will adopt a new interpretation during the Canberra visits this week by the U.S. President, George Bush, and his Chinese counterpart, Hu Jintao. Protesters will be free to speak as much as they like just as long as they can't be heard."[30] Demonstrators were shunted to an area away from the Federal Parliament building and prohibited from using any public address system in the area. Actually, when Chinese president Hu Jintao spoke the following day, protesters were allowed to get much closer to the Parliament building than when Bush spoke.[31]

The *Sydney Sunday Telegraph* noted that Bush "was kept in a cocoon" during the visit. The paper said, "Very few locals saw him, but all the signs were there"—including "sharpshooters on the roof of Parliament House" and "fighter planes patrolling overhead." Australian journalists were prohibited from photographing the helicopter the president used and were warned that their cameras would be confiscated if they violated the ban. Residents of Australia's capital, Canberra, "were kept 50 meters back from the roadside 'seclusion zone' which removed any slim chance of real people spotting the President."[32] Happily, the pervasive restrictions did not dampen the president's idealism. Bush told the Australian parliament: "It should surprise no one that the remnants and advocates of tyranny should fight liberty's advance. The advance of freedom will not be halted."[33]

For Bush's November 2003 visit to London, the White House initially demanded that British police ban all protest marches, close down the center of the city, and impose a "virtual three day shutdown of central London in a bid to foil disruption of the visit by anti war protesters," according to Britain's *Evening Standard.*[34] But instead of a "free speech zone," the Bush administration demanded an "exclusion zone" to protect Bush from protesters' messages.

Such unprecedented restrictions did not inhibit Bush from portraying himself as a champion of freedom during his visit. In a speech at Whitehall on November 19, Bush hyped the "forward strategy of freedom" and declared, "We seek the advance of freedom and the peace that freedom brings."[35] Bush sought to joke about the protesters: "I've been here only a short time, but I've noticed that the tradition of free speech—exercised with enthusiasm—is alive and well here in London. We have that at home, too. They now have that right in Baghdad, as well." But Bush-style freedom is less freedom than British citizens usually enjoy, aside from when he comes to town. And his mention of Baghdad is ludicrous: in the months after Bush's statements, U.S. and British troops shot and killed or wounded many unarmed Iraqis who were protesting the occupation.[36]

VIEWING DEMONSTRATORS AS WOULD-BE TERRORISTS

The Bush administration's attempts to sidetrack and suppress protesters becomes more ominous in light of the Homeland Security Department's recommendation that local police departments view critics of the war on terrorism as potential terrorists. In a May 2003 terrorist advisory, the Homeland Security Department warned local law enforcement agencies to keep an eye on anyone who "expressed dislike of attitudes and decisions of the U.S. government."[37] If police vigorously follow this advice, millions of Americans could be added to the official lists of "suspected terrorists."

Protesters have claimed that police assaulted them during demonstrations in New York, Washington, and elsewhere. Film footage of a February 2003 antiwar rally in New York showed a policeman on horseback charging into senior citizen protesters.

One of the most violent government responses to an antiwar protest occurred on April 7, 2003, when local police fired wooden bullets and tear gas at peaceful protesters and innocent bystanders at the port of Oakland, injuring a number of people. The Oakland police were extremely aggressive in part because, five days before the protest, they were warned by the California Anti-Terrorism Information Center (CATIC) that violence might occur at the event. The *Oakland Tribune* noted that "a warning of potential violence from the state's anti-terror nerve center, staffed with personnel from the FBI, Defense Intelligence Agency and other federal, state and local agencies, carries a strong imprimatur of danger." The federal and state experts are not necessarily focused on preventing another 9/11; the *Tribune* noted that "causing a traffic jam can be enough to trigger a CATIC analysis and bulletin" to local and state law enforcement.

When the police attack sparked a geyser of media criticism, Mike van Winkle, the spokesman for the California Anti-Terrorism Information Center, told the *Oakland Tribune:* "You can make an easy kind of a link that, if you have a protest group protesting a war where the cause that's being fought against is international terrorism, you might have terrorism at that protest. You can almost argue that a protest against that is a terrorist act." Van Winkle justified classifying protesters like terrorists: "I've heard terrorism described as anything that is violent or has an economic impact, and shutting down a port certainly would have some economic impact. Terrorism isn't just bombs going off and killing people."[38]

Aggressive state and local police tactics could become more common in the future. In its Patriot II draft legislation, the Bush administration advocates nullifying all judicial consent decrees restricting state and local police from spying on individuals and groups who may oppose government policies.[39] These judicial restrictions were put in place in response to pervasive abuses in the 1960s, 1970s, and after. Some local police departments are already covertly infiltrating organizations that are planning demonstrations.[40] In some cases, police undercover activities may be occurring as part of FBI Joint Terrorism Task Force operations.

The FBI may already be far more involved in directly infiltrating antiwar and other groups than it was in the recent past. On May 30, 2002, Ashcroft effectively abolished restrictions on FBI surveillance of Americans' everyday lives and political activities that were first imposed in 1976.[41] Prior to Ashcroft's announcement, FBI agents were free to enter mosques or attend political meetings, but only when there was some indication of criminal conduct. Ashcroft liberated FBI agents to spy on any nonprivate gathering they choose, based on their whims—or their malice.

The 1976 restrictions were imposed after a Senate committee report detailed how the FBI's COINTELPRO operations suppressed free speech, incited gang warfare, wrecked marriages, got people fired, smeared innocent people by portraying them as government informants, trashed the reputation of critics, and sought to destroy left-wing, black, communist, and other groups. One FBI internal newsletter had encouraged FBI agents to conduct more interviews with antiwar activists "for plenty of reasons, chief of which it will enhance the paranoia endemic in such circles and will further serve to get the point across that there is an FBI agent behind every mailbox."[42] The FBI took a shotgun approach toward protesters partly because of the FBI's "belief that dissident speech and association should be prevented because they were incipient steps towards the possible ultimate commission of acts which might be criminal," according to the Senate report on COINTELPRO abuses.[43]

On October 15, 2003, the FBI sent *Intelligence Bulletin #89* to 17,000 local and state law enforcement agencies around the country. The bulletin warned of pending marches in Washington and San Francisco against Bush's Iraqi policy and stated: "While the FBI possesses no information indicating that violent or terrorist activities are being planned as part of these protests, the possibility exists that elements of the activist community may attempt to engage in violent, destructive, or disruptive acts."[44]

The FBI catalogued some of the new threats to public safety: "Several effective and innovative strategies are commonly used by protesters prior to, during, and after demonstrations. . . . Protesters often use the internet to recruit, raise funds, and coordinate their activities prior to demonstrations. Activists may also make use of training camps to rehearse tactics and counter-strategies for dealing with the police. . . ."[45]

Suggesting that dissenters are attending a "training camp" implies that they are akin to the killers who attended Afghan terrorist training camps. And the fact that protesters use the Internet is as irrelevant as earlier generations of protesters using the U.S. mail. (Since FBI computers are far behind the technology curve,[46] FBI analysts may be unaware that Internet usage is pervasive among Americans of all political stripes.)

After warning about the danger that "extremist elements could engage in "vandalism," "trespassing," and "the formation of human chains," the FBI cast suspicion on almost anyone attending a protest: "Even the more peaceful techniques can create a climate of disorder, block access to a site, draw large numbers of police officers to a specific location in order to weaken security at other locations, obstruct traffic, and possibly intimidate people from attending the events being protested."[47] The FBI promulgated the doctrine of collective guilt for all demonstrators—as if anyone on the streets in the same city as a masked anarchist troublemaker is as guilty as the person who throws the brick through a Starbucks window.

The confidential FBI intelligence bulletin revealed to the nation's law officers that protesters may use "media equipment (video cameras, photographic equipment, audio tape recorders, microphones, and computer and radio equipment) . . . for documenting potential cases of police brutality and for distribution of information over the internet." Apparently, the FBI sees videotaping an arrest as an illicit infringement on a police officer's creativity.

The FBI also portrayed practically any defensive measures by demonstrators as highly suspicious:

> Extremists may be prepared to defend themselves against law enforcement officials during the course of a demonstration. Masks (gas masks, goggles, scarves, scuba masks, filter masks, and sunglasses) can serve to minimize the effects of tear gas and pepper spray as well as obscure one's identity. Extremists may also employ . . . body protection equipment (layered clothing, hard hats and helmets, sporting equipment, life jackets, etc.) to protect themselves during marches.[48]

Implying that "layered clothing" is an unfair or illicit tactic is bizarre—as if anything that blunts the impact of a policeman's baton should be considered aiding and abetting Al Qaeda. The FBI also implied that any self-defense measures should be considered a provocation.

The intelligence bulletin concluded: "Law enforcement agencies should be alert to these *possible indicators* of protest activity and report any *potentially illegal acts* to the nearest FBI Joint Terrorism Task Force." If local police take the hint and start pouring in information, the task force could build a "Total Information Awareness"–lite database on antiwar groups and activists.

The FBI intelligence bulletin was first publicly disclosed by the *New York Times'* Eric Lichtblau on November 23, 2003.[49] The *Times* added that the FBI intelligence Bulletin "appears to offer the first corroboration of a coordinated, nationwide effort to collect intelligence regarding demonstrations."[50] Michael Ratner, president of Center for Constitutional Rights, observed: "Routine spying on dissidents is a sign of a police state, and unless we stop this administration's cavalier attitude towards fundamental rights we face a serious threat to our democracy."[51] Herman Schwartz, a constitutional law professor at American University, commented: "If you go around telling people, 'We're going to ferret out information on demonstrations,' that deters people. People don't want their names and pictures in FBI files."[52]

An FBI official who insisted on anonymity told the *New York Times:* "We're not concerned with individuals who are exercising their constitutional rights. But it's obvious that there are individuals capable of violence at these events."[53] The "capable of violence" standard justifies surveillance of almost anyone except quadriplegics strapped into wheelchairs. The FBI in the late

1960s and early 1970s justified surveillance of Women's Lib meetings—including keeping detailed records of each attendee's sexual grievances—based on the fear that libbers might become violent.[54] Given the FBI's expansive definition of "potential violence" in the past, this net can snare almost any group or individual who falls into official disfavor.

In response to the *Times* article, the FBI sent a letter to the editor, which it publicly released along with the confidential intelligence bulletin. The FBI stated: "The bulletin is not focused on political protesters or others who exercise their first amendment rights to protest the policies of the government, but simply cites the fact that anarchists and others have used violent tactics to disrupt otherwise peaceful demonstrations. . . . The bulletin does not suggest that state and local law enforcement should collect information on peaceful demonstrators."[55]

But this sanitized interpretation is at odds with the intelligence bulletin's specific request that local law enforcement watch for "possible indicators of protest activity" and report to the FBI "potentially illegal acts." And the FBI's reference to "extremists" wearing "layered clothing" implies that most wintertime protesters north of the Mason-Dixon Line should be on the target list.

In February 2004, the FBI's Joint Terrorism Task Force issued subpoenas for information on an antiwar meeting held at the Des Moines, Iowa, campus of Drake University. The subpoena demanded "all records of Drake University campus security reflecting any observations made of the November 15, 2003 meeting, including any records of persons in charge or control of the meeting, and any records of attendees."[56] The feds also subpoenaed four antiwar activists, including the leader of the Catholic Peace Ministry, to compel them to testify before a grand jury. After controversy arose over the subpoenas, the feds issued a new subpoena muzzling Drake University officials from making any public comments about the prior subpoenas.[57] The feds also demanded "information about leaders of the National Lawyer Guild's Drake University chapter, the location of NLG's local offices, its membership rolls, and any annual reports issued since 2002."[58] The president of the guild, Michael Ayers, complained, "The law is clear that the use of the grand jury to investigate protected political activities or to intimidate protesters exceeds its authority."[59] According to several experts, this was the first time in decades that the feds had issued such a subpoena to a university.

The feds lost control of the spin on the investigation and, after widespread criticism, canceled the Drake University subpoenas. There is no way to know how many other subpoenas may have been quietly complied with by colleges or other organizations that eschewed a public confrontation with the feds.

The following week, two U.S. Army intelligence agents descended upon the University of Texas law school in Austin. They entered the office of the *Journal of Women and the Law* and demanded that the editors turn over a roster of the people who attended a recent conference on Islam and women. The editors denied having a list; the behavior of one agent was described as intimidating. The agents then demanded contact information for the student who organized the conference, Sahar Aziz.[60] University of Texas law professor Douglas Laycock commented, "We certainly hope that the Army doesn't believe that attending a conference on Islamic law or Islam and women is itself ground for investigation."[61] Though the Posse Comitatus Act of 1878 supposedly prohibited the use of the military for domestic law enforcement, the Bush administration is successfully pushing to have the U.S. military become more involved in domestic snooping.[62]

It took over a decade after the first big antiwar protests in the 1960s before Americans learned how far the FBI had gone to suppress and subvert public opposition to the Vietnam War. In the 1960s and early 1970s, the FBI and many congressmen vehemently denied that the FBI was systematically subverting free speech. There is no evidence that congressional oversight is more competent or courageous now than it was during the time of COINTELPRO. There have been no congressional hearings spurred as a result of *FBI Intelligence Bulletin #89*—despite the FBI's stark animosity to free speech therein.

Is the FBI now considering a similar order to field offices as the one it sent in 1968, telling them to gather information illustrating the "scurrilous and depraved nature of many of the characters, activities, habits, and living conditions representative of New Left adherents"[63]—but this time focused on those who oppose Bush's Brave New World?

Since the FBI admits surveilling antiwar groups and urging local police to send in information on protesters, how far might the feds already be going? Is the FBI following the standard that Ashcroft publicly proclaimed in December 2001—presuming that those who invoke "phantoms of lost liberty" are giving "ammunition to America's enemies"? Is the FBI following the Homeland Security Department's standard and assuming the worst of anyone who "expressed dislike of attitudes and decisions of the U.S. government"? Unfortunately, because of the Bush administration's secrecy policy, Americans cannot know how far it has already gone to suppress dissent.

CHAPTER FOUR

Hollow Steel
Bush vs. Free Trade

Free trade supports and sustains freedom in all its forms. When we open trade, we open minds.

—*George W. Bush, May 29, 2001*[1]

President Bush scapegoats foreigners for his decisions to pilfer Americans. While Bush loves to praise free trade, in reality, "free trade" is whatever George Bush says it is. For Bush, like other recent presidents, "fairness" is the magic word to sanctify almost any trade restrictions.

In his speeches, President Bush has made some of the most eloquent statements on the benefits of trade ever made by an American president:

- "We will work with our allies and friends to be a force for good and a champion of freedom. We will work for free markets, free trade, and freedom from oppression. Freedom is exported every day, as we ship goods and products that improve the lives of millions of people."[2] (February 27, 2001)
- "Free trade applies the power of markets to the needs of the poor. . . . We also know that free trade encourages the habits of liberty that sustain freedom over the long haul."[3] (July 17, 2001)
- "Free trade is also a proven strategy for building global prosperity and adding to the momentum of political freedom. . . . And greater freedom

for commerce across the borders eventually leads to greater freedom for citizens within the borders."[4] (August 12, 2002)

THE GREAT STEEL SHAFT

The steel industry has been heavily protected since the erection of the first steel mill in America in 1875. Trade restrictions on steel imports have cost American steel users $120 billion since 1971, according to the Institute for International Economics.[5] The federal government has also lavishly subsidized the steel industry with $17 billion in direct bailouts and other aid since 1977.[6]

Historically, the more handouts the steel industry received, the more indignantly it demanded further protection against competition. At the time Bush took office, more than half of all steel imports were restricted by federal price controls—penalties for foreign subsidies or penalties for low prices (so-called "dumping").[7] Steel lobbyists have had a major role in writing U.S. "fair trade" laws, thus helping ensure that foreign competition is routinely found guilty despite absence of wrongdoing. Even with subsidies and protection, many domestic steel mills continue to flounder. The steel lobby pushed Bush for additional barriers against foreign competition.

On June 5, 2001, Bush visited Capitol Hill and repeatedly declared his concern about foreign steel "unfair trade practices."[8] Bush ordered the U.S. International Trade Commission to commence investigating whether steel imports were harming domestic steel mills. Once Bush summoned the ITC study, it was a foregone conclusion that the ITC would find "material injury" or threat of injury because of steel imports. The ITC often acts as a wholly owned subsidiary of the steel lobby. Steel lobbyists have hand-picked many ITC commissioners over the years. To ask the ITC whether the steel industry deserves more protection is like asking the Pentagon whether it wants to give corporations money to build new weapons systems.

The Bush administration knew even before imposing tariffs that the steel industry's problems were not due to unfair trade. In early 2001, the Treasury Department hired the Boston Consulting Group to analyze the U.S. steel industry and world steel situation. *American Metal Market* reported that the study "highlighted inefficiencies in U.S. steel production compared with global competitors" and "measured U.S. steel industry efficiency in the bottom one-third of a global comparison." U.S. steel companies were outraged by the study and, as a result of their protests, the Treasury Department suppressed the report.[9]

Even though overall steel imports were still declining, the ITC concluded that the American steel mills were being injured by a "surge." The only product with sharply increasing imports was steel slabs—unfinished products being bought by American steel mills and transformed into finished, higher-value products.[10] The ITC effectively concluded that American mills were being badly injured by the foreign slab they voluntarily purchased and profited from. It didn't make any sense but, since it was U.S. trade law, it did not have to make sense.

Bush had no obligation to accept the ITC recommendation to impose steel tariffs. At a February 11, 2002 meeting of the National Security Council in the White House, almost all the top officials opposed slapping on tariffs. Secretary of State Colin Powell objected: "We can't even say this will improve our steel industry. It will hurt downstream producers."[11] Vice President Dick Cheney, who was chairing the meeting, stated that "imports are, in fact, way down from the surge."[12] (In a meeting with Treasury Secretary Paul O'Neill the day before, Cheney talked about the coming midterm congressional elections and how Bush had promised to give relief to West Virginia, a steel producing state, during the 2000 campaign.[13])

On March 5, 2002, President Bush lowered the boom on steel imports. Bush began the announcement by declaring: "Free trade is an important engine of economic growth and a cornerstone of my economic agenda." He then revealed how he would protect American workers from that cornerstone: "An integral part of our commitment to free trade is our commitment to enforcing trade laws to make sure that America's industries and workers compete on a level playing field. Free trade should not mean lax enforcement. . . . Today I am announcing my decision to impose temporary safeguards to help give America's steel industry and its workers the chance to adapt to the large influx of foreign steel." Bush first invoked U.S. fair trade laws and the "level playing field"—and then announced that he was providing special relief to steel producers that had nothing to do with laws that provide U.S. companies with relief from allegedly unfair imports. Bush justified the aid to U.S. steel companies in light of "the harm from 50 years of foreign government intervention in the global steel market."[14]

When asked about whether the new 30 percent tariffs should be seen as a tax increase, Bush replied, "We're a free trading nation, and in order to remain a free trading nation, we must enforce law. And that's exactly what I did. I decided that imports were severely affecting our industry, an important industry—had a *negative impact*—and therefore, provide temporary relief so that the industry could restructure itself. That's exactly what the World Trade

Organization allows for."[15] There is nothing in federal law that compels a president to erect trade barriers to benefit inefficient or lagging industries. By this standard, Bush would be justified in imposing tariffs any time rising imports negatively impact a U.S. industry—thus protecting American consumers from any benefits from world trade.

Under the World Trade Organization agreement (which the U.S. government voluntarily signed along with many other nations), a government can impose temporary restrictions on imports to protect a domestic industry against a surge of imports. But, in this case, there was no surge of imports at that time and Bush's action starkly violated WTO rules.

The Bush trade team brazenly misrepresented the 30 percent tariff on steel imports as little more than a paperwork formality of no concern to Americans. U.S. Trade Representative Robert Zoellick declared: "Now, the nature of the relief—and I think this is a key distinction—is focused on foreigners, not Americans. And so this does not affect the ability of the American companies and consumers [to purchase steel products]. So the safeguards are applied, obviously, to exports to the United States, not American production."[16] But there was no reason to assume that the import taxes would not be passed on to American buyers or that domestic steel mills would scorn the invitation to hammer their customers by jacking up prices. Bush administration officials, in their comments on the tariffs, continually referred to them as "trade safeguards"—as if Bush and Zoellick were so clever that they could enrich American steel companies without plundering American steel buyers.

Bush upheld a venerable tradition of Republican presidents praising free trade while restricting steel imports. When President Reagan imposed quotas on steel imports in 1983, he announced that the restrictions are "tailored to the needs of the industry as well as the objective of trade liberalization."[17] President George H. W. Bush's 1989 Steel Trade Liberalization Program extended steel import quotas for several more years. Bush, Sr. declared that his import quotas aimed "to end government interference in global trade in steel"— though maintaining U.S. government import restrictions was a peculiar way to achieve that goal.

With the tariffs imposed in March 2002, George W. Bush sacrificed the interests of nearly 13 million Americans working in steel-using industries to curry favor with 226,000 steel workers—thereby upholding another hallowed yet idiotic Washington tradition. Steel trade restrictions have perennially bushwhacked American industry. International Trade Commission chairwoman Paula Stern noted in 1989, "Inflated U.S. steel prices were an important factor in the erosion of U.S. manufacturing preeminence and employment from the

1960s to the mid 1980s."[18] A 1984 Federal Trade Commission study estimated that steel quotas cost the U.S. economy $25 for each additional dollar of profit for American steel producers.[19]

George W. Bush's administration knew its steel tariffs would destroy American manufacturing jobs but imposed them anyhow. Bush's chief economic advisor, Glenn Hubbard, "drafted detailed analyses against the tariffs, including state-by-state job losses that he forecast for manufacturing," the *Washington Post* later reported.[20] (The estimated job losses were never made public.) A late 2001 economic analysis by the Trade Partnership Worldwide consulting firm estimated that "new steel tariffs would cost about eight American jobs for every one steel job protected."[21] *Washington Post* columnist George Will derided the Bush tariffs: "Think of them as an $8 billion contribution coerced from manufacturers and consumers of steel products, for the benefit of about six Republican congressional candidates in steel-producing districts, and for Bush's reelection campaign."[22]

Administration officials predicted that the 30 percent tariffs would cause average steel prices to rise by only 5 percent—based on assurances received from domestic steel mill executives.[23] Instead, prices for hot-rolled steel almost doubled between the time the ITC recommended tariffs on imports in December 2001 and the summer of 2002. Prices for other steel products shot up by 50 percent or more. Manufacturers were also devastated by shortages of steel products, as the tariffs disrupted international trade and deterred exporters from delivering to the United States. In many cases, U.S. steel mills broke their contracts and forced their American customers to pay far higher prices.

Undersecretary of Commerce Grant Aldonas assured the media that the intent of the tariffs "wasn't to create any windfall profits."[24] This raises the question of whether Bush administration officials know what a tariff is, or whether they actually believed their hokum about "trade safeguards." The Bush trade team apparently presumed that the tariff would have little effect on anything aside from Bush's reelection odds.

U.S. steel prices surged much higher than world steel prices, decimating the competitiveness of many American manufacturers. An International Trade Commission report found that during the first year of tariffs, "one quarter of steel consuming companies reported that their customers had shifted to purchasing finished parts or assemblies overseas as a result of the steel tariffs."[25] Richard Clayton, president of Textron Fastening Systems, complained: "The automotive parts industry has been one of the industries hardest hit by the steel tariffs. After the steel tariffs took effect, we experienced skyrocketing prices, broken contracts, and problems with steel quality and delivery time."[26]

Sen. Lamar Alexander (R-Tenn.), a staunch Bush supporter, derided the tariff in a Senate speech on July 17, 2003: "The tariffs have become a job killer in the United States and a jobs growth program for Korea, Japan, Germany and other countries that produce quality auto parts. Since their institution in March 2002, the tariffs have already destroyed nearly as many jobs in the steel-consuming companies of America than exist in the entire steel-producing industry of America. Some auto parts plants in my state of Tennessee are already closing because of the higher costs of steel imposed by the tariffs."[27] Alexander cited a study done for the Consuming Industries Trade Action Coalition which found that "higher steel prices cost 200,000 American jobs and $4 billion in lost wages from February to November 2002."[28]

In September 2003, the *Washington Post* reported that "key administration officials have concluded that Bush's order has turned into a debacle."[29] A 2003 International Trade Commission analysis of the impact of steel tariffs concluded that the tariffs cost steel consuming industries $9 for every $1 in additional steel profits.[30] The *Post* noted that the hard numbers on job losses "may be less important than the perception in key states where the tariffs have been debilitating."[31] The high tariffs failed to achieve a primary goal when in August 2003 the United Steel Workers endorsed Democratic congressman Richard Gephardt, instead of Bush, for president.

The steel tariffs infuriated governments in Europe, Japan, Korea, and elsewhere. The *Wall Street Journal* noted in 2002: "Bush aides say they were surprised at the [foreign] uproar, but pronounce it more bark than bite."[32] Foreign governments filed complaints with the World Trade Organization, and the organization repeatedly ruled that the Bush tariffs violated WTO rules because there was no surge of imports to justify the tariffs.

The Bush trade team assumed that even if the World Trade Organization ruled against them, they could maintain the steel tariffs until after the 2004 election. Bush's trade experts wrongly expected foreign governments to dawdle before retaliating against U.S. exports.[33] The European Union shocked the Bush administration by promptly publishing a target list for punitive tariff retaliation in November 2003, picking out products from politically strategic states for the 2004 election, including textiles from North and South Carolina, Harley Davidson motorcycles from Wisconsin and Pennsylvania, and citrus from Florida. Japan, China, and South Korea also hustled to slap retaliatory tariffs on U.S. exports.

Bush surrendered to the threat of foreign retaliation and proclaimed victory in his December 4, 2003 announcement ending the tariffs. Bush rattled off some of the achievements the tariff produced: "Steel producers and workers have negotiated new groundbreaking labor agreements that allow greater flexibility and increase job stability."[34] American steel mills have been hobbled for decades by make-work job restrictions finagled by the United Steel Workers (USW). The new labor agreements permitted reducing the number of shift foremen by up to 90 percent. Bush did not explain why the USW deserved a federal bribe (i.e., higher steel prices) to stop sabotaging the productivity of American steel mills.

Citing another example of how life in America improved during the tariffs, Bush said, "The Pension Benefit Guaranty Corporation has guaranteed the pensions of eligible steelworkers and retirees and relieved the high pension costs that burdened some companies."[35] Instead, the high costs now burden American taxpayers, who are financing far more generous pensions for steelworkers than most taxpayers will collect. The Bush administration kindly transferred almost $10 billion in pension liabilities from sinking steel companies to struggling American taxpayers. Ironically, Trade Representative Zoellick, in the February 11, 2002, National Security Council meeting, had mentioned the danger of steel company pension defaults as a good reason to impose steel tariffs.[36]

Ending the steel tariffs did not stifle Bush's sanctimony:

- On November 17, 2003, Bush declared, "I am a fierce free trader. . . . In order for us to be free traders, we've got to enforce the rules of free trade, and I was doing so through the International Trade Commission's report."[37]
- In his December 4 "Mission Accomplished" speech, Bush declared that "an integral part of our commitment to free trade is our commitment to enforcing our trade laws."[38]
- Also on December 4, in a quick press comment before meeting Jordan's King Abdullah, Bush said the steel tariffs allowed the United States "to say to the world that we will trade, but we want to trade in a fair way."[39]

The tariffs never had anything to do with fairness. They were simply a sop to a domestic industry and an attempt to capture a union's endorsement and swing votes in the coming election. The temporary tariffs did permanent damage. Bill Adler, president of Stripmatic Products Inc., a Cleveland auto parts fabricator, observed: "When the tariffs came, they mortally wounded a significant percentage of the metal stampers. A lot of the damage has already been done."[40]

Regardless of the harm the steel tariffs inflicted, Bush expected to be applauded for his good intentions and compassion for steel workers. The Bush administration willingly endangered operations of thousands of companies and destroyed the jobs of an unknown number of American workers—solely for the president's own political advantage. Bush apparently expected steel users simply to "take a bullet" in honor of his reelection campaign.

BRA WARS

For almost two centuries, the U.S. government has vigorously protected Americans against low-priced foreign clothing. The United States maintains more than a thousand quotas on textile and clothing products. Many of the highest U.S. tariffs are on clothing and apparel. According to a Federal Reserve study, trade barriers add $33.6 billion to the price Americans pay for clothing and textiles each year.[41]

In 1994, as part of an international trade liberalization agreement, the United States and other nations pledged to remove all quotas on clothing and textile imports by December 31, 2004. In 2002, U.S. import quotas on bras were ended—in part because no American company manufactures bras. Bra imports from China had been restricted by U.S. quotas for over 20 years. After restrictions were lifted, Chinese bra exports to the United States swelled by 71 percent.

American textile companies were outraged by the Chinese bra surge. Some U.S. companies export fabrics and parts to Central America where low-paid workers assemble the components into bras; these are exported to the United States with zero tariffs (because they are made with U.S. components). The American Textile Manufacturers Institute petitioned the Commerce Department to reimpose quotas, aggrieved that the price of cotton Chinese bras in early 2003 declined from $6.53 to $5.56 per square meter.[42] (Happily, most consumers purchase by the piece rate instead of by the square meter.)

Even without quotas, bras must leap relatively high tariff barriers to enter the U.S. mainland. Bras made of cotton or polyester face a 16.9 percent tariff. The tariff burden is much lower—only 4.9 percent—on silk bras containing lace or embroidery. And for "respectable" silk bras with no lace or embroidery, the tariff is only 2.7 percent.[43] This tax on feminine accoutrements achieves nothing aside from boosting federal revenue and mulcting shoppers at Wal-Mart, Victoria's Secret, and elsewhere.

On November 18, 2003, the Commerce Department announced it was slapping import quotas on Chinese bras, dressing gowns, and knit fabric, restricting their growth to 7.5 percent in the following year. The decision was made by the Committee for the Implementation of Textile Agreements, the most protectionist cabal in the U.S. government. Commerce Undersecretary Gary Aldonas justified the restrictions: "Even with the Chinese figures built into the overall trade averages in these categories, the Chinese figures outstrip the average overall increase in trade."[44] Aldonas sounded as if the government is obliged to restrain anything that moves faster than average.

Commerce Secretary Don Evans said that the United States was simply "enforcing our trade laws" to "make it clear to the leadership of China and the people of America that we think free trade means more jobs for Americans. But it's got to be fair trade."[45] Evans did not reveal the secret formula by which the Bush administration deduced 7.5 percent as the "fair" brassiere expansion rate.

President Bush commented a few days after the quotas were decreed: "Free trade agreements require people honoring the agreements. And there are market disruptions involved with certain Chinese textiles; we're addressing those disruptions. . . . And as I have been saying publicly, that free trade also requires a level playing field for trade."[46] China has no import barriers against U.S. bras, and no bras are manufactured in the United States. Bush's comment illustrates how "level playing field" is a rote formula politicians invoke before clobbering consumers, akin to an obscure Latin phrase muttered by a priest before a medieval execution.

The United States never had any implied or explicit agreement with China that its bra exports would not rise after the U.S. government stopped repressing them. Bush and his trade team continually implied that the Chinese were guilty of bad faith, when it was actually the Bush administration doing a cheap shot.

The bra restrictions are far more likely to boost textile company profits than to save textile jobs. And a 7.5 percent import rise is unlikely to keep pace with the expanding U.S. market. (The average bra size in America rose from 34B to 36C between 1991 and 2003.)[47]

The Chinese restrictions amounted to little more than Bush pandering to textile workers and securing his southern electoral base. Perhaps the Bush administration also thought that its sacrificial gesture might inspire some American factory to begin making bras again.

The bra restraints may be the opening salvo of a new war on clothing imports. Aldonas said he is seeking a "broader" discussion with China regarding its other textile exports to the U.S. market.[48] The *New York Times* noted that "textile companies and unions are putting heavy pressure on President Bush to expand the agenda to cover nearly all of the $10.3 billion in imports of Chinese clothing and fabric."[49]

INSTEAD OF FREE TRADE

President Bush relishes huffing about free trade without actually putting American manufacturers and farmers at risk of competing with imports. So-called free trade agreements are one of his favorite devices to burnish his credentials without endangering his campaign contributions.

In his January 29, 2003 message to Congress seeking approval of a Free Trade Agreement (FTA) with Singapore, Bush declared: "The agreement we have negotiated promotes our commitment to secure a level playing field and open new opportunities for America's workers, farmers, businesses, and consumers in global trade."[50] But this was a sham. Even before the agreement was signed, Singapore had lower average tariffs than did the United States. The FTA specified that Singapore would have duty-free access for its clothing exports to the American market only if it purchased its yarn and fabric from American factories. This makes as little sense as forcing Italian companies to use American cowhide for their leather shoe exports, or forcing Japanese companies to use American sand for their semiconductor exports.

Bush's biggest FTA triumph came with Australia in February 2004. Australia is among the world's most efficient sugar, beef, and dairy producers. Bush took care, therefore, to see that those products were excluded from the Free Trade Agreement. In return, the United States agreed to exempt the Australian pharmaceutical industry and film industry from vigorous American competition. A *Los Angeles Times* analysis noted: "The pact gives the Bush administration an important domestic political win in an election year by placating the influential farm lobby and saving agricultural jobs in such key electoral states as California, Florida and Pennsylvania."[51]

The U.S.-Australia FTA victimizes New Zealand, Australia's most important trading partner and perhaps the world's most open economy. Greg Rushford, publisher of the best source of information on U.S. trade policy, the *Rushford Report,* noted that "the proposed U.S.-Australia FTA is designed to inflict some damage on New Zealand 's economy. By definition, Australians will be given special access to the American marketplace that will be denied to New Zealand. . . . The U.S.-Aussie FTA will obviously encourage potential investors in New Zealand to set up shop in Australia instead."[52] Australia sent troops to fight in Afghanistan and Iraq, while New Zealand—which has not always unquestioningly supported U.S. foreign policy—did not.

The Bush administration's fixation on free trade agreements is undermining progress toward a worldwide agreement that would provide vastly more benefits. In his May 17, 2002 World Trade Week proclamation, Bush noted, "Economists have calculated that lowering trade barriers by just one-third will strengthen the world's economic welfare by up to $613 billion and that of the United States by $177 billion. For the average American family of four, that amounts to $2,500 of annual savings."[53] But instead of concentrating on a broad international agreement, the Bush administration devotes itself to reaching FTAs with economic pipsqueaks such as Morocco and Swaziland.

One would presume that an honest free trade agreement would simply require little more than a handshake between the political leaders of the nations involved. If trade is free, then what is there to quibble about? But that would defeat the entire purpose of using free trade agreements to give preferences to favored nations and favored industries.

Free trade is not complex; it does not require an army of hair-splitting bureaucrats to achieve. Free trade agreements, on the other hand, usually outweigh the Bible and have more trick clauses than a Hollywood movie deal. (The U.S.-Australia FTA is nine hundred pages of wheedling, hemming, and hawing.)

Free trade minimizes the power of rulers to decimate the purchasing power of citizens. Free trade agreements allow politicians and bureaucrats to pick winners and losers with arcane formulas that guarantee that trade lawyers will never go hungry.

Free trade allows consumers and businesses to benefit from the best goods the world can produce at the lowest prices. Free trade agreements with a single nation divert trade. They give favored treatment to the producers whose governments sign deals with Washington and put the producers of all other nations at a disadvantage.

FTAs allow political clout to trump economic comparative advantage. FTAs seek to shift trade in whatever direction is most profitable to the politicians making the deals, rather than let trade flow from the decisions of producers and consumers.

Free trade agreements make borders more imposing and onerous for every nation except the one that politicians favor. Free trade aims to make national borders invisible for commerce.

The notion of "free trade"—but only with nationalities that American politicians bless—is a charade. This is like proclaiming freedom of the press, and then adding that people can buy books only from publishers specifically approved by the U.S. Congress.

CONCLUSION: BUSH'S FAIR TRADE FRAUD

At the March 2, 2001 swearing-in ceremony for his agriculture secretary, Ann Veneman, Bush declared: "Ann and I will carry out this equivocal [*sic*] message to the world: Markets must be open. The United States will not tolerate favoritism and unfair subsidies."[54] Bush was true to his word: his message could not be much more equivocal. The only unfair subsidies are the ones not awarded by American politicians. And the only favoritism that is impermissible is that which does not profit Bush and the Republican Party.

Bush is giving free trade a bad name. Bush is poisoning the well on trade—both abroad and at home—and spurring confusion and distrust. By talking as if free trade can be reconciled with imposing steel tariffs and restricting bras, Bush makes free trade a laughingstock. By wrapping protectionism in free trade rhetoric, Bush is legitimating protectionism and setting precedents for far greater trade restrictions in the coming years.

CHAPTER FIVE

Ed Fraud 101

The No Child Left Behind Act is historic, ushering in a new era of accountability
and education.

—*George W. Bush, March 2, 2002*[1]

Education reform was a premier topic in Bush's 2000 presidential campaign and probably the most popular part of his compassionate conservative platform. Bush promised to give America the benefit of his own
experience revolutionizing the Texas education system during his time as
governor. Bush, like Clinton, was determined to be seen as an "education
president."

When the president signed his landmark education act, he promised great
things from the

> most sweeping educational bill ever to come before Congress. It represents a
> major new commitment of the Federal Government to quality and equality in
> the schooling that we offer our young people. . . . By passing this bill, we
> bridge the gap between helplessness and hope for more than five million edu-
> cationally deprived children. We reduce the terrible time lag in bringing new
> teaching techniques into the nation's classrooms. And we rekindle the revolu-
> tion—the revolution of the spirit against the tyranny of ignorance. As Presi-
> dent of the United States, I believe deeply no law I have signed or will ever sign
> means more to the future of America.[2]

The president was Lyndon Johnson, the date was April 11, 1965, and the act was the Elementary and Secondary Education Act, a massive federal intrusion into local schools. Johnson's act was seen as "revolutionary." The Constitution provided no role for the federal government in education, and for more than 180 years, schooling was almost entirely a state and local responsibility. Title I of LBJ's act poured $250 billion in federal dollars into schools in relatively impoverished areas in the following decades, seeking to close achievement gaps between students from low-income and affluent homes and to reduce gaps between races.

Major evaluations have showed that Title I produced no lasting benefit to students.[3] Student performance in American schools deteriorated sharply in the 1970s. President Reagan appointed dignitaries to a commission whose 1983 report, *A Nation at Risk: The Imperative for Educational Reform*, warned: "If an unfriendly foreign power had attempted to impose on America the mediocre educational performance that exists today, we might well have viewed it as an act of war. . . . We have, in effect, been committing an act of unthinking, unilateral educational disarmament."[4]

The 1983 report spurred panic and fierce resolutions to improve American education. The most common response was to spend more money. Total government spending per student almost doubled in the subsequent two decades. But there was little or no sustained rise in educational achievement,[5] and reading scores of high school students continued to deteriorate. Some state governments began pressing for accountability from the schools.

President Bill Clinton capitalized on Americans' angst on education, making many appearances in classrooms and pushing legislation that would help bankroll the hiring of one hundred thousand new teachers and the modernization of schools around the country.[6]

Federal education policy has always been susceptible to politically inspired nonsense. Clinton appointees sought to use federal power to bury achievement gaps. In May 1999, Clinton's Education Department effectively proposed to harshly penalize the use of SAT scores by American colleges because of the continuing gap between the scores of white and Asian American students compared with the scores of black and Hispanic students. The proposal set off a firestorm in academia as university administrators recognized that the new policy could make it easier for the feds to impose racial quotas on student admissions. Clinton's Education Department also endorsed ten mathematics programs for schoolchildren that, in the words of two hundred mathematicians and scientists (including four Nobel laureates), aimed to "dumb down" school curricula to reduce racial gaps in student achievement.[7] The Clinton administration backed down on both issues.

Clinton's education efforts were policy failures and political triumphs. Clinton's "positive rating" on education in 1996 was five times higher than that of Republican presidential candidate Robert Dole.

At the time Bush became president in 2001, many public school systems across the country were mental wastelands. Only 13 percent of Philadelphia eleventh graders are "able to read a newspaper with any kind of comprehension."[8] The 2000 National Assessment of Educational Progress (NAEP, the only comprehensive national survey of student ability) found that "fewer than a third of fourth-graders can read proficiently." Only 3 percent of black and 4 percent of Hispanic fourth-graders were proficient at math.[9] Federal education spending had done little or nothing to remedy such problems in part because, as a General Accounting Office report noted, "federally funded programs have historically placed a low priority on results and accountability."[10]

Despite the failure of not only Clinton's education reforms but also almost all federal efforts on elementary and secondary education going back to Lyndon Johnson, George W. Bush resolved to expand federal control over local schooling. When Bush sent his legislative proposal to Congress on January 23, 2001, he declared: "Change will not come by disdaining or dismantling the federal role of education."[11] On July 7, 2001, Bush claimed his education bill was "the boldest plan to improve our public schools in a generation, a plan to raise educational standards for every child and to require new accountability from every school."[12]

Bush signed the No Child Left Behind Act (NCLB) at a public high school in Ohio on January 8, 2002. One staffer for Sen. Joseph Lieberman (D-Conn.) complained that the Bush education proposal "essentially plagiarized our plan."[13] Harvard education professor Richard Elmore called the NCLB "the single largest, and the single most damaging, expansion of federal power over the nation's education system in history." Chester Finn, assistant secretary of education under Bush's father, declared of NCLB: "It's Potemkin reform, a facade underwritten by billions in new spending."[14]

THE MECHANICS OF
BUSH EDUCATION FREEDOM

At the same time that NCLB purportedly imposes higher standards, it also supposedly liberates school officials and teachers. On June 20, 2001, Bush declared: "When these reforms become law, schools will have more freedom from needless meddling by Washington. There will be fewer mandates and regulations for schools to meet, more freedom and more flexibility, as schools live up to high standards they will now be required to meet."[15]

The NCLB requires all schools to annually test every child in reading and math from third grade through eighth grade. Schools separate out test scores according to race, level of poverty, special education status, and students with limited English proficiency. NCLB requires that all students be able to perform at "grade level"—that is, to pass minimal competency reading and math tests—by the year 2014. The act also requires that almost all students take the tests. Previously many state and local school systems' inflated average scores by arranging for low-scoring students not to take the tests.

The key to NCLB compliance is "adequate yearly progress" (AYP) as defined by state education plans and standards. Schools that fail to achieve AYP for two consecutive years will be labeled as "needing improvement"—that is, failing. The failure of a single ethnic or income group to meet a progress target means the school fails. If a school misses AYP for four consecutive years, the local school board is obliged to restructure the school. After five years of misses, all school staff can be fired and the state government must take over the school (or convert it to a charter school).

Bush freedom gives schools the freedom to meet NCLB deadlines or else be destroyed. The feds have vastly more punitive power over local schools than ever before.

DUMBING DOWN STANDARDS

In a July 2003 speech, Bush declared that the No Child Left Behind Act "essentially says . . . there is [*sic*] going to be high standards and strong accountability measures to every State in the Union."[16] Education Secretary Roderick Paige, speaking two months later at the National Press Club, announced that because of NCLB, "For the first time in the history of our nation, every state in our nation has an accountability plan that holds all schools and all students in their state to state-adopted high standards."[17]

By the time Bush and Paige boasted about high standards, the NCLB domino effect was already toppling standards and undermining expectations around the nation.

NCLB was a response to decades of local and state education bureaucrats conning parents into believing that the schools were performing well. School test data have been manipulated to allow "all 50 state education agencies to report above-average scores for their elementary schools, with most claiming such scores in every subject area and every grade level," as former Education Department official Larry Uzzell stated in 1989.[18] NCLB aimed to bring honesty to education statistics.

Because NCLB hinges on "adequate yearly progress," the lower the initial standards set by the states, the easier it becomes to show sufficient progress. Since NCLB's passage, many states have redefined failure downwards.

Michigan had some of the highest standards in the nation prior to NCLB. "Michigan [education] officials lowered the percentage of students who must pass statewide tests to certify a school as making adequate progress—to 42 percent, from 75 percent of high school students on English tests," the *New York Times* noted.[19] This slashed the number of Michigan schools tagged as NCLB failures from 1,513 to 216.

A headline in the Elmira, New York, *Star-Gazette* captured the soul of the standards game: "Schools Improve as Standards Go Down."

> Area schools made dramatic improvements on state English tests thanks mostly to lowered standards. . . . New York state this year lowered the level at which schools are considered to be performing satisfactorily as compared with last year. The outcome: fourth-graders at 46 of 50 area elementary schools met English test requirements, while eighth-graders at 25 of 26 middle schools met the requirements. Last year, 39 of 50 elementary schools and 12 of 26 middle schools met much higher standards.[20]

To avoid NCLB sanctions, Maryland abandoned a well-respected statewide assessment test and created a new NCLB-friendly test, the Maryland School Assessment (MSA). The *Baltimore Sun* noted in March 2003:

> Because it's the first year of MSA, teachers and principals are under no pressure to improve scores. Unfortunately, some would welcome mediocre results in this baseline testing so that progress would be easier to demonstrate later. For the same reason, Maryland officials will be pressured to set a low "proficient" score when they take on that all-important task next summer.[21]

Some states set their NCLB baselines at levels that should be satisfied by any random selection of people not in a mortuary. *National Journal* noted in 2003, "In Delaware this year . . . 33 percent [of students] must be at grade level in math."[22] In the District of Columbia, only 30.3 percent of elementary school students were obliged to pass the reading exam to satisfy the NCLB goal for 2003. The *Washington Post* reported that "school officials in the District, where scores have been low, anticipate that nearly 80 percent of their schools will hit the modest target for 'adequate progress' this year."[23]

Arkansas set a bottom-of-the-wagon-wheel-rut standard for NCLB compliance and progress. For the fall of 2003, even if 90 percent of a school's students failed to achieve math proficiency, the school would still satisfy statewide standards—only 9.3 percent of students had to score "proficient" or "advanced."[24] Alabama schools are among the nation's worst, yet Alabama's NCLB baseline ensures that its schools have one of the lowest failure rates—only 4 percent.[25]

NCLB deterred North Carolina from raising standards. North Carolina state standards are very low; even if students answer wrongly half the questions, they are still certified as "working at grade level." Though 84 percent of North Carolina fourth graders rated proficient in math scores under the state test, barely a quarter rated "proficient" on the NAEP.[26] State Superintendent Mike Ward conceded that the existing standard measures only whether a student is "minimally ready to move on." But Ward warned the state board of education that raising the standards could be politically disastrous. The *Charlotte Observer* noted, "Requiring students to get more questions right would reduce the number of N.C. schools that meet federal education standards and create an outcry from educators."[27]

The NCLB-sparked plunge in education standards was obvious shortly after Bush signed the law. Secretary Paige sent an angry letter to all state education commissioners in October 2002: "Some states have lowered the bar of expectations to hide the low performance of their schools. This is not worthy of a great country."[28] Paige warned that state plans to "ratchet down their standards in order to remove schools from their lists of low performers" were "nothing less than shameful." Paige declared: "Not only is this political tactic an embarrassment, it undermines the *public's trust in education*. Those who play semantic games or try to tinker with state numbers . . . stand in the way of progress and reform. They are apologists for failure."[29]

But, as far as undermining public trust in government schools, Bush's and Paige's subsequent statements about NCLB requiring high standards were as deceptive as anything done by state bureaucrats. Paige howled about states slashing standards in 2002 and then ignored the issue. The Bush administration thus helped hoodwink the American public one more time on the quality of government schools.

Many states reduced the number of failing schools by finagling statistics. Thirty-five states are using "margin-of-error" formulas that "give schools leeway—ranging from minor to dramatic—to meet math and reading standards that many parents and even some educators thought were set in stone," the

Chicago Tribune reported.[30] One Oregon high school finagled scores so that even though only 28 percent of students passed a reading test it satisfied the state NCLB-standard mandate that 40 percent of students pass. Maryland set a cutoff point for proficiency but permitted schools to miss the mark by up to 15 percent.[31] Kansas and Maryland reduced the number of failing schools by half by jiggering test results. The federal Education Department explicitly approved the dubious adjustment formulas used by states to slash the number of failed schools. University of Chicago mathematics professor Paul Sally observed that there was no "theoretical basis" for such adjustments: "What they're [states] trying to do is fake it, just plain and simple."[32]

In his 2004 State of the Union Address, Bush boasted that "the No Child Left Behind Act is opening the door of opportunity to all of America's children."[33] But the law's fixation of minimum competency is administering a coup de grace to many programs for gifted and advanced students. The *Wall Street Journal* noted in December 2003 that "a school faces no penalty if top students tail off as long as they remain proficient. To abide by the [NCLB], schools are shifting resources away from programs that help their most gifted students."[34] Illinois, Missouri, and California slashed statewide funding for gifted student programs, as did almost a quarter of Connecticut school districts in 2003. Stanford University education professor Michael Kirst observed that because all of NCLB's "incentives . . . are to focus on the bottom or the middle, reallocating resources there makes sense if you want to stay out of trouble."[35] Joyce Vantassel-Baska of the College of William and Mary Center for Gifted Education commented that NCLB "has almost taken gifted off the radar screen in terms of people being worried about that group of learners."[36] In December 2003, Deputy Secretary of Education Eugene Hickok dismissed criticism of NCLB's effect on gifted children: "It's a false dichotomy. If they get rid of the achievement gap, the entire school should improve."[37] But there is no reason to expect that concentrating resources on the lowest-scoring students will spawn sufficient karma to make the most talented students flourish. In March 2004, Hickok conceded to the *New York Times* that the shutdown of gifted education programs was an "unintended consequence" of NCLB.[38] But this adverse effect will never show up in the administration's score-keeping.

THE TRANSFER MIRAGE

Bush bragged on July 1, 2002: "Starting this September, as many as 3.5 million students across America who attend failing schools will have different options of transferring to another public school. It's part of being an account-able society."[39] NCLB gives students the right to transfer away from a school that misses AYP goals for two consecutive years into some other public school. Education Secretary Roderick Paige declared in September 2003: "When parents know their children's schools are failing, and they have the power to do something about it, they can control their family's own destiny."[40]

But the transfer option quickly turned out to be a mirage, obscured by conniving bureaucrats or ignored by apathetic parents. In Texas, almost a hundred thousand students were in schools that performed poorly enough to entitle the students to transfer elsewhere; only 107 students statewide switched schools.[41] In the fall of 2003, 20,000 parents in Oakland, California, received letters informing them of the right to transfer, but only 39 parents exercised the right. In East Palo Alto, 2,000 parents received letters, and not one family opted to move their kids to better schools.[42] The *San Jose Mercury News* observed: "Parents tend to be critical of education generally—but not of their own schools."[43]

The *Washington Post* noted in December 2003 that only a "minuscule" number of students have transferred schools nationwide because of NCLB.[44] The *Post* reported that "In rural areas, it is often difficult for parents to find more acceptable schools without traveling great distances. Even in urban areas, good schools are often crowded and reluctant to accept students from 'failing' schools."[45] In North Carolina, fewer than 50 students statewide transferred thanks to NCLB in the 2002–2003 school year. The Education Department has no information on how many students nationwide have taken NCLB-transfers.

NCLB also mandates that schools that have failed to achieve AYP for two consecutive years must offer paid tutors at no charge for low-income students. Companies that provide federally subsidized tutoring are bribing students to spur demand for their services.[46] In Baton Rouge, Louisiana, private companies are giving free cell phones, televisions, electric scooters, and video game consoles to "students who complete tax-paid after-school tutoring programs." John Hewitt of Louisiana Learning Circle commented: "If you think kids are going to sign on for this because it's a great program offered by the federal government, get real. You have to sell them on it."[47]

NCLB-mandated tutoring is stumbling in Chicago. Six thousand Chicago pupils enrolled for tutoring but less than half bothered to show up. "Companies are struggling with the same discipline, attendance and other problems that have kept failing schools from raising proficiency levels on their own," the *New York Times* reported. One disgruntled tutor commented: "It was extremely hard to get those kids' attention. They were boisterous and shouting from the day I walked into the class."[48] The Chicago school system is setting up its own teachers to offer tutoring services—which means that teachers will be receiving bonuses as a result of the schools' failure during normal working hours.

The tutoring has been still-born in some places because schools have done a lousy job of notifying parents of the option. "Detroit schools notified parents in August [2003] in a two-page letter full of jargon such as 'supplemental educational services.' The words 'free tutoring' were not mentioned," the *Detroit Free Press* reported.[49] Only 3 percent of eligible Detroit students accepted free tutoring. The tutoring is paid for out of federal education aid that otherwise goes to schools. The fewer kids who sign up for NCLB-mandated tutoring, the more money the school system can spend on its own priorities.

NCLB presumed that parents would take action once they learned of their school's failures. But a study entitled "Fumbling for an Exit Key: Parents, Choice, and the Future of No Child Left Behind" by Harvard professor William Howell, conducted for Boston's Pioneer Institute, found that "the vast majority of [parents] who in fact qualify for the Act's choice and supplemental services do not know that their child's school is on the state's list of underperforming schools." Howell scorned relying on school districts "to disseminate information about which schools have met AYP, and which students hence qualify for choice and supplemental services." Howell urged "state and federal governments . . . to find ways to communicate directly with parents to ensure that they know about the educational opportunities available to them."[50]

LIBERATING STUDENTS TO FLEE VIOLENCE

When Bush submitted his education proposal to Congress, he declared:

> We must face up to the plague of school violence. . . . American children must not be left in persistently dangerous or failing schools. . . . When children and teenagers go to school afraid of being threatened or attacked or worse, our society must make it clear, it's the ultimate betrayal of adult responsibility.[51]

In 2000, there were 700,000 violent crimes in public schools across the nation.[52] Inner city schools were especially prone to violence, though suburban and rural schools also had their gross abuses. Most states and localities made little effort to track school crime rates.

NCLB supposedly provided an escape hatch. NCLB requires that states establish a definition of a "persistently dangerous school" and permit parents to transfer their kids out of such snake pits. The Bush administration could have promulgated binding rules for the state definitions. William Modzeleski, the associate deputy undersecretary of education, warned states that "we are seriously considering regulating this."[53] Instead, the Education Department sent out 13 pages of non-binding guidance.

With a flurry of meetings and memos, state education officials dramatically ended the problem of school violence in America. In 2003, only 38 of the 90,000 schools in America were officially classified as "persistently dangerous."[54] Forty-seven states did not have a single persistently dangerous school in their domain.

Colorado's definition focuses solely on serious violence and provides school administrators ample leeway for little mishaps without schools being labeled persistently dangerous. "A school with 1,000 students could have 179 homicides every year and, without other offenses, still not qualify as dangerous," the *New York Times* reported. Dave Smith, a top official with the Colorado Department of Education, conceded that the 179 homicides yet not dangerous example was "technically correct." Smith blamed Washington: "Our problem was a total lack of guidance from the federal level. They just said, 'Define it as you like, and we'll tell you whether we like it or not.'"[55] The Colorado legislature considered a bill in April 2004 to change the standard, which Senate president John Andrews denounced as "absurd."[56] The bill was defeated because legislators feared that revising the standard could tar the reputations of schools with many violent incidents.

New York State ruled that an elementary or secondary school could be classified as persistently dangerously "if the school has in each of two consecutive years a 3 percent or greater ratio of weapons incidents to enrollment."[57] As long as less than 3 percent of an elementary school's students are caught with guns and knives, the school is NCLB-safe. Eli Silverman, a professor at John Jay College of Criminal Justice, criticized the state standard: "When you look at weapons incidents, they're small compared to actual assaults. If you ask people what they're most afraid of in the school system, they're most afraid of a fight."[58]

The New York standard was almost reasonable compared to that of Wisconsin, which requires that "the number of weapons-related suspensions exceeds 5 percent of the student body." A Wisconsin school can also be considered persistently dangerous if one percent of school's students are expelled for violent felonies three years in a row. Department of Public Instruction Deputy Superintendent Tony Evers explained: "Wisconsin schools are pretty safe."[59]

Illinois education officials were much more tolerant of recalcitrant students, requiring that violence-related expulsions exceed three percent of a school's enrollment for two consecutive years before labeling a school dangerous. North Carolina was even more liberal, requiring "two consecutive years of five or more violent criminal offenses per 100 students." But even this level of carnage will not trigger a "persistently dangerous" label unless the "state school board decides the conditions that contributed to these crimes are likely to continue into a third year."[60]

A middle school in Jacksonville had 478 crime and violence incidents in one year, including the sexual assault of a 12-year-old in a school bathroom by four students. Happily for the kids and parents, the school is not persistently dangerous because Florida sets a novel threshold which, aside from requiring many violent students, also requires that "a majority of students, parents and school personnel" agree to the "dangerous" label in a formal survey.[61] Permitting school officials to vote against the "dangerous" label means empowering them to suppress the evidence of their own failure to protect students.

One high school in Los Angeles was the scene of "28 battery cases, a robbery, two assaults with a deadly weapon and three sex offenses" in the 2001–02 school year.[62] But the school was not persistently dangerous, according to California education officials. The *Los Angeles Times* declared that "California's definition flunks any reasonable test. . . . Instead of addressing actual crime, the state measures how administrators reacted. If at least 1% of a school's students were expelled for violent crimes, the school is defined as dangerous. But only if there was also at least one incident involving a firearm in each of the last three years. A campus can come up clean even if students are regularly robbed at knifepoint or beaten."[63] Tim Buresh, the chief operating officer of the Los Angeles Unified School District, commented, "This is an index that almost rewards you for turning a blind eye to problems."[64] The *Times* reported that one of the school officials who helped craft the standard stated that "one concern among some school districts was that a broader definition of danger might have triggered too many transfers."[65]

Ohio officials initially considered a standard that would have labeled 36 schools persistently dangerous; lobbying by local school officials persuaded the state to set a standard that prevents any Ohio school from being labelled persistently dangerous.[66] Cleveland schools chief executive Barbara Byrd-Bennett commented: "I don't think you'll find one educator who would say that makes any bit of sense."[67]

Many states set the standard to practically guarantee no school would be found guilty. Missouri School Board member Jeannine Osborn admitted: "We don't ever anticipate having a school on the persistently dangerous schools list."[68] Sue Adams of the Alabama Department of Education commented: "We never expected any of our schools to meet the standard this year. We have schools that have incidents almost every day or certainly every week. But we don't have any schools that are persistently dangerous."[69]

Permitting kids to escape "persistently dangerous" schools was supposed to be one of the most humanitarian aspects of the NCLB. Instead, education officials defined the term to minimize students' freedom to escape violence. Bureaucrats refuse to permit children to flee from dangerous schools because that would damage the reputation of the school administrators and embarrass the teachers and other staff.

The only thing more ludicrous than many of the state definitions is the response of the Bush administration, which is both financing and countenancing the scams. In September 2002, William Modzeleski, who was also director of the federal Office of Safe and Drug-Free Schools, warned states: "It can't be that you raise the bar so high that it automatically excludes every school in your state."[70]

But after state governments did exactly that the federal overseers all of a sudden lost their voice.[71] In July 2003, after California's goofy standard provoked howls, Modzeleski commented: "There is no one right definition. One of the byproducts of this will lead to a debate between the public and state agencies. If there aren't any persistently dangerous schools, then why not?"[72]

In September 2003, as states announced one absurd definition after another, Modzeleski earned a gold medal for positive thinking: "Look, I'm less concerned about the number of schools [listed as persistently dangerous]. The numbers become sort of a secondary issue to the fact that we now have 50 states saying: 'Hey, as we concentrate on everything we do about teaching and learning, we also now have to ensure that the environments are safe.' . . . Not to say they haven't done so before, but now there are consequences."[73] But there were no adverse consequences from the Bush administration for states that deceived the public about school safety.

Some private experts believe NCLB will make schools more dangerous. Kenneth Trump, president of National School Safety and Security Services, commented, "The end result is another law that not only will not improve school safety, but will likely result in making schools less safe," because it "provides every incentive for school administrators not to report school crime and no incentives for them to actually report."[74]

Even after the system was proven to be a complete fraud, the Bush administration's point man continued chirping as if it was doing fine. Modzeleski commented in January 2004: "We feel very strongly that this should be done at a state level—not a federal level. If, in fact, we had a standard definition, we'd have more public outcry."[75] Avoiding a public outcry is more important than avoiding having the federal government be party to a massive school safety fraud. The feds acquiescence signals the Bush administration's willingness to tolerate as many shenanigans as state bureaucrats produce. A law that was supposed to result in honesty in education is instead producing more absurdities than ever. Perhaps the Bush administration is more concerned about maintaining public confidence in NCLB than in seeing that the law's lofty promises are fulfilled.

THE TEXAS MODEL SCAM

NCLB was based on what Bush proudly called the "Texas miracle"[76]—his education reform during his two terms as governor. Texas politicians in 1990 created a system of statewide education tests. When Bush was elected governor in November 1994, Bush pushed into law more rigorous testing and linked the pay of teachers and school administrators to dropout rates and students' scores on statewide tests. Bush won reelection in 1998 in part because he promised stricter standards for schools.[77]

The reforms produced stunning numbers. The dropout rate in Texas schools fell from 6.1 percent in 1989 to 1.6 percent in 2000, while the percentage of tenth-graders passing a statewide test rose from 58 percent in 1995 to 80 percent in 2000.[78] The Texas reforms supposedly proved how enforcing high standards can revolutionize school performance.

Nowhere in Texas was progress more dramatic than in Houston. Bush chose Rodney Paige as education secretary because of Paige's legendary achievements as superintendent of the Houston school system from 1995 to early 2001. Paige collected a $275,000 salary in Houston for his successes.[79]

But by 2003,the Houston miracle had been exposed as a scam. The Houston school system was in danger of losing its state accreditation in 1994 because of its high dropout rate before Paige took over, and was again in danger two years after he left, this time because of severe undercounting of dropouts. The *Houston Chronicle* noted, "In 1995, Paige told administrators to re-evaluate the way they were counting dropouts because some students were leaving school for reasons that did not meet the official definition of 'dropping out.' Later, he attributed the significant turnaround in dropout numbers to new training for employees who determine the 'leaver' codes that categorize the reasons students quit."[80] Texas writer Lou DuBose noted that the Texas Education Agency "even created an elaborate list of attendance and enrollment codes that allows (and even encourages) school administrators to identify 'leavers' as anything other than 'dropouts.'"[81]

The fraudulent nature of Houston dropout claims should have been obvious at first glance. The *New York Times* noted of one school under Paige's rule: "This poor, mostly minority high school of 1,650 students had a freshman class of 1,000 that dwindled to fewer than 300 students by senior year. And yet—and this is the miracle—not one dropout to report."[82] Robert Stockwell, the chief academic officer of the Houston school district, conceded in 2003, "The annual dropout rate was a crock, and we're not [using] it anymore."[83]

Some Houston inner-city high schools also claimed that 100 percent or almost 100 percent of their students planned to go to college. One former high school principal said that most of the students at his school "couldn't spell college, let alone attend."[84]

During Paige's reign, the passing rate of Houston tenth-graders on the Texas Assessment of Academic Skills soared.[85] Houston schools repeatedly flunked ninth-graders to prevent them from taking the tenth-grade test and hurting the school's image. One Houston high school had 1,160 ninth-grade students and only 281 tenth-grade students, thanks to the politically contrived "ninth grade pileup."[86] Many of the students locked down in ninth grade became discouraged and dropped out.

The "Texas miracle" was based on a very simple test. After George Bush became governor, the Texas Board of Education sharply lowered the number of correct answers required to pass the Texas Assessment of Academic Skills. A student could have worse reading skills than almost 95 percent of the students in the entire country and still be considered a Texas success story. Jeff Judson of the Texas Public Policy Foundation, a conservative think tank, observed: "Once you start digging, it's amazing how these scores can be manipulated for political purposes. It's raw politics. It's about making the system look good at the expense of students."[87] State officials slashed passing standards and then claimed schools turned water into wine.

There were warning signs of pervasive political-bureaucratic ed fraud. In 1999, the University of Texas warned of a "marked decline in the number of students who are prepared academically for higher education."[88] The Texas state comptroller created a Public Education Integrity Task Force in 1999 after widespread reports of schools sidetracking weak students away from statewide tests.[89] The 1.6 percent statewide high-school dropout rate was also treated derisively by some education experts.[90]

Paige, who ceaselessly preached "accountability" as Houston schools chief, responded to revelations of shenanigans by portraying himself as a martyr. Paige told the *Dallas Morning News,* "There's been an incredibly unfair examination of the issue."[91] When Paige appeared at the National Press Club in September 2003, he was asked by the moderator about the ongoing investigation of the Houston school system: "What does this say about your leadership of that district?" Paige righteously replied, "I think the way it was reported says more about the way it was reported than anything else."[92]

ABOLISHING RACE TEST GAPS

NCLB commands that all racial disparities in pass rates for math and English tests be abolished by the year 2014. Deputy Education Secretary Hickok told the *Wall Street Journal* in December 2003 that "the Bush administration's highest education priority is to narrow the achievement gap between minority and white students."[93] Secretary Paige declared, "I think the No Child Left Behind Act is probably this nation's greatest affirmative action program."[94]

Bush perennially denounces what he calls the "soft bigotry of low expectations," implying that prejudice is the primary reason for racial achievement gaps. Paige, speaking at a conservative think tank in Washington in January 2004, declared that "the No Child Left Behind Act . . . addresses latent segregation, a *de facto apartheid* that is emerging in our schools." Paige asserted that the act "is the logical step after Brown v. Board of Education ended segregation, and the 1964 Civil Rights Act promised an equitable society. . . . No Child Left Behind is about freedom and equality and justice." Paige even invoked the rhetoric of Lincoln's Gettysburg Address, orating, "Two score and 10 years have passed since Brown." Paige tarred opponents of NCLB as racists, warning, "If those who fear change defeat national reform, then division, exclusion, racism and callousness win."[95]

The gap that NCLB purports to close is much larger than most Americans realize. Black high school seniors "perform a little worse than white eighth-graders in both reading and U.S. history, and a lot worse in math and geography," as Harvard professor Stephan Thernstrom and his wife, U.S. Civil

Rights Commissioner Abigail Thernstrom, reported in their 2003 book, *No Excuses: Closing the Racial Gap in Learning.*[96] In Minnesota, one of the nation's most progressive states, 78 percent of white students pass the math portion of the high school exit exam, while only 33 percent of black students pass.[97]

The NAEP has four different categories of achievement; the lowest, "Below Basic," is "reserved for students unable to display even 'partial mastery' of prerequisite knowledge and skills."[98] Most black twelfth-graders perform at Below Basic in most NAEP test categories. The disparity between black and white achievement is even greater at the highest NAEP category. White and Asian-American students are 30 times more likely to score in the advanced level on the NAEP science test than are black students. (Hispanics also sharply lag behind white scores.) Though the gap between white and black test scores narrowed in the 1970s through the mid-1980s, it widened in the 1990s.

The racial test gap is not due to a shortage of government spending. The average school district with a majority of black or Hispanic students spends more per pupil than the average school district with a majority of white students.[99] "Impoverished Asian students at inferior inner-city schools outperform their black and Hispanic classmates. Same schools, same teachers, different results," the Thernstroms observed.[100] (Asian students also far outperform white students on math.)

Race is a far stronger predictor of test scores than income. As Harvard professor Nathan Glazer observed, "blacks with family incomes of $80,000 to $100,000 have lower average SAT scores than whites with family incomes below $10,000."[101] Though blacks have become far more educated in recent decades, "the disparity in academic performance between black and white children of highly educated parents is actually larger" than the disparity between black and white children.[102]

Though Secretary Paige hails NCLB as a strike against apartheid, black culture may be the largest source of the achievement gap. Black high school seniors are five times more likely to watch at least five hours of television a night than white high school seniors.[103] Black students are more than twice as likely to come from a single-parent household—often resulting in much less parental discipline and pressure to perform well in school. John McWhorter, a black professor at the University of California at Berkeley and the author of *Losing the Race: Self-Sabotage in Black America,* observed that "black students do not try as hard as other students. . . . All of these students belong to a culture infected with an anti-intellectual strain, which subtly but decisively teaches them from birth not to embrace schoolwork too wholeheartedly."[104] Harvard professor Henry Louis Gates, Jr. commented on a recent poll "where black kids were asked to list the things they considered 'acting white.'" The two most common responses were "making straight A's" and "speaking standard English." Gates observed, "If anybody had said anything like that when we were growing up in the '50s, first, your mother would smack you upside the head and second, they'd check you into a mental institution."[105]

The NCLB "equal scores" command is one of the most sweeping and foolish egalitarian dictates in the history of the federal government It is naive to expect that federal intervention will make all groups read equally well (or equally badly).

The fixation on closing the gap between races diverts attention from the fact that American students are falling further behind students of other nations. As Harvard professor Paul Peterson recently noted, international tests show that American 17-year-olds are among the weakest students in the advanced world, outscoring only Lithuania, Cyprus, and South Africa.[106] The longer American students are in school, the poorer their learning and understanding compares with foreign students. International surveys comparing the literacy of Americans of different age groups to foreigners shows "a simple, steady progression downward" from a near-top rating for 56-to-65-year-old Americans to a near-bottom rating for 16-to-25-year-old Americans.[107]

HOLLOW PROMISES, REAL DANGERS

In April 2002, three months after signing NCLB, Bush resurrected another failed Clinton promise when he proclaimed a federal goal that every child should be able to read by the third grade. Bush declared, "As we fight for freedom, I also understand that freedom means no child in America will be left behind. The new civil right in America is reading."[108] Bush draped his proposal for a new federal entitlement—the right to read, courtesy of Washington—in the patriotic language of his global war on terrorism. There is an old saying that if one person is oppressed, then no one is free. Bush's variation on that theme is: "If one child cannot read by the third grade, then all Americans are illiterate."

Bush proposed that the federal government finance training for all fifty thousand Head Start teachers nationwide and, as the *Washington Post* noted, "for the first time, evaluate how well those federally funded child development centers are teaching the low-income preschoolers they enroll."[109] It is ironic that Bush would portray this as a visionary reform, rather than a confession of perpetual gross negligence. The fact that the feds have bankrolled

Head Start for almost half a century without bothering to see if it worked apparently should not raise any doubts about the wisdom of expanding the federal role in forging young minds.

Bush declared: "If we expect achievement from every child, all our children need to begin school with an equal chance at achievement. *Every child must have an equal place at the starting line.*"[110] This was vintage LBJ: President Johnson promised in 1965 that Head Start would put children "on an even footing with their classmates as they enter school."[111] But there is no way to equalize the starting line between children of parents who are avid readers and children of parents who are TV-addicted lunkheads who would not recognize a book if it fell on them. Bush's "starting line" comments are the usual demagoguery that have long permeated Washington politicians' educational promises.

SPENDING AS TEACHING

Bush co-opted the liberal, Democratic message that boosting government spending will fructify young minds. In his January 20, 2004 State of the Union address, Bush declared, "We're providing more funding for our schools, a 36-percent increase since 2001."[112] When this assertion did not resonate loudly enough through the land, White House script doctors scrambled. Three days later, in a speech to the U.S. Conference of Mayors, Bush declared, "let me tell you my view of that important piece of legislation, since I was the person that asked Congress to pass it. I said, first of all, 'We'll increase the budgets,' which we have done by 49 percent since 2001."[113] While Bush bragged about how much spending rose, Democrats and liberals denounced Bush because spending did not increase even faster. In January 2003, a group of Democratic senators sent a letter to Bush demanding much more spending, huffing that "America's public schools cannot overcome the enormous obstacles they face on the cheap."[114]

The "more spending = more learning" equation has always been a charade. A 1999 report for the U.S. Department of Education concluded that "additional funding for education . . . in the past has not, in fact, generally led to higher achievement."[115] Many of the urban school systems that spend far more than the national average for education—such as Washington, D.C.—have among the lowest student scores in the nation. Montana, on the other hand, "spends only an average amount on education but achieved the second highest NAEP reading ranking out of the 40 states that administered the 1998 test."[116] A 2003 report for the Organization for Economic Cooperation and

Development compared education spending levels for industrial countries and concluded that the United States "is among the top spenders for elementary and secondary education—$10,240 per student in 2000—but American students compare poorly to many other nations that spend less for education."[117]

Secretary Paige declared in 2003, "No idea in politics has hurt children more than the false and misleading idea that the quality of education is determined by how much we spend."[118] Yet, Paige complained to the *Washington Post* that a critical piece on NCLB included "little focus on the unprecedented dollars flowing to the states to support the No Child Left Behind Act."[119] The Bush administration plays it both ways—first bragging about increased spending for education, and then denouncing critics who seek more spending.

The Bush administration recognizes the value of education activism as a political investment. Republican pollster David Winston informed Republican congressmen in early 2002: "When we talk about education, we move the numbers positively. When we don't, they tend to slip."[120] A January 2003 Republican National Committee memo to Republican leaders bragged of "a great turnaround" in the public's attitude toward Republicans and education."[121] But a survey a year later by a Republican pollster found that Democrats have an 11 percentage-point lead on the education issue. A January 27, 2004 memo from Rep. Deborah Pryce (R-Ohio), the House Republican conference chairman, and Rep. John Boehner (R-Ohio), the House education and workforce committee chairman, urged fellow Republicans in Congress to highlight and claim credit for "the 35 percent increase in federal teacher quality funding" and "the fact that federal funding for reading instruction programs has more than tripled since President Bush took office."[122]

THE TWO-TIER EDUCATION SYSTEM

In his September 2003 comments at the National Press Club, Secretary Paige declared: "We are facing an unrecognized educational crisis in our country. Our wide and sometimes growing achievement gap confirms this. There's a two-tiered educational system in this country."[123] Paige was referring to the gap in test scores between whites, on the one hand, and Hispanics and blacks, on the other.

But the clearest two tiers in American education are between government schools and private schools and home schools. The Bush education "revolution" almost completely ignores the vast successes of private schools and homeschooling. Almost every study comparing achievement shows that

private school students read better than public school students from comparable backgrounds.[124]

Though many education reforms in recent decades have concentrated on
the need for better-paid teachers, the stunning success of homeschooled kids
should cast doubt on this education establishment mantra. Parents who are
high school graduates are routinely more successful at teaching children how
to read than are college-educated teachers. A survey by University of Maryland
professor Lawrence Rudner found that "young home-schooled students test a
full grade level higher than their public- and private-school counterparts. By
the eighth grade, they're testing at four grade levels above their counterparts in
government schools."[125] Homeschooled students excel, compared with gov-
ernment-schooled kids, in part because home schools do not squander time on
the latest education fads and politically correct devotions. Up to two million
U.S. children are now being homeschooled.

Though Bush hinted at his support of vouchers for students from failed
government schools to attend private schools in the 2000 presidential campaign, his NCLB did nothing to aid parents who wanted to extradite their kids
from the public school morass. Bush dropped any talk of vouchers in order to
secure a broad-based political victory on education and to have Sen. Ted
Kennedy support his bill and appear at the signing ceremony.

NCLB UNDER FIRE

NCLB came under widespread criticism in early 2004. The Republican-
dominated Virginia House of Delegates passed a resolution by a vote of 98 to
1 in February 2004 denouncing NCLB as "one of the most sweeping intrusions into state and local control of education in the history of the United
States."[126] On March 24, 14 states requested that the Bush administration exempt them from NCLB standards because they already had a statewide set of
academic performance measurements and a "growth measurement" before
NCLB was enacted. The 14 chief state school officers warned: "Without any
changes to the law, calculations suggest that within a few years, the vast majority of all schools will be identified as in need of improvement."[127] But there
is nothing in the national assessment tests to indicate that the vast majority of
schools do not need to improve.

The Bush administration sought to mollify critics by relaxing standards
for special ed students' pass rate, by permitting more kids to miss taking tests,

by letting states jiggle the definition of "highly qualified teacher." But, as the 2004 election heated up, the concessions seemed to only fuel further criticism.

Secretary Paige denounced the National Education Association, claiming that the union was acting like "a terrorist organization" because of its resistance to NCLB. Education Department spokeswoman Susan Aspey explained: "The Secretary was responding to a question."[128] While the NEA has long been a primary cause of deteriorating school performance, Paige's smear was indicative of the blind righteousness that permeates Bush administration attitudes on many issues.

CONCLUSION

In order to be politically successful, federal education reform does not actually have to improve the quality of America's schools. Instead, it merely needs to persuade enough negligent or ignorant voters that the president is working hard to improve the schools. Few parents delve into the mechanics of NCLB but many parents can see Bush on television claiming credit for solving the problems of American education.

Bush talks about NCLB's deadline of 2014 for having all children's reading and math skills reach grade level. But the real deadline is the first Tuesday in November 2004. As long as NCLB avoids becoming a laughingstock until after Bush's reelection, the law will be a success.

Bush and Paige are correct that schools should be spending more time teaching reading than values clarification or other claptrap. Bush and Paige are correct that students should be rigorously tested to determine what they know. Bush and Paige are correct that many, if not most, public school systems are failing their students and that students should be learning far more. Paige is correct that previous federal education interventions have achieved little or nothing, and have often done more harm than good.

The Bush team accurately recognized some of the profound problems of government schools across America. But they offered a remedy that was three-quarters smoke and one-eighth mirrors, leaving little real substance. Nothing in NCLB will stop the pervasive bureaucratic racketeering that has long permeated government education policy.

To have Rod Paige leading a crusade for "honesty in reporting" by state education bureaucrats is like having Al Capone lead a temperance campaign. Paige rose to national fame after the school system he headed engaged in

brazen statistical manipulation to bury its failures. He has expressed no remorse for his negligence and shown no sense of personal responsibility for the
abuses under his watch in Houston. If Paige cannot be honest about what happened in Houston, what is the likelihood of his being honest about the national impact of NCLB? And if Paige was actually unaware of the Houston
shenanigans, what is the likelihood that he will be aware of similar scams occurring throughout the nation with federal education funds?

The failure to close the racial "test pass gap" could be a Pandora's box that
spurs endless demands for new federal interventions and more federal spending. It is folly to fixate on the racial achievement gap and ignore the ongoing
general deterioration in literacy and achievement by American students.

Though NCLB is a federal command for local school accountability, the
federal government itself has never been held responsible for its education failures. Instead, there is an unwritten "hold harmless" clause always entitling the
feds to at least as much power in the future as in the past, regardless of screw-
ups. Presidents, Congress and bureaucrats have prospered for decades by making lavish promises and deluging local and state school systems with money,
regardless of the failure of federal programs. There is nothing in NCLB to
change either the incentives or the characters of the politicians and bureaucrats
driving education policy.

CHAPTER SIX

AmeriCorps and Moral Reformation

I believe that in order to live in a free society, you need to give something back. . . .
In order to make a society vibrant, all of us owe something to America. And one
way to provide that is either through the military or through loving somebody and
showing it through actual deeds.

—*George Bush, March 12, 2002*[1]

President Bush portrays good deeds as practically a curative for terrorist attacks. "Since this is a war of good versus evil, those of—who want to participate in the war against terror can do acts of kindness to overwhelm the evil done to the country," Bush declared in a speech to Republican congressmen.[2]

Two months after the 9/11 attacks, Bush announced that he was expanding AmeriCorps and that "all of us can become a September the 11th volunteer by making a commitment to service in our own communities."[3] Bush had long been a fan of AmeriCorps, flaunting his enthusiasm for it during the 2000 presidential campaign as proof of his compassionate conservatism.

AmeriCorps was started by President Clinton in 1993 to hire a legion of people to perform federally designated good deeds. In Mississippi, AmeriCorps members went door to door to recruit people for food stamps. In Buffalo, New York, AmeriCorps members helped run a program that gave children $5 for each toy gun they brought in. In southern California, Ameri-Corps members busied themselves foisting unreliable ultra-low-flush toilets on poor people. In San Diego, AmeriCorps recruits carried out an undergarment drive to collect used bras and pantyhose for a local women's center.[4]

At the time Bush took office, many conservatives viewed AmeriCorps as incorrigible and demanded its abolition. Bush was far more interested in politically exploiting the program to showcase his own benevolence.

For their 1,700 hours of service, AmeriCorps members receive roughly $16,000 a year in cash and benefits, including a $4,725 education award that can be used for college costs or paying off college loans. Many AmeriCorps members are unskilled and earn as much or more on the federal payroll as they would in private employment. Despite their paychecks, Bush hails Ameri-Corps members as "volunteers."[5] The agency refers to its recruits as "stipended volunteers."[6] The political exploitation of the volunteer label epitomizes the false piety that has always seeped from AmeriCorps.

Bush chose Leslie Lenkowsky, a professor at Indiana University, to head the Corporation for National and Community Service, of which Ameri-Corps is the largest and most important program. Lenkowsky had been a member of the board of directors overseeing AmeriCorps. His comments at a public board meeting in September 1999 showed he had little or no familiarity with the inspector general reports on AmeriCorps problems that he, as a board member, was regularly sent.[7] Lenkowsky prides himself on being a man of ideas.

Bush's post-9/11 portrayal of good deeds as part of the national defense was a godsend for AmeriCorps. In an October 26, 2001 speech at the Franklin D. Roosevelt Memorial in Washington, D.C., Lenkowsky informed Ameri-Corps members that "the daily duties that you perform will also be helping to thwart terrorism itself. . . . Terrorists sow the seeds of distrust. You sow the seeds of trust, at a time your nation badly needs them."[8] Lenkowsky assured AmeriCorps members that their efforts are "as important to our nation's security and well-being" as the actions of American troops at that moment fighting the Taliban in Afghanistan.

In most areas of AmeriCorps activity, its effect is negligible—at best:

- In Louisiana, AmeriCorps members passed out free gun locks at Wal-Mart stores.[9]
- A team of 80 AmeriCorps members spent more than 20,000 hours hoeing corn and doing other tasks at the Garfield Farm Museum outside Geneva, Illinois.[10]

- AmeriCorps member Adrienne Blauser led a campaign to persuade the Idaho Transportation Department to rename parts of two state highways as the Sacajawea Historical Byway.[11]
- An AmeriCorps member helped organize a "Pink Prom," the first gay youth dance in Snohomish County, Washington.[12]
- AmeriCorps members in Worcester, Massachusetts presented lessons in half a dozen schools about "Super Bowl Surge"—the problems that occur when millions of people watching the big game use the bathroom during half time. "In one lesson, students were asked to consider what will happen if the New England Patriots football team makes it to the Super Bowl," the *Worcester Telegram and Gazette* reported.[13]
- In Buffalo, AmeriCorps members busied themselves repairing private lawns damaged by government snow plows.[14]
- In Pueblo, Colorado, an AmeriCorps team spent the first week of March 2004 sifting trash and other material in the basement of a local museum. AmeriCorps member Jane Howard Crutchfield beamed: "We're learning a lot of history, just going through and sorting through all the old magazines from 1940s till now, really."[15]
- In Knoxville, Tennessee, AmeriCorps members planted a few acres of vegetables to give to soup kitchens and food distribution centers. The program also involved three cats—Willow, Tiger Lily, and Lotus—to help with rodent control, according to the *Knoxville News Sentinel*.[16] Though this project may have filled AmeriCorps members with pride, a harvest the size of theirs could have been procured for poor folks at less cost at the nearest Safeway. AmeriCorps members are paid more than farmworkers, and based on my observations of AmeriCorps members and farmworkers, farmworkers are far more productive.
- AmeriCorps members worked with the Tobacco Free Coalition of Wood County, Wisconsin, calling up local residents to survey their attitudes on secondhand smoke. Local government will use the survey results when it decides whether to ban all smoking in restaurants.[17]
- The Huntington, West Virginia, *Herald-Dispatch* reported that a local AmeriCorps member "set up a 'March for Meals' campaign as part of Martin Luther King, Jr. week activities. As a result, 207 cans of food collected were donated" to a local food bank. The cost to taxpayers of the AmeriCorps member's salary during the canned food drive could easily have exceeded the value of the food collected (unless it was 207

cans of caviar). The same AmeriCorps member also "led students in coloring pictures to give to children" in a local hospital.[18]

Puppet shows are a favorite activity for AmeriCorps members. In Springfield, Illinois, AmeriCorps members presented a puppet show to edify three-year-olds at the Little Angels Child Care Center on the benefits of smoke detectors.[19] In Asheville, North Carolina, AmeriCorps members put on a puppet show for kids warning them about the dangers of child abuse. (The *Asheville Citizen-Times* report did not contain any graphic details of what the puppets did.)[20]

AmeriCorps is popular on Capitol Hill in part because it sometimes provides easy opportunities for members of Congress to flaunt their virtue. After some congressional folks showed up one day in March 2004 to hammer some nails at a Habitat for Humanity house-building project in Washington, D.C., AmeriCorps issued a press release hyping their participation in the good deed. The press release named eight members of Congress and noted, "Working alongside the elected officials were two dozen AmeriCorps members from the D.C. chapter of Habitat for Humanity and AmeriCorps."[21] The home they helped build was to be given to a single mother of three. Photos from the appearance at the Habitat project could prove helpful for some congressional re-election campaigns.

One of the most important tasks of AmeriCorps members is to be waiting on airport tarmacs when Air Force One arrives and Bush descends for local fundraisers and other public appearances. Bush routinely mentions Ameri-Corps members by name in the subsequent speech. Conservatives harshly criticized President Clinton for using AmeriCorps members as official greeters for his travels. Bush has not been scathed by similar complaints.

AmeriCorps is a government program which supposedly rectifies the failures of other government programs. According to the National Assessment of Educational Progress, most fourth-grade students in government schools are unable to read proficiently. School and literacy-related activities are the most frequent task for AmeriCorps members—despite the fact that they have no particular competence in these areas, special skills, or training as teachers.

Instead, AmeriCorps pretends that reading to kids is "close enough for government work" to teaching kids how to read. Many AmeriCorps literacy programs are little more than "fun with books"—activities that have as much lasting benefit as watching a few episodes of "Sesame Street." AmeriCorps members sometimes appear as "guest readers" in schools. Yet, some Ameri-Corps members may find even this task a bit daunting. AmeriCorps assistant teachers in Mississippi, for instance, were only required to read at an eighth-grade level. Many AmeriCorps members lack a high school degree.

Many AmeriCorps education activities have scant impact on learning. AmeriCorps members painted rainbows on the walls of an elementary school library in Pickens, South Carolina.[22] The South Carolina *Greenville News* reported that, among other noteworthy achievements, AmeriCorps member Kelly Jean Erwin "helped organize an arts closet so a teacher can more easily access materials for her students."[23]

AmeriCorps' efforts may be inspired by a "nearness to moral greatness" theory of education—i.e., that mere proximity to an AmeriCorps member will spontaneously generate literacy. Yet even the Bush administration now recognizes that AmeriCorps education activities often flop. President Bush issued an executive order on February 27, 2004, demanding that AmeriCorps activities in schools "employ tutors who meet required paraprofessional qualifications."[24] This could greatly reduce the number of AmeriCorps classroom interventions. On the other hand, it could work out well for urban beautification programs, since more AmeriCorps members may be shifted to litter pickup (a favorite agency activity to generate positive press coverage).

Though AmeriCorps abounds in "feel good" projects, it has never provided credible evidence of benefit to the United States. The Office of Management and Budget concluded in 2003 that "AmeriCorps has not been able to demonstrate results. Its current focus is on the amount of time a person serves, as opposed to the impact on the community or participants."[25] OMB noted in 2004, "AmeriCorps accomplishments are difficult to measure, but its reported impact is small."[26] The General Accounting Office noted in 2000 that AmeriCorps "generally reports the results of its programs and activities by quantifying the amount of services AmeriCorps participants perform."[27] GAO criticized AmeriCorps for failing to make any effort to measure the actual effect of its members' actions.

TRUST TRIPE

In a March 2002 speech, Bush kindly offered government aid to help Americans "bring a little discipline into your volunteer service": "One of the things that I have asked our White House staff to put together is a booklet that would give you an opportunity to record your service. And if you're interested in recording, not only for yourself but recording for your family or a child, perhaps, what you've done to make America a better place, this is a good go-by."[28]

Ironically, at the time of Bush's magnanimous offer, AmeriCorps itself was crashing and burning because of its gross incompetence in tracking its own "volunteers." Bush's high-profile appeals for people to join boosted the number of AmeriCorps enrollees. In its budget for fiscal 2002, the Bush administration requested and Congress approved funding for 50,000 AmeriCorps members. Though Bush proclaimed a goal of 75,000 AmeriCorps members shortly after 9/11, he never sought additional appropriations from Congress to pay the new members.

By August 2002, AmeriCorps had 60,000 members enrolled. The agency's director of planning e-mailed top officials warning of a potential budget shortfall. Agency chieftains brushed off his concerns because they saw the surging recruit totals as a good thing.

Even after AmeriCorps recognized its deficit spending and imposed an emergency freeze on new hires in November, the White House continued bragging about its rapid expansion. Bush beamed on December 10, 2002, that AmeriCorps is "expanding mightily,"[29] and a January 30, 2003, White House press release boasted that "the AmeriCorps program filled its enrollment goals faster than ever before."[30]

The Anti-Deficiency Act makes it a crime for a federal agency to spend more money than Congress has appropriated for it. AmeriCorps spent $64 million more than it was appropriated in fiscal year 2002. While a violation of the Anti-Deficiency Act is punishable by up to two years in prison, the agency's Inspector General concluded that there was no criminal intent because AmeriCorps bosses did not know what they were doing.[31]

The General Accounting Office reported that the AmeriCorps overenrollment resulted from "little or no communication among key Corporation executives, too much flexibility given to grantees regarding enrollments, and unreliable data on the number of AmeriCorps participants."[32] AmeriCorps chieftains had no idea how many members AmeriCorps programs had signed up because grantees were not obliged to notify Washington of their head counts.

"The ruse of hiring people in advance of funding is in fact a deliberate political effort to leverage more federal money," chided a *Wall Street Journal* editorial.[33] Sen. Barbara Mikulski (D-Md.) denounced AmeriCorps as the "Enron of nonprofits" and demanded Lenkowsky's resignation.[34] Sen. Kit Bond (R-Mo.), suggested that criminal prosecution might be appropriate but no one followed his lead.[35]

A $64-million error on an individual tax return would likely result in federal criminal prosecution. But Bush and Congress's response to the Ameri-

Corps debacle was: What's $64 million among friends? Besides, future generations of Americans will barely notice the additional government debt.

Neither AmeriCorps nor the Bush administration ever accepted culpability. Instead, they portrayed AmeriCorps as a victim of mass enthusiasm. USA Freedom Corps director John Bridgeland declared that "AmeriCorps was tested by overwhelming numbers of Americans who wanted to serve."[36]

Congress, working with the Bush administration, responded to the debacle by passing the Strengthening AmeriCorps Act. The "strengthening" part of the bill name was a charade. The primary change in the law was to make it easier for AmeriCorps to enlist recruits without having the full amount of their $4,725 education award in a special National Service Trust Fund. AmeriCorps was "strengthened" by being allowed to hire more people than it might be able to pay. (Many AmeriCorps recruits soon weary of righteousness and quit before their term is fulfilled, thus failing to earn an education award.)

Budgetary crack-ups did not deter AmeriCorps from generously rewarding its headquarters staff with bonuses for superior performance. The Corporation for National and Community Service gave $411,655 in employee bonuses to 265 officials (almost half of the agency's employees), including some of the officials responsible for the $64 million happenstance. Sen. Mikulski denounced the bonuses as "outrageous and unacceptable," saying, "Incompetence should not be rewarded under any circumstance."[37] AmeriCorps spokesman Sandy Scott justified the bonuses: "The corporation highly values its employees and believes it is important to invest in them. This is a sound human resource practice."[38]

VOLUNTEERING OTHER PEOPLE'S MONEY

Congress required AmeriCorps to pay for the extra members it enrolled in 2002 out of its 2003 budget, thereby creating a one-time reduction in spending. AmeriCorps curtailed its funding levels in June 2003 and lowered the enrollment cap for the year from 50,000 to 35,000 members.

Pandemonium ensued. A coalition of 12 organizations issued a press release declaiming that "Democracy is being thwarted" because the House of Representatives did not promptly approve additional funding for the program.[39] At a rally for AmeriCorps supporters in Boston, mayor Thomas Menino declared that Bush has "cut the heart out of volunteerism" and warned: "Something is wrong in America today when we forget that government is about improving the quality of life for people." Hundreds of local students held up placards with slogans such as "I want to serve."[40] Good deeds are apparently no longer conceivable without federal guidance and a federal reward.

In September, AmeriCorps advocates orchestrated a hundred straight hours of testimony on the program on Capitol Hill, with Washington media eminence and former White House aide David Gergen moderating the opening ceremony.

Sen. John McCain (R-Az.) denounced the "lack of good faith" in the AmeriCorps budget shortfall and hailed AmeriCorps recruits: "These good Americans have learned that *serving a cause larger than themselves* is as vital to their self-respect as it is useful to our country."[41] McCain implied that people would lose self-respect if the federal government did not certify their virtue. McCain advocates making national service compulsory, notwithstanding the 13th Amendment's prohibition on involuntary servitude.[42]

AmeriCorps' moral pretenses have long mesmerized most of the Washington press corps. *Washington Post* columnist E. J. Dionne whooped: "Who knew that the AmeriCorps program had—as we like to say here—such a deep political base? Indeed, the biggest political surprise of the past few months is that a very small program could roar. . . . Maybe 9/11 really did change us."[43]

In reality, it was Washington business as usual. The 2003 budget brouhaha illustrated how the bar for AmeriCorps is continually being lowered. The braying of beneficiaries is now sufficient proof of transcendent benefits. The dispute was a Washington version of a medieval morality play, with the federal budget determining the precise quantity of goodness to be unleashed onto the land.

While the budget cuts for AmeriCorps provoked a tidal wave of lobbying, the cuts did not spur donations to local programs aided by AmeriCorps. The National and Community Service Trust Act of 1993 envisioned AmeriCorps aid as a temporary boost to nonprofit groups that would be weaned of AmeriCorps funding after a few years. Some members of Congress hoped that AmeriCorps activities would be so good, wholesome, and helpful that they would attract wide funding from nonfederal sources. Instead, "once subsidized, forever entitled" appears to be the motto of many AmeriCorps grantees.

Many Republicans vigorously opposed the bailout. Rep. James Walsh (R-N.Y.) objected: "AmeriCorps has been sadly plagued by poor management and weak financial oversight. We shouldn't reward an agency that violates federal law and mismanages taxpayer dollars."[44] Bush's tacit support for AmeriCorps probably made the difference and swayed enough votes (or undermined enough resistance) for AmeriCorps to receive its largest budget increase ever—

rising from $327 million in fiscal 2003 to $452 million in 2004. The House Republican leadership—perhaps more than any other time during the Bush presidency—sought to take the high ground against wasteful government spending. The White House left them high and dry.

On February 2, 2004, the Bush administration released its proposed budget for fiscal 2005, which called for a 9 percent increase for the Corporation for National and Community Service. The agency's press release hailed the proposal: "President's 2005 Budget Would Engage Record Number of Americans in Service."[45] The administration reiterated its call for expanding AmeriCorps to 75,000 members.

Several weeks later, Bush issued an executive order that implied Ameri-Corps is badly mismanaged. Bush declared, "National and community service programs should make Federal support more accountable and more effective. . . . The Corporation should implement internal management reforms to strengthen its oversight of national and community service programs through enforcement of performance and compliance standards and other management tools." Bush demanded an assurance from the Corporation's CEO that its financial statements are "accurate and reliable" and called for "management reforms that tie employee performance to fiscal responsibility, attainment of management goals, and professional conduct."[46] Bush ordered the Corporation to report to him within 180 days on fulfilling the order.

After all the times Bush gushed over AmeriCorps in his speeches, after all the pictures with AmeriCorps members on airport tarmacs, after more than one billion dollars had been spent on the program during his watch, and after more than 3 years of being responsible for the program, Bush suddenly issued commands that looked like the administrative equivalent of ordering an alcoholic to go cold turkey.

BUSH'S FREEDOM TAX

In his January 29, 2002 State of the Union address, Bush sought to use 9/11 to achieve national moral reformation. Bush declared that "we have glimpsed what a new culture of responsibility could look like. We want to be a nation that serves goals larger than self." Bush issued a summons: "My call tonight is for every American to commit at least two years—four thousand hours—over the rest of your lifetime to the service of your neighbors and your nation."[47]

Bush felt entitled to call for 4,000 hours of service from every person in the country, regardless of how much that person had already served and regardless of that person's situation. It was as if the nation's moral life—and individuals' private moral existence—did not exist prior to Bush's summons. In a March 12, 2002 speech in Philadelphia, Bush declared: "One of the things I've asked the country to do is to think about 4,000 hours of public service, for the rest of your life or 2 years. That's not hard for some, I understand that. I bet you've already done that."

One audience member shouted: "I think so."

Bush replied: "Well, you've got another 4,000 to go."[48]

Bush upped the ante a few weeks later, announcing that he wants every American to volunteer for "4,000 *years*." The White House doctored the official transcript of the speech to shave the mandate back to a more manageable level.[49]

When Bush declares that people in a free society "need to give something back," he pretends that the government takes nothing from people when it only confiscates their paycheck. The Office of Management and Budget (OMB) estimated in 1994 that males born between 1980 and 1992 will have to surrender over half of their lifetime earnings to tax collectors. The average male born in 1967 will be forced to pay over $200,000 more in taxes than he receives from the government.[50] Yet, regardless of how much government takes from people, politicians can always demand another "pound of flesh."

Bush's "4,000 hours" mandate illustrates how the nation's most renowned Masters of Business Administration–degree recipient thinks like a government bureaucrat. Bush proposes to measure good deeds the same way federal workers snare their pensions. A person's service to humanity is gauged by a simple test: Did someone put in the time?

For Bush, because federal agencies failed to detect and derail a terrorist attack on 9/11, he becomes entitled to demand that all citizens serve 4,000 hours. Is the service to be penance to atone for the failures of the government? The more sacrifices the government demands, the more righteous the ruler appears.

Susan Ellis, president of Energize, a company that provides consulting on volunteers, pummeled Bush's call in the *Chronicle of Philanthropy*, noting that Bush's "surprise announcement . . . was crafted so poorly that a lot of time and money could be wasted building a new bureaucracy with no clear benefit or rationale. The president's plan was created so haphazardly that it seems almost guaranteed to discourage Americans who are inspired to volunteer." Ellis declared that "the White House has violated the fundamental rule of recruitment: Do not ask people to volunteer unless and until an assignment is ready for them to do. But President Bush is so concerned about generating interest that he does not seem to care about whether it leads to any real accomplishments."[51]

In his 2002 State of the Union address, Bush also announced the creation of USA Freedom Corps—a White House agency to oversee Americans' volunteer efforts and to supervise AmeriCorps, the Peace Corps, and other federal service programs. A White House booklet on the program entitled "A Call to Service" quoted President Lyndon Johnson: "Those who founded our country knew that freedom would be secure only if each generation fought to renew and enlarge its meaning."[52]

The Freedom Corps enlarged the meaning of freedom by recruiting for Operation TIPS (the Terrorist Information and Prevention System). TIPS aimed to sign up millions of informants—from truck drivers to letter carriers to cable television installers—who would report any "out of the ordinary" behavior to the feds.[53] No clear guidelines were ever issued on what could be considered "suspicious" and worthy of entry into someone's federal dossier. Rep. Bob Barr (R-Ga.) denounced TIPS as a "snitch system" and warned: "A formal program, organized, paid for and maintained by our own federal government to recruit Americans to spy on fellow Americans, smacks of the very type of fascist or Communist government we fought so hard to eradicate in other countries in decades past."[54]

Congress shot TIPS down. Bush's attempt to use the Freedom Corps to launch Operation TIPS should have provoked broad concern about his warped concept of freedom.

BUSH'S BOGUS MORAL REVOLUTION

Bush prides himself on how his post-9/11 exhortations made America a better place. In a December 20, 2003, radio broadcast, Bush bragged of how his efforts had spurred more Americans to volunteer:

> Just this week, a government report found that more than 63 million Americans volunteered over the past year—about 4 million more than in the year before. . . . This increase in volunteering is evidence of the new culture of service we are building in America, especially among young people. Nearly two years ago. . . . I asked every person in America to commit 4,000 hours over a lifetime—or about 100 hours a year—to serving neighbors in need. The response was immediate and enthusiastic, and has remained strong.[55]

A White House press release headline hyped Bush's success in "Mobilizing More Americans to Serve"—making it sound like a Soviet drive to boost the potato harvest.[56] USA Freedom Corps director Bridgeland declared that the government survey of volunteers "demonstrates that even more Americans are stepping forward to serve in their communities, which is what the president and his USA Freedom Corps set out to do."[57] Every additional American who volunteered became another Bush success story. The more Americans who obey Bush's summons, the more benevolent Bush appears.

The "4 million" new volunteers were surmised from a variance in responses between the first and second time the Labor Department's Bureau of Labor Statistics (BLS) surveyed Americans on volunteering. But the survey results are as dubious as the monthly unemployment numbers the same bureau issues.

The Bush "moral revolution" consisted of the purported increase in volunteering from 27.4 percent to 28.8 percent of the population. But the 1.4 percent increase in volunteering may have been smaller than the survey's margin of error (1.6 percent). BLS reported that there is "about a 90-percent chance, or level of confidence, that an estimate based on a sample will differ by no more than 1.6 standard errors from the 'true' population value because of sampling error."[58] The BLS expert who wrote the technical note was not able to provide a percentage estimate of the margin of error for the survey.[59]

The wording alone of the 2003 survey may have generated more affirmative responses than the 2002 survey. As a "technical note," the survey methodology explained: "In a redesigned question, non-volunteers were asked if they had ever volunteered. If they responded 'yes,' they were asked for the reason that they had not volunteered during the previous year." This question may have prompted some people's memories of brief volunteer gigs in the prior year—or encouraged them to "remember" something that they had actually done earlier and place it in the previous calendar year.[60] (The BLS survey did not count AmeriCorps recruits as "volunteers" since their paychecks disqualified them.)

The Bureau of Labor Statistics results conflict with the numbers and trends found by nongovernment surveys of volunteers:

- The Independent Sector, the nation's largest coalition of nonprofit organizations, estimated in a 2001 report that 84 million American adults—44 percent of all adults—volunteered with a formal organization during 2000.[61] (Bush's Office of Management and Budget relied upon Independent Sector volunteer numbers, not the Bureau of Labor Statistics reports, in its 2004 criticisms of AmeriCorps.)

- A 2002 survey conducted for non-profit organizations concluded that roughly 110 million American adults volunteer with nonprofit groups each year.[62]
- A November 2003 survey by the American Association for Retired Persons claimed that "51 percent of the middle-aged and older population reported volunteering."[63]
- University of Michigan psychologist Louis Penner reported that volunteerism surged only briefly after 9/11. *National Journal* reported in September 2003: "Tracking the activity of a national volunteer-placement center called VolunteerMatch, Penner found a threefold increase in volunteerism in the week after 9/11. Three weeks later, the rate of volunteerism fell back to its old level, where it has since remained."[64]

CONCLUSION

Shortly before his resignation in August 2003, Lenkowsky gave an interview to the *Wall Street Journal* editorial page, which had treated him with great respect and deference early in his time as AmeriCorps chief. Lenkowsky declared that AmeriCorps is just "another cumbersome, unpredictable government bureaucracy" and asked: "Even if [AmeriCorps] is well run, do we really need it? That's a good question."[65] The White House was furious when Lenkowsky's comments hit the street, and AmeriCorps spokesman Sandy Scott quickly announced that Lenkowsky's "words were taken out of context."[66] Lenkowsky never claimed he was misquoted.

AmeriCorps has always been grossly mismanaged. It is like a religious miracle that is continually exposed as a fake and a fraud—and yet people continue to make pilgrimages to the site and worship it—or at least to urge Congress to seize and spend other people's money for site maintenance.

AmeriCorps is the most visible symbol and proof of the hollowness of Bush's compassionate agenda. Bush is far more concerned about exploiting AmeriCorps' moral sheen than about preventing the waste of tax dollars. It is moral dementia to believe that government can create virtue simply by seizing some people's paychecks and paying other people to piously wander the land wearing gray t-shirts and hats.

CHAPTER SEVEN

Bush's Farm Fiasco

When George W. Bush took his oath of office, farm policy was widely perceived as perhaps the most persistent and abysmal federal sinkhole. The federal government had been mangling agricultural markets since the 1930s. The same blunders have been repeated decade in and decade out, and politicians laughed all the way to reelection.

Republicans responded to this perennial failure with the 1996 "Freedom to Farm Act" and solemn promises about ending farm subsidies once and for all. The Freedom to Farm Act turned out to be House Speaker Newt Gingrich's biggest fraud.

The 1996 farm act gave subsidized farmers more than three times as much in cash handouts in 1996 and 1997 as they would have received under the previous farm program. When crop prices went south, Congress scrambled to deliver extra billions of dollars to farmers in 1998, 1999, and 2000. With each new silo of handouts granted to farmers, Republicans recited their devotion to "freedom to farm."

In his 2000 presidential campaign, Bush declared that "the best way to ensure a strong, growing, and vibrant agricultural sector is through a more market-driven approach."[1] The Freedom to Farm Act was scheduled to expire in 2002, and the crafting of new farm legislation began shortly after Bush took office.

The debate over the 2002 farm bill rarely stooped to consider basic truths. The vast majority of the types of crops produced in the United States are unsubsidized, yet there is no shortage of output. The average full-time farmer has

a net worth of more than a million dollars.[2] Congressmen portray their interventions as correcting market failures. In reality, federal farm policy is like a
driver who perpetually has one foot on the brake and one foot on the acceler-
ator. But this is not a problem because the driver never has to pay for the
wasted gas or the burned-out brake pads.

Farm bills usually set policy and authorize subsidies for up to six years.
Historically, when farm bills are carved out, only the veto threats of a dutiful
president limit the budgetary carnage from farm-state congressmen fertilizing
their political future.

The Bush team, unlike most administrations, never bothered to write its
own farm bill. *National Journal* noted that the Bush administration was "re-
markably uninvolved" in the farm bill deliberations.[3] Four days before 9/11,
the *Wall Street Journal* reported: "Despite misgivings in the Bush administration, House Republicans are plowing ahead with a massive farm bill that
would more than wipe out what remains of non–Social Security surpluses projected for the next few years."[4]

When Office of Management and Budget director Mitch Daniels complained of the rising cost of the farm bill in early October 2001, congressman
Larry Combest (R-Tex.), chairman of the House Agriculture Committee, denounced him: "For you to come now at the last minute is an insult. How
could you dare do this to us?"[5] Agriculture Secretary Ann Veneman warned in
November 2001 that the congressional bill would spur overproduction, undermine U.S. exports, and create "pressure for more government payments,
thereby creating a self-defeating and ultimately unsustainable cycle."[6] Congress paid Veneman no heed.

The lofty tone of the farm bill debate was defiled by a nonprofit group's
website exposing the subsidies individual farmers reaped. The Environmental
Working Group revealed that the largest farmers are now snaring a higher percentage of handouts: "In 1995, the top 10 percent of American farmers received 55 percent of government subsidies; in 2001 their share rose to 67
percent."[7] The "top one percent of farmers—24,111 farms—collected $13.5
billion from 1996 to 2001, an average of $558,698 a pop."[8]

The *Los Angeles Times* weighed in belatedly with an excellent analysis of
farm subsidies in California:

> Only 9% of California's 74,000 farms have actually received subsidy payments
> and nearly two-thirds of the money since 1996—$1.8 billion—has gone to
> fewer than 3,500 farms. Most of the crops that fuel the state's $29-billion farm
> machine—grapes, peaches, plums, nectarines, strawberries, almonds, walnuts

and vegetables of every hue—don't get a penny of aid. They aren't eligible. Rather, the bulk of the money goes to support giant fields of cotton, rice, wheat and barley—crops that exist in surplus. Of the top 20 recipients in California, seven are big cotton growers and 11 are big rice growers. On average, they take in $596,000 in crop subsidies a year.[9]

The delicate legislative crafting of the farm bill benefited from many congressmen's personal experience with subsidies. Rep. Marion Berry (D-Ark.) raked in $750,449 from USDA between 1996 and 2001, and Sen. Blanche Lincoln (D-Ark.) pocketed $351,085. Rep Cal Dooley (D-Calif.) snared $306,903, while Rep. Tom Lathan (R-Iowa) harvested $286,862. Rep. Stenholm (D-Tex.) pulled down $39,298. Other members of Congress receiving farm subsidies included Rep. Doug Ose (R-Calif.), Sen. Charles Grassley (R-Iowa), Sen. Richard Lugar (R-Ind.), Rep. Bob Stump (R-Ariz.), House Speaker Dennis Hastert (R-Ill.), Sen. Sam Brownback (R-Kan.), Sen. Phil Gramm (R-Tex.), and Rep. Phil Crane (R-Ill.).[10] Perhaps to prevent any appearance of a conflict of interest, congressional ethics rules exempt congressmen from revealing how much in farm subsidies they collect. USDA refused to disclose how much it ladled out to individual farmers until a 1996 *Washington Post* lawsuit compelled the agency to open its books.[11] (Some members of Congress who received subsidies voted against the farm bill, including Lugar, Crane, Gramm, and Dooley.)

Congressmen responded to the embarrassing profiteering disclosures by seeking to turn farm subsidies into national secrets. Sen. Tom Harkin (D-Iowa) added a provision into the Senate farm bill to prevent the USDA from disclosing the names of recipients of farm conservation subsidies.[12] House Agriculture chairman Larry Combest championed a similar measure in the House bill. The provisions were dropped after the media howled.

The hottest controversy erupted over limits on how much subsidies individual farmers can collect each year. Until the late 1980s, farmers were limited to $50,000 in federal payments per year. However, the law at that time was written so that each farmer could get three separate $50,000 payments. And if a farmer included his wife and children on the title to the farm, each of them could also pocket $50,000 a year.[13]

Most farm-state congressmen agreed in 2002 that it was time to adjust the payment limitations to account for the high cost of rural living. The House Agriculture Committee authorized payments of up to $550,000 per year per farmer, while the Senate Agriculture Committee came in with a non-binding limit of $275,000 in handouts per year.

The Senate's parsimony caused great anguish. Sen. Jean Carnahan (D-Mo.) urged her colleagues to revise the bill "to protect rice and cotton growers" whom the payment limit would "disproportionately affect."[14] Rep. Charles Stenholm (D-Tex.), the patron saint of USDA boondoggles, whined, "The Senate payment limitation language was written by folks who don't necessarily appreciate the significant differences in agriculture among the various parts of the U.S. . . . Cotton and rice are more expensive to grow."[15] No one produced any evidence that rice and cotton plantation owners are being forced at gunpoint to grow those crops.

Members of the House and Senate conferred over the differences in their farm bills and reached a Solomonic compromise on how taxpayers would be sawed for farmers' benefit.[16] The new farm bill entitled farmers to snare up to $360,000 per year. This "limit" contains the usual King Kong-size loopholes so farmers can drive their harvesters back through the Treasury coffers for second and third loads.

Some Republicans were aghast at the final bill. Sen. Lugar complained that the bill creates "a huge transfer payment from a majority of Americans to very few" and also warned that the lavish new subsidies would result "almost inevitably" in "vast oversupply and lower prices."[17] Rep. Jeff Flake (R-Az.), complained that the "legislation will cost the average American household $4,377 over the next 10 years—$1,805 in taxes and $2,572 in inflated food prices because of price supports."[18] Flake observed that 90 percent of the $50 billion increase in handouts "will go to farmers producing just five crops: wheat, corn, rice, cotton and soybean. Two-thirds will go to just 10% of farmers."[19] The Congressional Budget Office estimated that the cost of subsidies would increase almost 80 percent over the following six years.[20]

The farm bill created new handouts for farmers producing apples, chickpeas, dry peas, lentils, onions, catfish, and other farm products. Congressmen may have sought to throw the subsidy cloak over more crops to hide the evidence that farmers can survive and thrive without government aid.

The bill was crafted by politicians representing many of America's least competitive farmers. *National Journal* noted: "The cornerstones of the plan were laid by two of the country's most troubled farm regions. At the northern end, Senate Majority Leader Thomas A. Daschle (D-S.D.) and Sen. Kent Conrad (D-N.D.) advocated the interests of the grain-dependent Dakotas. At the southern end were less-productive cotton- and rice-growing West Texas districts represented" by Rep. Combest and Rep. Stenholm.[21] This is like letting national high-tech policy be set by a bunch of folks who still have trouble figuring out how to use a cell phone.

Bush signed the Farm Security and Rural Investment Act of 2002 on May 13, 2002. (The farm bill was renamed a "security" act to capitalize on post 9/11 angst.) The farm bill's spending explosion offended some conservatives. White House senior advisor Karl Rove joked that Bush might sign it "by candlelight."[22] Instead, Bush signed the bill at 7:45 A.M. in a federal executive office building. The *Washington Post* noted: "Bush advisers said the timing was designed to minimize exposure in Washington and maximize it on early-morning crop broadcasts in farm regions."[23] A senior Republican official explained that Bush accepted the high spending levels "because the most fertile ground for gaining the one Senate seat needed for a Republican takeover lies in the farm states of South Dakota, Montana, Minnesota, Missouri, Iowa and Georgia."[24]

The signing ceremony was attended by lobbyists, big Republican donors, congressmen, and others who came to see and be seen.

Sounding like a king talking down to a group of awed peasants let into the palace to witness a coronation, Bush began by announcing, "And when I sign this bill, I'd like for you all to come up here and watch me sign it."[25]

He rattled off the reasons why this was a fine farm bill:

- Bush declared the bill "will provide a safety net for farmers." The farm bill entitles farmers to collect up to four times more in handouts each year than the total net worth of half of all the households in the United States. (The median household net worth in the United States was $86,100.)[26]
- Some provisions of the farm bill are means-tested, just like food stamps. Dairy farmers who suffer losses during a government-designated drought disaster are eligible for up to $40,000 in aid. But dairymen can collect this handout only if their gross income is less than $2.5 million a year.[27] (An individual can collect food stamps only if his income is less than $12,000 a year.)
- Bush asserted that the bill will give farmers ample aid "without encouraging overproduction and depressing prices." The farm bill raised support prices for most subsidized crops, assuring that taxpayers will be reamed. The bill had the same flaws that Bush's agriculture secretary denounced six months earlier.
- Bush asserted that the bill "reduces government interference in the market, and in farmers' and ranchers' planting decisions." But setting subsidies at higher levels guaranteed profound disruptions in rural America. Rep. Lathan complained two months later that the massive

handouts to large farmers were driving up land values in Iowa and "making it more difficult for young farmers to buy land and more costly to small family farmers who rent acreage."[28] The Environmental Defense Fund warned that the farm bill would provide big farmers "unprecedented funds to swallow up their smaller neighbors."

- Bush claimed that the bill "will promote farmer independence." But it does so in the same way that giving free Cadillacs to all poor people would promote "freedom of transportation." (After Bush signed the bill, the first hand he shook was that of Ken Hood, a Mississippi cotton baron whose plantation reaped $750,000 in subsidies in 2001.)[29]
- Bush declared that "this bill offers incentives for good conservation practices on working lands." But USDA's conservation efforts have often been a charade to dampen criticism of farm programs' environmental havoc. The 1985 farm bill, for instance, required subsidized farmers to follow strict conservation guidelines to reduce soil erosion and protect wetlands. The General Accounting Office reported in 2003 that almost half of USDA's Conservation Service offices did not bother enforcing the mandates on farmers "because they lack staff, management does not emphasize these provisions, or they are uncomfortable with their enforcement role."[30]

Bush mentioned three times in the signing ceremony that the bill was "generous." Who gave George Bush the right to be generous with other people's money? Bush talked as if farm subsidies were a personal dispensation from his own treasures—or perhaps a joint dispensation from his treasures and the personal stashes of congressmen. Bush and congressmen preened, expecting admiration and applause for seizing and delivering the paychecks of dishwashers and ditch diggers to millionaire land owners. The notion that a politician is being generous when he confiscates one person's paycheck to deliver to someone he considers a worthy recipient is one of the most pernicious delusions in contemporary political and moral thinking.

Bush admitted to one regret about the farm bill: "I thought it was important to have what they call Farm Savings Accounts to help farmers and ranchers manage the many risks they face. I thought that should be an important part of the bill. It didn't happen; I'm going to continue to work for it." Perhaps the farm lobby balked at this gambit because some farmers still cling to a few shreds of pride.

Bush sought to create savings accounts for individual farmers that would be managed by USDA. A farmer could deposit up to $10,000 a year, which the feds would match dollar for dollar. USDA would permit the farmer to make savings withdrawals only in years of relatively low crop prices.

Prior to the creation of federal farm programs, American farmers were renowned for their high savings rate. Perhaps Bush believes that farmers have become so dissolute (because of an addiction to subsidies) that they are now completely unable to save for a rainy day or a dry year. Thus, government must match their savings deposits the way parents do for a child they are trying to encourage to be thrifty.

Bush's "farm savings account" may have been a throwaway gesture to burnish his "compassionate conservative" credentials. Perhaps Bush hoped for a grandiose ceremony (modeled after a Super Bowl half-time show but without any breasts). In the full spotlight of the nation's media, Bush would accept the first "savings deposit" from a farmer (carefully chosen from a swing state with many electoral votes). Bush, standing in front of a giant "SAVINGS MISSION ACCOMPLISHED" banner, would then pat the hayseed on the head and, with studied theatrical gestures (choreographed by Karl Rove), formally deposit both the farmer's check and the federal government's matching money into a giant piggy bank that coincidentally resembles a Republican elephant.

Bush's concern for farmers' savings habits is misplaced. In reality, the typical farmer has far more financial savvy, at least as far as milking the government is concerned, then the feds could ever teach.

A few months later, Bush appeared before a farm-state audience and talked as if he deserved an Aggie Medal of Honor for his courage: "I want you to know I signed the farm bill, and I'm proud to have signed the farm bill. Some of us in this audience who supported a farm bill took a little heat over it. . . . We took heat over it because, I guess, some people didn't understand how important the farm economy is. But I said, when I signed that bill, there's $180 billion in that bill of taxpayers' money to help our farm and ranch community." Bush quickly reassured anyone in the audience who might be concerned about government waste: "It's important to watch our spending in Washington. It's important to set priorities and watch our spending."[31]

SUGAR SCAM

At the time the congressional agriculture committees began work on the farm bill, USDA was paying a million dollars a month to store piles of surplus sugar. The federal government also rewarded farmers in 2001 for plowing under tens of thousands of acres of sugar beets to try to stabilize the domestic sugar market.

There are roughly 8,000 U.S. sugar growers. More than 720,000 people work in U.S. industries that use sugar.[32] Thus, almost 90 times as many people rely on sugar for their jobs as actually grow it. The Sweetener Users Association estimated that up to 10,000 jobs were lost between 1997 and 2002 thanks to the federal sugar program.[33]

Congress recognized the problem and jiggled the program to make sugar subsidies more lucrative for farmers and more costly for taxpayers. Thanks to the 2002 farm bill, U.S. sugar prices are now triple the world sugar price.

GAO estimates that the sugar program costs American consumers almost $2 billion a year. GAO estimated that 17 of the nation's largest sugar cane farmers received more than half of all the benefits provided by the sugarcane subsidies. Nationwide, 1 percent of sugar growers captured almost two-thirds of the program's benefits. This is sound public policy—from Congress's perspective. The more concentrated the benefits, the more generous the recipients. The sugar lobby contributed $13 million to politicians, political action committees, and other political efforts in the 2000 election cycle and could break that record in the current presidential year.[34]

There is no need for a sugar program because the United States can buy all the sugar it needs at much lower prices than American sugar growers demand. Sugar is America's most uncompetitive crop: climate, land values, and labor costs ensure that America's farmers will never be able to compete with Third World farmers in tropical areas.

MILK MADNESS

When Bush signed the farm bill, USDA was the proud owner of a billion dollars worth of milk powder. Twenty million pounds of additional dry milk powder was arriving every week at USDA's specially made storage caves near Kansas City, Missouri.[35] The federal government bought and stored almost half of all the nonfat dry milk produced in the United States in 2000.[36] USDA judiciously keeps the milk powder in storage until it goes bad and then sells it at giveaway prices for use as animal feed. Seventy-five percent of Americans consume insufficient calcium,[37] but USDA's cut-rate sales ensure that cows and pigs get ample calcium.

The dairy program has been plagued by gluts of dry milk, butter, or cheese for 25 years. Congress perennially sets federal support prices above market prices—and the government sops up the resulting surplus.

Congress responded to the history of such debacles in 2002 by raising support prices and creating three new programs to bankroll dairy farmers. The combination of new subsidies and added complexity is mangling the dairy market, resulting in relatively low prices for farmers and soaring costs for taxpayers. Direct dairy subsidies cost more than $4 billion between 2002 and 2004, and domestic marketing restrictions cost consumers billions of dollars a year. California dairy farmer Charles Ahlem complained, "The government has sent the wrong signals, that there is an unlimited demand for commodity dairy products."[38] Rep. Cal Dooley (D-Calif.), who represents some of the nation's most efficient dairymen, declared: "It's time for us to have a serious analysis of whether a program like this makes any sense whatsoever."[39]

Federal policies encourage dairy farmers and much of the dairy industry to scorn consumer preferences. Constance Tipton of the International Dairy Foods Association testified to Congress that the dairy price support program "encouraged continued production of nonfat dry milk for which there was no market demand, instead of allowing market demand for high protein dairy ingredients which are increasingly used in new food products and product formulations to drive production of these products."[40] Dairy producers have "no incentive . . . to retool and produce other new products" as long as Uncle Sam is paying premium prices for nonfat dry milk, Tipton noted.

U.S. dairy product prices are double the world prices for key products. Americans could save $1.6 billion a year if the United States lowered its trade barriers against foreign milk, cheese, and butter.[41] But Americans should not be concerned about the dairy import quotas which keep out foreign dairy products because, as President Bush proudly proclaimed, "We've got the best cheese in the world here in America."[42]

HAIRBALL

The 2002 farm bill revived two of the biggest howlers in agricultural policy history—wool and mohair subsidies. Congress ended these programs in 1993. But, like serial offenders, the 107th Congress could not resist returning to the scene of earlier budgetary crimes. The wool program plowed more than a billion dollars into the pockets of sheepmen from 1954 to 1993. The program undermined the quality of American wool by encouraging farmers to rely on Uncle Sam for the bulk of their income.[43] USDA paid sheepmen the same price for their wool regardless of how many briars and other crap it contained—often making American wool unfit for American textile factories. The new mohair program bankrolls a smattering of Texas Angora goat farmers and indirectly subsidizes British factories (since no American textile factory dirties its hands with goat hair). Almost all the mohair produced in the United States is exported for production of fancy sweaters and coats that few American taxpayers can afford. The new programs will cost American taxpayers hundreds of millions of dollars in the coming years.

NUTS

Peanut farmers—already among the most heavily subsidized of all farmers—were honored with massive new windfalls. Prior to the 2002 farm bill, peanut farmers were required to have a federal license that would authorize each pound of peanuts they produced for domestic consumption. The lucky farmers with licenses collected a return more than eight times that of the average U.S. corporate profit.[44] The peanut program guaranteed American farmers prices that are roughly double world market levels, thereby forcing every person who bought a jar of peanut butter to pay tribute to Congress's favorites.

The 2002 farm bill abolished the feudal peanut licensing system. Congress should have recognized that there was no more need to subsidize peanuts than there is to subsidize pecans (which have long flourished without federal handouts). Instead, Congress created a new program to allow any peanut farmer to receive peanut subsidies. Congress also lavishly compensated the peanut quota owners. Many farmers had sold their nut license to doctors, dentists, or insurance companies, who then leased them back to farmers each year. The largest "peanut buyout" payments went to the John Hancock Insurance Company, which collected $2 million in 2002 and is scheduled to receive much more in the coming years. The Congressional Budget Office estimated that the peanut program and buyouts will cost $4 billion in the following decade.[45]

COTTON: EXPORTING DEATH AND MISERY

Cotton farmers receive among the most generous subsidies of all American farmers. Since 1990, the cotton program has cost taxpayers more than $20 billion—the equivalent of $6 million for each full-time cotton farmer. The 2002 farm bill authorized jacking up the subsidies the average American cotton farmer could receive by roughly 16 percent.[46]

Lavish subsidies spur bumper crops, which the U.S. government dumps on world markets, helping drive world cotton prices down by 50 percent between 1996 and 2002. Amadou Toumani Touré and Blaise Compaoré, the presidents of Mali and Burkina Faso, respectively, complained in July 2003 that "the payments to about 2,500 relatively well-off [American cotton] farmers has the unintended but nevertheless real effect of impoverishing some 10 million rural poor people in West and Central Africa."[47] Many cotton farmers in Africa have lower costs of production than their American counterparts, but U.S. subsidies trump comparative advantage every time. Mark Ritchie of the Institute for Agriculture and Trade Policy commented that the 2002 farm bill "will put millions of small farmers out of business in Africa. They will have to move to cities and become part of unemployed labor pools."[48]

The U.S. government, stung by the criticism, proposed a cotton remedy at international trade negotiations held in Cancun, Mexico in September 2003. U.S. government officials proposed encouraging African governments to seek World Bank aid "to effectively direct existing programs and resources toward diversification of the economies where cotton accounts for the major share of their GDP."[49] Greg Rushford, the editor of the *Rushford Report,* observed, "The Africans were told that if they objected to the American cotton program, they could tell their farmers to get out of cotton and into other commodities." Rushford labeled the gambit "an insulting colonial relic."[50] The U.S. proposal outraged Third World nations and helped spur the collapse of trade negotiations.

FREEBIES

The 2002 farm bill entitles American taxpayers to continue bankrolling food advertisements around the globe. In the 1985 farm bill, Congress created the Targeted Export Assistance program to pay for foreign advertisements for McDonald's and other multinational corporations. The program became such a disgrace that in the 1990 farm bill Congress changed its name to the Market Promotion Program. In 1995, after a scandal involving Japanese underwear advertisements, it was renamed the Market Access Program (MAP). MAP continues to pay for brand name ads abroad but no longer directly aids Fortune 500 companies. GAO found that the program's success claims are ludicrous and that there is no credible evidence that it boosts exports.[51]

Therefore, in the 2002 farm bill, Congress doubled MAP spending to $200 million a year. Yet, in many cases, federal policies are exporters' worst enemy. The feds gave the Cranberry Marketing Committee $736,959 for export ads in 2003, after the government rewarded cranberry farmers for slashing production. USDA is paying to boost exports of California almonds and raisins at the same time that federal marketing boards severely restrict the quantity of exports to inflate crop prices. The U.S. Dairy Export Council received more than $2 million to boost exports at the same time that federal policies make U.S. dairy products uncompetitive. The Chocolate Manufacturers Association received almost $1 million to boost chocolate exports, but their efforts are thwarted because U.S. chocolate makers must pay double the sugar price of foreign competitors. But it's the thought that counts. American teetotalers have the honor of helping finance MAP wine export efforts, which in 2003 included $3.7 million for the Wine Institute, $438,000 for the Northwest Wine Promotion Coalition, and $170,000 for the New York Wine and Grape Foundation.[52]

QUAINT

At the same time that the farm bill immersed farmers in political swamps that threaten their long-term viability, Congress also commanded the secretary of agriculture to "establish a historic barn preservation program . . . to assist States in developing a list of historic barns. . . . [and] to foster educational programs relating to the history, construction techniques, rehabilitation, and contribution to society of historic barns."[53] "Historic barn" was defined largely as a barn at least 50 years old that "retains sufficient integrity of design, materials, and construction to clearly identify the barn as an agricultural building." The farm bill barn mandate could signal a shift toward the French-style subsidies—turning farms into museums for visiting urban schoolchildren. Perhaps the next farm bill will gold-plate Tennessee outhouses.

CONCLUSION

In a June 7, 2002 speech at the World Pork Expo in Des Moines, Iowa, Bush assured the audience of his expertise: "I was from a—the Governor of the second largest agricultural State in the Union. I understand farm economics."[54] If Bush truly understands "farm economics," then he has no excuse for perpetuating a morass of programs and policies that decimate efficiency, blight innovation, and pulverize taxpayers and consumers. Even if Bush spoke falsely when he claimed to understand "farm economics," he has no excuse for not knowing the damage his actions inflict.

The Bush administration—like its predecessors going back to Herbert Hoover—appears to have learned nothing and forgotten nothing about farm policy. The main effect of farm programs is to force farmers to do inefficiently what they would have done efficiently without subsidies, to force Americans to pay more for food, to drive up the price of farmland (thereby decimating American farmers' competitiveness), and to pointlessly squander tens of billions of dollars a year. Every subsidized crop (except sugar) would still be grown in America even if USDA never handed out another bushel of greenbacks. The issue is not whether the United States will have ample food in the future, but whether politicians will continue manipulating American agriculture.

Farm programs have always cost taxpayers and consumers far more than they have benefited farmers. Agricultural policy has perennially squandered two, three, four, or more dollars to give one dollar in benefits, always wasting money and then spending more to camouflage the waste.

In 1930, the *New York Times,* surveying the wreckage of agricultural markets after the federal government tried to drive up wheat prices, concluded, "It is perhaps fortunate for the country that its fingers were so badly burned at the very first trial of the scheme."[55] Despite an unbroken string of failures, the federal government has continued to disrupt agriculture ever since. Almost all the mistakes of the past are being repeated: only the names of the presidents, secretaries of agriculture, and farm-state congressmen have changed. There is nothing that federal agricultural programs can do that markets cannot do better—except provide unearned handouts to farmers.

CHAPTER EIGHT

Spending as Caring

It is usually easy for a politician to buy a reputation for goodness with other people's money. Bush, like other recent presidents, offers lofty rationales for public spending binges that do little more than burnish his reputation or pad his expected vote totals. Unfortunately, Bush's spending sprees will cause lasting damage, both here and abroad.

BUSH-STYLE ANTI-CORRUPTION

President Bush has doled out more than $70 billion in foreign aid and loan guarantees to foreign governments, countries, and international organizations. Bush committed billions in new aid in large part to get the endorsement of a rock star and to garner applause at a United Nations summit.

Because roughly a minuscule percent of the aid will be paid out from a new program created to encourage foreign politicians not to steal, Bush talks as if his aid is revolutionizing the Third World. Early on, Bush and his top aides were honest and blunt on the failure of foreign aid:

- Treasury Secretary Paul O'Neill denounced the World Bank and International Monetary Fund for driving many poor nations "into a ditch" with excessive lending that governments wasted.[1]
- In an April 30, 2002, speech on compassionate conservatism, Bush declared, "The old way of pouring vast amounts of money into development

aid without any concern for results has failed, often leaving behind misery
and poverty and corruption."[2]

- A September 2002 White House report declared that foreign aid "has
  often served to prop up failed policies, relieving the pressure for reform
  and perpetuating misery."[3]

Foreign aid fails in part due to pervasive corruption. A 2003 report from
a leading Bangladesh university estimated that 75 percent of all foreign aid
received in that country is lost to corruption.[4] Northwestern University political economist Jeffrey Winters estimated that more than 50 percent of
World Bank aid is lost to corruption in some African countries.[5] Nigerian
President Olusegun Obasanjo announced in 2002 that African leaders "have
stolen at least $140 billion from their people in the decades since indepen-
dence."[6] An African Union study pegged the takings at a much higher rate,
estimating Africa's toll from corruption at $150 billion every year.[7] Lavish au-
tomobiles are so popular among African government officials that a word has
come into use in Swahili: *wabenzi*—"men of the Mercedes-Benz." Investment
guru Jim Rogers, who recently drove around the globe, declared: "Most foreign aid winds up with outside consultants, the local military, corrupt bureaucrats, the new NGO [nongovernmental organizations] administrators,
and Mercedes dealers. There are Mercedes dealers in places where there are
not even roads."[8]

A Brookings Institution analysis observed: "The history of U.S. assistance is littered with tales of corrupt foreign officials using aid to line their
own pockets, support military buildups, and pursue vanity projects. It is no
wonder that few studies show clear correlations between aid flows and
growth."[9] A Heritage Foundation report noted, "Most recipients of U.S. development assistance are poorer now than they were before first receiving
U.S. aid."[10] Former World Bank senior economist William Easterly estimates that World Bank and IMF loans "actually boosted poverty worldwide
by a total of 14 million people."[11]

Foreign aid breeds kleptocracies, or governments of thieves. A 1999 National Bureau of Economic Research study concluded that "countries that receive more [foreign] aid tend to have higher corruption."[12] A 2002 *American
Economic Review* study by the same authors concluded that "increases in aid
are associated with contemporaneous increases in corruption"[13] and that "corruption is positively correlated with aid received from the United States." Foreign aid can also spur civil wars. As Nobel laureate economist P. T. Bauer
noted, "The great increase in the prizes of political power has been a major fac-

tor in the frequency and intensity of political conflict in contemporary Africa and in the rest of the less developed world."[14]

Bush's comments on the failure of foreign aid have been among his more astute utterances. Since foreign aid is an indisputable failure, Bush resolved to start a new foreign aid program.

The propellant of Bush's foreign aid "conversion" was a UN summit on global poverty in Monterrey, Mexico, in March 2002. Bush agreed to come and speak to the meeting after being pressured by his buddy, Mexican president Vicente Fox. Because administration officials vocally criticized foreign aid, White House aides feared Bush could receive a hostile reception.

But Bush cleverly disarmed critics by promising to greatly increase U.S. foreign aid spending. Bush arranged to have the Irish rock star Bono present for his March 14, 2002 announcement; the *Washington Post* noted that the White House "clearly craved" Bono's support and that "Bono looked on approvingly" as Bush promised four days before the UN conference to boost foreign aid by $5 billion over a three year period.[15]

The White House was chagrined when Bush's proposal did not generate massive international applause. So, on the day before Bush left for Mexico, White House officials revealed that there'd been a glitch in the original announcement and that Bush actually planned to giveaway more than twice as much money under the new program. White House spokesman Ari Fleischer said the mistake was simply a result of "confusing" math.[16] National Security Advisor Condoleeza Rice explained: "We didn't want to go out there with essentially false or phony numbers."[17] The *New York Times* noted that "skeptics said the White House was just adding on billions to make sure that the president was a hit in Monterrey."[18]

Even before arriving in Monterrey, Bush bragged about the money he was bringing. In a March 20, 2002 interview with Peruvian radio, Bush declared, "I'm coming with this, what we call the Millennium Challenge Fund, which is $10 billion of new money."[19] (The name was later changed to Millennium Challenge Account.)

At that time, the United States was already the largest foreign aid donor in the world. But many foreign governments were miffed because the U.S. government did not give away a higher percent of the U.S. gross national product. The World Bank and other international organizations were beating the drums to double the amount of foreign aid by the year 2015. Perhaps the World Bank assumed that doubling foreign aid would finally resolve, once and for all, whether all that money really was vanishing into bottomless holes.

In his speech to the UN conference, Bush piously informed world leaders that foreign aid could harm: "Pouring money into a failed status quo does little to help the poor, and can actually delay the progress of reform."[20] Since the speech occurred after 9/11, Bush invoked antiterrorism to justify the largesse: "We fight against poverty because hope is an answer to terror." And, in a startling revelation that instantly altered humanitarian efforts around the globe, Bush revealed: "We must do more than just feel good about what we are doing; we must do good."

Less than three weeks after he slapped high tariffs on steel imports, Bush lectured the world that "to be serious about fighting poverty, we must be serious about expanding trade. . . . Trade brings expectations of freedom." Bush portrayed market openings as panaceas: "As one example, in a single year, the African Growth and Opportunity Act has increased African exports to the United States by more than 1,000 percent. . . ." In reality, the value of African exports to the United States decreased after the act was implemented (largely due to a fall in the price of oil).[21]

Bush said the aid provided through the Millennium Challenge Account (MCA) would be "devoted to projects in nations that govern justly, invest in their people, and encourage economic freedom." Bush assured the world that, "By taking the side of liberty and good government, we will liberate millions from poverty's prison."[22] Bush was confident that the new handouts and the new rhetoric gave both him and America the moral high ground.

Bush was hailed by dignitaries whose programs have long failed the world's poor. United Nations Development Program chief Mark Malloch Brown gushed: "There could be no more potent spokesman for increased aid than George W. Bush, the war leader."[23]

The White House did not bother submitting legislation to Congress to establish the new program until January 2003. Condoleeza Rice proudly declared in February 2004: "The Millennium Challenge Account is revolutionizing the way America provides aid to developing countries."[24] At that point, no MCA money had gone out and the State Department had not even bothered to publish the standards by which applicants for the money would be judged.

The State Department finally released the MCA aid criteria on March 10, 2004. Among the 16 factors by which applicants will be judged are political liberties, consumer price inflation, "regulatory quality," and "days to start a business." The U.S. government will base its assessment of an applicant's "government effectiveness" and "quality of public service provision" according to the assessments of the World Bank (which is like having the Soviet Union pass judgment on a country's agricultural policy). Governments will also be judged by their "performance in ensuring the rights of people with disabilities."[25]

When he first unveiled the visionary program, Bush made it clear that MCA would set the standard by which all foreign aid would be judged: "I think it makes no sense to give aid, money, to countries that are corrupt. . . . The money doesn't help the people; it helps an elite group of leaders. And that's not fair to the people of this particular country, nor is it fair to the tax-payers in the United States. And if a country thinks they're going to get aid from the United States and they're stealing money, they're just not going to get it out of this millennium fund—and hopefully not out of any fund."[26]

Though Bush implied in 2002 that the United States would cease bankrolling corrupt governments, he modified his tune in October 2003, characterizing the MCA as a program that "basically says we're willing to *add aid* if countries develop the habits necessary to be able to develop a just and honorable society."[27] The State Department codified the backtracking in early 2004: "The MCA is an incentive-based *supplement* to other U.S. aid programs."[28]

The MCA is based upon the revelation that it is unsound policy to give money to foreign leaders who steal, but the Bush administration is fastidiously avoiding applying the MCA "lesson" to other U.S. foreign aid. The idea of bribing foreign politicians to encourage honesty makes as much sense as distributing free condoms to encourage abstinence. The United States has doled out more than $500 billion in foreign aid since 1946, and Washington is knee-deep in foreign aid experts.

The largest foreign aid recipients also have poor ratings for corruption, oppression, or both:

- Israel ($14 billion in aid and loan guarantees in 2003): The chief prosecutor for the State of Israel recommended in March 2004 that Prime Minister Ariel Sharon be indicted for taking bribes.[29] U.S. aid to Israel has enabled the Israeli government to carry out repressive policies throughout the Occupied Territories, including building a wall that expropriates the land of thousands of Palestinians.
- Egypt ($1.9 billion in 2003): The U.S. government has perpetually financed Egypt's brand of authoritarian socialism and its brutal repression of reformers and democratic activists.[30]
- Pakistan ($300 million in 2003) has long been plagued by pilfering. Pakistani president Pervez Musharraf declared in April 2004: "The biggest chunk of corruption in Pakistan has been by the leaders them-

selves, they have been looting the wealth and stashing it in western banks, off-shore accounts, Swiss accounts." (Musharraf was referring only to his predecessors.)[31]

The State Department may rely on Transparency International, an international nonprofit organization, for assessing the corruption levels of governments that apply for MCA aid. However, according to Transparency's ratings, the U.S. government is already bankrolling many of the most corrupt governments in the world, including Nigeria, Bangladesh, Haiti, Tajikistan, Paraguay, Indonesia, Kenya, Azerbaijan, and Kyrgyzstan. Bush's launch of the MCA does nothing to reduce the corrupting effects of other existing aid programs.

Bush also boosted U.S. funding for the World Bank by $2.1 billion. Though administration officials had condemned the World Bank and the IMF for wreaking harm around the globe, Bush justified the aid boost: "We expect the World Bank to insist on reform and results, measured in improvements in people's lives."[32]

However, the World Bank has long been using measurements and insisting on results. But because it is continually trying to set new records for loans shoveled out, its conditionality is usually a hoax. Former World Bank senior economist William Easterly noted: "In the 1980s and 1990s, the IMF and World Bank made 958 conditional loans; during the past decade alone these institutions gave 10 or more conditional loans each to 36 poor countries. . . . The average per capita growth rate in this group during the past two decades was zero."[33] Easterly observed: "The World Bank has had in place 'performance ratings' as a basis for loans since 1977, yet still delivered more to bad performers than to good performers into the 1990s."[34] Bush decided that the World Bank's idle promises of reform are worth billions of Americans' hard-earned dollars.

Bush's portrayal of foreign aid as a silver bullet against terrorism was scoffed at by Sen. Christopher Bond (R-Mo.): "The premise that inadequate U.S. aid was the cause of the terrorist attacks is absolutely wrong. The terrorist hijackers were mostly from Saudi Arabia, one of the richest countries per capita in the Middle East. Others came from Egypt, one of the largest recipients of U.S. aid."[35] Regardless of whether foreign aid actually thwarts terrorism, Bush benefits from linking the two issues in his speeches.

Foreign aid has rarely done anything that countries could not have done for themselves. General Accounting Office senior economist Harold Blumm analyzed the impact of aid on a wide array of nations and concluded in 2003 that "foreign aid has a *negative* growth effect even where economic policy is sound."[36] The best foreign aid program is American citizens deciding which foreigners (or foreign governments) are worthy to receive their donations or investments. This is a far more effective check against waste, fraud, and abuse than anything the U.S. Agency for International Development will ever come up with. There are much better ways to help the poor people of the world than throwing more money at their rulers.

Bush profits from U.S. foreign aid regardless of how much damage the handouts inflict on the Third World. Foreign aid is usually judged as an abstract idea and as a moral ideal. All that matters is that an American politician cared enough to give away Americans' money abroad—and thereby earning the praise of rock stars, the media, and foreign leaders who have their hands in the till.

Bush preaches about how foreign politicians must prove their worthiness to receive bonus U.S. aid. But there is no requirement for American politicians to show that they have reformed, to prove that they are worthy to dole out other people's money to their foreign friends and lackeys. Bush talks about foreign corruption, but it is also corrupt for Bush to seize money from Americans and send it abroad when he knows the aid will finance corruption.

The louder Bush praises the MCA, the more he damns himself for failure to end traditional U.S. foreign aid. Since studies show that "corruption is positively correlated" with receiving U.S. aid, the surest way to reduce corruption is to end U.S. foreign aid

PROFITING FROM DEFAULTS

President Bush is determined to end the bias against people who want to buy a home but don't have any money.

Since Bush became president, HUD has spent more than $120 billion. HUD public housing projects continue to devastate poor neighborhoods. HUD largesse to local governments continues to finance the confiscation and demolition of private homes, and HUD programs continue to spur fraud and corruption around the nation.[37]

Bush has done almost nothing to reduce HUD's damage to America. Instead, Bush is devoting himself to expanding home giveaways. Bush proclaimed on June 16, 2003: "Homeownership is more than just a symbol of the

American Dream; it is an important part of our way of life. Core American values of individuality, thrift, responsibility, and self-reliance are embodied in homeownership."[38] In Bush's eyes, self-reliance is so wonderful that the government should subsidize it.

Bush could be exposing taxpayers to tens of billions of dollars of losses, luring thousands of low- and moderate-income people to the heartbreak of losing their first house, and risking wrecking entire neighborhoods. Bush's housing initiatives—especially his "American Dream Downpayment Act" to give free down payments to selected home buyers—are key planks in his re-election campaign.[39] Bush is also pushing Congress to enact a law to permit the feds to give zero down payment mortgages.

The Bush "Dream" act and the zero down payment plan are modeled after "down payment assistance programs" that have proliferated in recent years. These programs, often engineered by nonprofit groups, routinely involve a home builder giving a "gift" to the nonprofit, which provides the homebuyer with money for the down payment. The price of the house is sometimes increased by the same amount as the builder's "gift." Almost all the mortgages created with down payment assistance end up being underwritten or guaranteed by either the Federal Housing Administration or Ginnie Mae (the Government National Mortgage Association).

HUD's inspector general (IG) ruled in 2000 that seller-derived gifts to home buyers are illegal but HUD ignored the IG's opinion. An attempt to tighten the rules on the mortgages that the government guarantees was derailed by vigorous lobbying by organizations in the down payment assistance business.

Free down payments carry catastrophic risks. The default rate on mortgages from the largest down payment assistance organization, Nehemiah Corp., is 25 times higher than the nationwide mortgage delinquency rate, according to the HUD IG. The default rate on Nehemiah mortgages quadrupled between 1999 and 2002, reaching almost 20 percent.[40] The IG warned that permitting the Federal Housing Administration to insure mortgages made with gifts from down payment organizations is "endangering the FHA insurance pool."[41] HUD currently has no idea how many of the loans that the FHA is underwriting are closed with down payment gifts.

Bush began pushing his American Dream Payment plan in 2002. The administration's rhetoric echoed the 1968 Housing Act, which nullified state and local restrictions on where blacks and other groups could live. A June 17, 2002, White House Fact Sheet declared that Bush's agenda "will help tear down the barriers to homeownership that stand in the way of our nation's African-American, Hispanic and other minority families by providing down payment assistance. The single biggest barrier to homeownership is accumulating funds for a down payment."[42] The Bush administration sounded as if requiring down payments is the new version of Jim Crow laws.

The Bush administration finally got its "Dream" act pushed through Congress in the fall of 2003. The House leadership chose freshman congresswoman Katherine Harris (the Republican hero of the Florida 2000 recount) for the honor of sponsoring the bill. Harris declared, "As our nation continues to confront daunting threats both at home and abroad, we cannot neglect the most basic security of all, and that is a safe, clean, adequate place to live."[43] One congressional staffer raised the question of whether "HUD will soon send out maids to ensure our right to a clean house."[44]

When Bush signed the act on December 16, 2003, he declared: "One of the biggest hurdles to homeownership is getting money . . . so today I'm honored to be here to sign a law that will help many low-income buyers to overcome that hurdle, and to achieve an important part of the American Dream."[45] Bush plaintively added, "The rate of homeownership amongst minorities is below 50 percent. And that's not right, and this country needs to do something about it."[46] Bush did not specify the precise percentage of blacks and Hispanics that would be "right." His bill authorizes federal handouts of $5,000 each for 40,000 home buyers whose incomes are less than 80 percent of a local area's median.

The Bush administration and Republicans portray down payment giveaways as if they were primarily targeted to minorities:

- After Bush visited a black neighborhood in Atlanta in 2002 to hype his housing aid proposal, Bush's first HUD Secretary, Mel Martinez, explained: "We sell it that way, as a program for minorities, because we want minority buyers for these homes, but it's available to anyone" who qualifies under income guidelines.[47]
- When the House passed the American Dream Downpayment Act on October 1, 2003, House Speaker Dennis Hastert hailed the bill: "We will help lift up our African-American and Hispanic Communities."[48]
- HUD Secretary Alfonso Jackson declared in February 2004 that the Bush administration efforts "will help more Americans, *particularly minorities,* achieve that dream" of homeownership.[49]

If the down payment program actually specifically targeted minorities, it would violate numerous federal laws and the U.S. Constitution.

Bush talks as if people should be able to buy a house the same way they buy a couch at some dubious no-money-down furniture store. In a January 23, 2004, speech to the U.S. Conference of Mayors, Bush declared, "I'm asking Congress for $200 million to help people with their down payment. . . . Many citizens have the desire to own a home, but they *don't have the dough* to make the down payment. And therefore, they balk at making the decision."[50] But to portray this as a "balk" makes as little sense as criticizing the average wage earner for not purchasing a yacht.

Once Bush proclaims a national goal, he entitles himself to claim credit for the efforts of all Americans. At an October 15, 2003, talk at Ruiz Foods (the nation's largest manufacturer of frozen Mexican food) in Dinuba, California, Bush reminded listeners of his devotion to boosting homeownership: "And so I let out a goal. I said over the next decade, we want there to be 5.5 million new minority home owners." Then Bush informed his listeners of what he'd helped to achieve: "Last year, *we* did a pretty good job. There's now 809,000 new minority home owners in America."[51] Bush took credit for every black and Hispanic person who bought a home during his administration—even though the vast majority received no help from George W.

In the same way that Bush's comments on the No Child Left Behind Act imply that the gap in school achievement between races is the result of prejudice against blacks, Bush implies that the homeownership gap is caused by bias. But federal studies prove otherwise. A 1995 Federal Reserve Board study examined more than two hundred thousand mortgage loans and found that "blacks defaulted about twice as often as white borrowers."[52] Blacks are almost twice as likely as whites to have bad credit ratings even among people of the same income class, according to a 1999 survey by Freddie Mac (formerly the Federal National Mortgage Corporation).[53]

If Bush came out and called for equal homeownership percentages between groups with good credit ratings and bad credit ratings, people might wonder if our president was a halfwit. But as long as he refers to race instead of credit ratings, Bush is applauded as a visionary. There is no prejudice that compels blacks to have worse credit ratings on average than do whites. There is no prejudice that causes blacks and Hispanics to have much lower savings rates than Asians.

Bush exalts in the recent rise in the number of Americans who own homes as one of his greatest accomplishments: "It turns out that one of the fantastic statistics and one of the realities of our society today is more people own homes than ever before."[54] The percentage of Americans who own homes rose from 66.2 percent in 2001 to 68.6 percent in late 2003. But the foreclosure rate is rising much faster than the homeownership rate. The foreclosure rate for home mortgages has tripled since the early 1980s. The rate has especially "gone up a lot . . . in struggling neighborhoods in big cities," according to Federal Reserve Board governor Edward Gramlich.[55]

A month after signing the Dream act, Bush urged Congress to permit the Federal Housing Administration to begin making zero down payment loans to low-income Americans. The administration forecast that such mortgages could be given to 150,000 home buyers in the first year.[56] HUD Secretary Alphonso Jackson declared: "Offering FHA mortgages with no down payment will unlock the door to homeownership for hundreds of thousands of American families, particularly minorities."[57] Federal Housing Commissioner John Weicher said in January 2004 that "the White House doesn't think those who can afford the monthly payment but have been unable to save for a down payment should be *deprived* from owning a home," *National Mortgage News* reported.[58] While zero down payment mortgages have long been considered profoundly unsafe (especially for borrowers with dubious credit history), Weicher confidently asserted: "We do not anticipate any costs to taxpayers."[59] The Bush administration aims to make more dubious mortgages, even though the percentage of FHA single-family home loans that have defaulted rose 54 percent between 1999 and 2002, reaching 4.25 percent. Roughly 12 percent of all FHA mortgages are past due.[60]

Bush aims to expand the number of homeowners at a time when other government programs have already handed house keys to too many shaky buyers. Vincent Quayle, executive director of the St. Ambrose Housing Aid Center in Baltimore, observed, "Until five years ago, the typical reasons for people losing homes was because a marriage failed, they lost a job or they got sick. But now people are coming to us because they could never afford a house in the first place."[61] William Rohe, director of the Center for Urban and Regional Studies at the University of North Carolina, commented in 2003, "A lot of the affordable mortgages at this point are really pushing the envelope. They are qualifying people who really don't have a high probability of being a successful homeowner."[62]

Avoiding making unsound mortgages seems to be the last item on HUD's list of priorities. Weicher declared in January 2004, "We have been addressing our default rate, and we are now able to help half the families who go into default avoid foreclosure."[63] This merely suppresses the evidence of a failed policy and sticks taxpayers with a larger bill once the roof finally falls in. The House Appropriations Committee rejected a Bush-HUD proposal in 2003 to lower the standards to qualify people for FHA mortgages.[64]

Bush's policies are placing millions of American homeowners at risk of collateral damage. Bush's down payment program and proposals are similar to a program launched in 1968 to provide federally insured mortgages to poor people—with disastrous results. The *National Journal* reported in 1971, "The Federal Housing Administration . . . is financing the collapse of large residential areas of the center cities."[65] Since most families had almost no equity in their homes, it was often cheaper to abandon the houses than to repair them. The program resulted in scores of thousands of homes vacated and left to rot in previously stable neighborhoods. In 1973, President Richard Nixon bemoaned, "All across America the federal government has become the biggest slumlord in history."[66] Nationwide, the program cost the federal government more than $4 billion in direct losses from defaulted mortgages and demolition costs. It also inflicted billions of dollars of property damage to the value of non-HUD houses.

The FHA continues wreaking devastation in some neighborhoods and cities across the country. A 2002 study by the National Training and Information Center, a Chicago nonprofit organization, found that between 1996 and 2000 21 percent of FHA loans in low-income areas in Baltimore defaulted and 25 percent of FHA loans in low-income areas in Queens, New York, defaulted.[67] Eight of the 22 cities studied had default rates above 12 percent. The FHA paid out more than $5 billion in settlements on defaulted mortgages in 2001. More than forty-five thousand FHA homes were abandoned and vacant. The National Housing Institute noted that concentrations of FHA defaults in cities have "turned the American Dream of homeownership into the neighborhood nightmare. Community organizations around the country have witnessed firsthand the devastating effects of abandoned housing and the ensuing crime, drug trafficking, prostitution, child abuse, and disinvestment."[68]

Homeownership carries far more financial rude surprises (such as the cost of major repairs) than does renting. If people get into a house they cannot financially handle and go bankrupt, they are much worse off than if they had never received down payment assistance. Giving people a handout that leads them to financial ruin—as the Small Business Administration perennially does for people unfit to be small business owners—is wrecking ball benevolence.

The virtues of homeownership do not arise from living in a single-family dwelling and holding a piece of paper from a bank. Rep. Ron Paul (R-Tex.) commented: "In the original version of the American dream, individuals earned the money to purchase a house through their own efforts, oftentimes sacrificing other goods to save for their first down payment. . . .

That old American dream has been replaced by a new dream of having the federal government force your fellow citizens to hand you the money for a down payment."[69] Heritage Foundation analyst Ron Utt observed, "The absence of an owner-provided down payment that required some personal sacrifice to accumulate gives such subsidized buyers little incentive to be responsible owners."[70] Bush's freebie hype could make the millions of low- and moderate-income Americans who are saving and scrimping for a down payment feel like damn fools. Bush talks as if the federal government is obliged to relieve all Americans from the nuisance of ever having to accumulate any personal savings.

Down payment handouts and zero down payments are a great political strategy for Bush. He gets the applause and the political credit now, and the defaults from the program may not surge until after November 2004. Bush transfers the risk of homeownership from buyers to taxpayers and then pretends he has multiplied virtue in America. Bush preens as a great benefactor at the same time as he undermines those virtues that he is claiming to multiply.

In the early 1930s, shantytowns of destitute unemployed people were known as Hoovervilles. In the coming years, if neighborhood after neighborhood is wrecked by waves of defaults and foreclosures caused by the reckless new mortgage policies, the areas should be known as "Bush blights."

THE BIGGEST MEDICARE FRAUD EVER

Bush was determined to expand Medicare by including prescription drug subsidies for old folks. Medicare, which provides subsidies primarily for senior citizens' health care, is one of the fastest growing parts of the federal budget, rising from $31 billion in 1980 to $245 in 2003.[71] The value of the medical care that seniors receive far exceeds their contributions and previous taxes they paid in. But that was irrelevant to the political calculus. The Bush administration projected that its Medicare expansion plan would cost $400 billion in the first decade. Costs would then explode: the Congressional Budget Office estimated that the program's second decade could cost up to $2 trillion.[72]

Bush constantly portrayed the issue of new handouts in the loftiest moral terms. In a Florida speech on November 13, 2003, Bush declared, "The Medicare program is a basic trust that must be upheld throughout the generations."[73] And because it was an issue of trust, the Bush team was entitled to use deceit and any means necessary to ram the law through Congress.

The Republican leadership thought they could score victory in the House when the bill was brought to the floor on the evening of November 22, 2003. However, when the initial vote occurred at 3 A.M., the Bush proposal lost by two votes. The Republican leadership violated House rules, which limit votes to a half hour or less, and proceeded to carry out the longest floor vote in House history—dragging out the tally until 6 A.M., when two Republicans switched their "nays" to "yeas" and the bill passed.

Rep. Nick Smith (R-Mich.), a veteran congressman in his final term, caught intense heat for opposing the bill. Efforts to sway Smith's vote focused on his son, who was running for the congressional seat his father held. Columnist Robert Novak reported: "On the House floor, Nick Smith was told business interests would give his son $100,000 in return for his father's vote. When he still declined, fellow Republican House members told him they would make sure Brad Smith never came to Congress. After Nick Smith voted no and the bill passed, Duke Cunningham of California and other Republicans taunted him that his son was dead meat."[74] Smith complained widely about the threats and bribes in the days after the vote. The House Ethics Committee eventually grudgingly launched a bribery investigation.

Barely a month after Bush signed the bill, Bush's budget director, Josh Bolton, informed Congress that the estimated cost had jumped to $540 billion for the first decade, instead of the advertised $400 billion ticket price. The revision infuriated conservative Republican congressmen, but the congressional leadership tried to brush it off as a non-issue. Senate Majority Leader Bill Frist (R-Tenn.) declared, "In truth, nobody has any idea what the real figure will be at the end of the day, because we don't know what those assumptions should be as we go further."[75] If Frist actually believed no one had any idea of what the legislation would cost, then he and other supporters were grossly negligent or deceptive in the claims they made to the American people when Congress considered the bill. (A *New York Times* analysis noted that "no one knows whether the legislation will work as intended" because of all the vague terms and uncertain reactions by insurers, employers, and seniors to the new law.)[76]

The Bush administration intentionally deceived Congress over the estimated cost of the bill. Thirteen conservative House members had vowed to vote against any bill costing more than $400 billion.[77] Richard S. Foster, the top actuary at the federal Centers for Medicare and Medicaid Services, privately estimated in June 2003—5 months before the final vote—that the bill would actually cost $550 billion. Foster was contacted by Democratic staffers seeking estimates on the cost of the Bush proposal. By law, Foster was obliged to provide them the information. Thomas Scully, the chief Medicare administrator, reportedly threatened to fire Foster if he provided the information.[78] Foster later commented that "there was a pattern of withholding information for what I perceived to be political purposes."[79] The much higher estimate of the cost of the Medicare bill was apparently known by top officials at the White House. Eighteen Democratic senators requested the GAO to investigate the potential violation of a law prohibiting the use of federal funds to pay the salary of any official who "prohibits or prevents, or threatens to prohibit or prevent" another employee from communicating with Congress.[80] On April 1, House Republicans blocked an effort by Democrats to summon Scully and White House aide Doug Badger to testify before a congressional committee.[81]

On May 3, the Congressional Research Service released a legal analysis which concluded that "such 'gag orders' have been expressly prohibited by federal law since 1912." The Supreme Court, in a 1927 ruling on the 1912 law, declared that a "legislative body cannot legislate wisely or effectively in the absence of information regarding conditions which the legislation is intended to affect or change."[82] But the Bush administration was too astute to fall for such radical notions.

Republicans sought to pooh-pooh the suppression of the accurate estimate. House Majority Leader Tom DeLay declared that the actuary's numbers were "irrelevant to the policy that we passed."[83] Perhaps DeLay believes that Americans should feel lucky to have Republicans reelected at any price.

Bush insisted on a Medicare fix that rains the vast majority of benefits on non-needy elderly, on corporations, and on insurance companies. In his November 13 speech, he declared, "Three-quarters of seniors have some kind of drug coverage, and that's positive news. Yet seniors relying exclusively on Medicare do not have coverage for prescription drugs—for most prescription drugs and for many forms of preventative care. That needs to be fixed. This is not good medicine. It's not cost-effective."[84]

Bush never explained how it is more cost-effective to offer handouts to *all* the elderly because a quarter of them lack insurance coverage for drugs. Though this makes no economic sense, it makes perfect political sense. For politicians, it is not cost effective to let someone pay his own bills when his gratitude can be purchased.

The National Center for Policy Analysis estimated that only 6 to 7 percent of the expenditures in the Medicare reform bill will pay for additional drugs for the elderly.[85] In order to provide $1 for the elderly who could not afford pre-scription drugs, the Bush administration apparently felt obliged to spend $15 subsidizing non-needy elderly people and insurance companies. The new pro-gram also provides a huge windfall for corporations; the Congressional Budget Office forecast that "at least one-third of all private companies will dump their retirees into the Medicare system as a result of the new bill."[86]

Bush faced intense resistance on the Medicare expansion because some Republicans and some conservatives refused to abandon their principles sim-ply to help Bush get reelected. A group of 30 Republican congressmen favored a competing proposal that would have offered Medicare drug benefits only to seniors who lacked any private insurance coverage. The Bush team torpedoed this proposal. During the battle over the bill, Rep. Jeff Flake (R-Ariz.) de-clared, "I'm a Republican, and I didn't come here to create the largest expan-sion of an entitlement program in history."[87] During the Night of the Long Vote, Bush called to pressure Republicans. When he put the squeeze on Rep. Tom Feeney (R-Fla.), Feeney told him, "I came here to cut entitlements, not grow them." Bush angrily replied, "Me too, pal," and hung up the phone.[88] Republican aides made clear that conservatives who voted against Bush's bo-nanza would suffer.[89]

Throughout 2003, starting in his State of the Union address, Bush con-tinually invoked the bill's $400 billion price tag as proof of his benevolence. After meeting with congressmen on November 17, 2003, Bush boasted, "There's 400 billion additional dollars available for our seniors in this bill."[90] Once the bill's cost became a gauge of Bush's generosity, any reform that tar-geted benefits would make Bush look less compassionate.

Bush bragged on July 30, 2003, that "Medicare coverage has helped pro-tect the savings of our seniors."[91] Medicare is a major reason why the elderly are more affluent than other age groups in America. According to the Federal Reserve, the average household headed by someone between the ages of 65 and 74 has a net worth of $674,000—far higher than the average net worth of households headed by people aged 35–44 ($260,000) or below 35 ($91,000). The median household wealth—meaning 50 percent have more and 50 percent have less—for the entire population is $86,100.[92] The Bush Medicare expansion will cost "a 40-year-old head of household an average of $16,127 in taxes between now and the time he retires," according to a Her-itage Foundation study.[93] Insofar as Bush provides new drug benefits for all elderly (as opposed to only the needy), his plan punished the comparatively poor to benefit the comparatively affluent. He also punished those who aren't elderly at all.

Bush painted his Medicare expansion efforts as distinguished service to humanity. At a White House talk on Medicare, Bush announced, "We've all come to Washington, those of us who have been elected to office, to serve something greater than ourself."[94] But most treatises on ethics do not recognize "reelection" as a specific category of "service."

To publicize the new law, the Bush administration is spending tens of millions of dollars on television advertisements and other promotions. Some federally paid "information" advertisements show Bush receiving a standing ovation from a cheering crowd as he signs the act into law. The feds also distributed video news releases to local television stations' news programs that show someone pretending to be a reporter doing a phony news story about the wonderful new law. (Forty television stations aired the videos during news programs.) The TV ads and videos urge people to phone an 800 number; callers are obliged to say out loud the words "Medicare improvement" to hear recorded messages about new drug benefits. GAO concluded in May 2004 that the ads were illegal "covert propaganda." GAO noted that the videos suffered from "notable omissions and weaknesses" and were "not strictly factual news stories."[95] William Pierce, a spokesman for the Department of Health and Human Services, denied that the videos were covert: "TV stations knew the videos came from us and could have identified the government as the source if they had wanted to."[96] But the videos were targeted to viewers, not television producers, and there was nothing in them to warn people that they were seeing government propaganda. GAO also concluded that the ad campaign violated the Antideficiency Act, since it was not authorized by Congress. Sen. Kent Conrad (D-N. Dak.) said: "I have a hard time differentiating this 30-second television message from any partisan political ad."[97]

In July 2001, when Bush put forward his Medicare fix, he declared that any reform must "strengthen the program's long-term financial security."[98] But Bush's fix is the worst financial blow Medicare ever suffered. A report by the official board of Medicare trustees four months after Bush signed the bill warned that Medicare's finances have "taken a major turn for the worse."[99] Thanks in large part to the new law, Medicare is now forecast to go bankrupt seven years earlier than previous projections—in 2019, instead of 2026. The *Washington Post* noted that "the program has never before lurched seven years closer to insolvency in one year."[100] The trustees forecast that the new prescription drug benefit would cost up to $7 trillion over the next 75 years.[101] The trustees also warned that the combined Medicare–Social Security deficit (the gap between promised benefits and expected revenues) is now almost $50 trillion—almost triple the Bush administration's forecast in 2003 of $18 trillion.

The exorbitant cost of the new Medicare handout has thus far done little to boost Bush's November prospects. A March 2004 Gallup poll found that approval for Bush's handling of Medicare plunged after the law was enacted; only 35 percent approved of Bush's action on Medicare, while 55 percent disapproved.[102] The poll found that 40 percent of respondents believed that the Bush administration "deliberately misled the American public about the costs of the new Medicare law."[103]

The Bush administration was stunned by the criticism of its budget deceits and taxpayer-paid propaganda. White House Press Secretary Scott McClellan announced: "The Medicare issue is a prime example of how some in Washington are so wrapped up in how to use the issue for partisan gain, and so concerned about who gets the credit, that doing what is best for our seniors gets lost."[104] And the entire fracas was just one more example of how President Bush still has much work to do to change the tone in the nation's capital.

Bush talks about how the new law gives seniors more freedom. Bush is giving seniors "medical freedom" the same way he gave local schools "educational freedom" with the No Child Left Behind Act. The Supreme Court ruled in 1942, "It is hardly lack of due process for the government to regulate that which it subsidizes."[105] Bush's rhetoric will provide no protection against further restrictions as future Congresses and presidents struggle to control the soaring costs of his drug giveaway. Bush's Medicare expansion will inevitably increase government control over American medical treatment—a grave health danger to all Americans.

CONCLUSION

Perhaps Bush sees taxpayers as natural beasts of burden, created to support the glory of their rulers. The Bush throwaway attitude toward spending was illustrated by the administration's sudden enthusiasm for a moon-shot to pep up the president's reelection campaign. The *Washington Post* reported in December 2003 that "Bush's aides are considering a new lunar exploration program and other unifying national goals . . . as they sift ideas for a fresh agenda for the final year of his term." The *Post* noted that "the development of big ideas for Bush's 2004 agenda is being led by the president's senior adviser, Karl Rove." One official explained to the paper that "Bush's closest aides are promoting big initiatives on the theory that they contribute to Bush's image as a decisive leader even if people disagree with some of the specifics. 'Iraq was big.

AIDS is big,' the official said. 'Big works. Big grabs attention.'"[106] Bush subsequently proposed a big moon initiative, but after polls showed little public enthusiasm, the issue was shelved.

Bush's comments on government spending dripped with piety from the day he took office. In his first address to Congress on February 27, 2001, Bush declared that Washington budget debates "come down to an old, tired argument: on one side, those who want more Government, regardless of the cost; on the other, those who want less Government, regardless of the need."[107] Bush sought to place the moral onus on those who would not support his spending binges—and to portray himself as morally superior to conservatives who did not believe that federal spending was a panacea for what ails America.

Bush is giving America the largest budget deficits in history. Economists forecast deficits ranging in the $400 billion to $500 billion range for most of the next decade. Yet, Bush never stoops to publicly recognize the burdens he is foisting on young Americans and future taxpayers. Instead, any government spending that benefits Bush is presumptively cost-free.

CHAPTER NINE

The Political Profits
of Pointless Punishment

George Bush came to the presidency with more experience of illicit drugs than many recent Oval Office occupants. During his campaign for the presidency, Bush was widely rumored to have been a user of cocaine or other narcotics. When asked about his past drug use on August 17, 1999, Bush declared, "I made some mistakes years ago, but I learned from my mistakes." Bush explained: "As I understand it, the current FBI form asks the question, 'Did somebody use drugs within the last 7 years?' and I will be glad to answer that question, and the answer is no."[1]

Bush effectively admitted to being one of the more than 90 million Americans who, according to federally funded surveys, have used illicit drugs at least once in their lives.[2] Unfortunately, Bush's own experiences apparently did nothing to humanize drug offenders in his eyes. Instead, Bush's drug warriors are unleashing crackdown after crackdown to suppress vice and punish people guilty of the pursuit of illicit pleasure.

FREEDOM FROM BONGS

On February 7, 2003, as the U.S. government prepared to invade Iraq, Homeland Security chief Tom Ridge raised the terrorist alert to the orange level and declared that "specific protective measures will be taken by all federal agencies to reduce vulnerabilities." Ridge added comfortingly: "It's probably not a bad idea to sit down and just arrange some kind of a contact plan, [so] that if [a terrorist] event occurred . . . the family [can] get in touch with one another." Attorney General Ashcroft, at the same press conference, urged Americans to go about "with a heightened awareness of their environment and the activities [i.e., potential terrorist attacks] occurring around them."[3]

Seventeen days later, on February 24, Ashcroft proudly announced the most decisive attack ever on purveyors of bongs—pipes and bowls often used for smoking marijuana. At a time when political leaders warned that a terrorist attack on the homeland could be imminent, more than 1,200 federal law officers were involved in Operation Pipe Dreams, conducting raids in Pennsylvania, Texas, Oregon, Iowa, California, and Idaho.[4] Fifty-five people and ten companies were indicted in the biggest attack on glass bowls in American history. The feds confiscated 124 tons of alleged drug paraphernalia, including plastic baggies that could potentially be used to package illicit drugs.[5]

At the triumphal press conference announcing the raids, Ashcroft declared: "With the advent of the Internet, the illegal drug paraphernalia industry has exploded. Quite simply, the illegal drug paraphernalia industry has invaded the homes of families across the country without their knowledge."[6] (Ashcroft did not mention similar home invasions by federal e-mail and Internet surveillance.)

The feds used rarely enforced 1980s laws that criminalized the sale of drug paraphernalia. Seizure fever permeated the bong attack. U.S. deputy marshal Dale Ortmann commented: "This was the biggest push in asset seizures that I've seen in eight years." U.S. deputy marshal Gary Richards noted that, thanks to cash grabbed from businesses that were raided, "We have access to money that will pay for inventory and storage fees" for the 124 tons of goodies.

By far the biggest catch of Operation Pipe Dreams was 64-year old Tommy Chong, the older half of the legendary, Grammy Award–winning comic duo Cheech and Chong, who lampooned drug warriors from the 1960s to the 1980s. Chong's company, Chong Glass, sold ornate bongs that cost hundreds of dollars over the Internet; a Los Angeles art gallery had an exhibit on Chong's top-of-the-line products. The Drug Enforcement Administration set up a phony shop in Beaver Falls, Pennsylvania and ordered bongs and other material from Chong Glass.

The DEA hit Chong's Pacific Palisades, California house at 5:30 A.M., while Chong and his wife were asleep. Chong later commented: "It was a full-on raid. Helicopters, them bangin' on the door. They come in with loaded automatic weapons, flak jackets, helmets, visors, about 20 agents. They bust in the house. They took all my cash, took out my computers, and they took all the glass bongs they could find."[7]

Helicopters and SWAT teams were used in many Pipe Dreams arrests. Luckily, none of the G-men accidentally shot anyone during the raids. The U.S. Marshals Service magazine noted: "All of the arrests were without incident"—which was not surprising, since selling glass bowls and rolling paper is not usually indicative of violent tendencies.

Chong's arrest sparked ridicule far and wide, including barbs from both David Letterman and Jay Leno. The *Pittsburgh Post-Gazette* snipped, "With the nation on Orange Alert at the time, the only bearded men most Americans wanted to see in custody were members of al-Qaida."[8] Though Chong controlled much less than one percent of the national bong market, busting him guaranteed the feds massive publicity.

Chong continued doing his comedy routine pending his trial. When asked his views on Operation Pipe Dreams, Chong replied, "I feel pretty sad, but it seems to be the only weapons of mass destruction they've found this year."[9]

On September 11, 2003, the second anniversary of the infamous attacks, Chong appeared before federal judge Arthur Schwab in Pittsburgh for sentencing, after pleading guilty to "one count of conspiracy to sell drug paraphernalia." Chong's lawyer asked for probation, considering that this was Chong's first offense and that it was a nonviolent crime. U.S. Attorney Mary Beth Buchanan (a Bush appointee) urged a harsh sentence in part because of Chong's history of "trivializing law enforcement" with his humor.[10] But it is difficult to out-spoof political hacks who confiscate a few warehouses of glass bowls and then preen before TV cameras claiming to have made Americans safer.

Chong was sentenced to nine months in federal prison, fined $20,000 for selling bongs and other drug paraphernalia, and forced to surrender $103,514 in cash to the feds, as well as forfeiting his Internet domain name, Chongglass.com. Chong was also forced to promise the judge that he would not profit from his arrest and prosecution. This effectively destroyed Chong's freedom of speech to discuss his case in future comedy performances. At least in Chong's case, mocking the feds will now be a federal offense.

The Chong raids had no effect on the national marijuana market or on the vast majority of the 20 million Americans who use cannabis each year. Author Jacob Sullum observed: "Although the thought of a bong-bearing hippie under every bed may keep Ashcroft awake at night, it's hard to see how seizing marijuana pipes can be expected to have any impact on drug use. As long as there are paper and aluminum foil, pot smokers will have ready alternatives."[11] According to an employee of an Ithaca, New York store, the DEA crackdown actually helped business as customers raced to buy up paraphernalia before the government shut down the stores.[12] This is the same type of "Christmas sales rush" that gun stores experience when Congress considers gun control legislation.

The bong raids were widely seen as a publicity stunt by Ashcroft and federal drug warriors. The fact that all of the businesses were operating openly (some were members of the local chamber of commerce) proved that the SWAT teams and the helicopters were little more than theater designed to boost press coverage.

Subsequent enforcement efforts relied on low-key intimidation. In October 2003, DEA agents visited two stores in Potsdam, New York, that sold bongs and warned them that they were violating the law. DEA agent William Hebert commented to the *Watertown Daily Times:* "A lot of people are not familiar with the law. A lot of them are legitimate businesses that don't know. It's a fact finding mission, providing facts to the people."[13] To help the facts sink in, the DEA agents were accompanied on their courtesy call by police from the county drug task force.

PAIN AND PIETY

In October 2003, conservatives and Republicans across the land were crestfallen when talk show superstar Rush Limbaugh announced that he was addicted to painkillers and would be entering rehab. Limbaugh made his confession after a tabloid newspaper charged that Limbaugh had pressured his housemaid to buy tens of thousands of dollars worth of painkillers on the streets to feed his habit. News leaked out that Limbaugh was under investigation for "doctor shopping" (going to multiple doctors to get prescriptions for the same narcotics), a felony offense in Florida. Federal law classifies anyone who purchases a controlled substance painkiller such as Percocet or OxyContin without a prescription as a felon, eligible for a year in prison for each pill they illegally procure.

Limbaugh was one of the most prominent drug war champions. In 1995, Limbaugh bitterly complained that "too many whites are getting away with drug use. . . . The answer is to go out and find the ones who are getting away with it, convict them and send them up the river, too."[14] President Bush was reportedly deeply sympathetic on Limbaugh's plight. Bush announced at a White House staff meeting: "Rush is a great American. I am confident he can overcome any obstacles he faces right now."[15]

Unfortunately, Bush's compassion did not extend to non-Republican, non-talk show host, non-millionaire drug violators. The DEA is prescribing far more pain for millions of Americans by dropping the hammer across the nation on doctors who treat severe pain. Medical guidelines on the use of opiates to treat severe pain vary from state to state. Yet federal prosecutors are acting as if any doctor who deviates from the DEA's secret treatment guidelines can be treated like a crack dealer. Assistant U.S. Attorney Gene Rossi promised: "Our office will try our best to root out [certain doctors] like the Taliban."[16]

Heavily armed DEA teams raided many doctors' offices. Dr. Ronald Myers, president of the American Pain Institute, observed: "The war on drugs has turned into a war on doctors and pain patients. Such is the climate of fear across the medical community that for every doctor who has his license yanked by the DEA, there are a hundred doctors scared to prescribe proper pain medication for fear of going to prison."[17] The *Washington Post* noted that, thanks to the crackdown on doctors, "at least two have been imprisoned, one committed suicide, several are awaiting sentencing, many are preparing for trial, and more have lost their licenses to practice medicine and accumulated huge legal bills."[18]

The DEA pooh-poohed concerns about the crackdown, announcing in late 2003: "Doctors operating within the bounds of accepted medical practice have nothing to fear from the DEA." But there are no clear standards of "accepted medical practice" in pain treatment.[19] Dr. Jane Orient, chief of the Association of American Physicians and Surgeons, condemned the DEA: "Throughout the U.S., physicians are being threatened, impoverished, delicensed and imprisoned for prescribing in good faith with the intention of relieving pain. Law enforcement agents are using deceitful tactics to snare doctors, and prosecutors manipulate the legal system to frighten doctors who might be willing to testify on behalf of the wrongly accused doctors."[20]

The feds have launched more than four hundred investigations into doctors who prescribe OxyContin, a relatively new, very effective painkiller. OxyContin is sometimes abused by people seeking a cheap high. Attorney General Ashcroft proclaimed that the bust of one doctor for over-prescribing OxyContin showed "our commitment to bring to justice all those who traffic in this very dangerous drug."[21] The DEA sanctified its crackdown by vastly overstating the number of fatalities from pain killers, claiming that almost five hundred died from OxyContin overdoses in 2002. However, the *Journal of Analytical Toxicology* reported only a dozen cases in which OxyContin was the sole cause of death for 2002.[22] In all other cases, the fatality resulted from combining OxyContin with cocaine, alcohol, or other substances.

The DEA crackdown, by stifling doctors' willingness to prescribe strong painkillers, is creating despair among people with severe pain. Siobhan Reynolds, founder of the Pain Relief Network, said, "All over America, pain patients are committing suicide because of the DEA's campaign. . . . It's really astonishing the amount of human carnage that this campaign has already caused."[23]

In March 2004, the White House Office of National Drug Control Policy announced plans for a new crackdown to make it more burdensome for doctors to prescribe the most effective painkillers.[24] And the DEA is pushing to reclassify hydrocodone, the most frequently prescribed painkiller, to place it in the same severely restricted class of drugs as heroin and cocaine. The reclassification would make it much more difficult for patients (who could not get a prescription refilled without revisiting their doctor), for doctors (who would be prohibited from phoning in prescriptions to pharmacies), and for pharmacists (who would have far more paperwork burdens and risks and would be compelled to keep the drugs locked up at all times).

Unfortunately, with the way the American legal system works, Bush will never be held responsible for all the unnecessary pain his policies inflict upon innocent citizens. Instead, with each high-profile DEA bust of some hapless doctor, Bush will profit as the TV news reminds Americans that his administration cares enough to protect them from evil.

GLORIFYING DRUG MISEDUCATION

President Bush is an avid fan of Drug Abuse Resistance Education (DARE). In his National DARE Day proclamation on April 2, 2002, Bush declared that DARE "plays an important role in helping our young people understand the many reasons to avoid drugs. DARE helps build relationships among parents, teachers, law enforcement officers, and others interested in preventing drug use in their communities."[25] In his 2003 National DARE Day proclamation, Bush declared: "As we celebrate the 20th anniversary of this important program, we recognize DARE's proud record of helping millions of young people lead productive, drug-free, and violence-free lives. . . . DARE officers serve as supportive role models and encourage young people to develop healthy self-esteem."[26] In his 2004 DARE Day proclamation, Bush said, "By introducing students to local police officers and teaching them to become good citizens, DARE also strengthens communities."[27]

DARE, which relies on police officers as founts of drug wisdom—is taught in 80 percent of the nation's school districts, at a cost of more than a billion dollars a year. DARE is one of the most popular propaganda programs in modern times, a favorite of police, school officials, politicians, and many parents.

Bush's embrace of DARE epitomizes the "political cosmetics" approach to the drug war. Study after study proved DARE fails to deter drug use:

- In 2001, the U.S. Surgeon General concluded that DARE "does not work" and that "children who participate [in DARE] are as likely to use drugs as those who do not participate."[28]
- The National Academy of Sciences concluded in 2001 that DARE is one of the programs found "to have little impact on the targeted behavior and even to have counterproductive impacts among some populations."[29]
- The National Center on Addiction and Substance Abuse reported in September 2001 that there was "little evidence of any extended impact" from DARE.[30]
- The General Accounting Office reported in 2003 that there were "no significant differences in illicit drug use between students who received DARE . . . and students who did not."[31]

Because there is no scientific evidence that DARE is effective, the federal Department of Education has not permitted schools to use their federal Safe and Drug-Free Schools grants for DARE since 1998. Yet the U.S. Justice Department continues to finance DARE, as the program remains a good PR investment.

DARE is ineffective in part because it relies on the "just say no" mantra that thrills cops and politicians but misfires with many teenagers. DARE is widely perceived by teenagers as dishonestly exaggerating the danger of drugs. The government undermines its credibility and thereby blunts efforts to warn kids of the real dangers narcotics pose to their health.

A report by the federal Substance Abuse and Mental Health Services Administration noted, there are "several programs that show evidence of effectiveness in preventing youth substance abuse."[32] Yet, in part because of DARE's capture of the law enforcement and political establishment, the more effective drug education programs never penetrate the majority of American classrooms.

Bush's compassion for school kids does not stop with DARE. In his 2004 State of the Union address, Bush urged mandatory drug tests for students. Bush declared: "Drug testing in our schools has proven to be an effective part of this effort. So tonight I propose an additional $23 million for schools that want to use drug testing as a tool to save children's lives."[33] Bush aims to increase federal spending for school drug tests tenfold. Bush's drug czar, John Walters, hailed mandatory school urine tests as a "silver bullet" against teen drug abuse.[34]

Bush is wrong to portray drug tests as an effective deterrent: a study by the University of Michigan found no difference in drug usage rates at schools that required the tests and those that did not.[35] Some schools are also using urine tests to check whether students are using tobacco.[36]

A few weeks after Bush pushed teen drug testing, controversy was swirling over whether Bush effectively went AWOL before finishing his National Guard service. Though Bush promised on an NBC *Meet the Press* interview to disclose all his records from that time period, the White House quickly reneged. Reporters were especially interested in seeing Bush's medical records, partly because of rumors that he was a drug user in that time period.

White House Communications Director Dan Bartlett announced that a few reporters from the White House press corps would be permitted to step into a room for 20 minutes where 44 pages of Bush's medical records were laid out on a table. The journalists were prohibited from making copies or even taking notes from the documents. Bartlett justified the procedure to protect the president's "zone of privacy."[37]

At the same time Bush feels entitled to a "zone of privacy" that minimizes scrutiny of medical documents he promised to release, he is championing severe intrusions against all young Americans. Medical sociologist Marsha Rosenbaum observed, "As drug testing is currently practiced, students must be observed (by a teacher or other adult) as they urinate to be sure the sample they produce is their own. The collection of a specimen is a humiliating, invasive violation of privacy."[38] Mandatory urination-under-supervision policies treat all students like convicts on parole. By treating all kids as presumptively guilty, such policies breed servility or resentment.

There is far more hearsay evidence against Bush for past drug use than there is against the average 14-year-old girl who would be degraded by Bush's plan. Perhaps Bush believes that privacy is only for the rulers, not for the ruled.

BOTCHING THE AD WAR

Concerned about rising youth drug abuse, Congress and the Clinton administration in 1998 launched a five-year program of federally subsidized antidrug advertisements. Congress specified that unless the ads deterred drug use, the program would be terminated.

As a billion dollars' worth of ads blanketed the airwaves, teen drug use rose sharply in the late 1990s through 2002. Bush drug czar John Walters responded by making the antidrug ads far more menacing. The White House Office of National Drug Control Policy spent three million dollars for two television ads broadcast during the 2002 Super Bowl. One ad asked viewers: "Where do terrorists get their money?" The answer: "If you buy drugs, some of it might come from you." Drug users were portrayed as terrorist financiers—practically the moral equivalent of the hijackers who destroyed the World Trade Center towers.

But federally subsidized demagoguery failed to solve the drug problem. The Office of Management of Budget concluded in 2003 that "there is no evidence of direct effect on youth behavior" from the antidrug ads.[39] The strongest evidence of the failure of the antidrug ads came from the University of Pennsylvania, which was hired by the feds to do semiannual evaluations of the ads. Professor Robert Hornick testified to Congress in June 2003: "We have little or no evidence that the campaign has convinced youth to avoid marijuana use or to change their ideas about marijuana. . . . Early exposure to the campaign predicted more pro-drug beliefs at the second interview and more likelihood of initiation of use. . . . Girls with the highest campaign exposure at the start were more likely to initiate marijuana use than girls who were less exposed."[40] The dismal evaluations did not curb enthusiasm for more ads.

Walters also shifted the emphasis of some ads from the harm of drugs to the dangers of drug legalization. In May 2003, House Republicans (working with the drug czar's office) proposed to authorize federally funded advertisements directly attacking political candidates who opposed the war on drugs and to attack state and local referenda on medical marijuana. The measure was approved by the House Subcommittee on Criminal Justice, Drug Policy, and Human Resources. A Republican committee aide explained: "What we are simply trying to clarify is that the regular operation of the media campaign, when it gets into things that some people want to claim and construe as political, is not political."[41] In other words, congressmen used a legislative amendment to redefine the English language.

Steve Fox of the Marijuana Policy Project described the measure as "creating a political slush fund with a billion dollars of our tax money."[42] Bill Piper of the Drug Policy Alliance observed: "This would be like the IRS running ads against tax-cut proposals and the candidates that support them. Using public money to tell people how to think and feel about policy is the definition of propaganda."[43]

The provision to permit the drug czar to openly use tax dollars to attack politicians was stripped from the bill before its final passage in September 2003. But Congress increased the budget for the ads from $150 million to $180 million a year for the following five years, despite the lack of credible evidence that the ads deter drug use.

DRUGS AND BUSH FAMILY VALUES

President Bush does not have a family monopoly on drug war sanctimoniousness. Noelle Bush, the 25-year-old daughter of Florida governor Jeb Bush and niece of President Bush, was caught violating drug laws several times in 2002. The first arrest occurred on January 29 when she tried to buy Xanax, a DEA-controlled sedative, with a phony prescription. She could have been sentenced to five years in prison for prescription drug fraud. Instead, her case was handled by a pretrial diversion program and she was sent to a posh drug rehab facility, the Center for Drug-Free Living in Orlando.

In July 2002, she was caught by rehab center personnel with someone else's prescription drugs. This is also a felony, at least when done by non-governor's-family offenders. The drug rehab center dropped the hammer on Noelle, sending her to jail for three days. In September, in what became known as the "crack cocaine incident," the *Miami Herald* reported that "police were called by a fellow rehab patient who complained that the 'princess' gets caught repeatedly but is never punished."[44] Noelle was reportedly caught by rehab employees with crack in her shoe. Possession of any amount of cocaine is a felony. And, as part of her de facto parole from the first drug offense, she was prohibited from carrying any narcotics in her footwear. When the police arrived, one rehab employee had a written statement for them but tore it up after a supervisor barred disclosing the information.

When Orlando police sought to question the staff about Noelle's alleged criminal conduct, a rehab center lawyer rushed to court to block police from gathering evidence. After Orange County Chief Circuit Judge Belvin Perry, Jr. reined in the police, an *Orlando Sentinel* headline declared, "Judge Shuts

Down Investigation of Noelle Bush."[45] Assistant State Attorney Jeff Ashton criticized the judge's decision: "If this order is correct, then essentially drug-treatment centers are immune zones where you cannot be prosecuted for a drug crime."[46] Since the rehab employees refused to make sworn statements, Noelle could not be charged for the felony.

Gov. Jeb Bush was elated. During a campaign stop in his gubernatorial re-election campaign, Bush announced: "Putting aside my daughter for a second, this is a serious issue. . . . In the treatment facility, if counselors are required to report every violation, then it makes treatment very difficult to work."[47] Bush chirped to the *Miami Herald*: "The underlying function of drug treatment is that it is not a naturally progressive, always-moving-forward, never-stepping-back process."[48]

Bush's sudden scrupulousness for the rights of people in drug treatment was ironic, since shortly before his daughter's first arrest, he gutted spending for many Florida drug rehab programs.[49] Most poor folks, especially poor blacks and Hispanics, never get the option of rehab. Instead, they go straight to jail or prison. Since Bush became governor, tens of thousands of Florida residents have been jailed or imprisoned for drug offenses.[50]

The treatment center did send Noelle back to court for another wrist slap. At Noelle's sentencing hearing in October 2002, Circuit Judge Reginald Whitehead "didn't specifically give a reason in court for jailing Noelle Bush but told her that he was aware of allegations that she was found with crack cocaine in her shoe while at the treatment center."[51] For a judge to mention that he was "aware" of "allegations" that someone committed a federal felony— shortly after previous drug offenses—is curious. If a judge mentioned in passing to some defendant that he was "aware of allegations that you committed a murder" or "aware of allegations that you set a kindergarten on fire," the comments could raise eyebrows. But not for Noelle. Judge Whitehead awarded Noelle ten days in jail for "contempt"—a sentence much lighter than conservative advocates of "three strikes legislation" would have demanded for other serial offenders.

Neither Jeb Bush nor Columba, his wife and Noelle's mother, bothered attending the court hearing in which their daughter was sentenced. Jeb was busy doing a television interview and, later that day, had a big fundraiser. Bush did make time to denounce allegations that his daughter got special treatment as "completely unfair" and "absolutely wrong."[52]

Noelle did not deserve harsh punishment for her victimless crimes, but neither did all the other Floridians sent to prison for similar offenses. Jeb Bush rose to and perpetuated his political power in part by promising harsh treatment to nonviolent drug offenders. After his daughter got caught the first time, Jeb Bush pulled out his hankie and blubbered in front of a sympathetic audience at a Florida pro–drug war conference. Yet, as Stephen Heath of the Drug Policy Forum of Florida noted, Bush waged "a vigorous 12-month campaign against a proposed ballot initiative that would allow Floridians the right to drug treatment for first and second nonviolent drug possession offenses"—the same treatment Noelle received.[53]

No one in the White House press corps has ever asked President Bush whether Noelle's crimes and cushy treatment had any influence on his views on the war on drugs. Bush's piety on the drug issue has never been challenged during a press conference or in any interview transcript released by the White House.

THE PRISON INDUSTRIAL COMPLEX

Bush's drug crackdown marks an intensification of a war against drugs that was turbocharged by Ronald Reagan in the early 1980s. Since George W. Bush became president, five million people have been arrested in the United States for drug violations, including more than two million for marijuana possession.

Forty years ago, prisons were often seen as dark blotches on the landscapes. Now, economically depressed towns idolize prisons as the pot of gold at the end of the rainbow. Officials in Luzerne Township, Pennsylvania rejoiced when their locale was chosen for a new prison because it meant that they would receive $4 million dollars' worth of sewer line extensions.[54] A front-page article in the Lexington, Kentucky *Herald-Leader* promised that two new prisons would "invigorate" Kentucky's economy.[55] In small towns and depressed areas across the nation, politicos applaud government policies that turn other people into fodder because it keeps their own local prison-based economies humming.

Prior to the war on drugs, the U.S. incarceration rate was similar to that of other Western countries. But the number of people in federal and state prisons on drug charges has increased tenfold since 1980. Since 1987, drug defendants have accounted for nearly three-quarters of all new federal prisoners. Even former drug czar Barry McCaffrey conceded that the flood of drug violators has turned prisons into "America's internal gulag."[56] One Louisiana state senator observed that the situation has become so bad that "we had half the population in prison and the other half watching them."[57]

Federal policies and federal bribes to state and local governments have been the strongest force behind the prison boom of the last decade. President

Clinton rammed a crime bill through Congress in 1994 that opened up new floodgates of federal aid for state prison building. Since then, the federal government has awarded more than $8 billion to build state prisons, including more than $500 million since Bush became president.[58]

The prison industry is pump-primed by other generous federal policies. Towns that become sites for a new prison or that incorporate a prison as a result of annexation can double or triple their populations. Many federal grants are distributed based on raw population numbers, regardless of how many residents are locked away in solitary confinement. Prisoners become tokens redeemable for extra federal aid for housing, road building, environmental concerns, and social spending for residents. Local governments also collect federal windfalls because most prisoners have zero income—thus making the locales appear to be poverty zones. The *Wall Street Journal* reported that the town of Florence, Arizona receives almost two-thirds of its entire budget from federal grants keyed to the number of convicts within town limits. The *Journal* noted that the prison deluge is also reshaping the political landscape: "Although inmates aren't allowed to vote in most states, they are counted for legislative apportionment and redistricting. In states such as New York, the prison boom has helped to shift political muscle from minority-dominated inner-city neighborhoods to rural areas dominated by whites."[59]

U.S. DRUG WAR DEBACLES
IN LATIN AMERICA

In South America, the U.S. war on drugs helped topple the most pro-American ruler on the continent. In October 2003, Bolivian President Gonzalo Sánchez de Lozada was overthrown by violent protests that left 70 dead and hundreds wounded in the nation of 8 million. A U.S. embassy official labeled Sanchez de Lozada's fall as a "narco-coup."[60]

For the previous five years, Bolivia was the beneficiary of Plan Dignity, a $500-million, U.S.-financed campaign to crush coca farmers. Coca is the plant from which cocaine is derived. The Bolivian army took over the coca growing regions of the country, effectively ending civilian rule in those areas. Soldiers tore up coca plants by the roots. After soldiers sweep an area, agents from the U.S. Embassy's Narcotics Affairs Section descend to inspect the damage and determine if further eradication efforts are needed.[61] Soldiers have pillaged or abused hundreds, if not thousands, of peasants and Indians. Though eradicating coca production was supposed to make Bolivians feel dignified, placing peasants under the heel of military boots helped spur the violent uprising.

Bolivians also resented U.S. meddling in the 2002 presidential election against a socialist candidate, Evo Morales, who favored the legalization of coca growing. The U.S. ambassador to Bolivia, Manuel Rocha, warned shortly before the election: "The Bolivian electorate must consider the consequences of choosing leaders somehow connected with drug trafficking and terrorism. I want to remind the Bolivian electorate that if they vote for those who want Bolivia to return to exporting cocaine, that will seriously jeopardize any future aid to Bolivia from the United States." Rocha's warning infuriated Bolivians, and Morales called Rocha his "best campaign chief."[62]

Prior to the "narco-coup," Bolivia was the poster boy for the U.S. international war on drugs. Coca production fell sharply in the late 1990s but is now storming back. In neighboring Peru, mass resistance against the U.S. drug war also threatened to topple the government in October 2003, as thousands of peasants marched on the capital city, Lima, and demanded that the government cease its eradication campaign and related abuses. The government placated the protesters with promises to rein in the military.

Peru was also the scene of one of the biggest embarrassments for U.S. drug warriors. On April 16, 2001, U.S.-financed Peruvian fighter jets shot down a small plane carrying five American civilians, including several Baptist missionaries. Veronica Bowers, a 35-year-old missionary, and her infant daughter, Charity, were killed; her husband, Jim, was badly wounded. A CIA surveillance plane tipped off the Peruvian jets about what it claimed was a suspicious plane. The U.S. government initially sought to deny any role in the shootdown but the facts got out.[63]

The missionary's plane was blown out of the air as a result of a U.S.-financed automatic shoot-down policy. Controversy over the killings led to a temporary suspension of the policy. The CIA washed its hands of the program. When the policy resumed, the State Department took charge. The policy was again suspended briefly in September 2003 after a Colombian Air Force fighter jet, in the first interdiction of the revived program, forced a civilian plane down and then strafed it on the ground, completely destroying it. The U.S. government did not know if there were any casualties in the attack. No evidence of drugs was found at the site of the destroyed plane. News of the destruction of another civilian plane was kept under wraps until the *New York Times* broke the story in January 2004.[64]

In Colombia the U.S. government continues to bankroll the fumigation of the countryside. Coca production fell in 2003, after rising sharply in the

preceding years despite eradication efforts. The spraying is intensely controversial, and two Colombian judicial panels ordered a cessation until scientific
analysis can be conducted to determine if the spraying is harming humans.
The Colombian government, under U.S. pressure, ignored the rulings of its
own courts and continues dousing the countryside with herbicides. And while
coca production has fallen, poppy production in Colombia has almost doubled in the last four years, fueling a new U.S. heroin boom.

At the same time the United States is trying to put a tourniquet squeeze on
Colombia, Peru, and Bolivia, narcotics production in Mexico is booming. The
State Department estimated that Mexican marijuana production rose by 70 per-
cent and Mexican poppy production rose by 78 percent in 2003.[65] However, the
U.S. government historically tends to underestimate Mexican drug output.

U.S.-APPROVED MASS MURDER

The most exhilarating foreign drug crackdown is occurring in Thailand, a relatively new democracy emerging from the shadow of decades of military rule.
Police and government agents killed thousands of suspected drug dealers and
users in 2003 to honor King Bhumibol Adulyadej by making Thailand "drug
free" in time for the King's seventy-fifth birthday. Prime Minister Thaksin Shi-
nawatra set the tone for the campaign when he declared that "in this war, drug
dealers must die."[66] Interior Minister Wan Muhamad Nor Matha promised
that drug dealers "will be put behind bars or even vanish without a trace. Who
cares? They are destroying our country."[67]

The Thai government was concerned about the rising number of Thais
taking amphetamine-type pills—popularly known as Yaa-Baa. The crackdown
began in early February 2003. Within weeks, government officials were bragging about the number of bad guys killed. A New York Times article noted that
"the killings started right on cue. Many victims were on secret, but official,
'black lists.'"[68] Throughout Thailand, local officials set up black boxes or mail-
boxes and encouraged people to accuse anyone suspected of involvement with
narcotics—no evidence required. Many people used the anonymous system to
accuse business competitors or personal enemies. According to a 2004 U.S.
State Department human rights report, the interior minister warned "governors and provincial police that those who failed to eliminate a prescribed percentage of the names from their blacklists would be fired."[69]

The central government issued specific quotas for arrests for each state,
city, and village. Sunai Phasuk of Forum Asia, a Bangkok-based human rights

organization, noted: "Most of [the victims] got killed on the way back from the police office. People found their name on a blacklist, went to the police, then end up dead."[70] Thai Senator Tuenjai Deetes observed: "The justice system was destroyed. . . . Here, the government official or police judged immediately, 'you are doing drugs, you must be killed.'"[71] Many of the victims had drugs planted on their bodies after they were murdered. Amnesty International complained: "Authorities are not permitting pathologists to perform autopsies and bullets are reportedly being removed from the corpses."[72]

Interior Minister Matha even established an arrest quota for local politicians, warning governors: "To prove the government is serious and spares no one, in March and April you will arrest big dealers—suspects such as provincial councilors and local politicians—four to five in each province."[73] Governors were permitted to keep 35 percent of all the drug assets they confiscated, and police detectives were entitled to skim 15 percent of the loot.[74]

Many knowledgeable Thais believed the crackdown had little or no chance of permanently suppressing narcotics. Charan Pakdithanakul, secretary to the Supreme Court president, commented, "People may take one look at the death toll and hail the government, but if you scrutinize the names of those killed, there's not a single big-time dealer."[75] Many Thai drug gangs operate under the protection of politicians and the military and appeared to easily survive the Thaksin purge.

In early May 2003, the Thai government proudly announced that 2,275 suspected drug dealers had been killed and that 90 percent of the nation's drug trafficking had been eliminated.[76] The government insisted that it had no role in the vast majority of deaths of drug dealers, except for a small number of dealers whom police supposedly killed in self-defense.

Some of the killings did not enhance the government's image, including the police slayings of a 9-year-old boy as he and his mother drove along a Bangkok street; a 16-month old baby killed along with her mother when their car was riddled with bullets; a woman who was in the eighth month of her pregnancy; and a 75-year-old grandmother gunned down as she walked along a street.[77] Thaksin dismissed concerns about widespread violence in the drug crackdown, declaring that murder "is not an unusual fate for wicked people."[78]

The slaughter evoked muffled comments from the U.S. embassy in Bangkok. On May 7, a U.S. embassy spokesman, who insisted on anonymity, told the Associated Press that the Bush administration has "made very clear that we have serious concerns about the number of killings that may have been associated with Thailand's war on drugs" and insisted that the Thaksin government "needs to . . . investigate all unexplained killings and identify and prosecute those responsible."[79]

The Thai government ignored the anonymous State Department official's comments. The following month, Thailand's prime minister was invited to the White House to meet with Bush. Bush upgraded Thailand's status with the U.S. government into a "major non-NATO ally" (thereby entitling the Thai government to a bevy of U.S. government benefits and subsidies, including the right to buy depleted uranium ammunition).[80] A June 11, 2003 White House statement by the Thai and U.S. Governments declared:

> The two leaders recognized the long, successful history of cooperation between the United States and Thailand on law enforcement and counternarcotics. President Bush appreciated Thailand's leadership in hosting one of the largest and most successful U.S. Drug Enforcement Administration (DEA) operations in the world as well as the U.S.-Thai International Law Enforcement Academy (ILEA). President Bush recognized Prime Minister Thaksin's determination to combat transnational crime in all its forms, including drug trafficking and trafficking in persons.

The White House Joint Statement dismissed the allegations of anti-drug carnage:

> Regarding recent press allegations that Thai security services carried out extrajudicial killings during a counternarcotics campaign in Thailand, Prime Minister Thaksin stated unequivocally that the Thai Government does not tolerate extrajudicial killings and assured President Bush that all allegations regarding killings are being investigated thoroughly.[81]

The only reference to the slaughter was a brazen lie by the Thai prime minister that was sanctified in an official White House statement. The prime minister's pledge made as much sense as if he had promised to personally resurrect all the people wrongfully killed in the crackdown. *The Nation,* one of the most respected newspapers in Thailand, noted that "the American president saw the halos on Thaksin's head," including one from the "drug-suppression campaign."[82] Thai Interior Minister Matha said that Bush praised Thailand's antidrug campaign during the White House meeting.[83]

On October 27, Bush visited Thailand and proclaimed, "Thailand is also a force of good throughout Southeast Asia."[84] A month later, William Snipes, the Bangkok-based DEA regional director for East Asia, hailed the Thai crackdown: "'Temporarily, we look at it as successful." Snipes conceded that whether the reduction in drug activity "is a lasting effect, we will have to wait and see."[85]

By early December, the official bad-guy body count had risen to 2,625.[86] Speaking at a giant Bangkok victory rally of thousands of government employees, Thaksin proclaimed: "Today is a milestone. More than 90% of ordinary Thais can now lead an honest daily life free from narcotics in their communities. . . . We are now in a position to declare that drugs, which formerly were a big danger to our nation, can no longer hurt us."[87]

In his annual birthday message on December 5, 2003, King Bhumibol Adulyadej—the king in whose honor Thailand had been rendered drug free—first said that the alleged killings of drug dealers were a "small thing." Then he insisted that many of the killings were not the fault of the government. Then he called for an investigation of the killings. The king fretted that, unless the killings were cleared up, "the people will blame the King. This would breach the Constitution which stipulates that the King should not have to take responsibility for anything."[88]

But the government stonewalled such investigations. Deputy Attorney General Prapan Naiyakowit, the chief investigator of the killings, complained in early December: "In May I completed the probe report on drug-related deaths. Since then, police have not submitted a single report on any individual killing that happened during the anti-drug campaign."[89] A Thai senate committee concluded that "the government used rhetoric and ceremony to make people hate each other, to destroy the human dignity of suspected drug dealers, and incite people to handle the drug problem with violence and without mercy."[90]

The government's killing spree intimidated much of the populace. Thai National Human Rights Commissioner Charan Ditthaapichai complained of the plight of the 329,000 people on the blacklist: "They feel they are no longer safe and could be exterminated at any time."[91] Amnesty International reported that the government's murder spree left many Thais "afraid to leave their homes, and others avoided traveling to areas where they were not known for fear of being suspected as drug traffickers and shot dead."[92]

After 9/11, Bush repeatedly proclaimed that any nation or government guilty of aiding and abetting terrorists will be considered to be as guilty as the terrorists themselves. Yet the U.S. government helped bankroll a Thai government campaign that terrorized the Thai people. The Bush administration gave Thailand $3.7 million in antidrug aid in 2003[93]—thus compelling American taxpayers to bankroll Thai state terrorism.[94]

According to the U.S. State Department, 307 people were killed worldwide in international terrorist attacks in 2003.[95] The Bush administration endorsed and helped finance an antidrug crackdown that killed more than seven times as many people in a single country as were killed by all the international terrorists in the world last year.

Though the Thaksin crackdown caused the price of amphetamine pills to triple in Thailand, the price fell by two-thirds in Cambodia, where many of the pills (mostly made in Burma) were diverted. U.N. drug official Sandro Calvani warned that the surge of drugs into Cambodia, Laos, and India could breed new problems. Calvani explained: "It is the so-called balloon effect— you squeeze in one part and it bulges out somewhere else. Obviously dealers are looking for new markets."[96]

On February 28, 2004, Thaksin revealed that the drug problem was "coming back" to Thailand. He announced a new war on drugs, this time doing it for the children.[97] Thaksin explained: "Young people might fall prey to drug peddlers during their holidays. The government will make sure this does not happen. The new round of drug suppression will cover Bangkok and major cities."[98]

CONCLUSION

"We will continue to work toward a society in which all citizens are free from the devastating influence of drugs," President Bush proclaimed on April 7, 2004.[99] But there is no reason to expect Bush's heavy-handed campaign to free Americans from the devastating influence of drugs to be any more successful than the far harsher Thai campaign.

The Bush administration, like prior administrations, continues to lose the war on drugs and continues to deceive the American people about the futility of the federal drug war. Administration officials continue to portray the issue as a question of good versus evil rather than raise the obvious question: What is the sanity of perpetuating failed policies that punish vast numbers of Americans while failing to achieve their goal?

When Bush's DEA chief Asa Hutchinson was sworn in on August 20, 2001, he announced, "I would hope that we are judged by the lives that are touched and the hope that we give America."[100] Yet Bush and his drug-war team seem more devoted to frightening voters than to protecting public health. The drug war illustrates Bush's moralizing at its worst—running roughshod over the lives and rights of millions of people—simply to burnish the president's reputation as caring, compassionate, righteous, or whatever.

CHAPTER TEN

Government by Stealth
The New Iron Curtain

I think it's important for folks, no matter what your political party is . . . to look at
Washington and be proud of what you see.
—*George W. Bush, June 21, 2001*[1]

Everything secret degenerates, even the administration of justice.
—*Lord Acton*[2]

The Bush administration is seeking to lower an iron curtain around federal
agencies. Bush is championing doctrines more akin to a monarchy than to a
democracy. Bush's secrecy policies and mandates already prevented Americans
from learning of some of the worst government abuses in decades.

PRIVILEGED TO CONCEAL;
OR HOW BUSH PROTECTS LIBERTY

On December 12, 2001, Bush announced that he was invoking "executive
privilege" to withhold subpoenaed documents from Congress because their
disclosure would be "contrary to the national interest." Bush warned that the
congressional investigation threatened Americans' cherished freedoms: "The
Founders' fundamental purpose in establishing the separation of powers in
the Constitution was to *protect individual liberty.* Congressional pressure on

executive branch prosecutorial decisionmaking is inconsistent with separation of powers and *threatens individual liberty*."[3]

Bush invoked protecting individual liberty to cover up the FBI's role in mass murder in Boston and its perversion of justice throughout New England. Beginning in 1965, the FBI enrolled Boston mob murderers as informants and shielded these killers time and again from prosecutors seeking to nail them. The FBI helped send four innocent men to prison for life for a murder committed by one of the FBI's favorites. (Two of the men died in prison.) The FBI's prize informant, "Whitey" Bulger, absconded in 1995 and was quickly placed on the "Ten Most Wanted" list, thanks to his connection to more than 20 murders.

Bush's invocation of executive privilege perturbed Rep. Dan Burton (R-Ind.), chairman of the House Government Reform Committee, who was leading the investigation into FBI perfidy. When a deputy assistant attorney general appeared before the committee the day after Bush's statement, Burton blasted the guy: "This is not a monarchy. . . . We've got a dictatorial President. . . . Your guy's acting like he's king."[4]

Burton notified Attorney General Ashcroft that "it eludes me how it is in the national interest to cloak this dark chapter of the Justice Department's history in secrecy."[5] He later summarized the outrages: "The United States Department of Justice allowed lying witnesses to send men to death row. It stood by idly while innocent men spent decades behind bars. It permitted informants to commit murder. It tipped off killers so that they could flee before they were caught. . . . And then, when people went to the Justice Department with evidence about murders, some of them ended up dead."[6]

The House Government Reform Committee's final report on its investigation, released in November 2003, denounced the FBI's conduct in New England as "one of the greatest failures in the history of federal law enforcement." More than 20 murders were allegedly committed by FBI informants and "major homicide and criminal investigations in a number of states including Massachusetts, Connecticut, Oklahoma, California, Nevada, Florida and Rhode Island were frustrated or compromised by federal law enforcement officials intent on protecting informants." Countenancing murders by FBI informants was not a rogue Boston operation; instead, awareness of the killings extended "all the way up to the office of FBI chief J. Edgar Hoover." The committee also raised questions about "whether the FBI used its authority to protect former Massachusetts State Senate President William Bulger [the brother of 'Whitey' Bulger] from scrutiny by law enforcement or to advance his political career."[7]

The FBI office in Boston was continuing to deny any misconduct as late as 2001—shortly before Bush invoked executive privilege. Though two of the four people wrongfully sent to prison for life because of the FBI were still alive, the Justice Department treated this as an irrelevant closed case.

The Bush administration eventually dropped its claims of executive privilege and provided foot-dragging cooperation. The committee noted that "the President's claim of executive privilege was a drastic departure from the long-standing history of Congressional access to precisely the types of documents sought by the Committee." Congress had routinely had access to such documents going back to the Teapot Dome scandal of 1923.

No FBI agent was ever disciplined, let alone fired, for his role in fomenting and condoning mass murder in Boston. After the committee issued its report in November 2003, the FBI issued a statement: "While the FBI recognizes there have been instances of misconduct by a few FBI employees, it also recognizes the importance of human source information in terrorism, criminal and counterintelligence investigations."[8] The FBI did not specify how many murders it would countenance in the future by its informants.

The administration had tactical reasons to stonewall Burton's investigation. *The Hill,* a Capitol Hill newspaper, noted that even relatively ancient "revelations [of FBI misconduct] would be problematic for Ashcroft at a time when he is pushing to significantly expand the powers of law enforcement as part of the war on terrorism."[9] In a May 2002 announcement that he was unleashing FBI agents to conduct surveillance in any "public" place they choose (including churches, mosques, and political meetings), Ashcroft boasted: "In its 94-year history, the Federal Bureau of Investigation has been . . . the tireless protector of civil rights and civil liberties for all Americans."[10] At the time of Ashcroft's declaration, the Justice Department was still using trick after trick to block congressional discoveries of FBI atrocities. And in its response to the Burton investigation, the Bush administration did not hesitate to invoke the highest principles to cover up dastardly deeds. For Bush, preserving the good reputation of government was more important than exposing and deterring FBI profound and perennial abuses.

TOTAL TASK FORCE SECRECY

The Bush administration also revealed a novel interpretation of executive privilege in the case of Vice President Cheney's task force on energy policy. Cheney convened the task force shortly after Bush's election. Cheney refused to disclose the names of the advisors, even though the task force report was the basis for energy legislation that would profoundly affect the nation's economy. (After Enron went bankrupt, White House officials grudgingly conceded that Cheney or his staffers had six meetings with Enron officials during the crafting of the Bush energy policy.) Critics argued that the involvement of private companies in crafting legislation made the task force a federal advisory committee. And, thanks to a 1972 law, such committees are required to disclose membership and other information. The Clinton administration ran aground on this reef after a federal judge ruled that the secrecy of its health care task force violated federal law.[11]

The General Accounting Office, the investigative arm of Congress, initially requested all the energy task force records, including transcripts of the meetings. After the administration refused to provide any information, GAO sued to get a list of "who attended the energy task force meetings, the process that determined who would be invited, and how much it all cost."[12]

Bush portrayed the GAO's action as a threat to the survival of the presidency. Bush declared: "I am not going to let Congress erode the power of the executive branch. I have a duty to protect the executive branch from legislative encroachment. . . . Can you imagine having to give up every single transcript of what is advised me or the vice president? Our advice [from others] wouldn't be good and honest and open."[13] At the time of Bush's statement, GAO had long since dropped its request for transcripts. Bush invoked openness for his advisors as a pretext for closing government for everyone else.

The GAO lawsuit was dismissed by a pliant federal judge—John Bates Jr.—Bush appointed in 2001. Bates ruled that because GAO had not been injured, it had no standing to sue to get the documents. In a 1980 law, Congress explicitly authorized GAO to file such lawsuits, but Bates brushed aside this technicality. The *Washington Post* noted that the decision "could severely weaken the GAO and leave a president largely immune from aggressive congressional oversight unless the opposition party is in the majority."[14]

The Bush administration did not escape a similar lawsuit on energy task force documents filed by the Sierra Club and by Judicial Watch, a law firm renowned for its hounding of the Clinton administration. The White House claimed executive privilege to deny all information demands, seeking to close the White House to almost any outside oversight. Federal judge Emmett Sullivan slammed the Bush team: "The implications of the bright-line rule advocated by the government are stunning." Sullivan warned that accepting this doctrine "would eviscerate the understanding of checks and balances between the three branches of government on which our constitutional order depends."[15]

The Bush administration informed the court in September 2002 that it would not turn over the documents because they "are *all* presumptively privileged because they *all* involve sensitive communications between and among the president and his closest advisers."[16] However, in an October 2002 court hearing, Justice Department attorneys confessed that they had not reviewed the documents that they claimed all contained sensitive information. Judge Sullivan commanded the Bush administration lawyer: "You have to produce the non-privileged documents and assert the [executive] privilege for those that are. You refuse to assert the privilege and won't respond to court orders."[17] Deputy Assistant Attorney General Shannen Coffin explained that "we're not going to ask our clients to complete that review because it's an unconstitutional burden."[18] This notion of "unconstitutional burden" sounded like it might apply to a princess who did not wish to be compelled to make a ceremonial appearance.

Rather than comply with Judge Sullivan's order, the Bush administration trotted off to federal appeals court. Federal appeals judge Harry Edwards complained to a Justice Department lawyer: "You have no case . . . you have no authority to bring the case here."[19] The court refused to countenance the Bush administration's demand for blanket secrecy.

The Bush team took the case to the Supreme Court. After the court took the case, Sierra Club attorney David Bookbinder declared: "The American people have already waited far too long to find out exactly how energy industries influenced our national energy policy."[20] Justice Department spokesman Mark Corallo countered: "The administration's energy plan is available to the public for anyone to review, and the administration has provided 36,000 additional pages of documents relating to its development."[21] But it is irrelevant how many boxes of documents are dumped on plaintiffs if the key information is withheld. Not a single page of information was disclosed from the Cheney task force.

The Bush administration's arguments in the Cheney task force case were "strikingly similar" to its arguments for the president's power to unilaterally label people as enemy combatants and lock them up in perpetuity without a trial, the *New York Times* noted.[22] In both cases, the administration is "projecting a vision of presidential power in both war and peace as far-reaching as any the court has seen and posing important questions of the constitutional separation of powers." The administration claimed that the Federal Advisory Committee Act of 1972 is "plainly unconstitutional" in authorizing "unwarranted intrusion" and "extreme interference" with the president's "core" constitutional duties. Solicitor General Theodore Olson informed the court: "Congress does not have the power to inhibit, confine or control the process through which the president formulates the legislative measures he proposes or the administrative actions he orders."[23] The Bush administration warned that a broad interpretation of the Federal Advisory Committee Act turns the law "into a general warrant to search executive branch groups and committees for contacts with outsiders who might be deemed de facto members."[24] It is ironic for the Bush administration to complain about a general warrant, since that is its preferred method of dealing with American citizens.

On April 27, when the Supreme Court heard oral arguments on the case, Bush's solicitor general, Theodore Olson, declared that "the separation of powers issue in this case goes far beyond the assertion of executive privilege. Executive privilege concerns itself with particular documents or a concern over the relationship the particular documents refer to. The objection here is to the process." Olson declared that the president should not even have to bother to claim executive privilege in the case, since that "would have required the president and the vice president to *spend time with documents*." Olson declared that even permitting a private organization to seek White House documents would create "a process that's invasive to fundamental presidential prerogatives and responsibilities." He derided private groups' efforts to learn what White House officials have said or done, declaring that "the discovery itself violates the Constitution." Justice Ruth Bader Ginsburg asked: "All discovery?" Olson replied, "Yes." Olson propounded a doctrine of "constitutional immunity" that made it sound as if the White House deserves the same status that the Vatican enjoys in Rome.

Justice Scalia, in questioning a lawyer for the Sierra Club, propounded a sweeping doctrine that could satisfy even Bush absolutists: "I think executive privilege means whenever the president feels that he is threatened, he can simply refuse to comply with a court order. He has the power . . . to say, 'No, this intrudes too much upon my powers. I will not do it.'"[25]

The Supreme Court will rule in this case by the end of June 2004. Most commentators expected a Bush administration victory, based on the justices' questions and comments during the oral arguments.[26] The Bush administration's overreaching in this case was lampooned by comic Jay Leno, who characterized its view of "separation of powers": "That means that people who don't have any power shouldn't be allowed to find out what the people who do have power are doing."[27]

At the same time that the Bush administration was using every legal tactic to delay disclosures on Cheney's energy task force, it was pushing Congress full steam ahead to enact its energy bill. The administration desperately sought final judgment from Congress before it had to reveal the ingredients that helped make up its stew.

"FREEDOM FROM INFORMATION"

In a January 2004 speech to the rich and influential gathered for a conference in Davos, Switzerland, Attorney General John Ashcroft lectured the world: "Information is the most therapeutic resource we have in achieving integrity in our markets and in our government. When evidence of corruption is presented to the public, institutions are held accountable. In this way, open government becomes an essential tool to creating good government."[28] Ashcroft scrupulously avoided permitting such personal prejudices to bias his actions as the nation's chief law enforcement officer.

In 1974, as evidence of a torrent of Nixonian lies accumulated, Congress passed a sweeping expansion of the Freedom of Information Act (FOIA), originally enacted in 1966. Donald Rumsfeld, President Ford's chief of staff, and Dick Cheney, Rumsfeld's deputy, urged Ford to veto the act as "unworkable and unconstitutional."[29] Ford followed Cheney's advice, and Congress promptly overrode Ford's veto.

FOIA proved invaluable in disclosing government abuses across the board, and millions of citizens have also used the act to track down their personal records from the FBI, the Veterans Administration, and other federal agencies. In 1993, Clinton's attorney general, Janet Reno, notified federal agencies to interpret the act in a way to ensure that the government "is not unduly limiting the records found responsive to those requests" and to fulfill requests unless it was "reasonably foreseeable that disclosure would be harmful."[30] Some federal agencies followed Reno's dictum and provided fuller responses to citizens and media seeking government records.

Despite Reno's memo, FOIA continued to be one of the most frequently violated laws in Washington. FOIA requires federal agencies to respond to requests within 20 business days. However, many agencies have been notorious for taking years to respond to FOIA requests, if at all. As of 2001, the attorney general's average delay for responding to an FOIA request was 137 days, and the FBI took more than 500 days to process FOIA complex requests.[31] The Energy Department averaged more than five years to respond to FOIA requests.

Upon taking power, Ashcroft surveyed the situation and realized the problem was that some federal agencies continued to brazenly obey FOIA. One month after 9/11, Ashcroft issued guidance to all federal FOIA officers.

Ashcroft curtsied to "full compliance" with FOIA and then quickly reminded FOIA officers that the Justice Department "and this Administration
are equally committed to protecting other fundamental values that are held
by our society. Among them are safeguarding our national security, enhanc-
ing the effectiveness of our law enforcement agencies, protecting sensitive
business information and, not least, preserving personal privacy." Ashcroft
implied that these values somehow conflict with FOIA. Yet, FOIA already has
specific exemptions to prevent disclosure of documents in most of the categories he mentioned.

Ashcroft continued:

> I encourage your agency to carefully consider the *protection of all such values*
> and interests when making disclosure determinations under the FOIA. Any
> discretionary decision by your agency to disclose information protected under
> the FOIA should be made *only after full and deliberate consideration of the in-
> stitutional, commercial, and personal privacy interests that could be implicated by
> disclosure of the information.* . . . When you carefully consider FOIA requests
> *and decide to withhold records,* in whole or in part, you can be assured that *the
> Department of Justice will defend your decisions* unless they lack a sound legal
> basis or present an unwarranted risk of adverse impact on the ability of other
> agencies to protect other important records.[32]

Ashcroft effectively encouraged agencies to deny FOIA requests. Ashcroft
sounded as if he believed that Congress made a technical error in drafting the
original legislation, inadvertently neglecting to title it "The Freedom from Information Act." Ashcroft sought to create a presumption of non-disclosure,
backed up by the deep pockets of the world's largest law firm. The feds know
that few FOIA requesters have the means for lengthy legal battles with a federal agency to get the documents they seek.

GAO reported a year later that "agency backlogs of pending [FOIA] requests are substantial and growing government-wide."[33] Most agencies surveyed had an average of ten weeks backlog of unfulfilled FOIA requests.
Steven Aftergood, director of the Project on Government Secrecy at the Federation of American Scientists, said, "The greater the backlog, the longer the
delay, the less useful the law is in fulfilling its function."[34]

National Security Archive, a non-profit organization in Washington, filed
FOIA requests with federal agencies seeking information on the impact of the
Ashcroft memo. Almost 10 percent of the agencies "lost" the FOIA request
the organization submitted. Less than a third of the agencies responded
within the statutory twenty-day deadline. Thomas Blanton, director of the

National Security Archive, commented, "The administrative system that makes FOIA a reality is in grave disrepair, plagued with delays, and Byzantine in its complexity for the ordinary requester; and Attorney General Ashcroft seems only to have thrown sand in the gears."[35] On the other hand, a September 2003 GAO survey found that almost half of federal FOIA officers said that the Ashcroft memo had little effect, while 31 percent said that they believed less information is being released as a result of the directive.[36]

Ashcroft's FOIA hostility helped spur denials on almost all requests by the ACLU and other organizations and individuals on how the Justice Department is using the new powers provided by the Patriot Act. The Defense Department also stonewalled FOIA requests on the workings of its Total Information Awareness surveillance scheme.

The most important FOIA denials involved the Bush administration's claim of secrecy on the names of the 1,200 Arabs, Muslims, and others who were arrested as "suspected terrorists" in the wake of the 9/11 attacks. The Justice Department insisted on closed court hearings for all of the arrests and on closed immigration hearings for all the subsequent deportations. Even though not one of those arrested turned out to have any connection to the 9/11 attacks, the Bush administration continued to claim that disclosure of any of the names could provide a "mosaic" that could fatally aid terrorist plotters. Federal appellate judge Damon Keith ruled against the Bush policy in 2003: "Democracies die behind closed doors. . . . A government operating in the shadow of secrecy stands in complete opposition to the society envisioned by the Framers of our Constitution. When government begins closing doors, it selectively controls information rightfully belonging to the people. Selective information is misinformation."[37] Federal judge Gladys Kessler also trounced the Bush policy: "Secret arrests are a concept odious to a democratic society. . . . The public's interest in learning the identity of those arrested and detained is essential to verifying whether the government is operating within the bounds of law."[38]

Lower federal courts split on the issue, and the case landed at the Supreme Court. The issue was whether the government's unsubstantiated assertion that someone was suspected of a heinous crime can justify keeping secret in perpetuity all details of their case, regardless of their innocence of serious offenses. The Justice Department never explained how revealing the names of hundreds of non-terrorists arrested after 9/11 would aid terrorist groups.

The Supreme Court refused to hear the challenge. The *Washington Post* termed the Supreme Court's refusal to consider the secrecy of the 9/11 roundup as "a significant victory for the Bush administration."[39] Ashcroft said he was "pleased the court let stand a decision that clearly outlined the danger of giving terrorists a virtual road map to our investigation that could have allowed them to chart a potentially deadly detour around our efforts."[40] But it was a "road map" that would have shown little more than the number of federal wild goose chases. Kate Martin of the Center for National Security Studies commented: "We have a situation where the government arrested more than a thousand people in secret, and the courts have let them get away with it. There is no accountability for the abuses, and secrecy allowed the abuses."[41] Thanks to the Supreme Court's tacit approval, the federal government may merely need to repeat the "national security" mantra if it carries out another round of mass secret arrests.

Government officials often cite the cost of compliance with FOIA requests as a reason for violating the statutory deadlines. The Justice Department estimated in 2002 that responding to FOIA requests cost federal agencies $300 million in 2002.[42] Fees paid by people requesting information covered part of this cost. In contrast, the federal government spends almost $5 billion a year classifying documents to prevent their disclosure.[43] The federal government spends almost 15 times as much locking information away as it does responding to requests for information.

Federal FOIA officers violate the law on a regular basis yet the Justice Department has never sought criminal sanctions against federal employees who violate Americans' right to know how the government is using its power over them.

PROTECTING PRESIDENTS FROM HISTORY

On November 1, 2001, President Bush issued an executive order entitled "Further Implementation of the Presidential Records Act." Bush's order effectively overturned an act of Congress and a Supreme Court decision and could make it far more difficult for Americans to learn of government abuses. George Washington University law professor Jonathan Turley declared that Bush's executive order "effectively rewrote the Presidential Records Act, converting it from a measure guaranteeing public access to one that blocks it."[44]

In 1978, Congress passed the Presidential Records Act, declaring, "The United States shall reserve and retain complete ownership, possession, and control of Presidential records."[45] The act was a response to the titanic clashes between Congress, the Supreme Court, and the Nixon administration over who owned Nixon's records (especially those pesky tape recordings). The act requires that the unclassified papers of a president be routinely released 12 years after the president's term ends. There are provisions in the act to justify non-disclosure for information that could threaten national security.

Two months after taking office, Bush's White House counsel, Alberto Gonzales, issued an order delaying the release of sixty-eight thousand pages of records from Reagan's administration that archivists at the Reagan library had already confirmed did not threaten national security or violate personal privacy.[46] The release of records (including those on Iran-Contra) from the Reagan administration could have proven a profound embarrassment to many officials in George W. Bush's administration—including his father (who was vice president under Reagan).

The White House completely misrepresented both the 1978 law and the new executive order. Bush commented on the day after his surprise order: "We responded to a new law written by Congress that lays out a procedure that I think is fair for past Presidents."[47] (Most 23-year-old laws are no longer considered new.) At a press briefing on the day Bush's order was announced, White House press secretary Ari Fleischer said, "As a result of the new law that is now going into effect, and thanks to the executive order that the President will soon issue, more information will be forthcoming." Fleischer insisted that Bush's order was a triumph in open government because "under the existing procedures, existing law, a former President has the right to withhold anything for any reason, if they don't want to make it public." This was ludicrous, since a post-Watergate Congress would not have passed a law to make presidents czars in perpetuity over the records of their actions in office.

Fleischer insisted that there "will be a 90 day time limit" on presidents' right to review requests. Bush's executive order mentioned 90 days, but a former president will be entitled to dally as long as he pleases.

After a journalist asked Fleischer about the new requirement for "people having to demonstrate their need for the information" about a former president's actions, Fleischer snipped: "So you're making guesses and judgments, all of which would indicate malfeasance or withholding of information by this administration. And I just can't accept that; that's not the case."

The journalist responded: "So you are saying, trust us, it'll all be fine?"

Fleischer snapped: "You are saying, we don't trust you."[48]

Trust was the issue—regardless of whether Bush's order was legal or Constitutional, and regardless of how much information could be hidden in perpetuity because of the new restrictions. And none of Fleischer's inaccurate portrayals could ding the administration's credibility.

The *White House Weekly* summarized the changes in Bush's order:

- It prohibits the release of records unless and until both the former and incumbent president affirmatively consent to their release.
- It imposes no firm time limit on record reviews and assertions of privilege claims. It allows the former or incumbent president to extend the review period unilaterally and indefinitely.
- It requires the archivist to withhold records in response to any privilege claim by a former president, regardless of its merit. It thereby places the burden on the requester to sue to contest the privilege claim.
- It may be read to permit a former vice president to claim executive privilege.
- It asserts a very expansive view of the scope of executive privilege. It suggests that a requester under the Presidential Records Act must establish "*a demonstrated, specific need*" for records in order to overcome a privilege claim.[49]

The people's "right to know" has been replaced by former presidents' right to suppress. Bush's edict reversed the burden of proof in the law—as if a former president is presumptively entitled to have embarrassing facts and documents hidden forever.

Bush also sought to create a hereditary privilege not only for former presidents but for their wives and children and others to assert "state secrets privilege." Professor Turley noted that, under the order, "a former president can transfer the right to invoke executive privilege to anyone of his choosing. The order would also extend the privilege beyond the death of a former president, allowing the privilege to be passed on to anyone of his choosing: a half-wit nephew or a drinking buddy."[50]

Bush created a document review process custom-made to create massive bottlenecks. *National Journal* noted: "Bush's own order commits the White House to a task—reviewing millions of documents—that it is probably physically unable to perform in a timely way. And why this Administration has concluded that the archivist has no more expertise, independence, or standing than, say, a White House deputy chief of staff, is also perplexing to scholars and members of Congress alike."[51]

Bush's order infuriated many historians. American University historian Anna Nelson said that the order "sets up a minefield in front of what was a straightforward piece of legislation."[52] Vanderbilt University history professor Hugh Graham observed, "Unless this executive order of his is overturned, it will be a victory for secrecy in government so total that it would make Nixon jealous in his grave."[53]

Bush's order will make it easier for former presidents to perpetuate their cons on the American people. Presidents don't suppress news of their good deeds and successes. Steven Hensen, president of the Society of American Archivists, commented: "The order effectively blocks access to information that enables Americans to hold our presidents accountable for their actions."[54] In issuing this order, Bush sounded as if he had discovered a new constitutional right by which the president is entitled to be protected against the truth. Or perhaps it is merely a constitutional right entitling former presidents to a better reputation than they deserve.

Congress began consideration of a bill to overturn the executive order. Assistant Attorney General Daniel J. Bryant criticized one bill as "unnecessary and inappropriate and, more importantly, unconstitutional." The Bush administration sought to settle the dispute by releasing most of the sixty-eight thousand pages of requested Reagan records, thereby proving that no legislative remedy was needed. Bryant wrote that "Congress lacks the authority to regulate by legislation the procedures for exercising" executive privilege.[55] But Bush's privilege is not the highest law of the land. (The bill stalled out.)

In contrast to Bush's behavior, former President Clinton announced in early 2003 that he was waiving his rights to a 12-year delay in release of the vast majority of the confidential advice he received during his presidency (excluding arcane matters such as the Paula Jones, Monica Lewinsky, and Whitewater cases). Clinton declared: "The more information we can make available to scholars, historians, and the general public, the better informed people will be about the formulation of public policy and the decision-making process at the White House."[56] However, under the new executive order, Bush can veto the release of Clinton's papers.

President Clinton issued an executive order in 1995 decreeing that most government documents will be automatically declassified after 25 years. Clinton's order contained an exemption for material that continued to be sensitive for national security. On March 25, 2003, Bush issued an executive order that delayed for years public access to millions of pages of documents that were scheduled for release in the following weeks. Bush claimed that "sensitive information" needed to be reviewed prior to the release—though the feds had had years to get ready for this deadline. The Bush order reversed the Clinton order's presumption in favor of disclosure. Bush's order also awarded the vice president the prerogative to block disclosures. And, in a triumph of revisionism, Bush empowered federal agencies to reclassify documents that had already been publicly released.[57]

In April 2004, historians around the country became alarmed after the Bush administration nominated Allen Weinstein to be Archivist of the United States. Many historians believe that the Bush administration may have nudged the current archivist, John Carlin, into retiring early so that Bush could put his own man in the slot—and thereby perhaps make it more difficult to get access both to his records and the records of his father's administration (which were scheduled to be released in January 2005). Historians were concerned about Weinstein's close ties to Republican politicians and former Secretary of State Henry Kissinger's place on the board of Weinstein's Center for Democracy. Scott Armstrong, one of the founders of the National Security Archive, commented that Bush's choice of Weinstein is "the most cynical appointment of an Archivist possible. He has a very clouded, very complicated, self-promoting, neo-con, politically manipulative record."[58] Timothy Slavin, president of the Council of State Historical Records Coordinators, complained: "It's the equivalent of the administration's thumbing its nose at the nation's history. It seems to me that they were trying to bum-rush an appointment."[59] American University historian Anna Nelson observed of the administration's process: "This is pretty sneaky. There is only one motive here, and that is they [the White House] had to be worried that Bush was going to be defeated" in the 2004 election.[60]

CONCLUSION

In 1798, James Madison, the father of the Constitution, in a resolution attacking the Alien and Sedition Acts, championed "the right of freely examining public characters and measures, and of free communication among the people thereon, which has ever been justly deemed, the only effectual guardian of every other right."[61] Bush administration policies, by making it more difficult to learn of government's actions, place Americans' rights in danger.

Attorney General Ashcroft sounded almost Madisonian in January 2002, when he declared that "the best friend of freedom is information because information allows freedom-loving people to become the best line of self-defense."[62] However, Ashcroft was referring only to getting people's help to detect terrorists. Madison recognized the need for people to arm themselves with information for self-defense against the government. Ashcroft saw "freedom of information" largely as a way to create millions of amateur Barney Fifes.

Bush perennially justifies his foreign wars and incursions by proclaiming that they spread the light of liberty—because "freedom is God's gift to each and every person of the world."[63] Bush declared in April 2004: "A country that hides something is a country that is afraid of getting caught, and that was part of our calculation."[64] Bush was referring to Iraq and invoking Saddam's secrecy to justify war. But Bush acts as if spreading liberty abroad requires keeping Americans in the dark about the actions of their own government. Bush's solicitor general, Theodore Olson, informed the Supreme Court: "It's easy to imagine an infinite number of situations where the government might legitimately give out false information."[65] If Bush becomes entitled to invade a foreign nation because its government keeps secrets, what right do Bush's secrecy policies confer upon American citizens regarding how they may treat Washington?

Americans are supposed to presume that the more secretive the U.S. government becomes, the more secure their liberty will be. And the less people know, the safer they will become. But the fact that Bush would make a sweeping claim of privilege and prerogative in a case involving stunning FBI abuses indicates what Americans should expect from the "new secrecy." Perhaps the Bush legal team chose some of the worst abuses on which to establish the principle. Apparently, the worse the government misconduct, the greater the government's right to secrecy. The only way to understand all of the Bush administration's different Executive Privilege claims regarding secrecy is through a quasi-religious belief that the American public has no right to know the actions of their rulers. Preserving respect is more important than preventing misgovernment.

Bush preaches to Americans about the need to accept a "culture of responsibility." Yet his secrecy policies make it far more difficult to hold government and government officials accountable. Perhaps Bush wants the federal government to have a monopoly on irresponsibility. Bush is vastly more fastidious about the supposed constitutional rights of presidents and former presidents than he is about the rights of average Americans. Bush's secrecy policies—especially the Presidential Records Act—turn largely on whether government is the personal fiefdom of the rulers, and whether citizens have any other primary role aside from paying taxes and fighting in foreign wars.

The common theme to Bush secrecy policies is that it is in the national interest for the American people to have nearly boundless faith in the president and in the federal government. Whatever deters the worship of government threatens freedom, national security, and maybe apple pie as well.

Conservatives frequently dismiss concerns about government surveillance by asking: "If you haven't done anything wrong, then what have you got to hide?" One could also ask: "If the government hasn't done anything wrong, then why should politicians and bureaucrats work so hard to hide their deeds?" *Oregonian* columnist David Sarasohn observed: "Just like the Nixon administration, this White House bases its information policy on a clear principle: What you don't know won't hurt us."[66]

Preserving freedom requires leashing government. The less people learn about government policies, the less control people will have over government action. By preventing people from knowing what government is doing, secrecy unleashes government.

CHAPTER ELEVEN

Airport Antics
The TSA Attitude Police

Shortly before Labor Day weekend 2003, the Transportation Security Administration held press conferences at airports around the nation, putting on display some of the knives, box cutters, and other items seized from travelers at TSA checkpoints. (Fingernail clippers and cigar cutters were excluded from the trophy displays.) The agency announced that it had confiscated more than seven million sharp or pointy objects since formally taking over airport security in February 2002. TSA chief James Loy proudly declared, "Every day screeners are meeting the challenge of keeping flights secure, and all too often they are finding dangerous weapons that passengers are trying to take on flights."[1]

The press conferences generated laudatory media coverage. The TSA succeeded, at least briefly, in convincing some Americans they were safe when they traveled because TSA agents would protect them from evil.

Since 9/11, more than $10 billion has been spent by the federal government on upgrading airport security. The TSA was created in November 2001 to provide world-class security to American airports, fliers, and airlines. The TSA is perhaps the most visible "war on terrorism" change in Americans' daily lives.

TSA'S PUBLIC ENEMY NUMBER ONE

Two years after the 9/11 attacks, news leaked out that federal investigators had succeeded in smuggling box cutters and other potential weapons through TSA security checkpoints at every airport they tested.[2] TSA chief spokesman Brian Turmail explained why the breaches were good news: "We cannot afford in the U.S. to rest on our laurels. That is exactly why the TSA so rigorously tests every element of the security system. Because what might be good enough today for security is never going to be good enough tomorrow or the day after. So if we don't probe our system, Al Qaeda will."[3]

In reality, after 9/11, TSA shut down perhaps the most effective checkpoint testing system because it did not want to frighten its own screeners. In the late 1990s, the FAA created the Threat Image Projection System, which placed images of objects that might be threats on X-ray screens "during actual operations to record whether or not a screener detects a threat."[4] This was the most frequently used method to test airport screeners prior to 9/11. But the system "was shut down immediately following the September 11th terrorist attacks due to concerns that it would result in screening delays and panic, as screeners might think that they were actually viewing a threat object," the General Accounting Office reported in September 2003.

The TSA also sharply reduced the number of covert tests of its screeners, compared to what the FAA conducted prior to 9/11. By mid-2003, only 1 percent of TSA's screeners had been tested—and TSA magnanimously ignores those test failures when assessing a screener's competence. GAO noted, "TSA does not consider the results of these tests as a measure of screener performance, but rather a 'snapshot' of a screener's ability to detect threat objects at a particular point in time."

The Aviation and Transportation Security Act of 2001, which created the agency, required TSA to develop a short-term annual performance plan. The TSA plan, typical of Washington bureaucracies, ignored any effort to determine whether its screeners could actually detect weapons at checkpoints. TSA's plan "focused on progress in meeting deadlines rather than on the effectiveness of programs and initiatives," GAO noted.[5]

When the TSA began hiring screeners, Transportation Secretary Norman Mineta announced that the agency would "hire the best and the brightest" for the new jobs.[6] But not all TSA hiring processes are biased in favor of intelligence.

For instance, TSA screener applicants in New York were not required to show any ability to detect weapons and were given the answers to test questions before the test that determined if they would be hired. Clark Kent Ervin, the inspector general for the Homeland Security Department, complained that some of the test questions "are simply inane."[7] The test asked would-be screeners why they should bother looking for smuggled bombs:

Question: Why is it important to screen bags for IEDs [Improvised Explosive Devices]?

    a. The IED batteries could leak and damage other passenger bags.

    b. The wires in the IED could cause a short to the aircraft wires.

    c. IEDs can cause loss of lives, property, and aircraft.

    d. The ticking timer could worry other passengers.[8]

The inspector general report did not disclose how many TSA screeners chose a wrong answer.

Charles Slepian of the Foreseeable Risk Analysis Center, an Oregon-based organization that specializes on travel security issues, commented that the GAO and inspector general reports showed that airport security was a "national disgrace." He added: "The only conclusion is we are faced with a sham everyday we walk into an airport. They are either just negligent or worse."[9]

Few people pay attention to GAO and inspector general reports, so the TSA continued to relish a modicum of respectability.

Until October 17, 2003.

On that day, Americans learned how a 20-year-old college student made a mockery of Uncle Sam's fifty-thousand-member airport security army. Nathaniel Heatwole of Damascus, Maryland, carried concealed weapons— "two ash-colored box cutters, each complete with blade, approximately 10–12 oz. of a simulated plastic explosive (reddish molding clay), a few dozen strike-anywhere matches, and approximately 8 oz. of liquid bleach"[10]—through airport security and stashed the goods in airplane lavatories, first on a flight from Greensboro, North Carolina, to Baltimore, and then two days later on a return flight from Baltimore to North Carolina. Heatwole left a note specifying where and when the contraband was taken through airport security. Heatwole then e-mailed the TSA telling them exactly what he had done, the dates and flight numbers, and where the contraband was hidden on the planes. The subject line on the e-mail message announced: "Information Regarding 6 Recent Security Breaches." (Heatwole left similar stashes on two flights in April 2003, and also carted box cutters through airport security twice in February 2003 without leaving a deposit.) Heatwole signed the e-mail with his own name and included his phone number. TSA ignored the e-mail.

The massive security breach was discovered five weeks later when a Southwest Airlines jet had a toilet problem. A maintenance man was called in to fix the john and found Heatwole's souvenirs. A second search on another Southwest airlines plane discovered an identical surprise in the lavatory.

Southwest notified TSA on October 16. The TSA searched its e-mail database the following day and found Heatwole's message.

Heatwole is a student at Guilford College in Greensboro, North Carolina, and a Quaker who opposes war. In a sworn statement to the FBI after his arrest, Heatwole stated that his actions were "an act of civil disobedience with the aim of improving public safety for the air-traveling public."[11]

The TSA was outraged. Deputy TSA Administrator Steven McHale exclaimed: "Amateur testing like this does not in any way assist us or show us where we have flaws in our system."[12] TSA chief Loy announced on October 17 that Heatwole had been "under investigation for several months."[13] But neither Loy nor anyone else at TSA ever publicly produced any evidence to support this claim. Besides, if Heatwole was under surveillance, why did the TSA not bother reading the e-mail he sent the agency confessing his crime? Why did the agency not bother searching him before permitting him to fly? If this is how the TSA tracks people "under investigation for several months," then why do the feds even bother compiling a "terrorism watch list"?

TSA quickly announced plans "to update the agency's contact center software to trigger alarms on certain threatening communication."[14] TSA spokeswoman Yolanda Clark reassured the American public, "TSA will require contact center staff to flag messages that discuss illegal activity even if it does not contain threatening information, as in this case."[15] TSA seemed to consider Heatwole's massive security breaches as a nonthreat, except for PR. TSA spokesman Mark Hatfield, Jr. said: "We've set into motion changes that will not only create automatic flagging by the software itself that receives these e-mails, but dedicate analysts, people with law enforcement backgrounds, to the interpretation of e-mails." Rather than spending more money to bring in "people with law enforcement backgrounds," maybe the TSA should hire people who can read plain English. Perhaps the TSA should create a special e-mail address and require anyone notifying it of security flaws to send their message to fuckups@tsa.gov.

Hatfield made his comment during a verbal gymnastics display on the NBC *Today Show*.[16] Hatfield portrayed the breaches as "old news": "Well, the individual that we're talking about, Mr. Heatwole, was able to exploit a limitation of passenger screening that the TSA is on the record for over a year in testimony to Congress and discussions in public forum with the media identifying." But TSA press conferences never mentioned that airport security is a sieve. Nor did the agency drop any hints that screeners were not expected to notice a cache like the one Heatwole carted past them.

Hatfield sought to vindicate the TSA: "We've netted eight million pro-hibited items in the last 14, 15 months, including fifty-two thousand box cut-ters. So we're doing a better job." The fact that the TSA seized millions of items that posed no threat somehow whitewashes the agency's failure to detect potentially catastrophic threats.

Though TSA spokesmen talked as if Heatwole's action was an irrelevant prank, the Justice Department, seeking a harsh sentence for the college stu-dent, portrayed his actions far more ominously. U.S. Attorney Thomas DiBi-agio declared: "It was not a test. . . . It was not public service. It was a very foolish and very dangerous course of action, and very, very dangerous."[17] Rep. Edward Markey (D-Mass.), on the other hand, suggested that Heatwole should be "sentenced to working 20 hours a week for the TSA" as a security consultant.[18]

After the scandal broke, the TSA wasted no time in launching an inves-tigation to determine why Southwest Airlines did not promptly find the dan-gerous items that Heatwole carried past TSA security. TSA spokesman Turmail said: "One of the things we're going to be asking is, 'Are the air car-riers properly following through in the inspection requirements each morn-ing and are the measures in place appropriate?' We don't know the answers to that."[19] The TSA did not bother conducting any special analysis or investiga-tion into its own gross security lapses at the Baltimore-Washington and Greensboro airports.

In March 2004, the feds reduced the charge against Heatwole to entering an area of an airport in violation of security requirements. Heatwole pled guilty to a misdemeanor on April 23 in a deal with prosecutors that will likely mean zero jail time for him. As part of his extensive cooperation with the feds, Heatwole gave the government a videotape he made which could be used to enlighten TSA screeners.[20]

OTHER ONE-TIME FLUKES

Heatwole was not the only person who demonstrated TSA's fallibility. Luckily for the agency, most of the other brazen breaches of TSA security received no coverage in the national media.

A chronology:

On August 2, 2003, at Chicago Midway Airport, a woman passed through a metal detector but left the screening area before TSA agents could wand her up and down. TSA made up for its glitch by evacuating three terminals and ordering a thousand passengers to pass through the check-points again, delaying all departing flights for an hour. A TSA spokesman refused to provide a description of the culprit to the news media.[21]

On August 12, the largest airport on Maui Island, Hawaii, was evacuated for an hour and a half after a male passenger whose carry-on bag tested positive for TNT retrieved his bag and continued to his flight without having his bag defused.[22] TSA agents searched the airport but could not find the mad bomber.

On October 17, the largest terminal at Phoenix International Airport was evacuated because of confusion related to a possible knife in a man's carry-on bag. After noticing the potential weapon on the screen the first time the bag was sent through the X-ray machine, TSA screeners ran the bag through the machine again, saw nothing, and sent the man on his merry way. A few minutes later, screeners realized they had violated TSA protocol by failing to hand search the bag. Four thousand passengers were rescreened and forty flights delayed. *Airport Security Report* noted, "During rescreening, screeners discovered two knives, but could not determine if either of them was the knife originally identified."[23]

On November 24, a terminal at the Austin, Texas, international airport was evacuated after a passenger who set off the magnetometer alarm did not bother waiting around for secondary "hand wand" screening. The culprit was never found and the terminal reopened half an hour later.[24]

On November 30, five flights and a thousand passengers were delayed at New York John F. Kennedy International Airport after a passenger zipped through the exit lane to reach his flight, instead of dutifully entering through a security checkpoint. TSA agents lost the passenger in the crowd; a sweep of the airport turned up nothing.[25]

On December 12, the Providence, Rhode Island, airport was disrupted for two hours after screeners "noticed a suspicious item in a carry-on bag" but failed to stop the passenger before he retrieved it and went to his flight. *Airport Security Report* noted, "The item was not found during rescreening. Officials were satisfied that no threat existed."[26]

On Christmas Eve, 2003, the Delta terminal at New York's LaGuardia Airport was evacuated after a female passenger who set off the metal detector was not wanded before tromping on to catch her flight. Ten flights were delayed for up to two hours.[27]

On January 20, 2004, a third of Hartford's Bradley International Airport was evacuated after someone discovered a little knife (described in initial press reports as "a cutting instrument") in a bathroom trash can. TSA manager Dan

Lee commented that the knife was "the kind you can buy for 29 cents at the hardware store. The adjustable blade was housed in a plastic case."[28] Nine flights were delayed. Sgt. J. Paul Vance, a spokesman for the Connecticut State Police, explained the airport shutdown: "There was absolutely no threat whatsoever. It was a discovery, and as result of that discovery we instituted the plans we have in place."[29]

On January 27, the Providence, Rhode Island, airport was again disrupted after TSA screeners seized one prohibited item from a carry-on bag and sent the passenger on his way. A few minutes later the screeners reexamined the image on the X-ray machine and realized they had missed a second prohibited item. TSA agents could not find the suspect so they herded everyone in two concourses back through the screening process. TSA spokeswoman Ann Davis commented on the disruption: "It's not an everyday occurrence, but it's not that unusual either." The airport's PR director, Patti Goldstein, bragged, "It's always an inconvenience but it just shows the system works. People are doing their jobs."[30]

On February 10, hundreds of passengers were hustled off airplanes and out of a terminal at Washington's Reagan National Airport. TSA spokeswoman Amy von Walter explained: "We did have a woman wander away from the screening area as she was waiting to be secondary screened." The perpetrator was never caught.[31]

On February 19, a terminal at Newark International Airport was evacuated for more than three hours after screeners noticed an image on the X-ray scanner of what appeared to be a gun—but not until the passenger had fetched his bag and marched on to his flight.[32]

The TSA has yet to produce any visible evidence of a learning curve. On March 26, 2004, John Wayne Airport in Orange County, California was temporarily shut down due to a security breach; authorities refused to provide any details or explanation.[33] On April 1, the Albuquerque International airport was evacuated after TSA failed to confiscate a female passenger's Swiss Army knife that showed up on an X-ray image.[34] On April 2, a thousand people were evacuated and flights were delayed for two hours at the San Diego airport after TSA screeners permitted a traveler with a sharp object to proceed to his or her flight without searching the person's bag.[35] On April 5, 2004, a terminal at Baltimore Washington Airport was evacuated and 35 flights were delayed after TSA agents failed to hand search a bag whose X-ray image indicated it might contain a knife.[36]

Not all airport disruptions are TSA's fault. On October 4, 2003, a dozen flights out of Denver International Airport were delayed after an FBI agent reported that he had lost his handgun and badge somewhere in the secured area of the airport. Half an hour later, the weapon turned up in a restaurant where the agent had dined. TSA spokesman Mike Fierberg explained: "It had the potential to be something serious. Fortunately it wasn't, except for that poor FBI agent who's going to have some explaining to do."[37]

Though the TSA may view such security breaches as minor happenstances that merely require sending another memo to Washington, evacuations at hub airports can cost air carriers $2 million per hour and throw off flight schedules across the country.[38] The TSA does not keep track of how many Americans' trips have been disrupted by its follies.

Some TSA agents have been arrested for seizing cash from travelers' belongings at checkpoints.[39] At least one TSA operation may enter the cash seizure business on an official basis. At San Antonio International Airport, the TSA's acting chief of passenger screening notified checkpoint managers to report "any passengers carrying in excess of $10,000." The airport's assistant TSA security chief informed checkpoint managers to "let me know about the money at the checkpoint as I have worked out an arrangement with the local HIDTA [High Intensity Drug Trafficking Areas] narcotics unit for them to respond for possible money seizures."[40] The Bush administration formally proposed in October 2001 to allow law enforcement to confiscate the cash of anyone caught traveling with more than $10,000, unless the person could somehow prove his or her innocence.[41] Congress rejected criminalizing Americans transporting their own money within the United States but that may not be stopping the TSA. The *San Antonio Express-News* warned readers to be "prepared for some intense—and perhaps 'slightly unconstitutional'—scrutiny" from the TSA if they travel through the San Antonio airport with a large amount of cash that they cannot prove they legally acquired. (Some of the worst asset forfeiture abuses in earlier years occurred at airports, where police or federal agents would target and search people who fit a "drug-courier profile"—which basically meant almost anyone flying to certain cities and almost any black or Hispanic adult male.)[42]

The TSA's problems are not confined to a seemingly endless list of airport security breaches. The agency has stumbled massively in almost everything it has done. In June 2003, the agency admitted that it had grossly failed to screen its own screeners. Once hired, more than 1,200 TSA employees were fired after failing criminal background checks or other internal investigations. A 2004 inspector general report revealed that the raw numbers were only the tip of the iceberg. At a time when TSA officials were assuring the American public of the agency's savvy, 500 boxes of documents on the background checks for 20,000 TSA screeners were piled away and went unexamined for months.[43] The TSA used lower standards for security clearances than the FAA required for private screeners hired before 9/11. The inspector general found that at one airport, TSA hired 13 screeners with serious criminal convictions (rape, burglary, manslaughter, etc.). The TSA allowed a dozen of the felons to continue working for months even after the agency discovered that they had failed their criminal background checks.[44]

THE OTHER AIRPORT BOMBS

The Aviation and Transportation Security Act required that by December 31, 2002, all airline baggage be run through bomb-detection machinery or checked with hand-held bomb detectors. TSA spent billions of dollars buying minivan-sized machines and hand-held detectors to protect travelers from bombs. Unfortunately, the machines that TSA rushed to buy are very unreliable, giving false positives for almost a third of all luggage. After a machine signals a false alert, the bag has to be searched by hand. Such searches have spurred more than ten thousand complaints to the TSA about luggage allegedly lost, stolen, or damaged while under TSA jurisdiction. A TSA screener who was caught stealing $5,000 worth of jewelry from someone's luggage was fired and sentenced in April 2004 to five years probation and six months home detention, and was fined $2,000.[45]

False explosives alarms have disrupted many airports. On November 12, 2003, hundreds of people were evacuated from Indianapolis International airport after an explosives trace detection test gave a positive reading. The bag was held at the checkpoint while the owner left and caught his flight. A bomb squad later determined that the explosives alarm was triggered by an electric toothbrush and a hair care product.[46] On April 16, 2004, a terminal at Los Angeles International Airport was evacuated and flights were delayed after the TSA agents summoned the bomb squad over luggage containing a stack of poker chips and a Palm Pilot.[47]

Heart patients are often wrongly tagged by the TSA as would-be terrorists. Much of the Portland airport was shut down on January 5, 2004, in large part because screeners were spooked by an elderly man testing positive for nitroglycerin. TSA spokeswoman Jennifer Marty told the *Portland Oregonian* that the shutdown could have been avoided if the passenger "had promptly disclosed that he was taking heart medication containing nitroglycerin."[48]

The *New York Daily News* reported on January 13, 2004, that "many common brands of hand lotions set off the explosives trace detection machines at U.S. airports' new screening stations. Dozens if not hundreds of times a day, someone's bag or shoe tests positive for glycerin—a substance widely used to smooth skin but which is also found in nitroglycerin, a main component of dynamite." One TSA screener working at a Midwestern airport commented: "This happens five or six times during an eight-hour shift." TSA spokeswoman Ann Davis explained why hand lotion false alarms are another success story: "Passengers should be confident that [detection] machines are finding even a trace of this substance. It shows the system is working as it should."[49]

Even false alarms that do not shut down airport corridors can disrupt a traveler's plans. On October 25, 2003, TSA agents at Norfolk International Airport were alarmed, as *Airport Security Report* gravely noted, after "a novelty dog toy, which breaks wind as it bends over, set off an explosives detector. The life-size mechanical terrier alerted screeners and armed law enforcement officers after it registered as TNT on an explosives trace machine. FBI agents grilled the man in possession of the toy, a 31-year-old male from England. A series of swabs were taken from the replica animal's rear end. Officers were convinced an explosive was inside the dog. Officers eventually returned the dog but stopped the passenger from taking his planned flight to Charlotte, N.C., and rerouted him via Philadelphia."[50] It is unclear whether it is official TSA policy to automatically route potentially exploding canines through Philadelphia.

TSA has snubbed mandates by Congress to upgrade its bomb catching skills. In the 2003 appropriations act for TSA, Congress allotted $75 million for research to develop better explosives detection equipment. TSA ignored the law and instead spent $60 million of that money on salaries for TSA officials.[51] Rep. Mica (R–Fla.), chairman for the House Aviation Subcommittee, groused that instead of developing new technology, "TSA's become expert in taking nail clippers from little old ladies."[52] Several companies that may have developed far more accurate bomb detection technologies complained in late 2003 that the TSA is ignoring their efforts.[53]

FEDERAL ATTITUDE POLICE

While travelers may be slightly at less risk from hijackers, Americans are at much greater risk of being arrested or fined in the airport for not kowtowing to federal agents.

TSA agents are entitled to reverential treatment, regardless of how much damage they inflict on people's travel schedules or luggage. The TSA slapped almost five thousand people with fines in 2003 yet never made any public announcement that people faced fines for violations. There were no warnings and people who received a fine in the mail were never informed of their right to contest or appeal the fine. TSA waited until early 2004 to announce the fine system, at which time the maximum fine was raised from $1,100 to $10,000.

Susan Brown Campbell, a California lawyer, had a small steak knife confiscated from her briefcase by TSA agents at Baltimore-Washington International Airport. After she received a $150 fine in the mail, she called TSA seeking information on how to challenge the fine. A TSA lawyer phoned Campbell and, as she later stated, was "very, very intimidating," warning "that the penalty could be up to $10,000."[54] Campbell was told she would have to travel back to Baltimore to contest the fine. TSA punished Campbell's insolence by doubling her fine to $300.

Travelers can now be heavily fined for inadvertently possessing the same kind of object TSA now approves giving to first-class passengers during flights. TSA ruled in September 2003 that airlines would be permitted to provide metal knives to first-class passengers at mealtime. TSA spokeswoman Yolanda Clark said of a typical airline knife: "Even though it's stainless steel, it has rounded edges and the chances of it actually being used to bring down an aircraft are probably minimal."[55] The metal knives given to first-class passengers may be potentially more dangerous than most items seized at TSA checkpoints. But the agency has no plans to boost its seizure totals by launching raids on first-class cabins.

The fines are an extension of power the feds awarded themselves in a February 2002 *Federal Register* notice, which announced that people could be arrested if they act in a way that "might distract or inhibit a screener from effectively performing his or her duties. . . . A screener encountering such a situation must turn away from his or her normal duties to deal with the disruptive individual, which may affect the screening of other individuals."[56] Practically any comment or behavior that makes a TSA screener "turn away" from whatever he or she was doing can thus be a federal offense.

A thousand people were arrested in airports at TSA's behest in 2002, and roughly fifteen hundred were arrested in 2003.[57] (Many of those arrested were caught with firearms or bona fide dangerous weapons.) Since the TSA is now intercepting 15,000 prohibited items a day from travelers,[58] the new system of fines could raise enough money to pay for fancy new epaulets for every TSA agent's uniform.

TSA agents can fine Americans up to $1,500 for any alleged "nonphysical interference" at a TSA checkpoint. TSA does not have a formal definition for this offense. TSA spokeswoman Ann Davis said the offense included "any nonphysical situation that in any way would interfere with the screener and his or her ability to continue to work, or interfere with their ability to do their jobs."[59] This penalty would seem to be limited solely by the imagination or the malice of TSA agents.

TSA agents can slap fines on Americans based on "attitude," which TSA classifies as one of the "aggravating factors" in determining financial punishments. TSA has issued no guidance on the precise amount of obligatory groveling at airport checkpoints. People who question TSA commands are probably far more likely to be fined.

The TSA's system of fines is a travesty of the Administrative Procedures Act—which guarantees Americans due process rights in dealings with federal agencies. Instead, TSA simply concocted a system of fines, failed to give people warning or notice, failed to define the key terms, failed to notify violators of their right to appeal.

The TSA has made little or no effort to control the attitude or arrogance of many of its own screeners. In March, 2004, airline passengers filed almost 3,000 formal complaints with the federal government over the conduct of TSA screeners. Hundreds of people complained about the rudeness of TSA screeners. And yet, all of these complaints by taxpayers and citizens will not result in a single attitude fine for a TSA employee. (Air travelers filed four times more complaints against the TSA than against airlines.)[60]

These fines have nothing to do with preventing terrorist attacks. The 9/11 hijackers intensely studied American airport security procedures. Once the system of attitude fines becomes known, savvy hijackers will simply work around it—the same way that the hijackers learned how to bypass obstacles at airport checkpoints prior to the 9/11 attacks.

Attitude fines exemplify how TSA aims to rule airports by fear. Anyone who is not properly docile can be treated as a public enemy. The attitude fines illustrate how power has gone to the heads of TSA chiefs. Amidst a surge of private and congressional complaints about TSA abuses, the TSA aspires to shut the American people up, once and for all. Intimidating people is the same as protecting them, and exalting federal agents the same as protecting public safety, apparently.

MONOPOLIZING GUNS

In the wake of 9/11, many pilots called for the right to carry a sidearm to defend their cockpit against terrorists and hijackers. Capt. Steve Luckey, chairman of the Air Line Pilots Association's flight security committee, explained: "The only reason we want lethal force in the cockpit is to provide an opportunity to get the aircraft on the ground. We don't have 911. We can't pull over."[61]

In lieu of permitting pilots to arm themselves, the Bush administration authorized military jets to shoot down hijacked airplanes anywhere over the United States. The TSA also considered creating a toll-free phone number that passengers could call when their planes have been hijacked—and perhaps thereby expedite the shoot-down.[62]

The Bush administration staunchly opposed letting pilots defend their own planes. John Magaw, the first TSA chief, justified keeping pilots unarmed because "if something does happen on that plane, they really need to be in control of that aircraft." Magaw suggested that pilots could rely on "maneuvering [the plane] so it knocks people off balance that are causing the problem."[63]

Instead of permitting armed pilots, the Transportation Department promised to increase the number of federal air marshals and make airport checkpoints reliable. Federal air marshals have been a mixed blessing on many flights, either needlessly intimidating passengers or losing their guns.[64] Though Magaw stressed that "the use of firearms aboard a U.S. aircraft must be limited to those thoroughly trained members of law enforcement," he forgot to mention that newly hired air marshals are no longer required to pass an advanced marksmanship test.[65] And, as for airport checkpoints, stun guns, revolvers, and other weapons continue slipping through on a regular basis.[66]

Congress vetoed the Bush administration's devotion to disarmed pilots. Sen. Zell Miller (D-Ga.) asked: "Will someone please explain to me the logic that says we can trust someone with a Boeing 747 in bad weather, but not with a Glock 9-millimeter?"[67] A pro-armed pilots amendment passed the Senate by a vote of 87 to 6. The November 2002 law creating the Homeland Security Department compelled the TSA to set up a program to train and authorize pilots to carry firearms.

TSA scorned the law. Though it went through the motions of setting up a program, it did so in a way to discourage pilots from participating. Pilot

Tracy Price complained, "The TSA has very intentionally and successfully minimized the number of volunteers through thinly veiled threats and by making the program difficult and threatening to get into."[68]

TSA declared that any pilot who wishes to be a "federal flight deck officer" (FFDO)—meaning someone authorized to carry firearms in the cockpit—must attend a week-long training session, among other hoops and hurdles. The only place the TSA offers the training is in Artesia, New Mexico, four hours from the nearest airport in El Paso, Texas.

Nine months after Congress passed the law, TSA had certified only 44 pilots to pack heat while flying. The *Washington Post* reported in October 2003 that "advocates for pilots who carry guns said the pilots are barred from criticizing the program to the media. The TSA has offered the news media opportunities to interview pilots who are supportive of the program."[69] Brian Darling of the Coalition of Airline Pilots Associations condemned the TSA's slant: "They should not be trotting out federal flight-deck officers to say good things about the program while muzzling pilots who are critical of the program."[70] After grumbling about TSA's policies on armed pilots spilled into the media, a TSA official sent an e-mail warning all FFDO pilots that they were prohibited even from communicating to their congressmen about their concerns about the program.[71] Rep. Mica warned the agency: "Members of Congress will speak to anybody in the program anytime they like without interference from TSA or there will be hell to pay."[72]

TSA is also entangling the program with silly edicts that make it easy to cite pilots for violations. TSA requires pilots who step out of the cockpit during the flight to leave their gun behind in the cockpit, locked in a box. One FFDO pilot who contacted me as I was researching this book related that the TSA recently decreed that when pilots go to the bathroom, "a flight attendant must come and stand in the aisle between first-class seats and the lavatory. No person in first class may get out of their seat and into the aisle while the pilot is using the bathroom. The pilot is not permitted to use the bathroom before checking with a flight attendant and confirming that the bathroom is unoccupied."

Pilots are also concerned that if they fail to follow the new edicts, they could be fined for violating a federal security procedure and lose their pilot's license. The exasperated pilot who contacted me complained that the new rule "has created paranoia among cockpit crews and cabin crews. Big Brother is really watching—Can I go to the bathroom now?"[73] Capt. Dave Mackett, president of the Airline Pilots Security Alliance, says the recent TSA mandates make a pilot's visit to the bathroom "the most threatening time to a flight right now. The TSA has effectively told terrorists our worst fears: Buy a first-class ticket; you don't have to break down the door, just wait until it is opened and rush the cockpit."[74]

Though pilots are prohibited from packing heat if they step out to the john, agents from more than a hundred federal agencies—including the Peace Corps and the Library of Congress—are permitted to keep their guns with them during a flight.[75] Rep. Joe Wilson (R-S.C.) commented: "At every step there has been an effort by the TSA to sabotage the ability of pilots to be armed. There has been one roadblock after another to make it unworkable."[76]

The TSA apparently aims to keep pilots totally dependent on TSA screeners—and on federal air marshals, who fly on fewer than one in ten domestic flights. The TSA acts as if people should only be protected from terrorists in ways that increase government power.

After legions of complaints about the podunk location of the only training site, agency spokesman Hatfield revealed in March 2004 that "the TSA is looking into having a weekly charter flight from Dallas to make it easier for pilots to get" to Artesia, New Mexico.[77]

TSA TRAVEL DELAYS

TSA is making U.S. air travel more uncertain. Shortly after TSA was created, Transportation Secretary Norman Mineta proclaimed a goal that passengers would not have to wait more than ten minutes to clear TSA checkpoints. Mineta hyped the slogan: "No weapons, no waiting."

But delays are mushrooming. TSA security delays in June 2003 at Atlanta Hartsfield airport were up to 90 minutes, and the Seattle-Tacoma airport reported TSA delays of up to two hours.[78] At Los Angeles International Airport, lines sometimes took more than an hour to get through and, over four days' time, a thousand passengers of a single airline missed a flight because of TSA.[79] TSA spokesman Robert Johnson explained that the long delays were due in part to "too many people hitting the airport at one time."[80]

In early November 2003, TSA announced that people flying over the Thanksgiving and Christmas holidays should expect longer checkpoint delays; some airports urged people to arrive at airports at least two hours before domestic flights.[81] Some of the nation's busiest airports had 30 minute delays for TSA checkpoints, though delays in most places were not as bad as feared.[82] The official forecast of long backups meant that millions of people spent more of their time vegetating in airports and less time with families.

Tens of thousands of travelers leaving Las Vegas in early 2004 found themselves out of luck. The *Las Vegas Review-Journal* reported that airport checkpoint delays lasted up to four hours.[83] In fairness, two- and three-hour delays were much more common. The TSA director at the Las Vegas airport, Jim Blair, denied that TSA was to blame for the massive delays.[84]

The TSA quietly dropped its "ten minutes wait" goal in 2003 and now allows the standard for tolerable delays to vary from airport to airport. At the Jacksonville, Florida, airport, TSA set a goal of wait times no longer than 30 minutes.[85] Passengers are currently advised to arrive at John Wayne Airport in Orange County, California two and a half hours before their flights. Lines at the airport in March 2004 took up to an hour and 37 minutes to clear.[86]

On December 27, 2003, the TSA announced a revolutionary reform to speed up airport lines: passengers who caused a magnetometer to alarm when they passed through would henceforth be permitted to empty their pockets or take off a belt buckle or shoes and then try passing through the metal detector again. Prior to this edict, any passenger who set off the alarm was taken aside for intensive hand wanding. The TSA reported that a test found "significant reductions in wanding" as a result of the second-chance option, and that each person not wanded saved three minutes of TSA screeners' time. TSA's Hatfield declared: "It's an effort to increase the efficiency of the security screening process and at the same time, it's a gain for customer service."[87] If this is such a positive change, why did it take TSA wizards so long to make the reform? The TSA did not estimate how many billions of passenger hours were squandered because the agency delayed this obvious step.

The TSA's Soviet-style central command-and-control methods are the source of many delays. TSA airport directors (formally known as federal security directors, or FSDs) often have little or no influence over how many screeners work at their airports. GAO noted: "Initially, TSA headquarters determined screener-staffing levels for all airports without actively seeking input from FSDs." Most TSA airport directors GAO interviewed said that "they had limited authority to respond to airport specific staffing needs, such as reacting to fluctuations in daily and/or seasonal passenger flow." TSA airport directors also have little or no control over who is doing the screening. They complain that they have no "role in reviewing applications, interviewing applicants, or making hiring decisions."[88] Many, if not most, large airports have fewer screeners than TSA authorizes because of TSA's laggardly hiring and training process.

The continual staffing shortages undermine TSA work ethics and discipline. One TSA airport director told GAO that "the lengthy hiring process limited his ability to address screener performance issues, such as absenteeism or tardiness, and contributed to screener complacency because screeners were aware that they were unlikely to be terminated due to staffing shortages."[89] Although federalizing airport security jobs was supposed to almost automatically make Americans safe, TSA employees are already showing the character traits that have made government workers the butt of humor for hundreds of years.

CONSPIRING AGAINST COMPETENCE

The 2001 act that created TSA specified that after November 2004, airports can opt out, requesting that private firms provide airport security instead of the TSA. The federal government would still be monitoring the standards and paying the personnel, but the screeners would no longer be federal agents.

The 2001 act also specified that five airports would be permitted to carry out pilot projects relying on privately employed screeners. Unfortunately, the TSA is sabotaging the pilot projects. The TSA prohibits private companies from providing better training to their screeners than the TSA gives its own employees: private companies were specifically prohibited from giving additional hours of training to their screening personnel. The *Washington Post* noted that the companies running the pilot projects have been "frustrated that the TSA denied their requests to train screeners to identify bombs and interview suspicious passengers, and to bring up to speed screener supervisors, who hadn't been trained by the TSA."[90] TSA spokesman Turmail explained that the agency prohibited private companies from launching innovative security techniques without TSA approval because "we have an obligation to make sure all security procedures are well coordinated."[91] The TSA is more vigilant in undermining potential competition than in monitoring the competence of its own screeners. *Airport Security Report* concluded that TSA's restrictions "effectively gutted" the federally mandated test of private screeners, "rendering any comparison between private and federal screeners problematic." The TSA required that "the five pilot projects must be operated in the same manner as all TSA-operated screening locations."[92] Perhaps the TSA considers it a federal crime to treat airline passengers better than the TSA does. The General Accounting Office warned in November 2003 that a pending TSA report on the private pilot projects would be of little value because the TSA does not keep reliable data on its own screeners' performance.[93]

Stephen Van Beek of Airports Council International, a lobby group for U.S. airports, commented: "One of our great criticisms of TSA is they have not set a standard for customer service. That's probably the most frustrating thing for air-ports."[94] More than a hundred airports have expressed interest in privatizing screening. Passenger service and screening have gone significantly more smoothly at five airports with private screeners than at many TSA-controlled airports.

Some airports are concerned that, if they choose to opt out, the TSA may prohibit them from hiring additional screeners in order to expedite passenger flow. This would simply perpetuate the problem of central control. And, as Rep. Mica observed, "The ineptness of TSA to staff these airports is legendary already. They'll never get it right because it's big government."[95]

GAO issued its report on private vs. government screeners in April 2004. The report, as summarized by *Airport Security Report,* found that the TSA pro-vided little opportunity "to demonstrate innovations, achieve efficiencies and implement initiatives to go beyond the minimum regulatory requirements."[96] The private companies were also hogtied because the TSA prohibited them from hiring as many screeners as they would have liked. Yet, despite the restrictions, the private pilot programs still found many ways to upgrade. As Rep. Mica ob-served, the airports with private security did find better ways, including "100 percent cross-training of security screeners; hiring of a mix of full-time and part-time screeners; the provision of recurrent training locally; development of a com-puter learning lab; pre-screening of all candidates to ensure they meet minimum requirements set by TSA." Mica noted that some of these innovations "are now being implemented at all federal-screening airports. This is not a coincidence."[97]

There is no reason to expect private companies to provide faultless airport security. Yet, while many people see the success of the 9/11 hijackers as proof of the failure of trusting private companies to run security, 9/11 was a gross failure by the FAA to fulfill its duty to the American public. Before 9/11, the federal government was already responsible for airport checkpoint security. The FAA did an abysmal job, ignoring congressional laws and deadlines to im-pose higher standards to safeguard travelers.

CONCLUSION

In April 2004, the Homeland Security IG and a private consultant study both submitted reports to Congress on the quality of airport screeners that were "devastating" in their verdict, according to the *Washington Post.* (The reports were confidential.) The *Post* noted that "the two reports concluded that there is little difference between the current system and the system that was in place be-fore the TSA existed."[98] Rep. Peter DeFazio (D-Ore.), the ranking Democrat on the House Aviation Subcommittee, complained, "The failure rates [by airport screeners] are comparable from 1987 to today."[99] Homeland Security Inspector General Clark Kent Ervin testified that both TSA screeners and the screeners at the five airports with privatized security performed "equally poorly" in response to covert tests. Ervin said that the "result was not unexpected, considering the degree of TSA involvement in hiring, deploying, and training the pilot screeners." Ervin warned that the "TSA needs to develop measurable criteria to evaluate both contractor and federal screeners properly."[100]

The latest reports make stark that the TSA has produced little except long lines and the pointless harassment of millions of Americans. But at least the reports spurred agency brass to continue zealously working to prevent Americans from being misled by the facts. TSA spokesman Hatfield went on the NBC *Today Show* and brushed off the IG's statement, explaining that "the point of the matter here is that you hear these sort of inflammatory statements like they are performing poorly or the system is broken. It doesn't get to the heart of the matter, which is the system was broken on 9/11, and we've taken extraordinary steps to make it better." Hatfield pointed out that "the encouraging news from the report yesterday" is that the "performance levels are at a higher level that [sic] they've ever been."[101]

Bush bragged in 2002 that the law that created the TSA "greatly enhanced the protections for America's passengers and goods."[102] The TSA has always been profoundly irresponsible and dishonest. Rather than making Americans safe from terrorists, the TSA has made them prey to federal agents. There is no reason to expect the agency to turn over a new leaf.

The TSA has no liability to any American citizen. The TSA views itself as entitled to wreak as much damage on Americans' travel plans as it sees fit. Rep. Mica nailed the issue: "TSA created a monolithic bureaucracy that has shown an inability to adapt and keep pace with the ever-changing demands of the aviation industry."[103] As airline consultant Michael Boyd observed, "The TSA is a threat to the nation because it puts up a fraudulent smokescreen of security, wasting billions that should be spent on professional, anticipative security. Unless and until the TSA is replaced by a professionally staffed, politically isolated, and entirely accountable security system, we're easy meat for terrorism."[104]

The follies of the TSA are a warning to Americans not to expect safety from mindless, arbitrary power. The TSA offers proof after proof of the fraudulent nature of the federal security blanket.

CHAPTER TWELVE

John Ashcroft,
King of "Ordered Liberty"

What we are defending is what generations before us fought for and defended: a nation that is a standard, a beacon. . . . A land of justice. A land of liberty.

—*Attorney General John Ashcroft, November 15, 2003*[1]

Attorney General John Ashcroft declared that he found his "calling" after 9/11.[2] Ashcroft relies on piety and protestations of righteousness to debunk all criticisms of federal conduct in the war on terrorism.

In 1997, Ashcroft vigorously opposed a Clinton administration surveillance proposal, warning against granting government "the Orwellian capability to listen at will and in real time to our communications across the Web." Ashcroft declared that there was "no reason to hand Big Brother the keys to unlock our e-mail diaries, open our ATM records, read our medical records."[3]

But 9/11 made government absolutely trustworthy—at least in Ashcroft's eyes. Or perhaps the federal government had become pure as driven snow on January 20, 2001, when Ashcroft was sworn in as attorney general.

Ashcroft explained his vision for America in 2003: "Ordered liberty means neither license nor Big Brother. Rather, the concept embraces liberty and security as complementary, mutually reinforcing values. . . . The concept of ordered liberty acknowledges that for liberty to thrive in America, America must be secure."[4] Thus, whatever the government does to increase security is automatically pro-liberty.

Ashcroft now aims to persuade Americans that the more power the government possesses, the more secure the people's liberties become. *National Journal* reported that a key "basic tenet" of the "Ashcroft doctrine" is that "a powerful government is a prerequisite for real liberty."[5]

The key to Ashcroft's "ordered liberty" is that the government is entitled to near-absolute power over anyone accused of violating any law. Ashcroft declared in June 2003 that "when people violate the law, they don't have a right to remain free."[6] Ashcroft was not talking about major felonies. Instead, any violation of the law is apparently sufficient to nullify a person's freedom.

CONSTITUTIONAL BEATINGS

In a speech to Memphis police on September 18, 2003, Ashcroft boasted: "On my watch, the Department of Justice will perform its duties in a manner that reflects the noblest ideals and highest standards set by the United States Constitution."[7] Ashcroft's concept of nobility is a bit out of the mainstream, since it apparently includes federal employees beating people who have been convicted of no crime.

Nothing better exemplifies "Ashcroft freedom" than the great roundup after 9/11. William Blackstone, the eighteenth-century British legal philosopher who profoundly influenced the Founding Fathers, warned, "To bereave a man of life, or by violence to confiscate his estate, without accusation or trial, would be so gross and notorious an act of despotism, as must at once convey the alarm of tyranny throughout the whole nation; but confinement of the person, by secretly hurrying him to jail, where his sufferings are unknown or forgotten, is a less public, a less striking, and therefore a more dangerous engine of arbitrary government."[8]

But for Ashcroft, mass secret arrests are the apex of the new freedom. Secretly locking people up and holding them without formal charges is the same conduct that the U.S. government condemns when perpetrated by foreign regimes. But when Ashcroft & Co. do the same thing, it only proves the government's devotion to liberty via security.

After 9/11, it was understandable that the federal government would cast a broad net to round up suspects at a time of great fear of a second wave of terrorist attacks. It was understandable that the government would target and interrogate many people who would not have formerly aroused suspicion. But the post-9/11 roundup of more than 1,200 Arabs, Muslims, and others quickly became a profoundly dishonest political circus. And when complaints arose about the treatment of the detainees, Ashcroft was indignant that anyone dared criticize the government at such a time. In Senate testimony on December 6, 2001, Ashcroft denounced critics whose "bold declarations of so-called fact have quickly dissolved, upon inspection, into vague conjecture." Ashcroft thundered: "Each action taken by the Department of Justice . . . is carefully drawn to target a *narrow class of individuals— terrorists.*"[9]

In reality, the Justice Department Inspector General found that the only thing necessary for a Muslim or Arab illegal immigrant to be considered a "suspected terrorist" was to be encountered by FBI agents in New York or New Jersey carrying out a 9/11 investigation. Arab students were locked up as suspected terrorists for working at pizza parlors (in violation of their student visas), and a Pakistani immigrant was jailed after attracting attention because he and his Queens housemates failed to cut the grass and hung their underwear to dry on the fence. One Muslim was arrested because "he had taken a roll of film to be developed and the film had multiple pictures of the World Trade Center on it but no other Manhattan sites."[10]

A month after 9/11, allegations were already swirling that detainees were being beaten and prevented from contacting a lawyer. Ashcroft announced on October 16: "I would be happy to hear from individuals if there are any alleged abuses of individuals, because that is not the way we do business."[11] He promised that "we will respect the constitutional rights and we will respect the dignity of individuals."[12] Ashcroft's invitation fell on deaf ears, since many of the people being abused were locked away in solitary confinement.

At a November 27, 2001 press conference, Ashcroft proclaimed that it is "simply not true" that "detainees are not able to be represented by an attorney or to contact their families."[13] Ashcroft repeated the claim during his December 6, 2001 Senate testimony: "Our efforts have been crafted carefully to avoid infringing on constitutional rights while saving American lives. . . . All persons being detained have the right to contact their lawyers and their families."[14]

This was hokum. The Justice Department Inspector General reported in June 2003 that many of the detainees were held incommunicado for weeks after their arrest and prevented from contacting lawyers or family members. Lawyers hired by family members were repeatedly prohibited from meeting with detainees and wrongly told that their clients were not at prisons when the lawyers visited. The Supreme Court ruled in 1991 that "absent extraordinary circumstances," a failure to charge someone "within 48 hours of the warrantless arrest . . . violates the Fourth Amendment."[15]

The Inspector General reported evidence that prisoners were physically and mentally abused, quoting one federal prison guard who said he "witnessed officers 'slam' inmates against walls and stated this was a common practice before the [prison] began videotaping the detainees."[16] The FBI made almost no effort to investigate charges that prison guards had beaten prisoners.

The IG investigation was often thwarted by federal prison officials. Much of the evidence of the treatment of prisoners had supposedly been destroyed, especially videotapes which prison officials insisted had been erased.

The Inspector General's June 2003 revelation of abuses infuriated Ashcroft's team. Deputy Attorney General Larry Thompson sent a letter to the IG complaining that it was "unfair to criticize the conduct of my members of staff during this period."[17] Accurate criticisms by the Inspector General were apparently a far greater offense than Ashcroft's perennial bogus statements. Justice Department spokeswoman Barbara Comstock declared: "We make no apologies for finding every legal way possible to protect the American public from further terrorist attacks."[18] But the IG report contained example after example of federal officials illegally denying detainees rights that the Supreme Court declared that anyone arrested and locked up must have.

Three days after the IG report's release, Ashcroft made a rare appearance before the House Judiciary Committee and announced that the United States was in an "ideological war" against the terrorists. Despite the IG's stark findings, Ashcroft continued to deny that the Justice Department had violated anyone's legal rights: "In all of the conduct of the activities of the Justice Department, we have not violated the law, and we will not violate the law. We will uphold the law."[19] Perhaps people were supposed to conclude that unchecked government power is no threat to freedom because government agents only beat people who are suspected of crimes. And as long as you are not doing anything wrong, you will not be beaten, unless the government makes an innocent mistake.

The following month, speaking in Portland, Oregon, Ashcroft declared: "No person has been detained by the Department of Justice without filing charges. No person has been detained without access to a lawyer."[20] Many of the detainees were held and interrogated vigorously for long periods before being permitted to get a lawyer. Letting someone hire a lawyer only after they have been bludgeoned into pleading guilty was not what the Founding Fathers had in mind in the Sixth Amendment of the Bill of Rights.

At the same time as he continued to deny any federal wrongdoing, Ashcroft milked the mass roundup of 9/11 suspects to vindicate law enforcement in the war on terrorism. In a speech to a National Restaurant Association convention in Washington (a noncombative audience), Ashcroft bragged that "we have deported more than 515 individuals with links to the September 11th investigation."[21] Almost two years after it became obvious that the mass roundup after 9/11 was largely a farce, Ashcroft hyped hundreds of false accusations against foreigners as proof of the government's devotion and competence. If the feds had any reason to believe the deportees were actually terrorists, they almost certainly would have prosecuted them with great fanfare. Ashcroft has never explained how the punishment and deportation of people wrongfully suspected of 9/11 connections makes America safer.

The IG did not end its investigation after the June 2003 report. An IG agent visiting a federal prison in New York discovered rows of videotapes in a storage room that showed the treatment of the 9/11 detainees. The IG issued another report in December 2003 revealing that some federal prison guards at the Brooklyn Metropolitan Detention Center "slammed and bounced detainees against the wall, twisted their arms and hands in painful ways, stepped on their leg restraint chains and punished them by keeping them restrained for long periods of time."[22]

Shortly after 9/11, prison guards hung a t-shirt with an American flag and the motto "These Colors Don't Run" on the wall of the room where detainees were checked into the prison. The t-shirt became covered with bloodstains. According to one lieutenant at the prison, some stains appeared to be from "a couple of bloody noses smudged in a row, and other stains looked like someone with blood in his mouth spit on the t-shirt." Videotapes show many detainees' faces being pushed into the t-shirt or held next to the t-shirt. The tapes also revealed that some federal Bureau of Prison staffers lied to IG officials. The report noted that "we saw that some staff members engaged in the very conduct they specifically denied in their interviews." The report noted that "three staff members stated in interviews that they did not press compliant detainees against the wall because that would be inappropriate. In viewing videotapes, however, we saw these same officers pressing compliant detainees into walls. . . . Another former officer told us he never saw any officer bend detainees' wrists or pull their thumbs, but in one videotape we saw him bend a compliant detainee's fingers in a way that seemed very painful and did not appear to serve any correctional purpose."[23]

The prison videotapes had many suspicious gaps. The report noted that "many tapes start or stop in the middle of detainees' escorts. There also are no tapes from some 'use of force' incidents, even though these tapes should have been preserved for two years under [Bureau of Prisons] policy. Officials could not explain these omissions." The report added that the prison "officers were cognizant of the presence of the cameras." Inspector General Glenn Fine commented, "If these incidents are an indication of what was done in front of the camera, what may have occurred without them?"[24]

How many people do federal guards have to beat before John Ashcroft admits that someone's rights have been violated? Justice Department chief spokesman Mark Corallo issued a statement: "It is unfortunate that the alleged misconduct of a few employees detracts from the fine work done by the correctional personnel at MDC [Metropolitan Detention Center] and around the nation, who conducted themselves professionally and appropriately in dealing with the vast majority of the 762 alien detainees."[25] The press release stated that the Bureau of Prisons was being directed to review the IG report "and take appropriate action at the conclusion of their review" and that federal attorneys were reviewing the report to see "whether any prosecutions are appropriate."

Americans probably have not yet learned of even the tip of the iceberg of federal agents' abuses in the war on terrorism. In the vast majority of encounters between feds and suspects, there are no annoying videotapes to document possible misconduct. Yet, there is no reason to presume that Ashcroft's protestations of purity are any more credible regarding federal surveillance or other crackdowns than they have been regarding the treatment of detainees.

If a group of radical environmentalists had taken a bunch of federal employees hostage and beat and bloodied them, Ashcroft would have been the first to denounce the culprits and demand the harshest punishments. Yet, when it is government officials doing the beating, it will likely be treated as a harmless error and something that can be quickly eclipsed by a few diversionary high-profile media events.

DEFINING LIBERTY DOWN

Championing the Patriot Act requires redefining American freedom. Ashcroft announced in an August 19, 2003, kickoff speech for a national tour to promote the Patriot Act: "Our efforts have been rewarded by the trust of the American people. . . . Ninety one percent of Americans understand that the Patriot Act has not affected their civil rights or the civil rights of their families."[26]

Ashcroft was contorting the poll data. The poll, taken by the Fox News Network (the most pro-Bush network), asked people: "To the best of your knowledge have you or a member of your family had your civil rights affected by the Patriot Act?" The poll asked "to the best of your knowledge"—which Ashcroft converted into "understand."

The government first keeps the public ignorant and then invokes their ignorance to prove people are well-governed. Simply because 91 percent of respondents might not be aware of government intrusions proves that the government is not violating people's rights.

The Justice Department is being very secretive about how the powers of the Patriot Act are being used and how many people have been affected. The Patriot Act effectively empowers the FBI to vacuum up Americans' email. With Carnivore, an e-mail wiretapping system, the FBI can easily get a search warrant to track a single person's e-mail activity. After the FBI compels an Internet service provider to attach its Carnivore black box to its computer system, an FBI agent can hit a single button and automatically copy all of the e-mail of all of the customers of that Internet service provider.[27] Carnivore is custom-made for overreaching—and "accidently" violating the rights of vast numbers of citizens. Despite the FBI's record of gross abuses with catch-all surveillance schemes, Congress has done no oversight as to how Carnivore is being used.

The Patriot Act not only greatly expands federal surveillance powers but also makes it far more difficult for citizens and members of Congress to learn who is being surveilled, what methods are being used, and how many innocent Americans' words and lives are being swept up in covert information dragnets. The number of secret wiretaps approved by the Foreign Intelligence Surveillance Court (FISA) has almost doubled since the Patriot Act was enacted.[28] This court, which never holds public hearings, whose proceedings are almost all kept secret in perpetuity, and which never allows defense attorneys to challenge its surveillance approvals, is very popular with prosecutors. In 2003, the feds got three times as many wiretap orders from the Foreign Intelligence Surveillance Court than from federal judges in criminal cases. The ACLU's Timothy Edgar commented that the surge in secret FISA surveillance warrants for wiretaps illustrates that "the Bush administration is using spy-hunting tools to sidestep the basic protections that exist in criminal cases."[29]

The Patriot Act also makes it much easier for FBI agents to commandeer private information via National Security Letters. These subpoena letters compel individuals, businesses, and other institutions to surrender confidential or proprietary information without a court order—including records on bank accounts, Internet usage, phone calls, e-mail logs, lists of purchases, and so on. There is no judicial oversight of this power, and each FBI field office is entitled to issue its own National Security Letters. Congress expanded this power in November 2003, acceding to a Bush administration request to permit FBI agents to use National Security Letters to seize citizens' financial records.

Section 215 of the Patriot Act empowers federal agents to get warrants to vacuum up library records, bookstore records, business records, phone records—just about any type of records imaginable. In order to get a Section 215 subpoena, a federal agent has to fill out a request notifying the Foreign Intelligence Surveillance Court that the information is "sought for an authorized intelligence investigation."[30] The G-man does not have to provide any evidence of suspected criminal behavior. Instead, all that is necessary is to submit a "push-button form" to a court which almost always grants the government's request for search warrants and other intrusions.

For both Section 215 searches and National Security Letter subpoenas, the government muzzles those it searches, threatening five years in prison for disclosing a search. The government gags its targets and then brags that the lack of complaints proves the searches are not a problem.

The Patriot Act unrolls a red carpet for federal agents to search people's homes and offices. The only thing necessary to get a judge to sign off on a secret intrusion is a G-man's assertion that there is "reasonable cause to believe that providing immediate notification of the execution of the warrant may have an adverse result."[31] There are cases in which secret searches are necessary and justified, but the Patriot Act's standard for such searches is little more than the whim of a government employee.

Perhaps Ashcroft believes that if someone does not know that his house or his e-mail was secretly searched, the government has not violated his rights. Perhaps some conservatives believe that government intrusions and government surveillance are no violation of freedom because no one has a right to do what the government does not approve. Government spying on people is also supposedly irrelevant to freedom because it is assumed that government would never abuse the information it compiles in people's dossiers. Besides, after 9/11, people who want to hide things from the government are "with the terrorists," not "with us."

Despite the best efforts of Justice Department propagandists, opposition to the Patriot Act surged across the United States. By summer 2003, 200 cities, towns, and other jurisdictions had passed resolutions condemning the Patriot Act. A CBS News poll showed that more than half of Americans were "very concerned" or "somewhat concerned" about "losing your civil liberties as a result of recent measures enacted by the Bush administration to fight terrorism."[32]

THE PATRIOT ACT SALVATION TOUR

In response to rising criticism, Ashcroft began traveling around the country in June and July 2003, talking to groups of federal agents and prosecutors and heaping praise on their good deeds. In August, the Bush administration sent Ashcroft on a Patriot Act Salvation Tour. The purpose of the trip was to "talk to the American people directly," according to a Justice Department spokesman.[33] The "American people" turned out to be mostly local police and prosecutors.

At the launch of the tour, in a speech at a conservative think tank in Washington on August 19, 2003, Ashcroft proclaimed: "We have built a new ethos of justice."[34] At the time of this comment, the Justice Department's Bureau of Prisons was continuing to obstruct the IG's investigation into the beatings of prisoners. Everywhere he traveled, Ashcroft portrayed the Patriot Act as the salvation of American freedom. Ashcroft told Philadelphia police that without the Patriot Act, "America will pay the price in lost liberty."[35] Ashcroft told Minneapolis police that Americans are "freer today than at any time in the history of human freedom. . . . The lives and liberties of all Americans are protected by the Patriot Act."[36]

In speech after speech, Ashcroft angrily denounced critics' "hysteria." Ashcroft first withholds the evidence of what the feds are doing and then insists that any criticism is unfair because it is uninformed. Instead of disclosing how new powers are being used, Ashcroft sneered, "Some people cannot start their cars and say, 'Oh, it's the Patriot Act.'"[37]Rep. John Conyers, the senior Democrat on the House Judiciary Committee, declared that Ashcroft's tour appeared to violate federal law "preventing the use of Justice Department money for publicity or propaganda purposes not authorized by Congress."[38]

The Justice Department and Secret Service tightly controlled the media when Ashcroft came to town. Justice Department spokeswoman Barbara Comstock explained that Ashcroft would speak only to TV interviewers in order to explain "key facts directly to the American people and not having as much of a filter from people who are already invested in having a different view of it."[39] Comstock complained: "In some cases we can look at a local newspaper and some people have reported on it over and over and it hasn't been very accurate. Some news writers on this tend to be a little more editorial than news."[40] Perhaps the Justice Department wanted to make sure that Ashcroft was not exposed to people with good reading skills or whose memory extended beyond the last 24-hour news cycle.

The *Idaho Statesman* noted of Ashcroft's appearance, "Ashcroft's speech was closed to the public, and Ashcroft's office refused to allow Idaho newspaper reporters time to ask questions. Ashcroft did give on-camera interviews to local television stations and spent about 10 minutes with The Associated Press."[41]

Howard Altman, the editor of the *Philadelphia City Paper,* was forcibly blocked from attending an Ashcroft mini–press conference after his spiel to Philly police at the National Constitution Center. A Secret Service agent informed Altman that Ashcroft "is not talking to print. Only talking to television." Altman called the Justice Department for a comment on the policy but got no response. He was not surprised because, as he noted, "The Patriot Act allows the feds to listen into calls. It doesn't say anything about returning them."[42]

The Society of Professional Journalists complained to Ashcroft on September 13 that "the following ground rules have been enforced at your recent appearances in support of the Patriot Act: while print reporters are allowed access to the formal event, one-on-one opportunities are offered only to local broadcast outlets; protesters are kept outside the event; and public access is conditioned on agreement with your position on the Act."[43]

The Patriot Act Salvation Tour was akin to a king traveling through the provinces, ensconced amidst his underlings, speaking to audiences stuffed to the rafters with people beholden to government. Perhaps Ashcroft believed that to take questions after his pronouncements would have been like Moses, after he came down from Mt. Sinai, inviting listeners to debate the 10 Commandments. Or maybe Ashcroft's Salvation Tour appearances were not open to the public to avoid having his speeches interrupted by derisive laughter.

The tour backfired, generating more criticism than adulation. Intense controversy arose over the Patriot Act provision that entitles federal agents to secretly round up the records of library users and bookstore customers. The Justice Department sought to squelch criticism by announcing that the feds had not used the Section 215 search power in any cases.

This was a great surprise, because a University of Illinois survey of librarians in 2002 reported that federal or local lawmen had visited almost 10 percent of the nation's public libraries "seeking September 11–related information about patron reading habits."[44] Some libraries have been pressured to "voluntarily" give patron records to the FBI, according to the ACLU.[45] Carla Hayden, president of the American Library Association, noted that "in March 2003, Justice Department spokesman Mark Corallo said that libraries had become a logical target of surveillance."[46] The feds may be relying on National Security Letters to snare library records instead of Section 215 subpoenas, according to information Ashcroft provided to the House Judiciary Committee. The Justice Department's "zero search" revelation was also mystifying because its Patriot Act website, http://www.lifeandliberty.gov/, portrayed Section 215 as one of the most important tools in fighting terrorism.

THE FREEDOM LOOPHOLE

In a January 2004 speech at an international forum in Davos, Switzerland, Ashcroft declared: "Corruption saps the legitimacy of democratic governments. In its extreme forms, corruption even threatens democracy itself, because democracy lives on trust, and corruption destroys trust."[47] Ashcroft appealed to the elite audience's idealism: "With each prosecution of a corrupt government official, we reinforce the principle that the purpose of government is to serve the people."[48]

Ashcroft's rhetoric would be uplifting, excepting the source. Each time Ashcroft falsely testified to Congress that the post-9/11 detainees have not been abused or been deprived of legal rights, his violation of his oath to tell the truth could have earned him a prison sentence. The Justice Department launched a high-profile prosecution of home decorator superstar Martha Stewart in large part because she allegedly made bogus statements to federal investigators regarding the sale of stock. Ashcroft's bogus statements, by sanctifying the growing abuse of power, pose much greater danger for America. Yet no one suggested that Ashcroft should receive Martha Stewart treatment. (Ashcroft would likely deny intentionally misleading Congress.)

The usual penalty for overstaying a visa in the United States is deportation; in rare cases, violators are hit with 90 days in jail. Ashcroft's false testimony to Congress could be far more significant in the eyes of the law than were the offenses of the vast majority of people the feds rounded up after 9/11.

Likewise, the federal prison guards who beat detainees and the prison officials who lied to IG investigators were guilty of far more serious offenses than the vast majority of 9/11 detainees. Lying to a federal official carries a prison term of up to three years. Beating prisoners can result in convictions for violating the victims' civil rights and can result in several years in prison.[49] Yet, the Justice Department seems to be shrugging off the evidence the IG provided of Justice officials' wrongdoing.

Ashcroft's personal record is also something that should (but doesn't) curb his righteousness.

The Federal Election Commission in December 2003 levied a $37,000 fine on Ashcroft's unsuccessful 2000 Senate reelection campaign for four violations of federal campaign law. Ashcroft's campaign treasurer did not even contest the fine.[50] As of early May 2004, the Public Integrity Section of the Justice Department was investigating whether Ashcroft may have personally committed criminal offenses during his reelection campaign.[51]

Nor does Ashcroft have a spotless record as far as obeying explicit orders from a federal judge. One of the Justice Department's greatest courtroom antiterrorism successes occurred in the Detroit prosecution of an alleged cell of Arab terrorists. Justice Department lawyers persuaded Youssef Hmimssa, who was charged with credit card and other fraud charges in three states, to become a government witness against three Arabs arrested in Michigan after 9/11. Hmimssa was the crucial witness in snaring convictions of two of the accused on terrorism charges. (Two defendants were convicted of conspiring to support terrorism.) Defense lawyers charged that Hmimssa was lying. The *Detroit News* noted that Hmimssa was "a self-described scam artist and crook."[52] On the day after Hmimssa finished testifying, Ashcroft publicly declared his cooperation had been "a critical tool" in fighting terrorism and that "his testimony has been of value, substantial value." This was the second time Ashcroft publicly commented on the case. After the first time, federal judge Gerald Rosen issued a gag order on defense attorneys and all Justice Department officials. In October 2002, in a closed court session, Rosen warned Deputy Attorney General Larry Thompson: "If there are any more violations by the government, I will impose sanctions, which may include a request to the Office of Professional Responsibility to investigate."

On December 15, 2003, Ashcroft was formally sanctioned by the judge. Ashcroft sent a letter of apology to the judge, notifying him that he had "communicated to my staff our need to be more careful when including references to ongoing cases when drafting remarks."[53] The Justice Department had submitted a brief to Rosen explaining why Ashcroft should not be called into court for his breach: "Compelling the attorney general's appearance to address the defendants' allegations . . . is inadvisable because it would likely serve only to chill legitimate public briefings [by Ashcroft] in the future."[54] The judge could have held Ashcroft in criminal contempt for violating the original gag order but he let the attorney general off easy.

The Justice Department's Detroit victory proved fleeting. After the jury verdict, evidence surfaced that federal prosecutors had withheld from defense attorneys a key letter charging that Hmimssa was lying. The Justice

Department launched a formal investigation into possible misconduct by its lead prosecutor, Assistant U.S. Attorney Richard Convertino.[55] A few weeks later, Convertino sued Attorney General John Ashcroft, charging him with "gross mismanagement" in the war on terrorism. Convertino said that the Justice Department suffered from a "lack of support and cooperation, lack of effective assistance [to prosecutors], lack of resources and intradepartmental infighting" in handling terrorism cases."[56] The FBI also got a post-trial bloody nose as "investigators swooped down on the Detroit FBI office after Marwan Farhat, 34, an illegal immigrant and convicted drug dealer, accused an FBI agent of directing him to steal mail from Arab terrorism suspects and failing to follow through on a pledge to give Farhat 25 percent of any money confiscated as a result," as the *Philadelphia Inquirer* reported.[57] Judge Rosen was considering overturning the convictions because of the government's misconduct.

CONCLUSION

In his December 6, 2001, Senate Judiciary Committee testimony, Ashcroft denounced "those who scare peace-loving people with phantoms of lost liberty," claiming that their efforts "encourage people of good will to remain silent in the face of evil."[58] In reality, it is Ashcroft who, by seeking to silence criticism, aims to make people acquiesce to the government's evil.

Under Ashcroft, the "presumption of innocence" has been transferred from citizens to the government. Now it is government officials who are entitled to avoid saying anything that might incriminate the government.

The only way to reconcile the Patriot Act with freedom is to assume that unjustified government intrusions into people's lives are irrelevant to freedom. Because Bush and Ashcroft proclaim that they are defending freedom, then all of the government's methods, tactics, and abuses automatically become pro-freedom. Due process is now redundant. Ashcroft's own purity is the only safeguard American freedom needs—or deserves.

Perhaps the key to "Ashcroft freedom" is that only the government has the right to break the law. For Ashcroft, the key for preserving freedom is for people to respect the government, no matter what the government does. The government remains trustworthy, regardless of how many lies it tells or how many people it beats. The reputation of the government remains inviolable, regardless of how many rights it violates. For Ashcroft, there may be few greater threats to American freedom than to allow Americans to discover what the federal government is doing.

CHAPTER THIRTEEN

Antiterrorism
Abuses and Frauds

After 9/11, as long as politicians promised security, they could do almost anything. While the Bush administration portrays the war on terrorism as the president's noblest priority, the war itself continues to be a mixture of frauds, follies, and power-grabs.

MISSING THE WATCH LISTS

The feds have struggled unsuccessfully for many years to compile a list of terrorists and terrorist suspects. Law enforcement failed to stop the first bombing of the World Trade Center in 1993 in part because two of the people involved in the bombing "were on an FBI watch list but still managed to get visas because the State Department and the old Immigration and Naturalization Service didn't have access to the FBI data."[1] Before 9/11, the Central Intelligence Agency neglected to add the names of two known Al Qaeda members onto the terrorist watch lists until after they entered the United States and got in position to wreak havoc.

Defending against incoming terrorists was among the most neglected aspects of national defense. The 9/11 Commission noted in January 2004: "Between 1992 and Sept. 11, 2001, we have not found any signs that intelligence, law enforcement or border-inspection services sought to acquire, develop or disseminate systematic information about terrorist groups' travel and passport practices."[2]

Even after 9/11, the feds moved like molasses on a cold winter day to create one good watch list. In his State of the Union address on January 28, 2003, Bush announced the creation of a new federal bureau, the Terrorist Threat Integration Center, "to merge and analyze all threat information in a single location. Our government must have the very best information possible, and we will use it to make sure the right people are in the right places to protect our citizens."[3] The promise buffed up a speech otherwise fixated on the Iraq menace. On March 25, 2003, Bush notified congressional leaders that the Department of Homeland Security "will work to virtually consolidate or link watch lists from multiple agencies and create a homeland security portal for users at all levels of government."[4] However, little or nothing was done.

GAO warned in April 2003 that the government's terrorist watch lists continued to be "overly complex, unnecessarily inefficient and potentially ineffective."[5] Nine different agencies maintained their own lists. Unfortunately, they used incompatible software—thereby making it very difficult for agencies to coordinate their national defense efforts. GAO also found that agencies continued to hoard information, thereby preventing other federal agencies (and local and state law enforcement) from learning about potential terrorists.

In August 2003, the Homeland Security Department conceded that it had done little on the watch lists. Homeland Security Department official Gordon Johndroe explained, "The administration is getting closer to the end of its planning process [for combining the watch lists]. But this is a very complicated issue, and we're not going to rush something out that isn't completely effective."[6] Sen. Joe Lieberman (D-Conn.) denounced the lack of progress as "an intolerable failure that exposes the American public to unacceptable risk."[7]

On September 16, Bush issued Homeland Security Presidential Directive #6, ordering the creation of a single terrorist watch list in a new federal bureau, the Terrorism Screening Center.[8] Attorney General John Ashcroft, Secretary of Homeland Security Tom Ridge, Secretary of State Colin Powell, FBI Director Robert Mueller, and Director of Central Intelligence George Tenet were all part of the big announcement. The Justice Department proclaimed, "Today's action marks another significant step forward in President George W. Bush's strategy to protect America's communities and families by detecting, disrupting and disabling terrorist threats."[9] Ashcroft promised, "The Terrorist Screening Center will provide 'one-stop shopping' so that every federal anti-terrorist screener is working off the same page—whether it's an airport screener, an embassy official issuing visas overseas, or an FBI agent on the street."[10] The Justice Department press release announced that the new center will be "operational by December 1, 2003."[11]

Despite the grandiose opening of the Terrorist Screening Center in Crystal City, Virginia, just across the Potomac from Washington, little or nothing changed. The *Wall Street Journal* reported in early 2004 that according to FBI officials, "the center has yet to make any headway integrating all the lists."[12] One Democratic congressional staffer commented, "In reality, all that's been created is a hollow box."[13]

The dismal condition of the U.S. terrorism watch list was illustrated at Christmastime 2003, when the U.S. government, working with the French, blocked three Air France flights to the United States because there were six passenger names that matched names on the U.S. terrorism watch list. The passengers were detained and interrogated. But, as the *Wall Street Journal* noted, "According to French officials, what they uncovered wasn't an international terrorist plot, but a huge case of mistaken identities: one name matching that of the leader of a Tunisian-based terror group turned out to be that of a child. Another 'terrorist' was a Welsh insurance agent. Another was an elderly Chinese woman who once ran a restaurant in Paris. The remaining three were French citizens."[14] The *Journal* noted that federal "agencies are continuing to work from at least 12 different, sometimes incompatible, often uncoordinated and technologically archaic databases."[15]

On March 12, Donna Bucella, the director of the Terrorist Screening Center, testified to Congress that the database for the watch list would not be fully functional and accessible until the end of 2004. The Pentagon is refusing to turn over its own watch list of names, so the final product may continue to have gaping holes.[16]

MONEY MUFFS

The Patriot Act, in the name of antiterrorism, greatly increased the feds' power to investigate American's financial affairs. As *Newsweek* reported, "Law-enforcement agencies can submit the name of any suspect to the Treasury Department, which then orders financial institutions across the country to search their records for any matches. If they get a 'hit'—evidence that the person has an account—the financial institution is slapped with a subpoena for the person's records."[17] Most of the warrantless financial searches the feds have ordered under the Patriot Act have had no connection to terrorism. The Electronic Frontier Foundation's Kevin Bankston observed: "There is no probable cause here. There is no judicial oversight. Yet the government can immediately query financial institutions across the nation to find out where you have an account or who you've done business with. It's not just if you have an account there, but any record of a financial transaction."[18] The feds used Patriot Act financial sweep search powers in 2003 in "Operation G-String," an investigation of bribes involving Las Vegas strip clubs. Rep. Shelley Berkley (D-Nev.) complained: "It was never my intent to have the Patriot Act used as a kitchen sink for all of the law enforcement tool goodies that the FBI has been trying to get for the last decades. . . . It is Patriot Act creep."[19]

Though the Patriot Act vastly increased the feds' financial surveillance powers, the feds are not concentrating their artillery on the gravest threats to American security. The Treasury Department's Office of Foreign Assets Control has a lead role in tracking down supposedly dangerous money. Unfortunately, this office has ten times more agents assigned to track violators of the U.S. embargo on Cuba as it has tracking Osama Bin Laden's money. Since 1994, it has collected almost a thousand times as much in fines for violations of the Cuban embargo as it has for terrorism financing violations ($8+ million vs. $9,425).[20] Rep. William Delahunt (D-Mass.) complained: "We're chasing old ladies on bicycle trips in Cuba when we should be concentrating on using a significant tool against shadowy terrorist organizations."[21] Treasury spokeswoman Molly Millerwise responded: "There is no question where the administration stands on Cuba policy. We are equally dedicated to fighting the financial terrorism network." But to be equally dedicated to spiking Cuban bicycle tours and to thwarting an organization that knocks down American skyscrapers seems a bit demented. Millerwise stressed: "We do focus on Cuba. They are our nearest neighbor."[22] This raises questions of whether maps used by the Bush administration have expunged both Mexico and Canada. However, neither Mexicans nor Canadians will be large voting blocs in Florida in November's presidential election. (Many Cuban-Americans avidly support the embargo on Castro.)

SURVEILLANCE MANIA

The 9/11 attacks have sanctified unlimited federal surveillance on Americans—at least in the opinion of many Bush administration officials. Regardless of the reasons why the CIA and FBI failed to stop the hijackers, the solution has been far more snooping and the potential creation of hundreds of millions of dossiers on American citizens. Almost overnight, it became widely accepted that the government must have unlimited powers to search anywhere and everywhere for enemies of freedom. The worse the government's failure, the further it permitted itself to intrude.

For example, the Patriot Act created a new Information Office in the Pentagon that promptly launched work on the Total Information Awareness (TIA) system. TIA aimed to create a massive dragnet to build dossiers on American citizens—seeking "connections between transactions—such as passports; visas; work permits; driver's licenses; credit cards; airline tickets; rental cars; gun purchases; chemical purchases—and events—such as arrest or suspicious activities and so forth," according to Under Secretary of Defense Pete Aldridge.[23]

TIA set off alarm bells far and wide and Congress sought to rein in its development in early 2003. But by that time, the Pentagon had already awarded 26 contracts for dozens of private research projects to develop components for TIA. Even though TIA has been sidelined, the feds are pursuing massive data mining research closely akin to TIA—especially the Novel Intelligence from Massive Data (NIMD) project being conducted by the National Security Agency. Many of the companies and researchers previously working on TIA are now working on the NIMD project. Steven Aftergood of the Federation of American Scientists commented: "The whole congressional action looks like a shell game. There may be enough of a difference for them to claim TIA was terminated while for all practical purposes the identical work is continuing."[24] While Congress mandated that TIA develop privacy protection computer projects, there is no such "privacy protection" requirement for NIMD.[25]

One of the biggest new intrusions is the Transportation Security Administration's Computer Assisted Passenger Prescreening System, or CAPPS 2. CAPPS 2 was mandated by Congress in late 2001 after the failure of the original CAPPS program. The first CAPPS system triggered alerts on 9 out of the 19 hijackers on 9/11. However, FAA regulations required merely checking their baggage to confirm that they were not transporting explosives. Even though the feds had received numerous warnings of potential hijacks and Al Qaeda plans to use airlines, the FAA did not require any additional searches or other responses for CAPPS alarmees.

TSA will use CAPPS 2 to create a color rating and a "risk profile" of every airline passenger in America. The TSA initially planned to search the medical records and credit scores of every airline passenger but backed away after public protests. TSA spokesman Mark Hatfield announced reassuringly, "We are taking a very deliberate approach that is predicated on upholding the privacy rights of individuals."[26]

Though CAPPS 2 was sold as a way to stop terrorists from boarding airplanes, TSA quickly expanded the program's goals to trigger alerts for people wanted for other federal crimes. The *Washington Post* reported in early

September 2003, based on information on CAPPS 2 from TSA and other agencies, that an "estimated 1 to 2 percent [of airline passengers] will be labeled 'red' and will be prohibited from boarding. These passengers also will face police questioning and may be arrested."[27] TSA chief Loy denied that the number of detainees would be that high. The *New York Times* fretted about the Bush administration's "talk of turning [CAPPS 2] into an all-purpose law-enforcement tool."[28]

TSA spokesman Brian Turmail bragged about the benefits of casting a broad net with CAPPS 2: "Not only should we keep passengers from sitting next to a terrorist, we should keep them from sitting next to wanted ax murderers."[29] Given the savvy of TSA checkpoints, perhaps the agency believes it needs a backup in case people smuggle axes on board planes to silence overly talkative seatmates.

The TSA promised that the new security system would reduce the number of airline passengers targeted for additional scrutiny from 14 to 15 percent to around 5 percent. Hatfield said: "It will go a long way to reduce the number of people who miss their flights because they have to talk with an investigator."[30] But that is a massive *increase* in the percentage of passengers who could face police interrogations. Why should Americans expect TSA's list of accused criminals to be more reliable than anything else the agency does?

Many travellers were wary that CAPPS 2 could result in the feds compiling dossiers on more than a hundred million Americans. Such fears were fed when a leak from an off-the-record briefing by TSA chief James Loy revealed that JetBlue airline had turned over 1.5 million passengers' records to an Army contractor for testing a prototype system for airline passenger screening. The TSA angrily denied having any involvement in the JetBlue data transfer. TSA spokesman Brian Turmail denounced the hubbub: "People have used irresponsible scare tactics to stop the testing of CAPPS 2. The American people have the right to know whether this system will work. We should have a dialogue based on fact and not innuendo."[31]

A Department of Homeland Security investigation found in February 2004 that TSA had requested in writing that JetBlue turn over its passenger data to the Army subcontractor. The report concluded that "TSA employees involved acted without appropriate regard for individual privacy interests or the spirit of the Privacy Act of 1974."[32] The report evoked a few toothless howls on Capitol Hill.

TSA responded to its agents violating Americans' privacy and ignoring federal law by issuing a press release announcing that all TSA employees would take part in a "privacy education week" program entitled, "Respecting Privacy, Preserving Freedoms."[33] TSA also promised to hire a "privacy officer."

JetBlue was not the only airline squeezed for passenger data to feed the feds' maw. In January 2004, the Electronic Privacy Information Center revealed that Northwest Airlines also covertly turned over 10 million passenger records to the National Aeronautics and Space Administration (NASA) for testing for new airline passenger screening.[34]

Congress specified in 2003 legislation that CAPPS 2 could not be deployed until after the General Accounting Office investigated and certified it would effectively detect terrorist threats and included reliable privacy protection measures. However, when Bush signed the bill, he announced that he was nullifying that provision of the law, declaring that the "executive branch shall construe as calling solely for notification the provisions of the Act that purport to require congressional committee approval for the execution of a law."[35]

GAO reported in February 2004 that CAPPS 2 will be unable either to stop terrorists or protect privacy.[36] TSA's planning for CAPPS 2 was a complete mess. GAO concluded that TSA failed to adequately address seven out of eight key congressional concerns. CAPPS 2 will need to process over 3 million passenger records per day, but the TSA tested the system with only 32 contrived passenger records. The agency could not explain how this test would indicate how CAPPS 2 could handle a 100,000 times heavier workload.

TSA scorned the GAO report and announced that it could soon compel airlines to turn over personal data on all passengers—regardless that the Privacy Act of 1974 prohibits such a command.

Many private experts see CAPPS 2 as a train wreck in the making. The Electronic Frontier Foundation's Lee Tien warned that CAPPS 2 could produce "the worst of both worlds: no real security against dedicated attackers, but a massive social surveillance system which will affect every American."[37] The American Civil Liberties Union's Barry Steinhardt complained: "Instead of zeroing in on suspects based on real evidence of wrongdoing, it sweeps every airline passenger through a dragnet."[38]

CAPPS 2 epitomizes the arrogance and incompetence of Bush administration surveillance schemes. When TSA agents violate the law or make false statements, heads never roll and budgets always swell. The current CAPPS is only an opening bid. Once it gets established, it will be easy for officials to perenially invoke public safety to justify vacuuming up more of Americans' lives each year. And opponents to each expansion will be greeted with the taunt: "Do you want the terrorists to win?"

A PRESIDENT'S RIGHT TO DESTROY ALL RIGHTS

After 9/11, the word of the president is the only protection that the rights and liberties of the American people need. As a result of the 9/11 attacks, President Bush entitled himself to unlimited, unchecked power over anyone in the world suspected of being a terrorist. The mere unsubstantiated assertion of the president now trumps all of the judicial procedures and protections built up during more than two hundred years of this nation's history.

On November 13, 2001, Bush issued an executive order establishing military tribunals for the trial and potential execution of any person Bush has labeled an "enemy combatant." Bush dictated that people classified as enemy combatants "shall not be privileged to seek any remedy . . . directly or indirectly . . . in any court of the United States."[39]

Bush defined an enemy combatant as a person whom the president has "reason to believe" is a current or former member of Al Qaeda, or someone who "has engaged in, aided or abetted, or conspired to commit, acts of international terrorism, or acts in preparation therefore, that have caused, threaten to cause, or have as their aim to cause, injury or adverse effects on the United States, its citizens, national security, foreign policy, or economy."[40] A person can also be labeled an enemy combatant if they are suspected of having "knowingly harbored" such malefactors. At the time that Bush issued his edict, he specified that it would apply only to "non-citizens." Bush's order authorized the seizure of terrorist suspects within the United States and abroad and authorized the tribunal to "sit at any time and any place."

The only right of appeal from the verdict of a military tribunal would be to the president himself (not exactly reassuring, giving Bush's nonchalant oversight of Texas death penalty cases). Ashcroft justified the boundless power: "Foreign terrorists who commit war crimes against the United States, in my judgment, are not entitled to and do not deserve the protections of the American Constitution."[41] But Bush's order was not limited to terrorists who committed "war crimes." Instead, it could sweep in people *suspected* of threatening to cause "adverse effects" on the U.S. economy via alleged terrorist conspiracies—a potentially very expansive category.

Michael Ratner of the Center for Constitutional Rights noted that, under Bush's order, "Hearsay and even evidence obtained from torture will apparently be admissible." It will not be necessary to hire a press spokesman for the trials because "the entire process, including execution, can be conducted in secret," as Ratner noted.[42]

New York Times columnist William Safire denounced Bush's edict for seeking the "replacement of the American rule of law with military kangaroo courts." Safire declared that, under Bush's decree, "noncitizens face an executive that is now investigator, prosecutor, judge, jury and jailer or executioner. In an Orwellian twist, Bush's order calls this Soviet-style abomination a full and fair trial."[43] Wesley Pruden, the editor in chief of the *Washington Times*, denounced Bush's proposal as "drumhead justice" and declared that it would be less cynical for Bush simply to "order his generals to shoot whoever he thinks needs shooting" in Afghanistan instead of pretending that his tribunal system is "a triumph of the rule of law."[44]

Bush's order provided no due process rights for the accused; instead, all the procedures would be at the discretion of Bush and his hand-picked death-sentence friendly judges. This is profoundly different from the established system of U.S. military courts, which abound in due process and appeal rights. And Bush's order starkly ignored a famous Supreme Court ruling striking down as unconstitutional Abraham Lincoln's suspension of habeas corpus during the Civil War. The Court ruled in 1866 that the president may not rely on military tribunals unless civil courts are "actually closed and it is impossible to administer criminal justice."[45]

The order initially primarily applied to the roughly 600 people seized in Afghanistan during the U.S. invasion. These individuals were transported to Guantanamo Naval Base in Cuba and kept in sometimes harsh conditions.

In April 2002, the Pentagon revealed that one person being held at Guantanamo was actually a U.S. citizen. Yaser Hamdi, a Saudi who was born in Louisiana, was captured in Afghanistan by Northern Alliance forces and turned over to the U.S. military. Hamdi denied that he was a combatant. His family stated that he was in Afghanistan for missionary work. Hamdi's parents hired counsel for their son but the Bush administration insisted on holding Hamdi incommunicado.

On June 10, 2002, the president claimed even greater power. On that day, Attorney General Ashcroft announced during a visit to Moscow that the U.S. government had designated an American citizen arrested in Chicago as an enemy combatant. Jose Padilla, a Puerto Rican who grew up in Chicago and served time in Florida prisons, was transferred to a military brig after the feds realized that they had little or no evidence to justify his arrest. Ashcroft hyped Padilla as someone planning to explode a "dirty bomb" and cause "mass death and injury." While Ashcroft portrayed Padilla as having "trained with the enemy [in Pakistan], including studying how to wire explosive devices and researching radiological dispersion devices," federal officials later admitted that this "consisted largely of surfing the Internet."[46] Ashcroft was widely ridiculed for his exaggerations.

Padilla had been arrested on May 8 when he flew into Chicago from Pakistan. The Bush administration stripped Padilla of all rights and confined him to a military brig in South Carolina. As an enemy combatant, Padilla had no right to petition any federal court to review his case or challenge his status. Federal judge Michael Mukasey warned in 2003 that if the Bush administration continued denying all of Padilla's legal rights, "a dictatorship will be upon us, the tanks will have rolled."[47]

On July 3, 2003, the Bush administration announced that six detainees would be tried before tribunals.[48] Defense lawyers will be obliged to pay the government thousands of dollars for a security clearance before being permitted to represent clients. And, as the *New York Times* noted, defense lawyers "would have to tell the prosecution a week before the trial about all of its evidence, a stark departure from a civilian trial."[49] The National Association of Criminal Defense Lawyers announced that it could not recommend that any of its members act as defense counsels because of the pervasive and crippling restrictions the government imposed.

In January 2004, five uniformed military lawyers assigned to defend Guantanamo detainees filed a challenge to the Supreme Court, asserting that Bush's system would "create a legal black hole. . . . Under this monarchical regime, those who fall into the black hole may not contest the jurisdiction, competency or even the constitutionality of the military tribunals."[50] Bush's trial plans also generated a brief from 175 members of Britain's parliament, who warned that "the exercise of executive power without possibility of judicial review jeopardizes the keystone of our existence as nations, namely the rule of law."[51]

Bush's own standard for labeling people enemy combatants seems hazy, if not contradictory. In a July 17, 2003, press conference in Britain, Bush was asked whether his comments about "bad people" being held at Guantanamo "will merely fuel their doubts that the United States regards them as innocent until proven guilty and due a fair, free, and open trial." Bush replied: "Well, yes—let me just say these were illegal combatants. They were picked up off the battlefield aiding and abetting the Taliban. I'm not trying to try them in front of your cameras or in your newspaper."[52]

Yet, four months later, in an interview with BBC's David Frost, Bush justified the Guantanamo detentions by declaring that "these were illegal *non*-combatants picked up off of a battlefield."[53] In a November 20 press conference in London, Bush declared, "These are illegal *non*-combatants picked up off of a battlefield, and they are being treated in a humane fashion."[54] The White House sometimes marks corrections to Bush speeches and comments but it made no notations on these statements.

If someone is only a non-combatant, how can Bush justify holding them in perpetuity and denying them all legal rights because they are an "enemy combatant"? Bush may have assumed that whether a person was actually a combatant was a moot point after they were officially classified as enemies. Bush, commenting in January 2002, condemned all the people held at Guantanamo: "These are killers. These are terrorists. . . . The only thing they know about countries is when they find a country that's been weakened and they want to occupy it like a parasite."[55]

The Bush administration, in a January 2004 brief to the Supreme Court, reiterated the president's right to label American citizens as enemy combatants and nullify all of their rights. Bush's solicitor general, Theodore Olson, urged the Court to uphold this power because a lower federal court decision denying Bush's prerogative "undermines the president's constitutional authority to protect the nation."[56] For the Bush administration, the "constitutional authority to protect the nation" automatically nullifies the rest of the Constitution.

The Bush administration argued to the Supreme Court that a federal court can "only require the military to point to some evidence supporting its [enemy combatant] determination."[57] "Pointing" is not a high standard of proof. They claimed that a federal judge should have no right to examine the evidence provided by the military. In other words, it requires a mere memo to justify incarcerating someone in perpetuity with no escape.[58]

The Supreme Court heard oral arguments on two enemy combatant cases on April 28, 2004. Frank Dunham, representing Hamdi, sought a hearing that his client had been denied for the two years he was held at a Navy brig in Norfolk, Virginia.[59] The Bush administration refused to permit Hamdi to have any contact with legal counsel until shortly before the Supreme Court hearing. Dunham explained that he was prohibited by the U.S. military from revealing anything in court that Hamdi had told him.

Dunham complained that the term "enemy combatant" was vague: "We don't find it defined in any case, we don't find it defined in any statute, and it hasn't been defined by regulation or by anything that's been filed in this case." Justice Scalia sounded indignant at Dunham's quest for clarity: "I assume it means someone who is—has taken up arms against the armed forces of the United States. Isn't that—really, I mean, do we have to quibble about that word?" Dunham made clear that the question of whether Hamdi was fighting against American forces was in dispute.

The Justice Department's Paul Clement, arguing the case for the Bush administration, mentioned three times that 10,000 U.S. troops are still in Afghanistan. Clement declared, "I find it so remarkable that we have to confront this question when our troops are still on the ground in this case." But the issue was not whether Hamdi should be released to go fight in Afghanistan. The question was what rights an American citizen has. Clement implied that no one had a right to question Bush's power until after the government announced a final cessation of hostilities.

Clement repeatedly stressed that "the United States military has no interest in detaining any individual who's not an enemy combatant or who does not present a continuing threat." But President Bush and many other officials have often bragged about how many enemy combatants are being held, implying that the raw number is proof that the United States is winning. Once a person is labeled an enemy combatant, the government cannot release them without admitting that it made a mistake.

Several justices were concerned about the apparent total lack of due process that Hamdi—and any other U.S. citizen—might receive under the Bush administration's new system. Justice Breyer pushed Clement as to whether "a person who contests something of importance is entitled to a neutral decision-maker and an opportunity to present proofs and arguments." Clement stressed: "Let me say very clearly that these individuals have gotten military process." Clement explained that "it may not seem what you think of as traditional due process . . . but the interrogation process [at Guantanamo] itself provides an opportunity for an individual to explain that this has all been a mistake." Justice Ginsburg asked if "the person who is locked up, doesn't he have a right to bring before some tribunal himself, his own words"? Clement explained that "he has an opportunity to explain it in his own words." Justice Stevens asked: "During interrogation?" Clement confirmed: "During interrogation."

But the interrogations Clement practically idealized are not quite the same as taking a deposition in the office of some law clerk. As one U.S. government official who supervised the capture and transfer of accused terrorists declared in 2002: "If you don't violate someone's human rights some of the time, you probably aren't doing your job."[60] The *Washington Post* interviewed ten U.S. national security officials and reported, "While the U.S. government publicly denounces the use of torture, each of the current national security officials interviewed for this article defended the use of violence against captives as just and necessary." Suspected members of Al Qaeda receive especially vigorous treatment: "Captives are often 'softened up' by MPs and U.S. Army Special

Forces troops who beat them up and confine them in tiny rooms. The alleged terrorists are commonly blindfolded and thrown into walls, bound in painful positions, subjected to loud noises and deprived of sleep."[61] Such circumstances and treatment may impede a detainee's ability to explain his case to even the most impartial and lofty-minded interrogator.

Dunham responded to the Bush administration's rosy portrayal of its process: "Here there is no law. If there is any law at all, it is the executive's own secret definition of whatever 'enemy combatant' is. And don't fool yourselves into thinking that that means somebody coming off a battlefield, because they've used it in Chicago, they've used it in New York, and they've used it in Indiana."

The Court also heard the case of Jose Padilla.[62] The Court's consideration on this case turned in part on a sentence from a congressional resolution in September 2001: "The president is authorized to use all necessary and appropriate force against persons he determines planned, authorized, committed or aided the terrorist attacks." Justice Breyer asked Clement whether the phrase "necessary and appropriate" implied any type of limit on the Bush administration's power. Clement responded, "I certainly wouldn't read the authorization of force's use of the term 'necessary and appropriate' as an invitation for sort of judicial management of the executive's war-making power." Clement may have surprised some of the justices by declaring that the Bush administration would have had the same power to detain Padilla even if Congress had never passed the war resolution, declaring that "the president had that authority on September 10th" 2001.

Clement asserted that Padilla was the same as someone apprehended in Afghanistan, as far as the question of the government's authority over him. Clement insisted that "where the government is on a war footing, that there— you have to trust the executive to make the kind of quintessential military judgments." Jennifer Martinez, representing Padilla, framed the issue: "Today the government asked this court for a broad ruling that would allow the president unlimited power to imprison any American, anywhere, at any time, without trial, simply by labeling him an 'enemy combatant.'" Martinez stressed that the issues in the case "go to the core of what our democracy is about, which is that the government cannot take citizens in this country off the street and lock them up in jail forever without a trial."

During the Padilla hearing, the Court's attention returned to the question of how the government was treating enemy combatants. Justice Stevens asked Clement whether "there's anything in the law that curtails the method of interrogation that may be employed"? Clement alluded to an international treaty and to a federal law, the Torture Victim Protection Act (enacted to permit people to sue foreign governments). Clement added that the law "doesn't actually apply to the United States. So I'm not sure that there would be any other basis for bringing a private cause of action against the United States." Clement then sought to reassure the justices that the government recognized that torture was not a sound method: "If you did that, you might get information more quickly. But you're really wonder about the reliability of the information you were getting."

Justice Ginsburg returned to the issue a few minutes later, asking about cases in which the executive declares that "mild torture . . . will help get this information." Clement quickly replied: "Well, our executive doesn't." Ginsburg asked: "Is it just up to the goodwill of the executive? Is there any judicial check?" Clement declared: "Well, this is a situation where there is jurisdiction in the habeas courts. So if necessary, they remain open." Yet the Bush administration had adamantly closed the courts to everyone labeled as an enemy combatant—regardless of any allegations of abuse. Clement insisted that "the fact that executive discretion in a war situation can be abused is not a good and sufficient reason for judicial micromanagement and overseeing of that authority."[63]

The Supreme Court oral arguments on the enemy combatant cases occurred only a few hours before CBS News first broadcast the shocking photos of the abuse and torture of Iraqi detainees. At the request of Gen. Richard Myers, chairman of the Joint Chiefs of Staff, CBS had delayed for two weeks broadcasting the photos. (The Iraqi torture scandal is discussed at length in chapter 16.) Clement might have faced far more vigorous questioning if he had appeared before the Court after the torture scandal erupted. Rep. John Conyers (D-Mich.) on May 19 called for a congressional investigation on whether the Justice Department knowingly misled the Supreme Court regarding the use of torture on detainees.

The Bush administration continually sought to confuse the argument—pretending that any limit on the president's power would leave America defenseless. But there are ways to designate enemies without giving the president absolute power. The issue is not whether suspected terrorists should be set free: the issue is what standards should govern their detention, and what procedural rights suspected terrorists should have. It would not have been difficult for Congress to set legal standards to justify detention of many of the people apprehended in Afghanistan based on less evidence than is required to hold someone arrested in America suspected of similarly grave offenses. If Congress had passed a law establishing standards and procedures for such cases, the issue of enemy combatants would have been less perilous for the U.S. Constitution. But the Bush administration seized this issue early, and Congress took a dive.

The power to designate people as enemy combatants is the power to nullify all their rights. If the president is permitted to pick and choose who will have constitutional rights and who can be thrown into the brig forever without seeing a lawyer, constitutional rights are not what they used to be. Bush cannot be granted the power to nullify all the rights of anyone he chooses—based on his own unsubstantiated assertion—without imperiling everyone's rights.

The *National Journal*'s Stuart Taylor, one of the most respected legal writers in Washington, commented: "The administration's handling of the enemy-combatant cases has been so lawless as to smack of tyranny. Under the administration's view of the law, no court could intervene even if Bush were to order all 600-plus Guantanamo detainees lined up and shot."[64] It is naive to presume that Bush's dictatorial power is no threat to average Americans because he will only use it against bad guys. A dictatorship rarely begins with public announcements of planned future abuses. Instead, it is a gradual process, whittling away rights and establishing one sweeping prerogative after another.

The Supreme Court is expected to rule on two cases involving the enemy combatant designations by the end of June 2004. The president's power will either be curbed or consecrated. Top administration officials have repeatedly said that it is only a matter of time until another terrorist attack. If the Supreme Court consecrates Bush's power, a second major attack could result in a round of abuses that will make the post-9/11 actions look like a law school picnic.

CONCLUSION

Federal antiterrorism surveillance efforts have been short on success. Unfortunately, each new botch seems to produce demands for new powers and new programs—as if every failure entitles the government to intrude deeper into people's lives. Government follies are propelling the wedge that politicians are using to further splinter the Bill of Rights. If federal agencies had not failed across the board prior to 9/11, President Bush never could have proclaimed his prerogative to unilaterally destroy anyone's rights based on his mere assertion.

President Bush recognizes how the existence of boundless government power threatens every person within a society. "Every woman in Iraq is better

off because the rape rooms and torture chambers of Saddam Hussein are forever closed," Bush declared on March 12, 2004.[65] Even though only a minuscule percentage of Iraqi women were ever savaged in the rape rooms, the mere
existence of such places was a Damocles sword hanging over their heads. Placing people under the absolute power of government officials always poses the
risk of horrific results. If Bush recognizes this, then why does he not also recognize that his "enemy combatant" designation power endangers the freedom
of every American?

Bush invented his enemy combatant/rights-nullification power from a
simple decree. If this power is permitted to continue, it is only a question of
time until Bush or future presidents issue new decrees nullifying the rights of
other targets and groups. Once the premise is accepted that nullifying rights is
the path to safety, then government incompetence—the failure to stop attacks—will become the Grim Reaper of the Constitution. The Patriot Act created a new crime of "domestic terrorism"—defined as violent or threatening
private actions intended "to influence the policy of a government by intimidation or coercion." It could be only a question of time until presidential decrees strip all rights from alleged environmental extremists, or anti-abortion
protestors, or groups of gun owners who meet and shoot and talk about their
hatred of Washington.

Bush talks about his power to designate enemy combatants as if it were a
simple question of whether government should fight evil. But the genius of the
Founding Fathers was to recognize that the existence of private evil cannot justify or sanctify absolute power. The Constitution was created by a generation
of men who had fought not just a war against a foreign power but also, in
many places, a de facto civil war, thanks to the pervasive Tory sympathizers in
many parts of the colonies. The Constitution was not made for sunny days
and smooth sailing. Instead, it was crafted for hard times, with many provisions for dealing with deadly threats to the nation's survival. For Bush to effectively claim that he can no longer be bound by the Constitution is an insult
to the Founding Fathers who survived far harsher tests in their time than
America did on and after 9/11.

CHAPTER FOURTEEN

Protecting Democracy from Freedom

Congress has done little to check the abuses of the executive branch of government during the Bush presidency. Most of Bush's power grabs have evoked either silence or applause on Capitol Hill. The caliber of congressional oversight has sharply deteriorated, reaching a new low for the modern era.

Instead, many members of Congress have devoted themselves to restricting Americans' participation in the political process. In early 2002, Congress finally enacted campaign finance legislation that seeks to forcibly uplift American politics. Congress's fix will protect the government's reputation and make the ruling class even more unassailable in future years.

The source of the problem with campaigns, in the view of many incumbents, is the proliferation of so-called soft money—money not limited by federal restrictions on the amount of donations per individual or political action committee. Bush's solicitor general, Theodore Olson, told the Supreme Court that soft money is "a euphemism for money that's going around the system . . . money that is prohibited to go to Federal elections."[1] But the concept of "soft money" is itself a charade, based on the idea that politicians should have almost boundless control over anything that could affect their reelection.

At the same time that Congress imposed new restrictions on citizens' political activism, Congress doubled the amount of money that can be legally given to candidates (so-called hard money). During the last election cycle, 90 percent of the hard money went to incumbent congressmen.[2] Incumbents received almost ten times as much money as challengers because the incumbents are already in position to reward donors.

The pro-incumbent bias in campaign contributions helps members of Congress avoid bothersome relocations. While many Americans rightfully scoffed in 2002 when the Iraqi government announced that President Saddam Hussein was reelected after facing no opposition, the seats of most congressmen are almost as safe. As the *Wall Street Journal* noted in 2002, "After the last census, the people in state legislatures who map congressional districts—ostensibly to reflect demographic changes but often to push political agendas—stacked the vast majority of them to favor one side or the other. That has left only about 40 races to be seriously contested by both parties, fewer than one-third as many competitive seats as ten years ago, by the reckoning of political handicapper Charlie Cook."[3] In the 2002 elections, only four incumbent members of Congress who ran against nonincumbent challengers were defeated.[4] Incumbents usually have a reelection rate in the 98-percent range.

Though almost all congressmen get reelected, their victories are often tarnished by the indignities they suffer along the path to perpetuating their power. The most revolutionary element of the Bipartisan Campaign Reform Act is the de facto prohibition on most issue ads on radio and television during election season. Thanks to the new act, it can be a federal crime to expose the abuses of congressmen or presidents while they are seeking reelection—usually the only time their power can be effectively challenged. The act restricts nonprofit groups, corporations, and other entities' "electioneering communications" within 30 days of a primary election or 60 days of a general election. An "electioneering communication" is defined broadly enough to stifle most things that can adversely affect the voting totals of an incumbent member of Congress or president. It would have been indelicate for Congress to specifically prohibit ads criticizing incumbent politicians. Instead, Congress banned practically all issue ads from radio and television.

The Bill of Rights is not vague on this subject. The First Amendment states that "Congress shall make no law . . . abridging the freedom of speech, or of the press." Congress ignored this stark edict and imposed stranglehold restrictions on "electioneering communications."

Like a bunch of amateur actors in a small-town Shakespeare performance, one congressman after another proclaimed a lofty motive for knifing the First Amendment in the debate leading to the bill's passage. Rep. Chris Shays (R-

Conn.) claimed the restrictions are actually a triumph for free speech: "The reform legislation we introduce today strengthens First Amendment values. It will ensure that elected officials are more responsive to the voices of their constituents and do not appear beholden only to big money. As your own constituents would surely tell you, stemming the tide of soft money would improve their access to government—and enhance their First Amendment rights—by allowing them to participate in the process."[5] "First Amendment values" became an Orwellian substitute for freedom of speech.

Rep. Zach Wamp (R-Tenn.) also insisted that restricting criticism of congressmen is a victory for free speech: "We need to stand up for the First Amendment and treat these groups and these people playing politics in elections the same as the candidates themselves."[6] The Founding Fathers forgot to include a footnote to the First Amendment specifying the need for full disclosure to the federal speech police.

Many congressmen talk as if they have an unlimited right to regulate and muzzle anyone who wants to criticize them. Rep. Jim Davis (D-Fla.) praised one proposal that "subjects those people who *attempt to influence the outcome of an election* to the same requirements that congressional candidates face now when they spend money to influence the election. There will be meaningful full disclosure that will allow the voters to judge who is making the statement and I believe will force people to discontinue making these inflammatory, deceitful actions."[7]

But neither Davis nor any other incumbent proposed regulations to stop incumbents from making inflammatory, deceitful speeches or accusations against their opponents or organizations that they despise. In fact, no study has ever shown that independent "issue ads" or "attack ads" are more deceptive than the ads congressional candidates run.

Some members insisted that, by betraying the Bill of Rights, Congress would restore Americans' trust in government. Rep. Nancy Pelosi (D-Calif.) declared: "We have an opportunity today to send a valentine to the American people; to tell them they are important to us; that what they think matters to us; that they should have faith in government."[8] Rep. John Lewis (D-Ga.) commented: "We must pass [the campaign finance reform act] to lessen the people's growing cynicism. . . . It is time to restore the people's faith in their government."[9]

Nothing infuriated many senators more than negative ads. Sen. John McCain (R-Ariz.), a darling of the news media, declared: "I hope that we will not allow our attention to be distracted from the real issues at hand—how to raise the tenor of the debate in our elections and give people real choices. No one benefits from negative ads. They don't aid our Nation's political dialog."[10] While campaigning for the presidential nomination in December 1999, McCain announced, "If I could think of a way constitutionally, I would ban negative ads."[11]

Sen. James Jeffords (R/D-Vt.), who abandoned the party that helped elect him, declared: "These sham issue ads are corrupting our election system and are not better informing the voters about the candidates. The public can differentiate between electioneering communications and other types of communications done to purely inform the public on an issue."[12] Sen. Christopher Dodd (D-Conn.) promised that campaign reform legislation "will have the net effect of ending these issue-based ads that destroy people's reputations and destroy any sense of understanding of what that particular campaign may be about. To that extent, everyone is benefited—not the candidate so much, in my view, but the voting public who may learn more about what people stand for, rather than what some issue group dislikes about a candidate."[13] Sen. Paul Wellstone (D-Minn.) asserted: "I think these issue advocacy ads are a nightmare. I think all of us should hate them. . . . [By passing the legislation], [w]e could get some of this poison politics off television."[14] Democratic senators also denounced attack ads as the equivalent of "crack cocaine," "drive-by shootings," and "air pollution."[15]

Many Republicans, however, staunchly opposed the bill; some congressmen were adamantly opposed to the restriction on freedom of speech. But the White House sabotaged opposition among its own party. An hour before the House began debate on the bill, White House press secretary Ari Fleischer announced on February 14, 2002, that the efforts of Republican opponents were thwarting a bill that would "in the president's opinion, improve the system." Fleischer declared that, if the bill passed, "I believe that you can thank President George W. Bush."[16] The *Washington Post* noted that "the White House's actions proved to be a turning point in the House passage of campaign finance reform." A senior Bush administration official confided: "The president is very realistic about this. He knows that this is an issue that needs to be dealt with, both substantively and politically."[17]

Bush signed the law on March 27, 2002. Bush applauded the fact that the law "creates new disclosure requirements and compels speedier compliance with existing ones, which will promote the free and swift flow of information to the public regarding the activities of groups and individuals in the political process." Unfortunately, as Bush's secrecy mania shows, he does not cherish the same standard regarding the "free and swift flow of information" regarding the government's own activities. Bush declared, "All of the American electorate will benefit from these measures to strengthen our democracy."

Bush conceded that "the bill does have flaws. Certain provisions present serious constitutional concerns. . . . I believe individual freedom to participate in elections should be expanded, not diminished; and when individual freedoms are restricted, questions arise under the First Amendment. I also have reservations about the constitutionality of the broad ban on issue advertising. . . . I expect that the courts will resolve these legitimate legal questions as appropriate under the law."[18] Bush interpreted his oath of office as absolving himself of any duty to veto a bill he considered unconstitutional. It was as if Bush believed that there was a secret escape clause that excused him from doing anything that might dint his poll ratings. Bush's comment—that "when individual freedoms are restricted, questions arise under the First Amendment"—portrays him as an innocent bystander. For Bush to sign an act he considered unconstitutional and suggest that judges would fix the problem is as irresponsible as a drunk driver absolving himself for reckless driving because of tow trucks can cart off any car he hits on the way home.

The new law was quickly challenged in federal court. The case ended up in the lap of the Supreme Court, which heard oral arguments on September 8, 2003. The Bush administration sent its solicitor general, Theodore Olson, to persuade the justices that the new act was constitutional.

Dietary freedom was a major goal of the new law. Many incumbents were bitter about the burden of fundraising. Olson recited the tales of woe by senators "who describe what it's like, the breakfasts, the lunches, the receptions, the dinners, the endless cycle of campaign finance."[19] Chief Justice Rehnquist retorted: "I don't believe [it] is a permissible basis for a restriction, that you know, we're tired of having to go to these breakfasts and lunches." Some of the new law's supporters presumed that if members of Congress were not so busy raising money, they might even begin reading the bills they vote on and perhaps even become zealous at oversight. Such naiveté would be touching if it was not countenancing the sacrifice of some people's freedom to augment other people's leisure.

On December 10, 2003, the Supreme Court upheld most provisions of the law by a 5 to 4 vote. The ban on issue ads survived intact. The majority decision offered endless hairsplitting about "electioneering communications." The ruling did not deign to explain why Americans should have more unfettered access to bestiality videos than to information about what their rulers are doing to them.

The majority of the justices concluded that the pervasive new restrictions were justified to reduce the American political system's corruption or the appearance of corruption. The Court's decision repeatedly derided "so-called issue advocacy"—as if any comments on public policy during election season are inherently suspect. The Court justified greatly expanding federal restrictions on speech because "the presence or absence of magic words cannot meaningfully distinguish electioneering speech from a true issue ad." The Court noted that its earlier decisions exempting "express advocacy" from restrictions "has not aided the legislative effort to combat real or apparent corruption."

Public communications "that promote or attack a candidate for federal office . . . undoubtedly have a dramatic effect on federal elections. Such ads were a prime motivating force behind BCRA's passage," the Court noted. The court declared that "any public communication that promotes or attacks a clearly identified federal candidate directly affects the election in which he is participating." So, the Court reasoned, members of Congress were entitled to restrict such communications. The Court explained: "Congress enacted the new 'electioneering communications' provisions precisely because it recognized that the express advocacy test was woefully inadequate at capturing communications designed to influence candidate elections." But who entitled Congress to "capture" everything intended to influence an election? Does the Supreme Court believe that incumbents are practically entitled to mind control over the voters?

The Court, in the name of anticorruption, endorsed suppressing efforts to get Americans more involved in politics. The decision declared, "Because voter registration, voter identification, GOTV [get out the vote drives], and generic campaign activity all confer substantial benefits on federal candidates, the funding of such activities creates a significant risk of actual and apparent corruption."[20]

The Supreme Court ruled that pre-election issue ads can be criminalized even if "advertisements do not urge the viewer to vote for or against a candidate in so many words they are no less clearly intended to influence the election." The Court denounced "sham ads" but never defined the word "sham." Paul Jacob, the chief of U.S. Term Limits, a nonprofit group that seeks to fight corruption by ending congressmen's tenured status, commented, "Perhaps labeling an advertisement a 'sham' is like naming someone an 'enemy combatant'—all constitutional rights are then lost."[21] The Supreme Court sacrificed freedom to fairness—in this case, protecting politicians from potentially unfair criticism.

The profound philosophical issues in the decision were largely ignored in the media's coverage. Instead, most story lines simply portrayed the decision as a victory over conniving special interests. Justice Clarence Thomas rightly declared that the decision "upholds what can only be described as the most significant abridgment of the freedoms of speech and association since the Civil War."[22]

Justice Scalia, in a noble dissent, warned that the law "cuts to the heart of what the First Amendment is meant to protect: the right to criticize the government."[23] Scalia declared that "this legislation prohibits the criticism of members of Congress by those entities most capable of giving such criticism loud voice: national political parties and corporations, both of the commercial and the not-for-profit sort." Scalia hinted that some members of Congress "who voted for this legislation did so not to produce 'fairer' campaigns, but to mute criticism of their records and facilitate reelection." Scalia illustrated how the legislation seeks to entrench the ruling class:

> The present legislation targets for prohibition certain categories of campaign speech that are particularly harmful to incumbents. Is it accidental, do you think, that incumbents raise about three times as much "hard money"—the sort of funding generally not restricted by this legislation—as do their challengers?. . . . Or that lobbyists (who seek the favor of incumbents) give 92 percent of their money in "hard" contributions?

During oral arguments, solicitor general Olson insisted that justices should not be suspicious about the law providing additional protections for incumbents because "it would be hard to develop a scheme that could be better for incumbents" than the prior law.[24] Scalia noted, "While the [Bush administration's] briefs and arguments before this Court focused on the horrible 'appearance of corruption,' the most passionate floor statements during the debates on this legislation pertained to so-called attack ads, which the Constitution surely protects."

Scalia noted how the decision attacked both freedom of speech and freedom of association: "The freedom to associate with others for the dissemination of ideas—not just by singing or speaking in unison, but by pooling financial resources for expressive purposes—is part of the freedom of speech." Scalia captured the transcendent issue before the court: "This litigation is about preventing criticism of the government."[25] Preserving the government's reputation now trumps the people's rights.

Seth Waxman, a former Solicitor General who argued in favor of the law to the Supreme Court, hailed the verdict: "Congress is not handcuffed by the First Amendment."[26] But if Congress is not handcuffed by the First Amendment, then what could possibly curb its power?

A legal analysis by the AFL-CIO vivifies how the new law edifies American political discourse by suppressing criticism:

> Beginning 30 days before the first primary or caucus . . . December 14, 2003 . . . Section 203 will criminalize broadcast references to the President in a series of geographic blackouts that will continuously ripple through the Nation, blocking every broadcast outlet, wherever located, whose signal can reach 50,000 persons in an upcoming primary or caucus state until June 8, 2004.
>
> . . . . This blackout will become national in scope on July 31, 30 days before the August 30–September 2 Republican National Convention . . . and it will then continue without interruption throughout the remaining 60 days until the November 2 election. Thus, from July 31, 2004 until the election, it will be a crime for a union, corporation, or incorporated non-profit organization to pay to broadcast any "reference" to the President by "name," "photograph," "drawing" or other "unambiguous" means anywhere in the United States.[27]

The law protects citizens from exposure to a sweeping array of messages. The AFL-CIO noted that the act prohibits pre-election ads that "call upon a Member of Congress to support or oppose imminent legislation, or ask viewers or listeners to urge the member to do so; inform the public, or express an opinion, about a Member of Congress's votes, legislative proposals or performance otherwise; respond directly to a Member [of Congress] who has criticized the [independent] organization or taken issue with its activities or policies; or encourage candidates to commit that, if elected, they will support or oppose particular legislation or policies."[28] The issue ad ban strikes across the board, muzzling the National Abortion Rights League and the American Life League, the National Rifle Association and the Brady Campaign to Ban Handguns, the Sierra Club and the American Civil Liberties Union.

On March 11, 2004, the Federal Election Commission proposed sweeping rules that could reclassify thousands of nonprofit organizations as federal "political committees" if they spent more than a thousand dollars on any type of activity related to a presidential or congressional election. The Coalition to Protect Nonprofit Advocacy, an organization with 600 members from across the ideological spectrum, complained: "Under the proposed rules, nonprofits would be virtually prohibited from criticizing or praising President Bush until after the November election."[29] The proposed regulations are so sweeping that "a church . . . could not publish a legislative report card during an election year. . . . The NAACP would have to stop its 2004 voter registration campaigns," the Coalition declared.[30] A group of 120 House Democrats protested to the FEC: "There has been absolutely no case made to Congress, or record established by the commission, to support any notion that tax-exempt organizations and other independent groups threaten the legitimacy of our government when criticizing its policies."[31]

The Drug Policy Alliance warned that the proposed rules "represent one of the worst assaults on the freedoms of speech and association ever proposed in the United States." The Alliance complained that the "proposed rules make clear that the federal government may selectively interpret any of the Alliance's communications that mention a candidate's positions on a drug policy issue as 'opposing' or even 'attacking' that candidate." And this could "silence our work to end the government-funded War on Drugs."[32]

The FEC proposed to determine the "major purpose" of a nonprofit organization—whether it was actually a federal political committee—based on an examination of its previous four and a half years of activities. This spurred howls of retroactive enforcement of the 2002 campaign reform act. If the FEC classified a nonprofit as a "political committee," the organization would face a vast increase in the reporting and regulatory burdens, and restrictions on donors. And there would be a profusion of new criminal penalties hanging over the heads of both the organization's officials and its donors.

The Bush legal team quickly used the new law to seek to suppress private groups from criticizing the president any time during an election year. In early 2004, left-wing and antiwar groups launched advertisements criticizing Bush and his record. The Republican National Committee on March 5, 2004 formally warned 250 television stations not to play the ads. RNC chief counsel Jill Holtzman Vogel asserted that the ads by MoveOn.org violated the new campaign finance act. Vogel declared, "Between now and November, our nation will engage in a debate that pits President Bush's strong and steady leadership against others who seek to attack the President and engage in a vicious, negative campaign." Vogel hinted that the stations' survival could be on the line: "As a broadcaster licensed by the Federal Communications Commission, you have a responsibility to the viewing public and to your licensing agency to refrain from complicity in any illegal activity." Vogel explained that under the new campaign law, "any entity that spends or raises more than $1,000 in a calendar year 'for the purpose of influencing any election for federal office' must register as a federal political committee" with the FEC.[33] Vogel asserted that MoveOn.org could not use "soft money" for its allegedly illegal ad campaign.

A few days later, Bush's reelection campaign formally requested the Federal Election Commission to launch an investigation of the Media Fund, another group running advertisements critical of Bush. The Bush campaign's general counsel, Tom Josefiak, condemned the ads as "an attempt to blow up the ban on the newly passed campaign finance reform bill."[34] Media Fund spokesman James Jordan denounced the Bush campaign's allegation as "a lie, a deliberate misrepresentation of the law. This is nothing more than a cynical and transparent attempt to intimidate our donors and silence dissenting voices."[35] On April 5, Bush campaign chairman Marc Racicot urged supporters to contact the FEC to urge them to crack down on the ad campaigns criticizing the president.[36] Racicot's appeal generated 66,000 e-mails to the agency.

However, on May 13, the FEC voted to postpone imposing restrictions on groups like MoveOn.org and the Media Fund until after the current election. The refusal to crack down on "soft money" was denounced as "shameful" by the *New York Times,* which warned that it "will unleash a fresh torrent of unregulated donations to pollute the presidential election."[37]

At the same time that Republicans pressured the FEC to ban the activities of the new groups, they hinted that they could file criminal referrals directly with the Justice Department. The new campaign law includes prison time for types of offenses previously punished only by fines. *The Hill* reported on March 25 that "some Republican operatives, including a senior Bush adviser, have said they expect complaints to be filed directly with the Department of Justice."[38] Some Republicans suggested criminal prosecution would be appropriate for the large donors to the new groups.

At the same time the Republican National Committee sought to suppress the Moveon.org ads, Bush was traveling around the country on taxpayer-financed fundraising gigs. The president has the right to dishonestly send hundreds of Americans to their deaths in foreign wars, but American citizens have little or no right to expose the president's lies during a time when the president is seeking to perpetuate his power over them.

At the same time the Bush campaign and the Republican National Committee sought to use federal law to bludgeon critics into silence, the president's reelection campaign began running television ads hyping Bush's leadership and showing a dead person being carried out of the World Trade Center wreckage. If a private group ran an ad with exactly the same video images and different audio comments criticizing Bush, the president's lawyers almost certainly would have used the new law to seek to suppress the ads.

PURGING THE APPEARANCE OF CORRUPTION

By banning the mention of politicians' names in ads in the months before an election, the act makes it far more difficult to inform Americans about who is responsible for what the government has done. It could be a federal crime for a private group to pay to broadcast in September and October of this year the fact that a congressman voted for the Patriot Act. Even a simple "tombstone" television ad—stating in large print—"Rep. Smith Voted for the Patriot Act"—may be judged illegal. Regardless of how much power the Patriot Act confers upon the government, it could be a criminal offense to publicize a congressman's support for it. Similarly, an October television advertisement merely listing Attorney General John Ashcroft's mildly deranged statements will be illegal—because it is effectively categorized as an unfair attack on the president's reelection campaign.

Though independent groups are prohibited from criticizing congressmen, congressmen have unlimited freedom to attack such groups and anyone else they please. U.S. Term Limits' Paul Jacob noted that an incumbent congressman "could run ads at election time slamming that group and wildly distorting the truth. While spot after spot by the congressman plays on television screens mercilessly smearing the organization, the federal speech Gestapo will be there to make certain that the insolent group is not permitted to air a single ad which dares mention the powerful congressman by name or, heaven forbid, show his or her royal likeness."[39] This is Congress's idea of a level playing field.

Congressmen rail against "poisonous" issue ads. But no "issue ad" ever impacted as many Americans as did the film footage of FBI tanks smashing into the Branch Davidians' home in Waco, Texas. No "issue ad" shook as many people as the photograph of a federal agent pointing a submachine gun towards terrified six-year-old Elian Gonzalez, whom Attorney General Janet Reno sent 130 G-men to seize in the middle of the night on April 22, 2000.

The Supreme Court sacrifices freedom to protect Americans against "sham ads." But this does nothing to ban or rein in sham politicians. And what about the sham war? What about the sham TSA? What about the other sham antiterrorism efforts? What about the sham farm subsidies?

Regardless of how many shams politicians concoct, a purity test is now required for all critics. Or more accurately, the Supreme Court approves a broad ban on any criticism because of the risk that some of the critics may be impure. Censorship is not censorship if it is labeled "reform"—and if government officials promise to protect against TV ads that can jolt people watching Seinfeld re-runs. Freedom of speech is presumed to be most harmful at a time when it could be most powerful.

The Supreme Court presumes that it is the harsh criticism of politicians that causes the appearance of corruption, and not the corruption that causes the appearance. The Supreme Court decision ignores how the actions of congressmen and presidents corrupt American democracy. Instead, it tacitly accepts that the problem is that the government and the rulers don't get enough respect. The problem is what outsiders, what private citizens say, not what government officials do. Instead of making government less corrupt, the act authorizes harsh penalties for private citizens who accuse their rulers of corruption.

Congress acted as if the torrent of negative ads was the equivalent of a national emergency requiring a drastic response. During the 2000 election cycle, the total expenditures for all congressional campaigns and the presidential race was about $2.5 billion. During that same time period—from early 1999 through the end of 2000—the federal government spent over $4 trillion. The federal government spent more than fifteen hundred times as much as was spent to seek to influence who would hold the reins of power.

A more accurate comparison is the amount of money spent on issue ads during the 2000 campaign. According to the Center for Responsive Politics, $204 million was spent on issue ads in the seven months before the 2000 election.[40] This is barely more than the current annual PR budget for a single federal program—the drug czar's anti-drug ad campaign.

The best baseline is how much is spent on issue ads versus how many tax dollars politicians spend to seek to perpetuate their power. Thanks to the farm bill, farmers will collect more than $180 billion in handouts. Since farm programs make no economic sense, it is fair to consider the subsidies as compulsory contributions to incumbents' reelection campaigns. Bush endlessly hypes how his Medicare drug benefit bill will purportedly provide $400 billion in benefits for the elderly. This alone is almost two thousand times the amount spent on issue ads in the last presidential election cycle. Politicians can forcibly confiscate people's paychecks to use for their own campaign spending at the same time they prohibit people from spending their own money to expose politicians' money grabs.

There is no way to clean up American politics without greatly decreasing the power of politicians to buy votes. This is the heart of the corruption, and nothing in the campaign reform act comes within a million miles of touching that power. The fundamental problem with the federal government is that its power is nearly boundless. The campaign reform act expands that power by suppressing criticism of government.

While congressmen portrayed the campaign reform act as a strike against greedy special interests, there was no recognition that government itself is the most powerful and most dangerous special interest. In the name of curbing special interests, Congress made it more difficult to curb government power.

It is a felony for a citizen to make any false statement to a federal agent. However, the statements of congressmen and the president to the American people are effectively immune from prosecution. We now have a situation in which politicians have a de facto right to lie to the public, yet citizens can become criminals if they spend more than a thousand dollars to pay to broadcast ads exposing the falsehoods during election season.

At the same time that Congress enacted a law to suppress free speech in order to reduce "the appearance of corruption," the House of Representatives perpetuated a system that practically encourages corruption. House members have enjoyed an "ethics truce" since 1997, which effectively prevented almost any investigations into ethical, criminal, or other abuses by House members.[41] After a decade of intense political battles over alleged wrongdoing, starting with House Speaker Jim Wright (D-Tex) and concluding with House Speaker Newt Gingrich (R-Ga.), leading Republicans and Democrats rigged the system to prevent further controversies. The rules for ethics complaints were "reformed" to prevent private citizens or private groups from filing complaints about misconduct by members of the House. Instead, only members of Congress can file complaints about the ethical conduct of other members. And Republican and Democratic congressional leaders agreed not to permit any such complaints to be filed. Trevor Potter, a former Republican political appointee who now heads the Campaign Legal Center, commented, "The ethics oversight process in the House is completely paralyzed."[42] Tom Fitton, the president of Judicial Watch, bemoaned, "Rather than change the regime and create a rigorous ethics system as promised, Republicans over the last 10 years have eviscerated the ethics process."[43]

If Congress and the Supreme Court truly want to reduce the "appearance of corruption," one easy step would be to apply the Freedom of Information Act to all correspondence between congressmen and donors. Congress exempted itself from FOIA. This simple reform would do wonders for proving that congressmen are never unduly influenced by the people and groups that give them millions of dollars.

The issue ad ban is nothing more than unilateral political disarmament of the victims of the federal government. Congress criminalized the effective exposure of its own wrongdoing. Instead, groups can criticize members of Congress only during times when most voters are not paying attention. In most elections, political illiterates are the largest single voting bloc. The issue ad ban will help to maximize the number of Americans who haven't got a clue.

The Supreme Court effectively decreed that the American people will be better served if their rulers are less criticized. This is not a doctrine fit for a free people. As Scalia noted in his dissent, "The premise of the First Amendment is that the American people are neither sheep nor fools, and hence fully capable of considering both the substance of the speech presented to them and its proximate and ultimate source. If that premise is wrong, our democracy has a much greater problem to overcome than merely the influence of amassed wealth."[44]

CONCLUSION

Congress, Bush, and the Supreme Court have turned back the clock to an era prior to that of King George III. In 1734, John Peter Zenger was arrested and charged with seditious libel because of articles in his newspaper attacking the abuses of the New York appointed colonial governor, William Cosby. Zenger spent eight months in jail before his case went to trial. The authorities likely expected an easy conviction, since the ruling maxim at that time regarding criticism of government officials was "the greater the truth, the greater the libel." But a courageous New York jury nullified the law and found him not guilty, thereby helping establish the principle that "truth is an absolute defense against libel." The Zenger verdict unleashed a torrent of free speech and helped pave the way to the American Revolution.

Now, thanks to the Bipartisan Campaign Reform Act, Americans have less freedom to criticize their rulers than the colonials had to criticize royal governors prior to the Revolution. Even if a coalition of citizens publish an ad that honestly lays out a congressman's actions and votes during election season, it is now a federal crime.

The attitude of Bush, Congress, and the Supreme Court appears to be that freedom of speech is a favor that the government bestows upon the governed. And since freedom of speech is a gift, the government may rightfully impose as many restrictions on its use as it sees fit.

Perhaps the Washington political establishment has forgotten how the federal government came into existence. A 1937 Senate report declared that "the Constitution . . . is the people's charter of the powers granted those who govern them."[45] The Declaration of Independence radicalized the world by recognizing that rights preexist government and are inalienable. The citizens of the Revolutionary era, having fought and defeated British armies, permitted the creation of a new government in Washington only upon the government's solemn pledge to respect the preexisting rights of the citizens. The power granted to the federal government was severely limited because Americans refused to replace King George with new masters.

Few Washington politicians have earned the trust of the American people, at least as far as respecting the Constitution. Few politicians have earned the trust of taxpayers, as far as not wasting the dollars the government seizes. And no congressman has earned the right to silence the American people.

What gives our rulers the right to dictate how and when they may be criticized? The fact that Congress would pass, Bush would sign, and the Supreme Court would uphold the ban on issue ads is itself proof of profound corruption in Washington. Former Congressman Tom Coburn, in his 2003 memoirs, accurately warned: "In Washington, power is like morphine. It dulls the senses, impairs judgment, and leads politicians to make choices that damage their own character and the machinery of our democracy."[46] The campaign reform law illustrates how much damage Bush, Congress, and the Supreme Court will inflict on Americans' liberties to maintain the prestige of government.

With the stratospheric reelection rates of incumbent congressmen, reform can only marginally increase their job security. But the real issue is rulers' right to adulation. Why not just formally classify all criticism of incumbents as violations of *Lese Majeste* and have done with the pretense of freedom?

Tragically, despite the vigorous new preemptive censorship, the American electorate continues to be exposed to falsehoods and smears. The *New York Times* reported on May 25, 2004, that television viewers were seeing a "hail of televised exaggerations, omissions and mischaracterizations" on both Bush and Democratic presidential nominee John Kerry. The Bush campaign is running ads falsely claiming that Kerry has a plan to raise taxes by $900 billion in his first 100 days in office, while the Kerry campaign is running ads falsely claiming that Bush "says sending jobs overseas makes sense for America."[47] But the FEC has no jurisdiction over the content of these ads. Apparently, only candidates for high office have a right to deceive the American people.

Maintaining trust in government is not more important than preserving freedom. We cannot "clean up democracy" by making political speech more regulated than hazardous waste disposal. Has "good government" become nothing more than "don't disturb the natives"—preventing utterances that might make people restless about the actions of their rulers?

CHAPTER FIFTEEN

Afghan Absurdities

George W. Bush is the first president of the United States to attack and overthrow a foreign regime because of its elementary school policies. Actually, this was not the justification for the war against the Taliban at the time U.S. troops charged in. But in the months after the war, Bush constantly contorted the war into a tale that would thrill soccer moms and political illiterates.

The hyping of the opening of schools to girls was part of an effort to exploit the Afghan war as proof of American moral greatness and Bush's benevolent leadership. The Bush administration sought to make Americans perceive this war as a grandiose good deed, rather than as the usual bombing, killing, and subjugating.

We will briefly consider a few Bush administration Afghan myths.

A NUCLEAR FALSEHOOD

In the wake of the U.S. military victory, President Bush warned America in his State of the Union address on January 29, 2002: "Our discoveries in Afghanistan confirmed our worst fears. . . . We have found diagrams of American nuclear power plants and public water facilities. . . . What we have found in Afghanistan confirms that, far from ending there, our war against terror is only beginning."[1]

The news that Al Qaeda was targeting American nuclear reactors was the most chilling revelation in Bush's speech. Senior CIA and FBI officials gave "background" briefings to the Washington media in the wake of Bush's speech, amplifying the threat that Afghan-based Al Qaeda fighters were targeting U.S. nuclear power facilities.[2] This news made the terrorist threat far more ominous and may have spurred support for Bush's preemptive war policy.

Two years later, the Bush administration admitted that the president's statement was false and that no nuclear power plant diagrams had been discovered in Afghanistan. A senior Bush administration official told the *Wall Street Journal,* "There's no additional basis for the language in the speech that we have found."[3] Nuclear Regulatory Commissioner Edward McGaffigan, who had testified in 2002 on this issue on closed hearings on Capitol Hill, commented that Bush was "poorly served by a speechwriter."[4]

When word began circulating that the nuclear power plant story was a hoax, at least one White House official refused to raise the white flag. *Nucleonics Week* reported that National Security Council spokesman Sean McCormack denied that Bush ever claimed the nuclear power plant diagrams were found in Afghanistan. McCormack told *Nucleonics Week:* "'We stand by the line in the president's speech."[5] McCormack stressed that, although Afghanistan was mentioned in sentences before and after the bombshell about discovering U.S. nuclear power plant diagrams, the word "Afghanistan" did not appear in that specific sentence. McCormack revealed that Bush's comment was merely referring to the possibility that terrorists might access the web sites of U.S. nuclear power plants. McCormack said, "In terms of wording of the president's speech, at the time we didn't want to talk in public about what we knew about the ability of al Qaeda to access the Internet and download information from the Internet." But the FBI had revealed months earlier that the 9/11 hijackers routinely used the Internet to communicate with one another.

The news that Bush's Afghan nuclear claim was bogus popped up in the news for a day or two and then vanished. Almost no one on Capitol Hill showed any interest in investigating.

DOING IT FOR THE SCHOOL GIRLS

The White House political machine decided that vanquishing the Taliban was not enough. Instead, the war needed a grandiose, redeeming purpose. And the Bush administration found it in the admission of girls to school. Bush continually sought to give the bombing of Afghanistan the PTA seal of approval.

One of the Taliban's many barbaric practices was to prohibit girls from attending school. After the U.S. conquest, schools in most parts of Afghanistan were—at least temporarily—officially open to girls.

Bush milked the school issue at every opportunity:

- "I want to remind you all that, as a result of our military action in Afghanistan. . . . For the first time, many young girls got to go to school. I'm so proud of the compassion of America. I'm proud of our strength, but I'm equally as proud of the compassion of this great nation."[6] (April 2, 2002)
- "There are young girls going to school in Afghanistan for the first time, thanks to the mighty government—mighty United States military and our friends and allies."[7] (August 7, 2002)
- "We continue to help the Afghan people lay roads, restore hospitals, and educate *all* of their children."[8] (May 1, 2003)

Bush's "girls school mythology" is a charade for much of Afghanistan. The United Nations estimates that only 3 percent of Afghan girls attend school in some southern provinces (in which almost all boys attend school).[9] Nationwide, more than twice as many boys go to school as girls. Human Rights Watch reported that "millions of girls—many more than the number currently enrolled—are not in school."[10] Many girls schools have been attacked; arsonists have emptied some classrooms.[11]

Even in places in Afghanistan where girls attend school, it is rare for them to continue beyond elementary school, while it is common for boys to receive years of additional schooling. The *Washington Post* noted in 2003 that "the idea of female study beyond sixth grade is far more controversial, particularly in traditional, rural areas steeped in social and gender taboos that existed long before the Taliban took power in 1996."[12]

The Afghan government cracked down in 2003 to reduce the number of females in school. Many Afghan females are forced to marry at an early age. A recent U.S. State Department report noted, "Government regulations prohibit women who are married from attending high school classes and . . . the education ministry ordered all regions to enforce this rule. During [2003], thousands of young women were expelled from school because they were married. . . . Supporters of the legislation say it protected unmarried girls in school from hearing 'tales of marriage' from their wedded classmates."[13]

SHAM WOMEN'S LIB

In his State of the Union address on January 29, 2002, Bush, listing the achievements of the Afghan invasion, declared: "The mothers and daughters of Afghanistan were captives in their own homes. . . . Today women are free."[14]

But most Afghan women have yet to experience the Bush deliverance. A January 2003 United Nations report on conditions in rural Afghanistan concluded that "the situation of women has not changed to any great extent since the removal of the Taliban."[15]

The U.S. State Department, in a February 2004 report on Afghanistan,[16] noted the following imperfections in Afghan equal rights:

> Kabul police authorities placed women under detention in prison, at the request of family members, for defying the family's wishes on the choice of a spouse.
>
> Tribal elders resolved murder cases by ordering the defendant to provide young girls in marriage to the victims' family, in exchange for the murder.
>
> In some areas, women were forbidden to leave the home except in the company of a male relative.
>
> Some local authorities excluded women from all employment outside the home, apart from the traditional work of women in agriculture.

In Herat province, ruler-warlord Ismael Khan closed down all beauty parlors and banned women from working as tailors. The government of the Nangarhar province banned all women entertainers from radio and television in April 2004.[17]

New York Times columnist Nicholas Kristof, who visited Afghanistan in early 2004, reported that "many Afghan women are still captives in their homes. . . . The rise of banditry and rape has had a particularly devastating effect on women. Because the roads are not safe even in daylight, girls do not dare go to schools or their mothers to health centers."[18] One international aid worker commented that during the Taliban era "if a woman went to market and showed an inch of flesh she would have been flogged—now she's raped."[19] The State Department cited reports that "women and older girls could not go out alone and that, when they did go out, they wore a burqa for fear of harassment or violence."[20] Judy Benjamin, a former advisor on gender issues for the U.S. government in Kabul, commented, "The legal opportunities have improved, but the day-to-day life for women, even in Kabul, isn't any better."[21]

Nancy Lindborg, who works with a nongovernmental organization in Afghanistan, commented that outside of Kabul, "everywhere I go, from Kunduz to Kandahar, I see no change for most women, and security for everybody has fallen apart since November of 2002."[22]

BARBARITY OVERSOLD

Like a knight in Mark Twain's *A Connecticut Yankee in King Arthur's Court,* Bush continually inflates the size of the dragons he supposedly slayed. In a speech in Louisville, Kentucky, on September 2, 2002, Bush bragged, "We went in to liberate people from the clutches of the most barbaric regime in history."[23] This was an upgrade for the Taliban, since Bush usually characterized them as only "the most barbaric regime in *modern* history."

The Taliban were brutal and killed tens of thousands of civilians during their five-year rule over most of Afghanistan. On a year-to-year basis, the Taliban may have been less bloodthirsty than the Northern Alliance, which ruled most of Afghanistan in the mid-1990s and whose factions killed more than 25,000 civilians in Kabul alone.[24] The Taliban's brutality never approached that of the Soviet military, which killed one to two million Afghans between 1979 and 1989.

Many governments have far exceeded the Taliban's carnage. Three million North Koreans have perished because of their government's brutal repression and its destruction of the agricultural sector. More than a million people were killed by government forces and rampaging paramilitaries carrying out ethnic cleansing campaigns in Rwanda and Burundi in 1994. The Khmer Rouge killed an estimated two to three million Cambodians beginning in 1975—almost a third of the population. Nor does the Taliban's grisly record compare with that of Hitler's Germany, Stalin's Russia, or Mao's China. And many conquerors in earlier history—from the Mongol hordes to medieval Christian crusaders—make the Taliban look like pikers.

AMERICAN-MADE VICTIMS DON'T COUNT

The Taliban's barbarism does not absolve America of its abuses. Though the Bush administration continually portrays the U.S. defeat of the Taliban as a triumph for human rights, the U.S. military has routinely covered up its abuses of Afghan civilians.

The Bush administration continually seeks to ignore, shrug off, or misrepresent actions of U.S. forces that kill innocent Afghan civilians. After the United States killed 15 Afghan children in two separate bombing incidents in December 2003, the Afghan government, the United Nations, and other organizations demanded a public accounting. The military conducted its own investigation of an incident in which nine children were killed and discovered that it was blameless. The results were top secret, but, according to U.S. military spokesman Bryan Hilferty, "The investigating officer said we used appropriate rules of engagement and did follow the law of conflict."[25]

Human Rights Watch condemned U.S. practices in a March 2004 report, noting that "civilians are being held in a legal black hole—with no tribunals, no legal counsel, no family visits and no basic legal protections."[26] The report declared, "There is compelling evidence suggesting that U.S. personnel have committed acts against detainees amounting to torture or cruel, inhumane, or degrading treatment." The deaths of two Afghans being held at the U.S. Bagram air base were officially classified by military doctors as homicides resulting from "blunt force injuries."

As the Iraqi prison abuse scandal exploded in late April and May 2004, alleged abuses of Afghan prisoners again became a hot issue. The *New York Times* reported that two men held at the Bagram air base declared "that they were tortured and sexually humiliated by their American jailers; they said they were held in isolation cells, black hoods were placed over their heads, and their hands at times were chained to the ceiling."[27] U.S. forces have prohibited anyone—including the Afghan government or Red Cross—from visiting its detainees held at 20 smaller prisons scattered around Afghanistan.

OPIUM-FREE AFGHANISTAN

The Taliban government profited heavily from taxing poppy growers until it banned the crop as a violation of Islam in September 2000. Poppy production fell by 95 percent the following year—one of the greatest antidrug successes in world history. Poppy is used to make opium and heroin.

Bush vowed that Afghan narcotics would never again bankroll dark deeds. Bush proclaimed on November 15, 2001 that "The Taliban Government and Al Qaeda—the evil ones—use heroin trafficking in order to fund their murder. And one of our objectives is to make sure that Afghanistan is never used for that purpose again."[28]

The Taliban's poppy prohibition ended with the Taliban's collapse. The new Afghan government installed by the United States tried several measures to suppress poppy production, including rewarding farmers for destroying their crop or not growing poppy at all, and, in a few cases, sending out troops who shot growers. U.S. Drug Enforcement Administration chief Asa Hutchinson bragged that Afghan poppy production would be slashed by up to 30 percent in 2002.[29] Instead, production rose twenty-fold,[30] and soared again in 2003.

Free food from abroad is spurring poppy production. The *Washington Post* reported in July 2003: "Because aid groups have made food more plentiful, some farmers are feeding their families donated wheat, leaving their fields free for planting poppy. In the northern province of Faryab, World Food Program workers said they noticed the greatest poppy cultivation in areas where they distributed wheat most heavily."[31] The United Nations estimates that farmers can earn almost 40 times as much growing poppy as they do growing wheat. Food donations have also driven down the price of locally grown wheat in Afghanistan, making it more difficult for farmers to survive without turning to poppy.

Working in the poppy fields or in drug labs pays up to $10 a day, outbidding all other jobs. A United Nations official in Badakhshan, Afghanistan, complained: "Almost all the U.N. projects have stopped because there is no labor. People are working with the poppy. Roof construction, school projects—all stopped. Everybody is affected."[32]

Many of the U.S. government's warlord allies and even some soldiers in the U.S.-trained Afghan government army are involved in drug trafficking. The International Monetary Fund estimates that opium production provides the equivalent of almost half of Afghanistan's gross domestic product. The IMF warned: "A dangerous potential exists for Afghanistan to progressively slide into a 'narco-state' where all legitimate institutions become penetrated by the power and wealth of drug traffickers."[33] A United Nations survey found that almost 70 percent of farmers intended to greatly boost their poppy plantings in 2004.

On the other hand, the resurgence of opium production in 2002 may have done more than foreign aid to prevent starvation in Afghanistan. Many foreign countries, including the United States, largely defaulted on their pledges to provide prompt, massive aid to Afghanistan after the fall of the Taliban. The United Nations estimated that opium generated more money for Afghans in 2002 than the total international aid Afghans received that year. The vast majority of the opium money ends up in private pockets, while much of the international aid goes for setting up new government bureaucracies, fattening

American consultants, and hiring enforcement agents to take the place of the Taliban's God Squad.

At a March 2004 conference of international donors in Berlin, Afghan president Hamid Karzai proclaimed a "holy war" must be launched against "warlordism and poppy cultivation." Karzai warned that Afghanistan could not be secure "unless the society is free of narcotics and irresponsible armed groups."[34] But there is little reason to expect a massive crackdown on farmers to produce any more freedom in Afghanistan than a similar crackdown in Thailand produced.

THE MIRAGE OF THE AFGHAN ARMY

On August 14, 2003, Bush bragged, "We've also helped to build an Afghan national army."[35] Technically, Bush's statement was not false. The United States, along with France and Britain, have trained an Afghan army of roughly seven thousand troops. They all have uniforms with the insignia of the Afghan National Army and they all have (or had) army-issued boots and socks.

However, this army is almost irrelevant to stabilizing the nation or protecting it from terrorist incursions from Pakistan or elsewhere. Almost half of the soldiers trained thus far have deserted. Experts estimate that it may take seven more years to get the army up to its goal of seventy thousand troops.[36] Afghan warlords have one hundred thousand men under their command[37]— more than ten times as many fighters as in the Afghan army. The U.S. government continues financing some of the warlords, despite the warlords' long records of atrocities and their scorn for the Afghan central government.

Afghan soldiers are sometimes a pox on their countrymen. Human Rights Watch reported that government "troops and police in many parts of the [southeast] region, and parts of Kabul itself, are invading private homes, usually at night, and robbing and assaulting civilians. By force or by ruse, soldiers and police gain entry into homes and hold people hostage for hours, terrorizing them with weapons, stealing their valuables, and sometimes raping women and girls. On the roads and at proliferating official and unofficial checkpoints, local soldiers and police extort money from civilians under the threat of beating or arrest."[38]

THE TALIBAN FOREVER VANQUISHED

On November 30, 2003, in a speech to U.S. Army troops at Fort Carson, Colorado, Bush declared: "Working with a fine coalition, our military went to Afghanistan, destroyed the training camps of Al Qaida, and put the Taliban out of business forever."[39]

Shortly after Bush's announcement, the U.S. military launched Operation Mountain Blizzard to fight Taliban elements and terrorist suspects in the southern part of Afghanistan. Mountain Blizzard was so successful in putting the Taliban "out of business forever" that the United States brought in thousands of reinforcements and launched Operation Mountain Storm in March 2004.[40]

On the main road in the Zabul province, "the Taliban have set up daytime road blocks. They scrutinize vehicles for potential targets to kill or kidnap. Four engineers working on that road have been kidnapped, and 15 Afghans working for the central government have been killed in the past three months," according to a February 2004 report in Canada's *Globe and Mail.*[41]

The Taliban continue to pose a mortal threat to many Afghans who seek progress and stability in their country. As of March 2004, the Taliban and cohorts controlled roughly a third of Afghanistan, primarily in the southern areas adjacent to Pakistan. General James Jones, the U.S. commander of NATO forces in Afghanistan, testified to Congress in January 2004 that enemy forces "have some military capability to psychologically demoralize us."[42] The U.N. Development Program warned in March 2004 that Afghanistan may again become a "terrorist breeding ground" unless it receives far more international aid.[43]

HIGHWAY TO NOWHERE?

On December 16, 2003, dignitaries from the U.S. government, the Afghan provisional government, the United Nations, and other organizations gathered for a ribbon-cutting ceremony. President Bush issued a statement from Washington bragging that "the first phase of paving the Kabul-Kandahar leg of the highway is completed under budget and ahead of schedule. This new road reduces travel time between Kabul to Kandahar to five hours. It will promote political unity between Afghanistan's provinces, facilitate commerce by making it easier to bring products to market, and provide the Afghan people with greater access to health care and educational opportunities."[44]

Bush's notion of "under budget" is unusual; the U.S. government spent more than three times as much on the road as it originally planned ($270 million instead of $80 million).[45] On the other hand, compared to the U.S. overspending on the occupation of Iraq versus prewar forecasts, this Afghan highway is under budget and a great bargain.

Though the announcement and the ceremony were widely portrayed in the U.S. media as a triumph for the Bush administration, the reality was less cheery. The *Los Angeles Times* reported that "it took hundreds of U.S. and Afghan troops, backed by attack helicopters, antitank weapons, snipers and bomb-sniffing dogs to make it safe for President Hamid Karzai to cut the ribbon on the Kabul-to-Kandahar highway." Prior to the signing ceremony, "troops set up roadblocks to stop traffic in both directions for more than three hours. That was just long enough for dignitaries to arrive in heavily guarded convoys and on Chinook helicopters, celebrate a job well done and rush back to safer ground in Kabul, the capital, 25 miles northeast."[46]

The trip from Kabul to Kandahar is much faster now—unless a person gets killed or kidnapped along the way. Andrew Natsios, the director of the U.S. Agency for International Development, bragged: "We built this road right through a war zone."[47] But the road is doing nothing to end the war. Though the road itself is a vast improvement over the horribly potholed road first built by the United States in the 1960s, the *Chicago Tribune* noted that "all but about 40 miles of it are off-limits to the United Nations agencies and international aid workers" because of the high risk of attacks.[48] The soaring crime rate can make the road too perilous even for Afghan taxi drivers.

THE AFGHAN PEOPLE ARE FREE

President Bush never tires of reminding listeners that the Afghan people, just like Americans, are free. In a February 5, 2004, speech in Charleston, South Carolina, Bush declared, "Thanks to the United States and our friends, thanks to the bravery of many of our fellow citizens, Afghanistan is no longer a haven for terror. Afghanistan is a free country."[49] The Afghans costar in one of Bush's favorite fundraiser lines: "Fifty million people in those two countries [Afghanistan and Iraq] once lived under tyranny, and today, they live in freedom."[50] On September 17, 2003, Bush asserted that the United States "liberated the . . . Afghan people from oppression and fear."[51]

It takes more than the abolition of weekly public executions in the Kabul soccer stadium to make Afghans free. If freeing people was as simple as toppling a bad government, then almost all of the people in the world would have long since been free.

Perhaps Bush assumes that the Afghan people are free because their ruler is under the U.S. thumb. The Afghan central government (which has little power outside Kabul) is headed by a man widely perceived as a puppet of the

U.S. government. *Time* noted in March 2004 that, because of "fear of assassination," Hamid Karzai "rarely leaves the palace" and "almost never sees" the country he purportedly governs.[52] Karzai is constantly surrounded by a bodyguard of American soldiers.

Karzai is dominated by U.S. ambassador Zalmay Khalilzad, according to an April 17, 2004, *New York Times* report.[53] The *Times* reported how a day starts in the seat of power in Kabul:

> "So what are we doing today?" Afghanistan's president, Hamid Karzai, asked the United States ambassador, Zalmay M. Khalilzad, as they sat in Mr. Karzai's office.
>
> Mr. Khalilzad patiently explained that they would attend a ceremony to kick off the "greening" of Kabul—the planting and seeding of 850,000 trees—in honor of the Afghan New Year. . . .
>
> The genial Mr. Karzai may be Afghanistan's president, but the affable, ambitious Mr. Khalilzad often seems more like its chief executive. With his command of both details and American largesse, the Afghan-born envoy has created an alternate seat of power since his arrival on Thanksgiving. As he shuttles between the American Embassy and the presidential palace, where Americans guard Mr. Karzai, one place seems an extension of the other.

Meanwhile, most of Afghanistan is dominated by warlords who have traditionally plundered and exploited whatever fell under their sway.

Bush's proclamation that Afghan is free provides more insight into Bush's concept of freedom than it does into the daily sufferings of Afghans at the hands of their government. The U.S. State Department noted, "Arbitrary arrest and detention are serious problems. . . . Procedures for taking persons into custody and bringing them to justice followed no established code. . . . Limits on lengths of pretrial detention were not respected. . . . There were credible reports that some detainees were tortured to elicit confessions while awaiting trial." On the bright side, the State Department noted that "defendants . . . were permitted attorneys in some instances."[54]

Afghan freedom mimics *Bush freedom*. The Afghan government created a National Security Court to try terrorist and other cases but did not disclose any details on how the court will actually function. The new court could provide the appearance of a court while permitting maximum political manipulation of charges and verdicts. The Karzai government also expanded the number of judges on the Afghan Supreme Court from 9 to 137.

Afghans' freedom to engage in political activity turns on the government's pleasure. The October 2003 government directive decrees that all political parties must "register with the Ministry of Justice and requires political parties to pursue objectives that are in line with the principles of Islam."[55] If the government refuses to permit a political party to register, then the party is illegal and its members can be arrested as criminals.

Freedom is flattening for some Afghans unlucky enough to live near high-ranking government officials. The State Department reported: "Government forces demolished homes and forcibly removed populations from and around the homes of high government officials and other government facilities, without any judicial review. In September, police officers, led by Kabul Chief of Police Salangi, destroyed the homes of more than 30 families in Kabul." Since June 2003, the Afghan Independent Human Rights Commission has "investigated and registered approximately 300 cases of police arbitrarily destroying homes."[56]

Freedom of speech and freedom of press are sparse in many parts of Afghanistan. The State Department noted: "Government intimidation and surveillance of journalists continued to inhibit open, public discussion of political issues. . . . the Government maintained departments that were pre-disposed to crack down on journalists. Members of the intelligence service, National Directorate of Security, reportedly staked out journalists' homes, followed them on the street, visited their offices, and delivered threats to stop publishing critical articles." The threats pack a punch because the Afghan intelligence service runs its own prisons, completely separate from judicial meddling. Police arrested and interrogated the two top editors of a weekly newspaper, *Aftaab,* after it "criticized senior leaders of the Northern Alliance, called for a secular government, and questioned the morals of Islamic leaders."[57] The government banned the newspaper.

The government and political forces have a stranglehold on broadcast media and also dominate much of the print media. The State Department noted, "The State owned at least 35 publications and almost all of the electronic news media. All other newspapers were published only sporadically and for the most part were affiliated with different provincial authorities. Some government officials through political party ties maintained their own communications facilities."[58] Considering the high rate of illiteracy in Afghanistan, the government broadcast media monopoly assures that few Afghans will hear a discouraging word—at least regarding their rulers.

The government also censors in the name of Islam. The Afghan Supreme Court "banned cable television, calling its content offensive to the moral values of Islamic society. Following an April inquiry by the Afghan Ministry of Information and Culture, the Government eased the ban on most news and sports cable broadcasters. . . . but prohibited cable operators from airing West-ern movie and music channels."[59]

Other freedoms have yet to blossom in Afghanistan. The State Depart-ment noted that "authorities in Pagham and Shakar Dara arrested and beat musicians and persons dancing."[60]

In early 2004, Bush gushed about the provisional constitution recently ap-proved by a meeting of Afghanistan's Loya Jirga. Bush told the U.S. Confer-ence of Mayors on January 23: "Afghanistan has now got a constitution which talks about freedom of religion and talks about women's rights. . . . Democ-racy is flourishing."[61] In a January 22 speech, Bush beamed that "the people of Afghanistan have written a constitution which guarantees free elections, freedom, full participation in government by women. Things are changing. Freedom is powerful."[62]

But the new Afghan constitution has thus far had about as much effect on the average Afghan as Stalin's 1936 constitution, which generously proclaimed a panoply of freedoms, had on the typical Soviet citizen. The constitution is largely a list of positive-sounding aspirations—the type of public relations slo-gans that Washington lobbies emit all the time for their foreign clients. The new constitution has thus far done little more than make regular appearances in Bush's speeches.

CONCLUSION

As long as the Taliban have not reentered Kabul in triumph, Bush can con-tinue to portray the U.S. invasion of Afghanistan as one of the greatest hu-manitarian triumphs in history. Bush inflated the victory over the Taliban to make himself appear as not only a great military conqueror but also a savior of part of humanity. Bush is playing on the ignorance of Americans who vaguely recall the television news broadcasts showing the U.S. troops' victories but otherwise followed few, if any, of the details of what happened in Afghanistan since late 2001.

Bush was permitted to transform the war into a "feel good" experience for uninformed or gullible Americans—dousing the citizenry with borrowed virtue and permitting them to feel benevolent at no cost or inconvenience to themselves. Politicians and the media talked as if freedom were the automatic aftereffect of a U.S. invasion. The triumph of the United States was presented as the triumph of human rights and democracy—so there was no point in quibbling over a few lingering petty problems.

After the United States and its allies defeated the Taliban, the president became entitled to distort the victory however he chose. And the more glorious the victory in Afghanistan became, the more inviting the invasion of Iraq appeared. But there are no harmless political lies about a war. The more war lies citizens tolerate, the more wars they are likely to get. Every lie that is tolerated about one war becomes an engraved invitation to launch another war.

One can fervently wish for freedom and prosperity for the long-suffering Afghan people without buying into Bush's nonsense about how U.S. intervention has already delivered the Promised Land unto them.

CHAPTER SIXTEEN

Iraq
The Iron Fist of Freedom

Freedom is happening in Iraq.

—*George Bush, Roswell, New Mexico, January 22, 2004*[1]

On March 24, 2004, President Bush treated attendees at the Radio and Television Correspondents annual dinner to a light-hearted slide show entitled the "White House Election-Year Album." One series of slides showed a perplexed Bush crawling around on his knees, checking behind a curtain and moving chairs in the Oval Office. Bush quipped for the crowd: "Those weapons of mass destruction have got to be somewhere . . . Nope, no weapons over there . . . Maybe under here?"[2]

The president's jests got a hearty laugh and applause from the government and media dignitaries. The president's skit epitomized that, for Bush and many broadcast journalists, the primary fraud that led to war is now a big joke. The fact that almost 600 Americans had been killed in Iraq did not dampen the spirits of the Washington elite.

Bush's war against Iraq may be his greatest abuse of power. But the Iraq war is far larger than George Bush, whether or not the current president retires to his ranch early next year. Bush has set precedents that threaten American security and world peace.

THOSE PESKY MISSING WMD

In the lead-up to the U.S. invasion, no issue was stressed as heavily as Saddam's possession of weapons of mass destruction (WMD). Bush and his team were very specific as to the quantities and types of weapons; Defense Secretary Donald Rumsfeld even declared that the United States knew where the illicit arms were hidden. In a speech on March 17, 2003, in which he gave Saddam 48 hours to abdicate power, Bush declared, "Intelligence gathered by this and other governments leaves no doubt that the Iraq regime continues to possess and conceal some of the most lethal weapons ever devised."[3] Bush justified the invasion of Iraq by appealing to UN resolutions that, he said, "authorized" the United States and other governments "to use force in ridding Iraq of weapons of mass destruction." A day earlier, Vice President Dick Cheney announced on national television that "we believe [Saddam] has, in fact, reconstituted nuclear weapons."[4]

Over the following year, Bush fought doggedly to defend his WMD claims, continually confusing the issue and making transcendent appeals to other subjects. Bush usually carried out his verbal sleights of hand more suavely than did "Baghdad Bob," the PR spokesman for Saddam's regime who continually announced great Iraqi military victories.

At a May 29, 2003, exchange with the press corps, Bush was asked how the war was justified since no WMDs had been found. Bush stunned listeners: "We found the weapons of mass destruction. We found biological laboratories. . . . They're illegal . . . They're against the United Nations resolutions, and we've so far discovered two. . . . But for those who say we haven't found the banned manufacturing devices or banned weapons, they're wrong. We found them." CIA experts later concluded that the alleged mobile "biological laboratories" were actually used to produce hydrogen for Iraqi artillery shells during the Iraq-Iran war.[5] Bush's vindication was a far cry from his shrill tones the previous September, when he misrepresented a UN report, claiming it said Iraq was only six months away from developing a nuclear weapon.[6] And the truck trailers did not quite fulfill Secretary of State Colin Powell's "conservative estimate," when he assured the UN Security Council the previous February that "Iraq, today, has a stockpile of between 100 and 500 tons of chemical weapons agent."[7]

On June 10, 2003, when asked by a reporter if the failure to find WMDs damaged U.S. credibility, Bush replied, "I'm not exactly sure what that means. I mean, Iraq had a weapons program. Intelligence throughout the decade showed they had a weapons program. I am absolutely convinced with time we'll find out that they did have a weapons program." Bush then veered off to higher ground:

> The credibility of this country is based upon our strong desire to make the world more peaceful—and the world is now more peaceful after our decision; the strong desire to make sure free nations are more secure—our free nations are now more secure; and the strong desire to spread freedom. And the Iraqi people are now free and are learning the habits of freedom and the responsibilities that come with freedom.[8]

Bush sounded as if fixating on WMDs somehow deterred the advance of freedom.

In a June 17, 2003, speech at a community college in northern Virginia, Bush sneered, "I know there's a lot of revisionist history now going on, but one thing is certain: [Saddam] is no longer a threat to the free world, and the people of Iraq are free."[9] In a speech in New Jersey the day before, Bush also denounced "revisionist historians."[10] In Bush's worldview, the revisionists were those unable to rise above history, petty-minded people mired in irrelevant ancient quibbles.

In his June 21, 2003, weekly radio address, Bush blamed Saddam for the missing WMDs: "For more than a decade, Saddam Hussein went to great lengths to hide his weapons from the world. And in the regime's final days, documents and suspected weapons sites were looted and burned. . . . We are determined to discover the true extent of Saddam Hussein's weapons programs, no matter how long it takes."[11] Bush allocated $600 million for teams of experts to comb Iraq searching for vindication.

Before audiences where Bush ran no risk of hoots and catcalls, he simply proclaimed success. Speaking at a military reenlistment ceremony on July 1, 2003, Bush bragged: "We ended a regime that possessed weapons of mass destruction."[12]

At a July 2 press conference, a reporter asked whether "there is a discrepancy between what the intelligence community and you and your top officials described as the threat from Saddam Hussein, and what was actually there on the ground?" Bush replied: "But he played his hand—Saddam Hussein—when he used chemical weapons. And then he played his hand by not letting people come in and inspect for the weapons. He had them, and it's just a matter of time. It's a matter of time. The man was a threat to America."[13] But Saddam *did* permit UN inspectors to enter Iraq in late 2002 and early 2003. The inspectors were going gangbusters, according to UN officials, until Bush invaded.

On July 3, 2003, in an interview session with African journalists, Bush was asked about the missing WMDs. The president replied: "We found a biological lab, the very same lab that had been banned by the United Nations. It will be a matter of time."[14] The two biological labs of late May had by then dwindled to one, and the Bush administration's chief weapons investigator in Iraq labeled the bogus charge a "fiasco."[15]

As controversy swirled over the missing WMDs, National Security Advisor Condoleezza Rice played the race card against those who opposed invading Iraq. In a September 7, 2003, speech to the National Association of Black Journalists, Rice scorned the view that some nations should not be liberated: "We've heard that argument before. And we, more than any, as a people, should be ready to reject it. That view was wrong in 1963 in Birmingham and it is wrong in 2003 in Baghdad and in the rest of the Middle East."[16] But the fact that the Klan bombed a black church in Birmingham in 1963 does not justify Bush bombing Baghdad 40 years later.

In an October 9, 2003, speech to a chamber of commerce in New Hampshire, Bush justified the invasion: "Our investigators have found evidence of a clandestine network of biological laboratories, advance design work on prohibited longer-range missiles, an elaborate campaign to hide illegal programs. . . . It is undeniable that Saddam Hussein was a deceiver and a danger."[17] But the "advance design work" consisted simply of diagrams and other information contained on a couple of computer diskettes.[18] It was little more than one engineer's fantasy—barely more of a threat than a bored tenth-grade student's doodlings in the margins of his notebook.

The obstinate refusal of the WMDs to divulge themselves prompted other higgling questions. At an October 28, 2003, press conference, Bush was asked about the giant "Mission Accomplished" banner hung on the aircraft carrier *USS Abraham Lincoln* for his fly-in and victory speech on May 1, 2003. Bush replied: "The 'Mission Accomplished' sign, of course, was put up by the members of the *USS Abraham Lincoln,* saying that their mission was accomplished. I know it was attributed somehow to some ingenious advance man from my staff—they weren't that ingenious, by the way."[19]

The design of the banner had the same design, typeface, and background as a large "Jobs and Growth" banner hung at a Bush speaking event in Ohio a week earlier. A few days after Bush's *Abraham Lincoln* speech, the *Washington Post* noted that Bush's "aides say the slogan was chosen in part to mark a presidential turn toward domestic affairs as his campaign for reelection approaches."[20] After Bush's October 28 comment on the banner, White House spokesman Dan Bartlett asserted that the slogan was thought up by sailors who then asked the White House to create the banner. The White House arranged for the banner to be created and delivered to the aircraft carrier. But Bush was correct that the banner was not hung up on the carrier by his press secretary, Ari Fleischer.

In a November 12, 2003, interview, the BBC's David Frost asked Bush, "Do you think that you were the victim of a failure of intelligence in a way?" Bush replied: "No, not at all. I think our intelligence was sound." Bush then mentioned that he sent a team to Iraq "to find the weapons or the intent of weapons."[21] Bush did not offer any insight into how he defined "the intent of weapons."

Other administration officials continually probed the limits of public gullibility on WMDs. In a CNN interview on December 7, 2003, Andrew Card, the White House chief of staff, was asked about the WMDs: "Was U.S. intelligence going into the war faulty?" Card recited a few Saddam crimes and then shrugged off the issue: "So, I think that's a moot point."[22]

In a December 16, 2003, interview with ABC News, Diane Sawyer pressed Bush on whether he had gone to war on false evidence. Bush replied by insisting that Saddam had sought to acquire weapons.

Sawyer asked incredulously: "But stated as a hard fact, that there were weapons of mass destruction as opposed to the possibility that he could move to acquire those weapons still—"

Bush replied: "So what's the difference?"

Sawyer responded: "Well—"

Bush said: "The possibility that he could acquire weapons. If he were to acquire weapons, he would be the danger. That's, that's what I'm trying to explain to you."[23]

In his January 20, 2004, State of the Union address, Bush vindicated his war, declaring that "had we failed to act, the dictator's weapons of mass destruction programs would continue to this day."[24] But postwar investigations found no evidence that such programs were making significant progress or posed any threat. Bush claimed inspectors had discovered "dozens of weapons of mass destruction-related program activities." But sometimes a memo is just a memo. And regardless of how many memos U.S. investigators found, there was nothing to justify Bush's fear-mongering when he told Americans in September 2002 that "Each passing day could be the one on which the Iraqi regime gives anthrax or VX—nerve gas—or someday a nuclear weapon to a terrorist ally."[25]

A few days after the State of the Union address, David Kay—the man Bush chose to head the search for WMDs in Iraq—testified to Congress that "we were almost all wrong," as far as Iraq possessing WMDs.[26] Kay had been selected as chief WMD finder in part because of his staunch advocacy of the war, and his testimony turned up the heat on Bush. White House spokesman Scott McClellan reassured the media that the Bush administration still believed Saddam had WMDs "and yes we believe they will be found. We believe the truth will come out."[27]

Attorney General John Ashcroft jumped into the fray, summing up the squabble in a way that made George Bush look like a Rhodes Scholar. Pontificating during a European tour, Ashcroft proclaimed that the war against Saddam was justified because of the dictator's use of "evil chemistry" and "evil biology."[28] Ashcroft put the entire controversy in fundamentalist terms, potentially sanctifying a U.S. invasion of any country whose leader Bush hates and whose high schools offer chemistry classes.

Bush sent Condoleezza Rice to the talk shows in late January to respond to the gathering storm caused by Kay's revelations. Rice told one TV interviewer: "Nobody could count on the good will of Saddam Hussein to tell us that he did not have anthrax or botulinum toxin. He didn't even try."[29] But Saddam was apparently more honest about Iraqi WMD than Bush. The 12,000-page Iraqi government report to the UN in late 2002 was probably more accurate than any public statement by Bush or his top people in the same period. In another television interview, Rice helped Americans see the Big Picture: "What we have is evidence that there are differences between what we knew going in and what we found on the ground. But that's not surprising in a country that was as closed and secretive as Iraq, a country that was doing everything that it could to deceive the United Nations, to deceive the world."[30] And what were Bush and his top officials doing in the same period?

The decision to invade Iraq based on little or no evidence morphed into proof of Bush's courage. In a February 5, 2004, speech in Charleston, South Carolina, Bush continually congratulated himself for his courage in attacking a foreign nation on false pretenses: "When you're the Commander in Chief, you have to be willing to make the tough calls and to see your decisions through."[31]

On February 8, 2004, Bush revealed that invading Iraq was justified because Saddam "had the ability to make weapons at the very minimum."[32] This is like justifying a violent no-knock raid on someone's house because they live in a state where it is possible to purchase gunpowder and tin cans.

Bush sought to dodge responsibility by insisting that Congress was equally culpable. In a March 18, 2004, speech to soldiers at Fort Campbell, Kentucky, Bush declared: "In Iraq, my administration looked at the intelligence information, and we saw a threat. Members of Congress looked at the intelligence, and they saw a threat."[33] But the "look-see" defense is a fraud because the Bush administration fed bogus information to Congress. Sen. Bill Nelson (D-Fla.) revealed in December 2003 that, prior to the vote by Congress, endorsing the war effort, Bush administration officials told senators in a closed briefing that Saddam had the ability to send unmanned aerial vehicles (UAVs) to dump anthrax or other chemical and biological weapons on cities on the East Coast. Nelson commented that weapons inspectors "have not found anything that resembles an UAV that has that capability."[34] This threat was far more specific and imminent than Bush's public statements. Nelson stated that the threat of anthrax-laden UAVs wreaking havoc on American cities contradicted other intelligence senators received.[35] In contract law, a fraudulent representation is routinely invoked to void a contract. But Bush assumed that Congress's consent was irrevocable, regardless of the falsities upon which it was gained. (Congress, however, did a dismal job of oversight both before and in the year after the war. Congress received a 92-page classified assessment of Iraq's alleged WMD in the fall of 2002. The *Washington Post* reported that "no more than six senators and a handful of House members read beyond the five-page National Intelligence Estimate executive summary."[36])

In a March 19, 2004, speech celebrating the first anniversary of the invasion, Bush declared, "It is a good thing that years of illicit weapons developed by the dictator have come to the end." But the evidence indicated that the Iraqis had ceased development of biological and chemical weapons shortly after the 1991 war. Weapons inspector David Kay concluded that Iraq apparently disposed of its stockpiles by the mid-1990s. Bush then sought to portray critics as enemies of humanity, or perhaps simply as pro-tyranny: "Who would begrudge the Iraqi people their long-awaited liberation?"[37]

Bush claims that his war against Iraq increased the credibility of the U.S. government. Bush continually assured audiences in early 2004 that "This Nation is strong and confident in the cause of freedom. No friend or enemy today doubts the word of America."[38] At that time, international opinion polls showed a sharp decrease in U.S. credibility in almost every country where polls were taken.[39]

In April 2004, *Washington Post* editor Bob Woodward's book, *Plan of Attack,* was published, featuring material from Woodward's personal interviews with Bush a few months earlier. Woodward asked Bush about the failure to find WMD. Bush replied, "I don't want people to say 'Aha, we told you so.' I want people to know that there is a process that's ongoing." Bush stressed that not a single person had urged him to acknowledge publicly that WMD had not been found—and then admonished Woodward: "But you run in different circles than I do. Much more elite."

Woodward replied "It's really lots of business groups."

Bush explained: "The realism is to be able to understand that nature of Saddam Hussein, history, his potential harm to America." He then settled the issue: "The person who wants the president to stand up and declare that [Iraq had no WMDs] publicly is also the person who wants to say, 'Shouldn't have done it.' And there is no doubt in my mind we should have done this." Bush even questioned Woodward: "Why do you need to deal with this in the book? What's this got to do about it?" Woodward explained that the issue of the missing WMDs "was a key question" in the aftermath of the war.[40]

In March 2, 2004, comments to federal employees commemorating the first anniversary of the creation of the Department of Homeland Security, Bush again justified the invasion of Iraq and declared, "America will not allow terrorists and outlaw regimes to threaten our Nation and the world with the world's *most dangerous technologies.*"[41] This was a change from Bush's 2002 constant refrain that "We cannot let the world's most dangerous regimes threaten us with the world's *most dangerous weapons.*"[42] Now, the mere suspicion that a nation might have "dangerous technologies" is enough to justify attacking them.

Bush also offered a new standard to justify the war: "September the 11th, 2001, taught a lesson I have not forgotten. America must *confront threats before they fully materialize.*"[43] Prior to invading Iraq, Bush portrayed Saddam's threat as so dire that "we cannot wait for the final proof—the smoking gun—that could come in the form of a mushroom cloud."[44] Now, he is practically claiming to be justified in going to war against imagined—if not bogus—threats. At what point have threats materialized enough to justify preemptively killing a large number of foreigners?

The new Bush standard for preemptive wars is far more dangerous than the old lies. Bush is claiming that the war against Iraq was justified by a far lower standard of evidence, a far lower standard of threat, than what he initially claimed. With the "Not Fully Materialized' standard, Bush can declare dozens of nations a threat to the United States and justify attacking them—no evidence required. This is the war-making equivalent of the president's power to declare anyone an enemy combatant and strip them of all rights.

Bush has never shown an iota of contrition for his prewar falsehoods. Nor has he ever admitted any remorse for continually misleading the American people and the world. In an April 13, 2004, press conference, a reporter asked Bush whether it was a "fair criticism" that "you never admit a mistake" on issues such as "WMDs in Iraq"? Bush never wavered in his belief in the purity of his innocence, replying, "The people know where I stand, I mean, in terms of Iraq. I was very clear about what I believed. And, of course, I want to know why we haven't found a weapon yet."[45] The fact that Bush was both clear and consistent apparently made his false claims irrelevant.[46]

Some people believe Bush was misinformed by aides or staffers prior to the invasion of Iraq and that he bears little or no blame for the false statements. But Bush now tells lies of the same breadth and brightness as he did before he invaded Iraq.

Bush sought to quash the growing controversy over the missing WMDs by appointing a commission to investigate the problem. Bush decreed that the commission would finish its report in March 2005—regrettably, not in time to offer insights for voters in the November election.[47] Bush cited his creation of an "independent" commission as proof of his devotion to learning the truth about Iraq. Sen. Robert Byrd (D-W.Va.) ridiculed this notion:

> This commission is 100 percent under the thumb of the White House. Who created the panel's charter? The President. Who chooses the panel members? The President. To whom does the panel report? The President. Whom shall the panel advise and assist? The President. Who is in charge of determining what classified reports the panel may see? The President. Who gets to decide whether the Congress may see the panel's report? The President.[48]

The commission has no subpoena power. Bush's order creating the commission specified: "The President may at any time modify the security rules or procedures of the commission to provide the necessary protection to classified information."[49] This Bush-created commission is unlikely to receive information that tarnishes Bush.

Bush selected Sen. John McCain (R-Ariz.) as one of the seven commission members. On the day Bush announced McCain's appointment, McCain publicly declared, "The president of the United States, I believe, would not manipulate any kind of information for political gain or otherwise."[50] Bush appointed Laurence Silberman as co-chairman of the commission. Silberman was prominently involved in conservative efforts to have President Clinton removed from office during the Monica Lewinsky scandal. Ivo

Daalder, a former National Security Council advisor and Brookings Institution fellow, commented: "This is the most ill-prepared snow job I have seen in a long time. The commissioners he has named know absolutely nothing about the subject matter."[51] When asked about the missing WMDs at his April 13, 2004, press conference, Bush replied: "That's why we set up the independent commission. I look forward to hearing the truth as to exactly where they are."[52] But the purpose of the commission is to delay the truth, not to reveal it. Bush appears to believe he can siderail the matter with a commission only slightly more independent than a gaggle of White House interns.

Bush's WMD assertions are also suspect because he was determined to find any pretext to attack Iraq. Former Treasury Secretary Paul O'Neill commented in January 2004: "From the very beginning, there was a conviction, that Saddam Hussein was a bad person and that he needed to go. Going after Saddam was topic 'A' ten days after the inauguration—eight months before Sept. 11."[53] Bush made it clear in his first cabinet meetings that he wanted a pretext to invade Iraq: "It was all about finding a way to do it. That was the tone of it. The president saying, 'Find me a way to do this.'"[54] O'Neill was stunned that no one attending an early 2001 National Security Council meeting even bothered to ask why the United States should invade Iraq. In May 2003, Deputy Defense Secretary Paul Wolfowitz explained to a sympathetic journalist that the Bush team emphasized WMDs for "bureaucratic reasons . . . because it was the one reason everyone could agree on."[55]

BUSH'S IRON FIST FREEDOM

From the start, Bush immersed his attack of Iraq in freedom verbiage. The invasion was named Operation Iraqi Freedom, and the occupation costs are being paid out of the Iraqi Freedom Fund. Bush continually told listeners that the United States was "liberating" a foreign country and setting free 25 million Iraqis. Bush declared in July 2003 that, because of U.S. action in Iraq, people are "going to find out the word 'freedom' and 'America' are synonymous."[56] The constant invocation of freedom sanctified the war—at least in the minds of tens of millions of Americans who never read good newspapers.

Many Iraqis were confounded by Bush's promise of liberation. At the time U.S. forces entered Baghdad, hospitals were in pitiful shape, with shortages of everything. (The UN sanctions imposed on Iraq from 1990 to 2003, at the behest of the U.S. government, wrecked the Iraqi health care system.)[57] American troops effectively took over the hospitals but provided few supplies. However, U.S. troops did vigorously enforce a new "no smoking" rule inside hospitals. Capt. John Margolis, the U.S. commander, explained, "This is freedom and freedom can mean different things, and in this case freedom means we are going to have to enforce our values on them."[58]

In November 2003, the White House continually hyped the fact that Iraqis had new paper money to pay for their pomegranates. In a November 14, 2003, interview with British journalists, Bush declared, "On the humanitarian side, in seven months we've got a new currency moving through the system, which is pretty remarkable when you think about it."[59] Five days later, in an interview with an Arab journalist in London, Bush bragged, "They've got new currencies, and that's hard to do. And yet, we're making good, steady progress in replacing the currency."[60] It was a fiat currency—something that had value solely because of the dictate of the U.S. occupying army. The fact that Iraqis used the new currency was no more an acceptance of U.S. authority than the cessation of smoking in hospitals when in the presence of heavily armed American soldiers.

On July 2, 2003, asked about continuing attacks on American troops, Bush issued a taunt: "My answer is: Bring 'em on. We've got the force necessary to deal with the security situation."[61] Iraqi attacks intensified, killing hundreds of Americans in the following months.

Bush gushes over one "Operation Kick Ass" after another. On June 21, 2003, Bush hailed Operation Peninsula Strike and Operation Desert Scorpion, targeting terrorist organizations and "Ba'ath party loyalists."[62] In a September 13, 2003, radio address, Bush hailed American soldiers carrying out Operation Longstreet, "seeking and finding our enemies wherever they hide and plot."[63] In a November 1, 2003, radio address, Bush lauded "Operation Ivy Focus, a series of aggressive raids by the Army's 4th Infantry Division that in a little over a month has yielded the capture of more than 100 former regime members. . . . In other operations, our soldiers have also seized hundreds of weapons."[64] Bragging about seizing hundreds of weapons in a nation with millions of rifles is lame. Six months later, Bush proudly told radio listeners about Operation Vigilant Resolve in Fallujah and Operation Resolute Sword in southern Iraq.[65]

Bush at times portrayed practically any Iraqis who did not kowtow to the military occupation as terrorists. On November 11, 2003, Bush bragged to a conservative audience in Washington: "Last month alone, we made 1,500 raids against terrorists."[66] Anyone targeted by the U.S. military automatically earned the terrorist label.

In a March 6, 2004, radio address, Bush boasted, "A year ago, Iraq's only law was the whim of one brutal man. When the new law takes effect, Iraqis will, for the first time in decades, live under the clear protections of a written bill of rights."[67] But in the meantime, Iraqis live and die according to the whims of American soldiers. The Iraqis have a written bill of rights but the rights are null and void against the U.S. military.

Many American military tactics in Iraq are patterned after the heavy-handed methods used by the Israelis in their occupied territories. U.S. Brigadier Gen. Michael Vane reported in July 2003 that he and other U.S. military officers "recently traveled to Israel to glean lessons learned from their counterterrorist operations in urban areas."[68] U.S. military officials also expressed interest in Israeli software "instructing soldiers on how to behave in the West Bank and Gaza."[69] These are not the only "lessons learned": the *New York Times* reported in December 2003 that "American soldiers are demolishing buildings thought to be used by Iraqi attackers. They have begun imprisoning the relatives of suspected guerrillas, in hopes of pressing the insurgents to turn themselves in."[70]

After an American soldier was killed by a rocket-propelled grenade in the town of Abu Hishma, a U.S. jet destroyed the house where the attackers hid with a 500-pound bomb. U.S. troops arrested "eight sheiks, the mayor, the police chief and most members of the city council."[71] U.S. Army Major Darron Wright beamed: "We really hammered the place."[72] U.S. forces incarcerated the entire population of 7,000 by surrounding the area with five miles of razor wire. Signs in front of the fence notified residents: "This fence is here for your protection. Do not approach or try to cross, or you will be shot."

Every Iraqi male from the age of 18 to 65 was required to get an identification card with a mug shot, his name, and a description of his car. Any male without a card was prohibited from entering or leaving the town. The writing on the cards was only in English, so few Iraqis could understand their badges of servitude. One bitter Iraqi complained: "I see no difference between us and the Palestinians. We didn't expect anything like this after Saddam fell."[73] The *New York Times* described the constraints placed on the townspeople: "Residents complain that the village is locked down for 15 hours a day, meaning that they are unable to go to the mosque for morning and evening prayers. They say the curfew does not allow them time to stand in the daylong lines for gasoline and get home before the gate closes for the night. But mostly, it is a loss of dignity that the villagers talk about."[74] Capt. Todd Brown, one of the U.S. commanders whose troops locked down Abu Hishma, explained, "You have to understand the Arab mind. The only thing they understand is force—force, pride and saving face."[75]

On March 19, 2004, the first anniversary of the invasion, Bush proclaimed: "It's a good thing that the men and women across the Middle East looking to Iraq are getting a glimpse of what life in a free country can be like."[76] But Middle Easterners are seeing *Bush freedom,* not old-fashioned American freedom. Rather than establishing individual rights for an oppressed people, the U.S. military has created a nation of people classified as "enemy combatants."

The *New York Times* reported on March 7 that "Iraq has a new generation of missing men. But instead of ending up in mass graves or at the bottom of the Tigris River, as they often did during the rule of Saddam Hussein, they are detained somewhere in American jails."[77] More than 10,000 men and boys are locked up, ranging in age from 11 to 75. Some are being held on suspicion of planting bombs or attacking U.S. forces. But the *Times* noted that U.S. officials "acknowledge that most of the people captured are probably not dangerous."[78]

U.S. methods are maximizing fear in the conquered populace. Arrested men are often "led away in the middle of the night, with bags over their heads and no explanation. Many people have said that when they asked soldiers where their family members were being taken, they were told to shut up," the *Times* reported.[79] A U.S. raid on one village effectively shut down the schools, since most of the school teachers were rounded up and carted off.

Many Iraqis were reportedly arrested because they fired guns in the air at wedding celebrations, a common practice in the country. Other Iraqis have been arrested because troops conducting no-knock searches found firearms in their homes. Brig. Gen. Mark Kimmitt, the deputy director of operations for the occupying military forces, insisted that the U.S. military was being "careful" in its operations: "We don't want to arrest an entire village and come out with one rifle."[80] Adil Allami, a lawyer with the Human Rights Organization of Iraq, complained, "Iraq has turned into one big Guantánamo."[81] The only right most detainees have is for their wives and mothers to beg at prison gates for their release.

LIBERATION VIA COLLECTIVE PUNISHMENT

In his May 1, 2003 victory speech on the USS *Abraham Lincoln,* Bush declared, "When Iraqi civilians looked into the faces of our service men and women, they saw strength and kindness and good will." Bush was especially proud that "with new tactics and precision weapons, we can achieve military objectives without directing violence against civilians."[82] But such careful tactics did not impede U.S. commanders from inflicting collective punishment on an Iraqi city. On March 29, 2004, four American security contractors were killed and brutally mutilated in the streets of Fallujah, a city long hostile to American forces.

An Iraqi group known as the Brigades of Martyr Ahmed Yassin claimed responsibility for the killings. The group's statement declared: "This is a gift from the people of Fallujah to the people of Palestine and the family of Sheikh Ahmed Yassin who was assassinated by the criminal Zionists."[83] Yassin, the spiritual leader of Hamas, was killed a week earlier by missiles from an Israeli helicopter as he was leaving a mosque in his wheelchair. After Israeli leader Ariel Sharon okayed the killing of Yassin, many experts feared that the attack would further inflame Arabs against both Israel and the United States. Juan Cole, a University of Michigan history professor, commented: "Just as the Israelis and their American amen corner helped drag the US into the Iraq war, so they also have inflamed Iraqi sentiment against the US by spectacular uses of state terror against Palestinians. Both the Sunni and the Shiite uprisings in Iraq in the past week in a very real sense were set off by Sharon's whacking of Yassin, a paraplegic who could easily have been arrested."[84]

After the killings, the bodies of the Americans were dragged through the streets of Fallujah, surrounded by cheering crowds. Bush reportedly gave the order: "I want heads to roll."[85] Brigadier General Mark Kimmitt announced that the U.S. response "will be overwhelming. We will re-establish control and will pacify that city."[86]

The Bush administration tried to make an example out of the rebellious city. U.S. forces soon placed the entire city under siege. The British *Guardian* reported: "The US soldiers were going around telling people to leave by dusk or they would be killed, but then when people fled with whatever they could carry, they were stopped at the US military checkpoint on the edge of town and not let out, trapped, watching the sun go down."[87] Marine Lt. Col. Brennan Byrne announced on April 11: "What is coming is the destruction of anti-coalition forces in Fallujah. . . . They have two choices: Submit or die."[88]

The city was blasted by American F–16 jets and by AC–130 Spectre planes, which pumped 4,000 rounds a minute into selected targets. Residents were warned that they could be killed if they stepped out of their homes, and U.S. snipers made good the promise many times. Several Arab members of the Iraqi Governing Council—the front group carefully chosen by U.S. officials to add legitimacy to the occupation—resigned, denouncing the "collective punishment" of the residents of Fallujah. Al-Jazeera, an Arab television network, broadcast the carnage that the military attack inflicted on civilians, helping stir outrage and opposition to the occupation throughout Iraq. U.S. military officials demanded that the Al-Jazeera correspondents be expelled from Fallujah before they would agree to a ceasefire.[89]

A fragile ceasefire was finally reached in late April, and President Bush declared that "most of Falluja is returning to normal." But the city's largest hospital had been destroyed by American bombs and more than 400 Iraqis were killed during the U.S. retaliation for the killing of the 4 U.S. contractors.

Brutal crackdowns may gratify Bush but the hatred they generate may doom American efforts. Army Major General Charles Swannack, the commander of the 82nd Airborne Division, declared in May 2004 that he believes that the United States is losing "strategically," even though U.S. forces win most of the tactical battles.[90] Army Colonel Paul Hughes, who directed strategic planning for the military occupation authority in 2003, warned that "Unless we ensure that we have coherency in our policy, we will lose strategically." Hughes voiced the danger that "we will win every fight and lose the war, because we don't understand the war we're in."[91]

TORTURE: "THE PEARL HARBOR OF PR"[92]

Bush has long flaunted his opposition to torture. Bush proclaimed on June 26, 2003, on the UN International Day in Support of Victims of Torture, "The United States is committed to the worldwide elimination of torture, and we are leading this fight by example."[93] As the months passed after the fall of Baghdad and no WMDs turned up, Bush increasingly invoked Saddam's use of torture to justify the U.S. invasion. Bush mentioned Saddam or the Iraqi government's torture more than 20 times in speeches:

- October 8, 2003: "Iraq is free of rape rooms and torture chambers."
- January 12, 2004: "One thing is for certain: There won't be any more mass graves and torture rooms and rape rooms."[94]
- February 4, 2004: "Saddam Hussein now sits in a prison cell, and Iraqi men and women are no longer carried to torture chambers and rape rooms."[95]

Bush had been informed in January 2004 that the military had launched an investigation into abuses by U.S. soldiers of Iraqi detainees.

On April 28, CBS broadcast photos of graphic prisoner abuse, including forced simulation of sexual acts, the stacking of naked prisoners, mock electrocution, and grinning U.S. soldiers. A few days later, the *New Yorker* published extracts from a report by Major General Antonio Taguba. It described abuses inflicted on prisoners by Americans at Abu Ghraib, Saddam's most notorious prison, including:

> Breaking chemical lights and pouring the phosphoric liquid on detainees; pouring cold water on naked detainees; beating detainees with a broom handle and a chair; threatening male detainees with rape . . . sodomizing a detainee with a chemical light and perhaps a broom stick, and using military working dogs to frighten and intimidate detainees with threats of attack, and in one instance actually biting a detainee.[96]

The Taguba report was submitted in early March 2004. Top Pentagon officials did not read it prior to the photos becoming public in late April.

Because a number of U.S. hostages were being held in Iraq in early and mid April, General Richard Myers, chairman of the Joint Chiefs of Staff, personally implored CBS news to postpone their broadcast of the photos of prisoner abuse. CBS held off the broadcast for at least two weeks. During the time that CBS delayed its bombshell story, Bush continually bragged about how well the American soldiers were treating Iraqis and how wonderful it was that torture had been abolished.

In a May 1, 2004, radio address on Iraq, Bush boasted, "At the most basic level of justice, people are no longer disappearing into political prisons, torture chambers, and mass graves—because the former dictator is in prison himself."[97] In his next weekly radio address on May 8, Bush sought to explain away the torture by American soldiers in Iraqi prisons, stressing that it had been done by "a small number of American servicemen and women. These individuals had been given the responsibility of overseeing Iraqis in American custody, and doing so in a decent and humane manner, consistent with U.S. law and the Geneva conventions."[98] But the Pentagon reportedly explicitly allowed some of the harsh techniques used on prisoners.

In reality, the torture scandal arose from one of Bush's most audacious edicts. In early 2002, Bush issued a ruling that could prevent the War Crimes Act from applying to many actions taken by U.S. officials against Al Qaeda and the Taliban.[99] The War Crimes Act, passed in 1996, applied to all Americans and defined war crimes in part as acts that would be "grave breaches" of the Geneva Conventions on the treatment of prisoners. White House counsel Alberto Gonzales advised Bush: "The nature of the new war places a high premium on other factors, such as the ability to quickly obtain information from captured terrorists and their sponsors in order to avoid further atrocities against American civilians. In my judgment, this new paradigm renders obsolete Geneva's strict limitations on questioning of enemy prisoners and renders quaint some of its provisions." Gonzales pointed out that formally ruling that the Geneva Conventions did not apply would help the president "preserve his flexibility." Bush declared that the Al Qaeda and Taliban forces did not have protection under the Geneva Conventions. Gonzales urged such a ruling, since it "substantially reduces the threat of domestic criminal prosecution under the War Crimes Act. . . . It is difficult to predict the motives of prosecutors and independent counsels who may in the future decide to pursue unwarranted charges based on Section 2441 [the War Crimes Act]." *Newsweek*, which first reported the memos, noted, "There is some reason to believe that administration lawyers were worried that the [War Crimes Act] could even be used in the future against senior administration officials" who authorized policies used in Afghanistan, Guantanamo, or elsewhere. Bush signed a secret directive that "authorized the CIA to set up a series of secret detention facilities outside the United States, and to question those held in them with unprecedented harshness," *Newsweek* reported.[100]

The Bush administration policy was shaped by a legal analysis done by John Yoo and Robert Delahunty of the Justice Department's Office of Legal Counsel. Yoo and Delahunty advised the Pentagon's general counsel that "Bush could argue that the Taliban government in Afghanistan was a 'failed state' and therefore its soldiers were not entitled to protections accorded in the conventions," as the *New York Times* summarized the confidential document.[101] Apparently, the amount of rights an individual possesses depends on the type of government they live under—or, more accurately, whether the U.S. government disparages it as a "failed state." Yet, no one has explained how U.S. disapproval of a foreign regime can create a license to torture the people who live in the territory of that nation.

The Bush administration proceeded to define torture almost out of existence. *Newsweek* noted, "One Justice Department memo, written for the CIA late in the fall of 2001, put an extremely narrow interpretation on the international anti-torture convention, allowing the agency to use a whole range of techniques—'including sleep deprivation, the use of phobias and the deployment of stress factors'—in interrogating Qaeda suspects."[102] One popular persuasive method included pushing a detainee's head underwater and making him believe he would be drowned. *Newsweek* noted that experts developed a "72-point matrix for stress and duress" at Guantanamo Bay, including "the use of harsh heat or cold; withholding food; hooding for days at a time; naked isolation in cold, dark cells for more than 30 days, and threatening (but not biting) by dogs. It also permitted limited use of 'stress positions' designed to subject detainees to rising levels of pain." After vigorous interrogation methods produced results in Afghanistan and Guantanamo Bay, Defense Secretary Rumsfeld "seemingly set in motion a process that led to their use in Iraq, even though that war was supposed to have been governed by the Geneva Conventions," according to *Newsweek*.[103]

After the photos from Abu Ghraib became public, Bush sought to defuse the controversy by granting an interview with Alhurra Television, an Arabic network owned and controlled by the U.S. government. Rather than apologizing for the gross abuses, Bush insisted that the scandal proved the superiority of democracy: "It's also important for the people of Iraq to know that in a democracy, everything is not perfect, that mistakes are made. But in a democracy as well those mistakes will be investigated, and people will be brought to justice. We're an open society. . . . That stands in stark contrast to life under Saddam Hussein. His trained torturers were never brought to justice under his regime." Perhaps Bush believes that Saddam's torture was always evil because it was in the service of tyranny, while American torture is by definition pro-freedom. Bush stressed: "We have nothing to hide. We believe in transparency, because we're a free society. That's what free societies do. They—if there's a problem, they address those problems in a forthright, upfront manner. And that's what's taking place." A minute later, Bush effectively announced what the results of the thorough investigation would be: "We're finding the few [U.S. troops] that wanted to try to stop progress toward freedom and democracy."[104] But the Pentagon had not begun a serious investigation of detainee abuse in Iraq until it became clear that the photos would leak out to the public.

In a May 24 speech at the Army War College, Bush repeated his assertion that Abu Ghraib's outrages involved actions "by a few American troops who disregarded our country and disregarded our values."[105] But, as of late May, the Pentagon was formally investigating the deaths of 37 men during their detainment by U.S. forces in Afghanistan and Iraq. One investigation targeted National Guard interrogators who had "forced into asphyxiation numerous detainees in an attempt to obtain information" in the spring of 2003.[106] The *Denver Post* reported in late May that "five prisoner interviews resulted in deaths at four different interrogation sites, and no prosecutions have been initiated in the cases." U.S. military personnel abused detainees "by stripping them of their clothing, beating them and shocking them with a blasting device," according to a Pentagon investigation. The penalties for Americans convicted of abuses were light, including prohibitions of visiting a local Internet cafe.[107]

Some military intelligence soldiers sent to conduct interrogation at Abu Ghraib prison "had only one day of training on how to pry information from high-value prisoners," the *Baltimore Sun* reported. Many of the people seized and locked up waited for months before being interrogated. The prison guards and interrogators developed their own lingo. One military intelligence soldier commented that Military Intelligence officials "would drop off a guy who wasn't talking, and the MP would say, 'So looks like I'll be going cowboy on him' or 'Looks like he needs some wild, wild west'"—slang for beatings.[108]

Defense Secretary Donald Rumsfeld complained in a Senate hearing in early May that "people [in Iraq] are running around with digital cameras and taking these unbelievable photographs and then passing them off, against the law, to the media, to our surprise, when they had not even arrived in the Pentagon."[109] But the "crime" of taking and passing around photographs was not the moral equivalent of the torture itself.

Some Bush supporters denounced the critics of prison abuses. At a Senate Intelligence Committee hearing on May 10, 2004, Sen. James Inhofe (R-Okla.) angrily complained: "I'm probably not the only one up at this table that is more outraged by the outrage than we are by the treatment." Inhofe explained why the detainees got what they deserved: "These prisoners, you know they're not there for traffic violations. If they're in cellblock 1-A or 1-B, these prisoners, they're murderers, they're terrorists, they're insurgents. Many of them probably have American blood on their hands and here we're so concerned about the treatment of those individuals."[110] Sen. Evan Bayh (D-Ind.), though not quite as fanatical as Inhofe, complained that the scandal "goes directly to the heart of how we hope to win the war against terror and what we're hoping to accomplish in Iraq. And that is that we are morally superior to our adversaries. . . . We don't torture people. We stand for freedom."[111]

CASKETS AND MISCOUNTS

The Bush administration prohibited the media from taking photos at Dover Air Force Base of returning caskets of soldiers killed in Iraq. White House spokesman Trent Duffy justified the ban: "The message is that the sensitivities and the privacy of the families of the fallen must be the first priority."[112] But other administration actions have scorned the wishes of families of dead soldiers. *Newsweek* noted, "For a year now, according to the *Army Times,* the military has put every obstacle possible in the way of family members who want to go to Dover to receive their loved ones. One family specifically asked for media coverage of a burial at Arlington. Request denied."[113] *Army Times* editor Robert Hodiern commented: "The military is so concerned they will have to fight without the support of the American people that they will do anything they can to limit the release of information or images they fear would erode that support."[114]

The ban on casket photos may be an expression of Bush family values. On the eve of the invasion of Iraq, Bush's mother, former First Lady Barbara Bush, commented during a television interview: "Why should we hear about body bags and deaths and how many, what day it's gonna happen? . . . It's not relevant, so why should I waste my beautiful mind on something like that?"[115]

Perhaps because of the lack of photos of caskets, at least one top Bush administration official had trouble keeping track of the war's toll. Paul Wolfowitz, testifying to Congress on April 29, 2004, was asked how many American soldiers had been killed in Iraq. Wolfowitz replied: "It's approximately 500, of which—I can get the exact numbers—approximately 350 are combat deaths." As of the day of Wolfowitz's testimony, 722 American soldiers had died in Iraq, including 521 killed in combat.[116] *New York Times* columnist Maureen Dowd commented: "What can you say about a deputy defense secretary so eager to invade Iraq he was nicknamed Wolfowitz of Arabia, so bullish to remold the Middle East he froze the State Department out of the occupation and then mangled it, who doesn't bother to keep track of the young Americans who died for his delusion?"[117]

BUSH-STYLE FREEDOM OF THE PRESS

U.S. policy in Iraq vivifies *Bush freedom*. In a January 29, 2004, interview with the U.S.-government-owned and controlled Middle East Television Network, Bush declared, "I recognize not every government is going to fashion a free society in the vision of America."[118] Bush sees freedom as something fashioned by government—or perhaps something government forces upon a backward populace. Bush portrays freedom as a "top-down" enterprise—something wise, benevolent rulers impose upon the people for their own good.

As proof of his devotion to spreading freedom in the Middle East, Bush bragged about the increase in funding for a federal bureaucracy created to meddle in foreign nations. On March 12, 2004, Bush declared, "The momentum of liberty is building in the Middle East. . . . I proposed doubling the budget for the National Endowment for Democracy to $80 million. We will focus its new work on bringing free elections and free markets and free speech and free labor unions to the Middle East."[119] Bush portrayed a surge in U.S. propaganda as a triumph of freedom: "By radio and television, we're broadcasting the message of tolerance and truth in Arabic and Persian to tens of millions of people on that initiative. We're pursuing a forward strategy of freedom—that's how I like to describe it, a forward strategy of freedom in the Middle East."[120]

According to Bush, the best way to achieve freedom of the press is to expose Iraqis and other Muslims to more U.S.-government paid propaganda:

> Freedom of the press and the free flow of ideas are vital foundations of liberty. To cut through the hateful propaganda that fills the airwaves in the Muslim world and to promote open debate, . . . we are telling the people in the Middle East the truth about the values and the policies of the United States, and the truth always serves the cause of freedom.[121]

Such broadcasts represent freedom because they are controlled by the U.S. government—which Bush sees as synonymous with freedom. But Bush's devotion to freedom of the press does not extend to newspapers or broadcasters that criticize the U.S. military. The U.S. military vigorously shut down independent Arab television operations in Iraq that criticized the coalition military government.

BAIT-AND-SWITCH WAR PRICING

Bush refused to provide any estimate of the cost of the war prior to the invasion. In a March 10, 2003, press conference, Ed Chen of the *Los Angeles Times* asked respectfully: "When it comes to the financial costs of the war, sir, it would seem that the administration, surely, has costed out various scenarios. If that's the case, why not present some of them to the American people so they know what to expect, sir?" Bush smugly replied: "Ed, we will. We'll present it in the form of a supplemental to the spenders. We don't get to spend the money, as you know. We have to request the expenditure of money from the Congress, and at the appropriate time, we'll request a supplemental. . . . In terms of the dollar amount, well, we'll let you know here pretty soon."[122] By refusing to disclose any estimate of the war cost, Bush prevented some Americans from recognizing that this would not be a cheap adventure in moral glory. A few days after U.S. troops surged across the Iraq border, Bush sent Congress a bill for $63 billion.

The Bush administration portrayed the rebuilding of Iraq as practically cost-free. Andrew Natsios, the chief of the U.S. Agency for International Development, announced on April 23, 2003, that "the American part of this will be $1.7 billion. We have no plans for any further-on funding for this."[123] Wolfowitz informed Congress on March 27 that Iraq "can really finance its own reconstruction, and relatively soon."[124] On the other hand, Pentagon budget experts predicted a first-year price tag for the invasion and occupation of up to $95 billion.

The war and occupation quickly proved vastly more expensive than Natsios or Wolfowitz predicted. By early 2004, the Bush administration had sought more than $150 billion for operations in Iraq.[125] But the administration quickly made Bush-style amends for underestimating the cost. Both the AID website and the White House website removed all traces of Natsios's $1.7 billion forecast. AID explained that the deletion was made "to reflect current statements and testimony on Iraq reconstruction."[126] The $150 billion that the feds have already budgeted for Iraq is more, in nominal dollars, than the cost for building the interstate highway system in the United States from the late 1950s through the early 1970s.

SOVEREIGNTY SHAM

The ultimate proof that Bush is a great liberator and that the United States freed the Iraqi people is the plan to formally transfer sovereignty back to the Iraqi people. In his April 13, 2004, press conference, Bush declared: "On June 30th, when the flag of a free Iraq is raised, Iraqi officials will assume full responsibility for the ministries of government. . . . One central commitment of that mission is the transfer of the sovereignty back to the Iraqi people. We have set a deadline of June 30th. It is important that we meet that deadline. We will not step back from our pledge."[127]

But Iraqi sovereignty, like Iraqi freedom, is a sham. The Iraqis will have self-government—and the proof will be that the American military will constantly remind them that they have self-government, damn it. The U.S. government does not intend to permit Iraqis to govern themselves in any way that does not suit the interests and demands of the Bush administration. When Wolfowitz was asked on April 2, 2004, what effect the June 30 sovereignty arrival would have upon the U.S. military, he replied: "There's not going to be any difference in our military posture on July 1st from what it is on June 30th, except that we will be there then at the invitation of a sovereign Iraqi govern-

ment."[128] This is akin to the sovereignty that the Soviets awarded East European nations after World War II. U.S. government officials have made it clear
that they intend to maintain 14 permanent military bases in Iraq. Iraqis will
be made to understand that sovereignty means "do what we say and you won't
get hurt."[129]

Bush apparently defines self-government for a foreign country as being
under benevolent American domination. This is another case of Bush assuming that people are dumb enough to fall for a bogus label. Bush believes he can
prove that the war was fought in the name of freedom, and prove that the Iraqi
people are now liberated and free, by having a power-handover facade—simply finding a new group of front men. There is no Iraqi government to which
sovereignty can be transferred. Besides, many Iraqis have never recognized
United States' sovereignty over them (as opposed to having enough force to
suppress resistance). Columbia University professor Rashid Khalidi derided
Bush's claims: "Sovereign power will be in the hands of the only military force
in the country, which is the United States. It is ludicrous . . . to talk about a
transfer of sovereignty."[130] Professor Juan Cole commented that the sovereignty handover "was always nothing more than a publicity stunt for the benefit of Bush's election campaign."[131]

DRAFT REVIVAL

Americans may soon suffer a major dose of military slavery in order to pay for
Bush's world liberation crusade. Since 1973, American males have been required to register with the Selective Service Board when they turn 18. Now, as
the U.S. military forces come closer to the exhaustion point, there is growing
enthusiasm in Washington for reviving conscription. A few weeks before Bush
invaded Iraq, the Pentagon's Selective Service System proposed compelling
women to register for the military draft and raising the upper age of eligibility
for the draft from 25 to 34. The Pentagon agency also proposed compelling
young Americans to formally notify the government any time they acquired a
new skill that might be useful for the military or other agencies. The agency
would add this into a database that would provide "a single, most accurate and
complete national inventory of young Americans with special skills."[132]

There is growing speculation that Bush might propose reviving the draft if
he wins reelection. White House press secretary Scott McClellan, when asked
if the president supports a return to the draft, replied, "That is just not something that's under consideration at this time."[133] Sen. Chuck Hagel (R-Neb.)

urged the Bush administration to "start realistically exploring" the draft to help fight "a generational war" against terrorism.[134]

IRAQ AND BUSH'S WAR AGAINST EVIL

Bush's catechism on terrorism is very simple and very dangerous. In his March 19, 2004, anniversary speech, Bush declared, "There is no neutral ground in the fight between civilization and terror, because there is no neutral ground between good and evil, freedom and slavery, and life and death. . . . The terrorists are offended not merely by our policies, they're offended by our existence as free nations. No concession will appease their hatred. No accommodation will satisfy their endless demands." The logical result of Bush's thinking would be a war of extermination against evil.

Bush cannot admit that U.S. policies might create new terrorists without invalidating much, if not most, of what he does. So instead, Bush assumes that people he labels as terrorists are all practically incurable homicidal maniacs—and that nothing can be done to influence their behavior except killing or capturing them. This allows Bush to exonerate himself from any action that might increase foreign hatred of the United States and thereby increase the number of people determined to kill Americans. Regardless of how many innocent Iraqis are killed by American troops, Bush is blameless for any surge in foreign hatred.

In his April 13, 2004, press conference, Bush proclaimed, "The violence we are seeing in Iraq is familiar. The terrorists who take hostages or plants a roadside bomb near Baghdad is serving the same ideology of murder that kills innocent people on trains in Madrid, and murders children on buses in Jerusalem, and blows up a nightclub in Bali and cuts the throat of a young reporter for being a Jew."[135] Bush then asserted that it was the "same ideology of murder" in the 1983 attack on U.S. troops in Beirut, in the attack on the USS *Cole* in October 2000, and in the 9/11 attacks. With his inclusion of the roadside bomb example, Bush portrayed all the Iraqis who resisted U.S. domination as the equivalent of the 9/11 hijackers. Bush declared: "All are the work of a fanatical political ideology. The servants of this ideology seek tyranny in the Middle East and beyond. They seek to oppress and persecute women."[136] Thus, Bush would have people believe that all who resist American power in Iraq are anti-female, anti-civilization, and anti–all good things. This is the soul of the post-9/11 Bush: anyone who does not submit is the incarnation of all evils. Insofar as Bush portrays this as a pure clash between good and evil, he represents himself as the Supreme Leader of Goodness.

Bush claimed transcendent benefits from the invasion: "By helping secure a free Iraq, Americans serving in that country are protecting their fellow citizens. . . . Above all, the defeat of violence and terror in Iraq is vital to the defeat of violence and terror elsewhere and vital, therefore, to the safety of the American people."[137] It is tripe to claim that violence in Iraq is linked to violence everywhere in the world. Iraq was no hotbed of terrorism before the United States invaded. Bush has turned a California-sized country into the world's largest terrorist training camp. And the actions of American forces are creating the best recruiting advertisements for terrorist groups. When Bush claims Americans are more secure because of the toppling of Saddam, he presumably does not mean the more than half million people with family members serving in Iraq—people whose daily lives are suffused with fear, if not dread, for the survival of their loved ones.

In his March 19, 2004, anniversary speech, Bush declared that one of the terrorists' "ultimate ambitions" is "to control the peoples of the Middle East." But a few weeks later Bush, with Ariel Sharon at his side in the White House Rose Garden, endorsed permitting Israel to permanently retain much of the West Bank. Israeli human rights abuses—including the torture and killing of innocent civilians, lockdowns on towns and villages, confiscation of land, and destruction of thousands of people's homes—have been denounced around the world.[138] Bush's decision is certain to stir up far more Arab hatred and help destroy whatever credibility the United States might have gained in some Arab minds from overthrowing Saddam. Perhaps Bush believes that the effect of his decision to endorse the Sharon plan—which breached U.S. policy since the 1967 war when Israeli seized the occupied territories, and which conflicted with many UN resolutions—can be rectified either by financing more U.S. government Arabic propaganda or by supressing a few more Arab television stations.

IRAQ VS. THE WAR ON TERRORISM

In January 2004, the Army War College published a report by professor Jeffrey Record that concluded that the war on Iraq undermined the war against Al Qaeda. Record warned, "The global war on terrorism as currently defined and waged is dangerously indiscriminate and ambitious, and accordingly . . . its parameters should be readjusted." Record concluded that the Bush administration's anti-terrorism campaign is "strategically unfocused, promises more than it can deliver, and threatens to dissipate U.S. military resources in

an endless and hopeless search for absolute security."[139] Record concluded
that most of the Global War on Terrorism's (GWOT) "declared objectives"—
such as "the eradication of terrorism as a means of irregular warfare"—"are
unrealistic and condemn the United States to a hopeless quest for absolute security. As such, the GWOT's goals are also politically, fiscally, and militarily
unsustainable."[140]

Record noted that the Bush administration

> has postulated a multiplicity of enemies, including rogue states; weapons of
> mass destruction (WMD) proliferators; terrorist organizations of global, re-
> gional, and national scope; and terrorism itself. It also seems to have conflated
> them into a monolithic threat, and in so doing has subordinated strategic clar-
> ity to the moral clarity it strives for in foreign policy and may have set the
> United States on a course of open-ended and gratuitous conflict with states
> and nonstate entities that pose no serious threat to the United States.
>
> The result has been an unnecessary preventive war of choice against a de-
> terred Iraq that has created a new front in the Middle East for Islamic terror-
> ism and diverted attention and resources away from securing the American
> homeland against further assault by an undeterrable al Qaeda.
>
> Moreover, to the extent that the GWOT is directed at the phenomenon
> of terrorism, as opposed to flesh-and-blood terrorist organizations, it sets itself
> up for strategic failure. Terrorism is a recourse of the politically desperate and
> militarily helpless, and, as such, it is hardly going to disappear.[141]

Record believed that the "forward strategy of freedom" justification for Iraq
was especially dubious: "The potential policy payoff of a democratic and pros-
perous Middle East, if there is one, almost certainly lies in the very distant future. The basis on which this democratic domino theory rests has never been
explicated."[142]

CONCLUSION

On January 22, 2004, Bush justified his war against Iraq as creating a free society: "Free societies do not breed terrorism. Free societies are peaceful nations."[143] Bush's own record as U.S. president refutes his doctrine. Yet, in
another sense, recent American experience confirms his thesis. To the extent
that the United States has strayed from the freedom vision of the Founding Fathers, thus far is the U.S. government becoming a warmonger. Insofar as Bush
abuses his executive powers, intimidates and shunts aside Congress, stonewalls

the courts, and deceives the American people—thus far America is not a free nation, and thus far Bush makes this a war-making nation.

Bush continually appeals to idealism to sanctify sacrificing American lives to his political agenda. Bush declared in early 2004: "I know the decency of our people. I know the willingness of the American citizen to serve a cause greater than themself."[144] But dying for Bush's lies should not be considered a lofty cause. "Service to a greater cause" is a constant theme of Bush's—a greedy politician encouraging everyone to sacrifice himself so that he can extend his power.

In his April 13, 2004, press conference, Bush proclaimed that "as the greatest power on the face of the earth, we have an obligation to help the spread of freedom." Bush lauded how Americans soldiers were sacrificed "in the name of security for America and freedom for the world."[145] When Bush was sworn in on January 20, 2001, he did not become entitled to send Americans off to die for "world freedom." The Constitution does not make Americans pawns to be sacrificed to prove a president's moral greatness.

To accept that Bush's bogus WMD allegations were a simple "intelligence failure" would be a profound failure by the American people. Bush was determined to demagogue the American people into war—to frighten them, to cajole them, to constantly exaggerate threats, to pretend that he was far more certain than the intelligence reports prepared by the government's best experts. The fact that Bush simply told new and different lies, made new and different misrepresentations after the search for WMDs came up empty is proof of the moral culpability of his earlier statements. Bush showed boundless bad faith—followed by boundless righteousness after his lies were exposed.

Bush is still expecting to be cheered and revered for his courage in "making a tough decision"—despite his lies to the American people. It is as if the more Americans die from Bush's folly, the more undeniable his greatness becomes. Regardless of how Bush seeks to distort or exploit the Iraq war, the American people will be paying for this debacle for many years to come.

Conclusion

We're in the Capital of the most powerful nation on Earth, yet we recognize the limits of all earthly power.

—*George W. Bush, February 5, 2004*[1]

President Bush commented shortly before 9/11: "A dictatorship would be a heck of a lot easier; there's no question about it."[2] Bush used the same phrase to tout dictatorships as paragons of efficiency a month before taking office.[3] Bush has always seemed oblivious to why dictatorships drag nations to ruin. Instead, all that matters is the prompt obedience and the reverence, enforced or otherwise, for the leader.

Since January 2001, America has suffered one dollop of *Bush freedom* after another. Bush does not respect the freedom to protest in his presence, does not respect the freedom from being searched without a warrant, and does not respect people's right not to be perpetually detained without being charged. Because Bush is devoted to government secrecy, Americans are obliged to take Bush's word when he says he is championing freedom.

Many of the follies and failures of the Bush administration stem from the president's view of his own exalted role. Bush declared in 2002: "I'm the commander—see, I don't need to explain. . . . That's the interesting thing about being president. . . . I don't feel like I owe anybody an explanation."[4] And his prerogative extends—at least in his own mind—to giving marching orders to hundreds of millions of Americans. In an October 29, 2003, speech, Bush declared, "A President must set great goals worthy of a great nation. We're a great nation. Therefore, a President must set big goals."[5] But most Americans who venture into a polling booth are not seeking someone to impose goals upon them. Bush described himself in April 2004 as "the ultimate decisionmaker for this country."[6] But Bush is not the ultimate decision-maker for America. He may be the ultimate decision-maker for the federal government, but only within the constraints of both the federal statute book and the U.S. Constitution.

WORLD SAVIOR DELUSIONS

We have drifted far from the visions and wisdom of the Founding Fathers. Neither Washington, nor Jefferson, nor Madison ever intended for the president of the United States to become the Torturer-in-Chief. Regardless of whether Bush had personal knowledge of the outrages committed by his agents around the globe, he is culpable for the results of his doctrine of absolute righteousness sanctifying absolute power—at least over those Iraqis, Afghans, or others unlucky enough to be suspected of something.

Bush is dangerous in part because of his supposed mandate from God. Bush declared that, at the time he launched the invasion of Iraq, "I was praying for strength to do the Lord's will. . . . In my case, I pray that I be as good a messenger of His will as possible."[7] Bush's attitude brings to mind the old quip about "a fanatic is someone who does what God would do if God knew the facts of the matter." Bush's personal religious views appear to fuel his intolerance and his belief that all opposition to his efforts is evil.

The Bush administration's missionary zeal on antiterrorism is a threat both to America and to the world. Defense Secretary Donald Rumsfeld told graduating West Point cadets on May 29, 2004, that "we are closer to the beginning of this struggle with global insurgency than to its end."[8] Rumsfeld's use of the term "global insurgency" as a synonym for terrorism should set off alarm bells. The Iraqi occupation has become mired in part because of Bush's assumption that anyone who resists American power is automatically a terrorist. To extend the same assumption to the entire world will guarantee both endless conflicts and an eventual, devastating U.S. defeat.

It will take more than the crushing of infidels to make America safe. America needs a supply-side antiterrorism policy. We should cease breeding new enemies at a time when the government is unfit to defend Americans against existing enemies.

Like Roman citizens long ago, many Americans are ignoring home front abuses as long as their government claims to be making foreign conquests. But how many more unnecessary wars can American freedom survive? We must recognize that every invasion to "liberate" a foreign nation puts our own rights and liberties at greater peril. Imperial habits, once cultivated and exalted, will not be confined outside our national borders.

The more arrogant and righteous Bush becomes about spreading democracy, the more the American Republic becomes a parody of the vision of the Founding Fathers, who did not intend to permit presidents to "hock" American rights for foreign conquests. Rather than leading a crusade to forcibly im-

pose democracy on the rest of the world, Americans must recognize the profound flaws in their own government.

BUSH LESSONS

Terrorism too easily becomes an entitlement program for politicians. The
worse government fails, the more credulous scores of millions of people become. One of the starkest lessons of the Bush presidency is how easily politicians exploit government failures to expand government power. There may be
no limit to political mendacity the next time the government fails to prevent
a terrorist attack.

Bush's compassionate conservatism schemes are little more than velvet
wrapping for the iron fist. Compassionate conservatism pretends the state does
not raise its own money via coercion and harsh threats against taxpayers.
Compassionate conservatism presumes that since the government just happens to have all this cash in the treasury coffers, why not do some good deeds
with it? Handouts become symbols of generosity rather than acts of redistrib-
ution at gunpoint. Compassionate conservatism portrays government as a font
of moral greatness, rather than a primary source of corruption, manipulation,
and degradation.

Bush's compassionate conservatism is little different than President Clinton's perennial portrayals of government as an engine for uplift. Bush and
Clinton both profited greatly from prattling about moral issues and making
moral appeals, regardless of whether their own policies were responsible or
honest. Bosh about virtue and compassion is sufficient to persuade many voters that a politician is a good man.

Bush's precedents are far more important than his intentions. These precedents, established after 9/11, will not vanish if Osama Bin Laden is captured
or if Iraq once again becomes the Garden of Eden. Americans became far more
deferential to the federal government after 9/11. Though some of this docility
is dissipating, the government continues to seek new powers. Americans must
cease deluding themselves that they are immune to the political deterioration
that history shows is the fate of most nations in most eras.

LEGITIMACY

For many people, the issue of the legitimacy of Bush's presidency was settled
once and for all by the Supreme Court's December 2000 ruling on the Florida

election returns. Prior to becoming president, Bush was required to take an oath to uphold the Constitution. Bush may have considered the oath as a few throwaway words of no more meaning than checking the consent form for a new software program. Bush, like many other Washington politicians, acts as if his right to rule is practically irrevocable for the duration of his term.

The monarchization of America is proceeding by leaps and bounds under Bush. It is time to pay heed to lessons from our English forefathers. More than 350 years ago, at the trial of King Charles I, a major charge against the king was that he had violated the Petition of Right. Parliament had permitted the king to continue ruling on condition that he assent to the Petition of Right and cease oppressing the English people. The king reneged, clinging to power and brutalizing far and wide. A few decades later, Britain's Glorious Revolution of 1688 established that the king forfeits his right to rule if he violates his coronation oath.

We should not treat the president and members of Congress with more unquestioning deference than the English people treated their kings a third of a millennium ago. What does representative government become when the president and congressmen are permitted to scorn their sacred pledge to honor the Constitution? To knowingly violate their oaths of office is to forfeit their legitimacy. The only alternative is to assume that whoever wins an election is entitled to as much power as they can grab in the following years.

THE ELECTION AND THE NEXT FOUR YEARS

Almost four years ago, America and the world became transfixed by the dangling chads of Florida's ballots. Unfortunately, far less attention likely will be paid this year to something far more pernicious. Thanks to the Bipartisan Campaign Reform Act, the federal government will suppress many, if not most, of the issue ads that citizens groups would have run on radio and television criticizing political leaders. The greater the censorship, the more illegitimate the results of the 2004 elections will be. And, insofar as citizens acquiesce to the government suppressing criticism of the rulers, Americans are unfit for self-government.

The Supreme Court justified restricting freedom of speech in order to prevent "the appearance of corruption." The more important question is: How much "appearance of democracy" does Washington need to perpetuate its power over the American people? How many gestures do the rulers need to make to lull Americans into thinking that they still control the federal government?

Regardless of who wins the November election, America will likely have a lousy president for the next four years. There is no indication that either major party candidate has recognized or understood why a meddling foreign policy will bring grief to America and strife to the world, or why the constant growth of federal power is irreconcilable with American liberty.

No one is entitled to the amount of power that the winner of the November election will possess over the American people. There is no candidate who should win the right to start unnecessary foreign wars or to unleash the Justice Department on targeted groups. The more power a politician receives, the less trustworthy he usually becomes. Becoming the most powerful man in the world rarely induces sainthood.

In February 2004, President George W. Bush endorsed a constitutional amendment to ban gay marriage. This cheered many of his conservative supporters. But what we really need is a constitutional amendment to make the federal government obey the Constitution. As long as the president, the Congress, and federal agencies can trample the Bill of Rights with impunity, then all other reforms are little more than whiffs of smoke. At this point, the government has far more power to enforce its exactions than citizens have to compel the government to respect their rights. As long as the rulers are permitted to scorn the rightful limits on their power, a mere rotation of elective dictators achieves little.

If the president is reelected, the more cynical Americans become, the less dangerous Bush will be. If Bush wins a second term, his grandiose schemes might be curbed if his proclamations on "good versus evil" are greeted with catcalls and laughter, rather than awe and submission. At this point, Bush is as qualified to talk about freedom as former President Clinton is to speak of chastity. Bush taints liberty every time he verbally embraces it.

QUESTIONS FOR NOVEMBER

Americans should ask themselves: Are you more free than you were four years ago? Obviously not—unless one equates pervasive government surveillance and mass secret arrests with liberation.

Americans should ask themselves: Are you more secure than you were four years ago? Again, obviously not. There are far more fears of terrorist attacks now than there were when George Bush took office. Bush's foreign policy, especially the invasion of Iraq, is multiplying the number of people with homicidal rage toward Americans.

Americans have reaped no profits from their lost freedoms. Sacrificing freedom usually only makes it easier for governments both to deceive and to oppress.

Americans must cease hoping for some politician to ride in on a white horse and suddenly solve all the nation's problems. It is time for Americans to have the maturity to recognize that no one is coming—that fatally flawed government programs and policies cannot be fixed by someone who claims to care more, or who is smarter, or who has (or doesn't have) an MBA. Americans should cease looking to a president as a savior and instead view him as a hired hand, put on the payroll for a fixed period to fulfill certain specific tasks.

Trying to end misgovernment in Washington merely by changing the ruling political party is like an alcoholic trying to solve his problem by switching from whiskey to rum. It will take more than a change in quack doctors to solve the problems of the American Republic.

If Americans desire better political leaders, Americans must become better citizens. Elections cannot protect people's liberties if voters have no understanding of how the government is abusing their rights. It is foolish to expect citizens to control the government when citizens docilely expect government to benevolently control their lives. Politicians will not become more honest until Americans become less gullible. The more lies citizens tolerate, the more abuses they will suffer.

People have been taught to expect far more from government than from freedom. How much affection or devotion do Americans still have for freedom? There may be more Americans reciting the Pledge of Allegiance now than before Bush became president—but fewer Americans concerned about government trampling their rights. There may be more Americans with U.S. flag decals on their autos—but fewer Americans who support the right of people to publicly oppose government policies. There are more Americans who revere the president—but fewer Americans who recall the Founding Fathers' warnings about the corrupting nature of political power.

The issue is not which political party should hold the reins, but whether the American people should be leashed by Washington. Some future Patriot Act or some other sweeping law may finally make Americans recognize the dangers posed by their would-be saviors. The arrogance of power is the best hope for the survival of freedom.

Acknowledgments

I want to thank Greg Rushford for his invaluable help in understanding Bush's trade policy. I appreciated the *American Conservative*'s Scott McConnell and Kara Hopkins encouraging me to write a piece for them late last year on the Bush administration's suppression of protests. I want to thank Claire Wolfe and two good friends who wished to remain anonymous for helpful suggestions on the style of this book. My research and thinking on Bush administration policies got big boosts from some excellent websites, including Antiwar.com, LewRockwell.com, FFF.com (the website of the Future of Freedom Foundation), and http://www.mapinc.org (a website devoted to drug policy reform).

At Palgrave Macmillan, I much appreciated editorial director Michael Flamini's early interest and enthusiasm for this book. After he exited to become an executive editor at St. Martin's Press, Garrett Keily, the president of Palgrave Macmillan USA, took over and did a superb job of advancing the book to print. Production Director Alan Bradshaw did a great job as always of helping the book come together as a coherent whole while all the time maintaining his cheerful disposition. I appreciated his keen eye and the multitude of excellent suggestions he made. Copy editors Norma McLemore and Bruce Murphy also made many excellent suggestions and thankfully caught plenty of glitches. I want to thank Rick Delaney for batting clean-up on the manuscript. I appreciate the long hours and overtime worked by folks at Palgrave to bring this book to market so quickly.

Updated information on this book and on Bush's latest achievements are available at www.palgrave-usa.com/blog/bovard and www.jimbovard.com.

Notes

CHAPTER 1. INTRODUCTION

1. "Remarks at the Iftaar Dinner," *Public Papers of the Presidents,* October 28, 2003.
2. "President Discusses War on Terrorism," White House Office of the Press Secretary, November 8, 2001.
3. "President's Radio Address," White House Office of the Press Secretary, December 20, 2003.
4. Bob Woodward, "Interview with the President," *Washington Post,* April 22, 2004. (The interview occurred on December 10, 2003.)
5. Dexter Filkins, "Tough New Tactics by U.S. Tighten Grip on Iraq Towns," *New York Times,* December 7, 2003.
6. Ken Auletta, "Fortress Bush; How the White House Keeps the Press under Control," *New Yorker,* January 19, 2004.
7. Shaun Waterman, "Al Qaeda Still Poses Risk to America, Legislators Say," *Washington Times,* January 5, 2004.

CHAPTER 2. 9/11: CANONIZATION AND COVERUP

1. "Address Before a Joint Session of the Congress on the State of the Union," *Public Papers of the Presidents,* January 29, 2002.
2. Will Lester, "9/11 Images Said Inappropriate by Voters," Associated Press, March 12, 2004.
3. Howard Kurtz and Dan Balz, "TV Ads Portray Bush Tackling Tough Times," *Washington Post,* March 4, 2004.
4. Dan Froomkin, "Ads Raise Issue of Bush Testimony," washingtonpost.com, March 5, 2004.
5. Scot J. Paltrow, "Government Accounts of 9/11 Reveal Gaps, Inconsistencies," *Wall Street Journal,* March 22, 2004.
6. Ibid.
7. Ibid.
8. Ibid.
9. Ibid.
10. Ibid.
11. "Remarks on the Terrorist Attacks at Barksdale Air Force Base, Louisiana," *Public Papers of the Presidents,* September 11, 2001.
12. Bob Woodward, *Bush at War* (New York: Simon & Schuster, 2002), 19.
13. Paltrow, "Government Accounts of 9/11 Reveal Gaps, Inconsistencies."

14. "Statement by the President in His Address to the Nation," White House Office of the Press Secretary, September 11, 2001.

15. Stephen Barr, "Survey Finds Americans Looking Favorably on Government and Its Workers," *Washington Post,* October 11, 2001.

16. Pamela Paul, "Faith in Institutions; Americans Find New Hope in Their Government," *American Demographics,* January 2002.

17. Ibid.

18. R. W. Apple, "Bush Presidency Seems to Gain Legitimacy," *New York Times,* September 16, 2001.

19. Francine Kiefer, "Antiterror War Speeds the Maturing of a President," *Christian Science Monitor,* January 2, 2002.

20. Ibid.

21. Chuck Raasch, "God, Government Both Offer Comfort in These Times of Stress," Gannett News Service, October 18, 2001.

22. Bernard Weinraub, "In Movies, Terrorism Is Making Government Look Good," *New York Times,* October 10, 2001.

23. Tom Shoop, "Bold Government; America Has Regained Its Love of Big Government. But Can the Romance Last?" *Government Executive,* February 2002.

24. Michael Kilian, "Attacks Awakened Nation's Patriotism, Mrs. Bush Says," *Chicago Tribune,* November 9, 2001.

25. Woodward, *Bush at War,* 277.

26. Charles Babington, "Bush: U.S. Must 'Rid the World of Evil,'" *Washington Post,* September 14, 2001.

27. "Remarks by President George W. Bush to Employees of the Federal Bureau of Investigation," Federal News Service, September 25, 2001.

28. "Remarks by the President upon Arrival on the South Lawn," White House Office of the Press Secretary, September 16, 2001.

29. "President Visits Logan High School in Lacrosse," White House Office of the Press Secretary, May 8, 2002.

30. "Remarks to Employees of Albers Manufacturing Company in O'Fallon," *Public Papers of the Presidents,* March 18, 2002.

31. "Remarks on the Citizens Corps in Knoxville," *Public Papers of the Presidents,* April 8 2002.

32. "Remarks at a Dinner for Gubernatorial Candidate Bill Simon in Los Angeles," *Public Papers of the Presidents,* April 29, 2002.

33. "Remarks at a Luncheon for Gubernatorial Candidate Bill Simon in Santa Clara, California," *Public Papers of the Presidents,* April 30, 2002.

34. "Remarks at the Republican Party of Florida Majority Dinner in Orlando, Florida," *Public Papers of the Presidents,* June 21, 2002.

35. "Remarks at East Literature Magnet School in Nashville," *Public Papers of the Presidents,* September 17, 2002.

36. "Investigators Think Terrorist Ordered Crash of Flight 93," Associated Press, August 9, 2003.

37. William Brunch, "Three Minute Discrepancy in Tape," *Philadelphia Daily News,* September 16, 2002.

38. Ibid.

39. Dan Balz and Bob Woodward, "America's Chaotic Road to War," *Washington Post,* January 27, 2002.

40. For detailed outtakes from the joint inquiry's staff reports and initial comprehensive report, see James Bovard, *Terrorism and Tyranny* (New York: Palgrave, 2003), 40–63.

41. "Commissioner: Bush Deliberately Delayed Inquiry Report Until After Iraq War," United Press International, July 28, 2003.

42. "Appendix—Access Limitations Encountered by the Joint Inquiry," Report of the Joint Inquiry into the Terrorist Attacks of September 11th," athttp://news.findlaw.com/usatoday/docs/911rpt/

43. Michael Isikoff, "The Informant Who Lived With the Hijackers," *Newsweek*, September 16, 2002.

44. "Appendix—Access Limitations Encountered by the Joint Inquiry." Quotes in following paragraphs are also from this source.

45. Michael Boyd, "Bureaucracy, Politics, Incompetence . . . Plus a Lot of Drivel," February 2, 2004. Posted at the website of his consulting firm, http://www.aviationplanning.com.

46. Ibid.

47. "The Ad Campaign: A Focus on the President's Leadership," *New York Times*, March 4, 2004.

48. The transcript is available at Limbaugh's website: http://www.rushlimbaugh.com/home/daily/site_030904/content/see_i_told_you_so.guest.html.

49. Breitweiser's comments were posted at http://tomflocco.com/modules.php?name=News&file=article&sid=42.

50. Adam Entous, "Bush Defends His Sept. 11 Ads, Economic Policies," Reuters News Service, March 6, 2004.

51. "Bush's Remarks Following His Cabinet Meeting," Federal News Service, March 23, 2004.

52. Dana Milbank and Walter Pincus, "Declassified Memo Said Al Qaeda Was in U.S.," *Washington Post*, April 11, 2004.

53. "Text: President's Daily Brief on Aug. 6, 2001," *Washington Post*, April 11, 2004.

54. "Bush Plays Down Importance of Pre-9/11 Intelligence Memo," Associated Press, April 12, 2004.

55. "Excerpts—Bush: 'Had I Known, We Would Have Acted,'" *Washington Post*, April 12, 2004.

56. Fred Kaplan, "The Out-of-Towner," *Slate*, April 14, 2004.

57. Walter Pincus, "9/11 Panel Seeks Author of Brief," *Washington Post*, April 13, 2004.

58. Dana Milbank and Mike Allen, "Bush Gave No Sign of Worry in August 2001," *Washington Post*, April 11, 2004.

59. Ibid.

60. Quoted in "Clarke: 'White House is Papering Over the Facts,'" CNN.com, March 23, 2004.

61. Staff Statement No. 10, "Threats and Responses in 2001," National Commission on Terrorist Attacks Upon the United States, April 2004.

62. David Johnston and Jim Dwyer, "Pre-9/11 Files Show Warnings Were More Dire and Persistent," *New York Times*, April 18, 2004.

63. Maureen Dowd, "Head Spook Sputters," *New York Times*, April 15, 2004.

64. Kaplan, "The Out-of-Towner."

65. Bradley Graham, "Pentagon Crash Scenario Was Rejected for Military Exercise," *Washington Post*, April 14, 2004.

66. Steve Fainaru, "Clues Pointed to Changing Terrorist Tactics," *Washington Post*, May 19, 2002.

67. Dan Eggen and Dana Milbank, "9/11 Panel Questions Bush and Cheney," *Washington Post*, April 30, 2004.

68. "Bush Says He Answered Every Question from Sept 11 Panel," Agence France Presse, April 29, 2004.

69. Dan Eggen and Dana Milbank, "9/11 Panel Questions Bush and Cheney."

70. Shaun Waterman, "Truth Squad," *American Prospect*, April 2004.

71. Eggen and Milbank, "9/11 Panel Questions Bush and Cheney."

72. "Transcript: 9/11 Commission Hearing," Federal Document Clearing House, April 13, 2004.

73. Ibid.
74. "Text of Bush's Press Conference," Washingtonpost.com, April 13, 2004.
75. Philip Shenon, "Early Warnings on Moussaoui Are Detailed," *New York Times,* October 18, 2002.
76. "The FBI's Handling of the Phoenix Electronic Communication and Investigation of Zacarias Moussaoui Prior to September 11, 2001: Statement of Eleanor Hill," Joint Intelligence Committee investigation, September 24, 2002.
77. "FISA Implementation Failures," Interim Report on FBI Oversight in the 107th Congress by the Senate Judiciary Committee: Senator Patrick Leahy, Senator Charles Grassley, and Senator Arlen Specter, February 2003.
78. Dan Eggen, "Publicizing Arrest Could Have Halted Sept. 11 Hijackers," *Washington Post,* April 17, 2004.
79. Ibid.
80. Philip Shenon and Lowell Bergman, "9/11 Panel Is Said to Offer Harsh Review of Ashcroft," *New York Times,* April 13, 2004.
81. Staff Statement No. 9, "Law Enforcement, Counterterrorism, and Intelligence Collection in the United States Prior to 9/11," National Commission on Terrorist Attacks Upon the United States, April 2004.
82. Staff Statement No. 12, "Reforming Law Enforcement, Counterterrorism, and Intelligence Collection in the United States," National Commission on Terrorist Attacks Upon the United States, April 2004.
83. "Transcript: 9/11 Commission Hearing," Federal Document Clearing House, April 13, 2004.
84. "Attorney General John Ashcroft Testimony before the Commerce, Justice, State and Judiciary Subcommittee of the Senate Appropriations Committee April 1, 2003," Justice Department Office of Public Affairs, April 1, 2003.
85. "Transcript: 9/11 Commission Hearing," Federal Document Clearing House, April 13, 2004.
86. Eric Lichtblau and Charles Piller, "War on Terrorism Highlights FBI's Computer Woes," *Los Angeles Times,* July 28, 2002.
87. Ibid.
88. Staff Statement No. 9, "Law Enforcement, Counterterrorism, and Intelligence Collection in the United States Prior to 9/11."
89. Ibid.
90. Ibid.
91. Ibid.
92. Ibid.
93. "Transcript: 9/11 Commission Hearing," Federal Document Clearing House, April 13, 2004.
94. Staff Statement No. 9, "Law Enforcement, Counterterrorism, and Intelligence Collection in the United States Prior to 9/11."
95. Shenon and Bergman, "9/11 Panel Is Said to Offer Harsh Review of Ashcroft."
96. Ibid.
97. "Transcript: 9/11 Commission Hearing," Federal Document Clearing House, April 13, 2004.
98. Ibid.
99. Eric Lichtblau and David Sanger, "Bush Was Warned of Possible Attack in U.S., Officials Say," *New York Times,* April 10, 2004.
100. "Transcript: 9/11 Commission Hearing," Federal Document Clearing House, April 13, 2004.
101. Maureen Dowd, "Sorry, Right Number," *New York Times,* February 29, 2004.
102. "Extraordinary Measures," *Newsweek,* February 18, 2004.

CHAPTER 3. A WAR ON DISSENT?

1.   "Remarks at Concord Middle School in Concord, North Carolina," *Public Papers of the Presidents,* April 11, 2001.
2.   "Hearing of the Senate Judiciary Committee—Subject: The Department of Justice and Terrorism," Federal News Service, December 6, 2001.
3.   *Free Speech under Fire: The ACLU Challenge to "Protest Zones,"* American Civil Liberties Union, September 23, 2003.
4.   Milan Simonich, "Judge Clears Bush Opponent," *Pittsburgh Post-Gazette,* November 1, 2002.
5.   Dave Lindorff, "Keeping Dissent Invisible," *Salon,* October 16, 2003.
6.   Ibid.
7.   Ron Hutcheson, "Protests Tightly Restricted," *Tallahassee Democrat,* February 23, 2003.
8.   Editorial, "See No Protest," *St. Petersburg Times,* October 28, 2003.
9.   Bruce Rushton, "Hell No, They Won't Go," *Phoenix New Times,* April 23, 2003.
10. Ibid.
11. *Freedom under Fire: Dissent in Post-9/11 America,* American Civil Liberties Union, 2003.
12. "Remarks by the President at Columbia, South Carolina, Welcome," White House Office of the Press Secretary, October 24, 2002.
13. "Protester Brett Bursey, Who Has Been Arrested Again for Protesting Outside of a Free-Speech Zone at a Presidential Appearance," *All Things Considered,* National Public Radio, July 25, 2003.
14. Henry Eichel, "Speech Zone Case Pulls Eyes to S.C.," *Charlotte Observer,* August 31, 2003.
15. Chris Haire, "America is a Free Speech Zone," *MetroBEAT,* October 21, 2003.
16. Eichel, "Speech Zone Case."
17. "Reporter's Notebook," *White House Weekly,* November 12, 2003.
18. Clif LeBlanc, "Critics Say Ruling Threatens Free Speech," *The State* (Columbia, S.C.), January 11, 2004.
19. Henry Eichel, "Restricted Presidential Access Trial Wraps Up," *Charlotte Observer,* November 14, 2003.
20. All statements in this paragraph from http://homepage.ntlworld.com/jksonc/docs/bursey-docket-dsc–03cr309.html#d75. This superb web page was constructed by Charles Judson Harwood, Jr.
21. Henry Eichel, "Bush Protester Gets $500 Fine," *Charlotte Observer,* January 7, 2004.
22. All statements in this paragraph from http://homepage.ntlworld.com/jksonc/docs/bursey-docket-dsc–03cr309.html#d75.
23. Clif LeBlanc, "Bursey Found Guilty," *The State* (Columbia, S.C.), January 6, 2004.
24. Eichel, "Bush Protester Gets $500 Fine."
25. LeBlanc, "Bursey Found Guilty."
26. Ibid.
27. Charles Levendosky, "Keeping the Protesters Out of Sight and out of Hearing," *International Herald Tribune,* November 6, 2003.
28. "Protester Brett Bursey, Who Has Been Arrested Again," *All Things Considered.*
29. "Secret Service Ordered Local Police to Restrict Anti-Bush Protesters at Rallies, ACLU Charges in Unprecedented Nationwide Lawsuit," American Civil Liberties Union press release, September 23, 2003.
30. Mark Riley, "Say What You Like, But Don't Expect Bush to Hear," *Sydney Morning Herald,* October 20, 2003.
31. Mark Phillips, "Presidential Protest Switches from Rowdy Violence to Silent Vigil," *Courier Mail* (Queensland, Australia), October 25, 2003.

32. Adam Harvey, "Mister Untouchable—The Secrets of George Bush's High-Security Visit," *Sunday Telegraph* (Sydney, Australia), October 26, 2003.

33. Jennifer Hewett, "Life Squeezed Out of Choreographed Set Piece," *Australian Financial Review,* October 24, 2003.

34. Patrick Sawer, "Yard Fury over Bush Visit," *Evening Standard* (London), November 10, 2003.

35. "President Bush Discusses Iraq Policy at Whitehall Palace in London," White House Office of Press Secretary, November 19, 2003.

36. "US Urged to Investigate Excessive Use of Force in Iraq Shootings," Agence France Presse, June 18, 2003.

37. Jack Douglas, "U.S. Security Memos Warn of Little Things," *Fort Worth Star-Telegram,* May 25, 2003.

38. Ian Hoffman, Sean Holstege, and Josh Richman, "State Monitored War Protesters," *Oakland Tribune,* May 20, 2003.

39. "Domestic Security Enhancement Act of 2003—Section-by-Section Analysis," Justice Department, January 9, 2003.

40. Michelle Goldberg, "Outlawing Dissent," *Salon,* February 11, 2004.

41. "Remarks of Attorney General John Ashcroft," Justice Department Office of Public Affairs, May 30, 2002.

42. Mark Wagenveld, "25 Years Ago, Before Watergate, a Burglary Changed History," *Philadelphia Inquirer,* March 10, 1996.

43. *COINTELPRO: The FBI's Covert Action Programs against American Citizens,* final report of the Senate Committee to Study Governmental Operations with respect to Intelligence Activities, Book III, April 23 (under authority of the order of April 14), 1976.

44. "Tactics Used During Protests and Demonstrations," *FBI Intelligence Bulletin #89,* October 15, 2003.

45. Ibid.

46. Eric Lichtblau and Charles Piller, "War on Terrorism Highlights FBI's Computer Woes," *Los Angeles Times,* July 28, 2002.

47. "Tactics Used during Protests and Demonstrations."

48. Ibid.

49. Eric Lichtblau, "F.B.I. Scrutinizes Antiwar Rallies," *New York Times,* November 23, 2003.

50. Ibid.

51. Jim Lobe, "FBI Plans for Antiwar Movement Spur Opposition," *Antiwar.com,* November 26, 2003.

52. Nat Hentoff, "J. Edgar Hoover Back at the 'New' FBI," *Village Voice,* December 4, 2003.

53. Lichtblau, "F.B.I. Scrutinizes Antiwar Rallies."

54. *Intelligence Activities and the Rights of Americans,* report of the Senate Select Committee to Study Governmental Operations with Respect to Intelligence Activities, April 14, 1976.

55. "Response to Media Misinterpretation of its Law Enforcement Sensitive Intelligence Bulletin, dated 10/15/2003," Federal Bureau of Investigation, November 25, 2003.

56. Jim Lobe, "Feds Back off Case Targeting Antiwar Activists," *Antiwar.com,* February 11, 2004.

57. Jeff Eckhoff and Mark Seibert, "Fourth Activist in D.M. Ordered to Testify," *Des Moines Register,* February 6, 2004.

58. Lobe, "Feds Back off Case."

59. Ryan J. Foley, "Feds Win Right to War Protesters' Records," Associated Press, February 7, 2004.

60. Janet Elliott, "Presence of Army Agents Stirs Furor," *Houston Chronicle,* February 13, 2004.

61. Eric Allen, "Army Intelligence Agents Inquire about UT Islam Conference," News 8 Austin, February 12, 2004.

62. Robert Block and Gary Fields, "Is Military Creeping into Domestic Spying and Enforcement?" *Wall Street Journal,* March 9, 2004.

63.   *COINTELPRO: The FBI's Covert Action Programs.*

CHAPTER 4. HOLLOW STEEL: BUSH VS. FREE TRADE

1.   "Bush Remarks to Los Angeles World Affairs Council," White House Office of the Press Secretary, May 29, 2001.
2.   "Address of the President to the Joint Session of Congress," White House Office of the Press Secretary, February 27, 2001.
3.   "Remarks by the President to the World Bank," White House Office of the Press Secretary, July 17, 2001.
4.   "Remarks on Signing the Trade Act of 2002," *Public Papers of the Presidents,* August 12, 2002.
5.   Neil King Jr., and Robert Guy Matthews, "So Far, Steel Tariffs Do Little of What President Envisioned," *Wall Street Journal,* September 13, 2002.
6.   Greg Rushford, "Bush Steps in a Steel Trap," *Wall Street Journal,* March 6, 2002.
7.   See James Bovard, *The Fair Trade Fraud* (New York: St. Martin's Press, 1991).
8.   "Remarks Prior to a Meeting with the Senate Education Working Group and an Exchange with Reporters," *Public Papers of the Presidents,* June 5, 2001.
9.   Greg Rushford, "Paul O'Neill's Steel Cover-Up," *Rushford Report,* April 2002. Rushford filed a Freedom of Information Act (FOIA) request for the report. The Treasury Department delayed responding for five months (even though the FOIA requires responses within 20 business days). The bureaucrats finally sent Rushford 84 sanitized pages from the report, with almost all the information blacked out—but only after Bush announced new tariffs.
10.   Rushford, "Bush Steps in a Steel Trap."
11.   Ron Suskind, *The Price of Loyalty* (New York: Simon & Schuster, 2004), 220.
12.   Ibid.
13.   Ibid., 216.
14.   "President Announces Temporary Safeguards for Steel Industry," White House Office of the Press Secretary, March 5, 2002.
15.   "President Bush Welcomes President Mubarak to White House," White House Office of the Press Secretary, March 5, 2002.
16.   Greg Rushford, "Pinocchio Bob," *Rushford Report,* April 2002.
17.   "Letter to the Speaker of the House and the President of the Senate," *Public Papers of the Presidents,* July 5, 1983.
18.   Paula Stern, "VRAs Seen Costly for Steel Users," *American Metal Market,* June 5, 1989.
19.   David Tarr and Morris Morke, "Aggregate Costs to the United States of Tariffs and Quotas on Imports: General Tariff Cuts and Removal of Quotas on Automobiles, Steel, Sugar and Textiles," U.S. Federal Trade Commission, 1984.
20.   Mike Allen and Jonathan Weisman, "Steel Tariffs Appear to Have Backfired on Bush," *Washington Post,* September 19, 2003.
21.   Editorial, "Man of Steel?," *Wall Street Journal,* March 4, 2002.
22.   George Will, "Bending for Steel," *Washington Post,* March 7, 2002.
23.   Warren Vieth, "Steel Prices Stoke Tariff Backlash," *Los Angeles Times,* June 24, 2002.
24.   Neil King, Jr. and Robert Guy Matthews, "U.S. Feels the Pain of Steel Tariffs," *Wall Street Journal,* May 31, 2002.
25.   "American Institute for International Steel Calls on Bush Administration to End Steel Tariffs; ITC Report Reveals Tariffs Cost Steel Consumers Over $1 Billion," American Institute for International Steel, press release, September 22, 2003.
26.   "Automotive Parts Manufacturers and Other Steel-Consuming Industries Urge Termination of Steel Tariffs," Motor and Equipment Manufacturers Association, press release, October 1, 2003.

27. Alexander's July 17, 2003 speech in the Senate was posted at http://alexander.senate.gov/news/205533.html.
28. Editorial, "Bush's Steel Opening," *Wall Street Journal*, November 11, 2003.
29. Allen and Weisman, "Steel Tariffs Appear to Have Backfired on Bush."
30. "American Institute for International Steel Calls on Bush Administration to End Steel Tariffs. "
31. Allen and Weisman, "Steel Tariffs Appear to Have Backfired on Bush."
32. King and Matthews, "So Far, Steel Tariffs Do Little of What President Envisioned."
33. Warren Vieth, "In the End, Bush Was Pressed," *Los Angeles Times*, December 5, 2003.
34. "Statement on Signing the Proclamation to Provide for the Termination of Action Taken with Regard to Imports of Certain Steel Products," *Public Papers of the Presidents*, December 4, 2003.
35. Ibid.
36. Suskind, *The Price of Loyalty*, 220.
37. "Interview with Trevor Kavanagh of the *Sun*," *Public Papers of the Presidents*, November 17, 2003.
38. "Statement on Signing the Proclamation."
39. "Remarks Prior to Discussions with King Abdullah II of Jordan and an Exchange with Reporters," *Public Papers of the Presidents*, December 4, 2003.
40. Vieth, "In the End, Bush Was Pressed."
41. "2002 Annual Report—The Fruits of Free Trade," Federal Reserve Bank of Dallas, 2002.
42. Information available at http://otexa.ita.doc.gov/fr2003/cat349649sg.htm.
43. U.S. International Trade Commission—2004 Tariff Database, available at http://dataweb.usitc.gov/scripts/tariff2004.asp.
44. Kristi Ellis and Scott Malone, "Bush Imparts Quotas on Some China Imports," *WWD*, November 19, 2003.
45. Evelyn Iritani and Warren Vieth, "China Adds Threat to U.S. Trade Tensions," *Los Angeles Times*, November 21, 2003.
46. "The President's News Conference With Prime Minister Tony Blair of the United Kingdom in London," *Public Papers of the Presidents*, November 20, 2003.
47. "Breast Size: Bigger Isn't Always Better," *Arizona Republic*, September 12, 2003.
48. Heather Scott, "US to Impose Safeguards to Stem China Textile Imports," *Main Wire*, November 19, 2003.
49. Edmund L. Andrews, "U.S. Moves to Limit Textile Imports from China," *New York Times*, November 19, 2003.
50. "Message to the Congress Transmitting Notification of Intention to Enter into a Free Trade Agreement with Singapore," *Public Papers of the Presidents*, February 3, 2003.
51. Evelyn Iritani, "Australia Pact a Win for U.S. Farm Interests," *Los Angeles Times*, February 9, 2004.
52. "Bush's 'Economic Coalition of the Willing,'" *Rushford Report*, August 2003.
53. "Proclamation 7564—World Trade Week, 2002," *Public Papers of the Presidents*, May 17, 2002.
54. "Remarks at the Swearing—In Ceremony for Ann M. Veneman as Secretary of Agriculture," *Public Papers of the Presidents*, March 2, 2001.

CHAPTER 5. ED FRAUD 101

1. "Radio Address by the President to the Nation," White House Office of the Press Secretary, March 2, 2002.
2. "Remarks in Johnson City, Texas, Upon Signing the Elementary and Secondary Education Bill," *Public Papers of the Presidents*, April 11, 1965.

3. Abigail Thernstrom and Stephan Thernstrom, *No Excuses: Closing the Racial Gap in Learning* (New York: Simon & Schuster, 2003), 215 .

4. Edward B. Fiske, "Commission on Education Warns 'Tide of Mediocrity' Imperils U.S.," *New York Times,* April 27, 1983.

5. Kirk A. Johnson, Ph.D., and Krista Kafer, "Why More Money Will Not Solve America's Education Crisis," Heritage Foundation, June 11, 2001.

6. "The Nation's Mayors Applaud President Clinton's bold New Initiatives That Will Better Prepare Our Cities for the 21st Century," U.S. Conference of Mayors, press release, February 4, 1999.

7. Richard Lee Colvin, "Experts Attack Math Teaching Programs," *Los Angeles Times,* November 18, 1999.

8. William McGurn, "Philadelphia Dims Edison's Light," *Wall Street Journal,* March 20, 2002.

9. "National Press Club Luncheon with Education Secretary Rod Paige," Federal News Service, September 24, 2003.

10. "Federal Education Funding: Multiple Programs and Lack of Data Raise Efficiency and Effectiveness Concerns," General Accounting Office, November 6, 1997.

11. "Remarks on Submitting the Education Plan to Congress," *Public Papers of the Presidents,* January 23, 2001.

12. "The President's Radio Address," *Public Papers of the Presidents,* July 7, 2001.

13. Andrew Rudalevige, "The Politics of No Child Left Behind," *Education Next,* Fall 2003.

14. Paul Gigot, "Beltway 101: Teddy Takes George to School," *Wall Street Journal,* May 4, 2001.

15. "Remarks at the Summit on the 21st Century Workforce," *Public Papers of the Presidents,* June 20, 2001.

16. "Remarks at Highland Park Elementary School in Landover, Maryland," *Public Papers of the Presidents,* July 7, 2003.

17. "National Press Club Luncheon with Education Secretary Rod Paige," Federal News Service, September 24, 2003.

18. Lawrence A. Uzzell, "Education Reform Fails the Test," *Wall Street Journal,* May 10, 1989.

19. Sam Dillon, "States Cut Test Standards to Avoid Sanctions," *New York Times,* May 22, 2003.

20. Matthew Meritt, "Schools Improve as Standards Go Down," *Star-Gazette* (Elmira, NY), May 21, 2003.

21. Editorial, "Bye-bye, MSPAP, hello, MSA," *Baltimore Sun,* March 5, 2003.

22. Brian Friel, "Making the Grade?" *National Journal,* September 13, 2003.

23. Rosalind S. Helderman and Ylan Q. Mui, "Comparing Schools' Progress Difficult," *Washington Post,* September 25, 2003.

24. Deann Smith, "School board votes to keep test standards," *Kansas City Star,* April 17, 2003.

25. Mike Bowler, "No Complaint Left Unvented," *Baltimore Sun,* March 21, 2004.

26. Thernstrom and Thernstrom, *No Excuses,* 242.

27. Ann Doss Helms, "Top N.C. Students May Be Losing Out," *Charlotte Observer,* January 8, 2004.

28. Alexandra Starr, "Why Johnny Can't Fail," *Business Week,* November 25, 2002.

29. Seanna Adcox, "Educators: AYP Results Misleading," *Post and Courier* (Charleston, S.C.), September 26, 2003.

30. Diane Rado and Darnell Little, "Schools Toying with Test Results," *Chicago Tribune,* September 28, 2003.

31. Adcox, "Educators: AYP Results Misleading."

32. Rado and Little, "Schools Toying with Test Results."

33. "Address before a Joint Session of the Congress on the State of the Union," *Public Papers of the Presidents,* January 20, 2004.
34. Daniel Golden, "Initiative to Leave No Child Behind Leaves Out Gifted," *Wall Street Journal,* December 29, 2003.
35. Ibid.
36. Diana Jean Schemo, "Schools, Facing Tight Budgets, Leave Gifted Programs Behind," *New York Times,* March 2, 2004.
37. Golden, "Initiative to Leave No Child Behind Leaves Out Gifted."
38. Schemo, "Schools, Facing Tight Budgets, Leave Gifted Programs Behind."
39. Dana Milbank, "Bush Urges Wide Use of School Vouchers," *Washington Post,* July 2, 2002.
40. Perry Bacon, "Struggle of the Classes," *Time,* September 22, 2003.
41. Terrence Stutz, "34 Low-Rated Schools Could Lose Students," *Dallas Morning News,* January 7, 2004.
42. Nanette Asimov, "Few Parents Seize Chance to Transfer Schools," *San Francisco Chronicle,* October 9, 2003.
43. Editorial, "No School Left Unpunished," *San Jose Mercury News,* October 20, 2003.
44. Michael Dobbs, "School Choice, Limited Options," *Washington Post,* December 22, 2003.
45. Ibid.
46. Kate Grossman and Art Golab, "Plenty of Grumbling over Reform Law," *Chicago Sun-Times,* December 19, 2003.
47. "Tutoring Services Court Students with Gifts," Associated Press, December 26, 2003.
48. Sam Dillon, "For Children Being Left Behind, Private Tutors Face Rocky Start," *New York Times,* April 16, 2004.
49. Lori Higgins, Chastity Pratt, and Peggy Walsh Sarnecki, "Kids Are Missing Out on Tutoring," *Detroit Free Press,* February 21, 2004.
50. William Howell, "Fumbling for an Exit Key: Parents, Choice, and the Future of No Child Left Behind," Pioneer Institute, 2004.
51. "Remarks on Submitting the Education Plan to Congress," *Public Papers of the Presidents,* January 23, 2001.
52. Phyllis Schafly, "Children Left Behind Despite Bush Education Act," *San Diego Union Tribune,* October, 24, 2003.
53. Erik W. Robelen, "Unsafe Label Will Trigger School Choice," *Education Week,* October 23, 2002.
54. Diane Stepp, "Police See Increase in School Crime," *Atlanta Journal-Constitution,* February 12, 2004.
55. Sam Dillon, "Threshold for Dangerous Schools Under New Law Is Too High, Critics Say," *New York Times,* September 28, 2003.
56. John J. Sanko, "Dangerous 'Schools Bill Clears Committee," *Rocky Mountain News,* April 15, 2004.
57. "Persistently Dangerous Schools: No Child Left Behind Update," Research and Educational Services, New York State United Teachers, August 12, 2003.
58. Elissa Gootman, "List of 'Dangerous' Schools Lists Few, Puzzling Many," *New York Times,* August 19, 2003.
59. Amy Hetzner and Sarah Carr, "Few Schools May Be Called Dangerous," *Milwaukee Journal Sentinel,* June 23, 2003.
60. Greg Toppo, "'Persistently Dangerous,'" *USA Today,* March 10, 2003.
61. Laura Diamond, "School Not a 'Danger' Despite Safety Record," *Florida Times-Union* (Jacksonville, FL), October 11, 2003.
62. Editorial, "State's Safe School Definition Is Laughable," *Sacramento Bee,* July 21, 2003.

63.   Editorial, "Tell Truth on School Crime," *Los Angeles Times,* July 11, 2003.
64.   Duke Helfand, "School Danger Narrowly Defined," *Los Angeles Times,* July 8, 2003.
65.   Ibid.
66.   Scott Stephens, "'Dangerous' Label Scares Educators," *Cleveland Plain Dealer,* July 27, 2003.
67.   "Schools Not 'Persistently Dangerous' Despite Danger," Associated Press, November 9, 2003.
68.   Jake Wagman, "No School Is Likely to Meet Definition of 'Persistently Dangerous;' State Panel Planned It that Way," *St. Louis Post Dispatch,* April 17, 2003.
69.   Charles J. Dean, "No Alabama Schools Persistently Dangerous," *Birmingham News,* December 8, 2003.
70.   Erik W. Robelen, "Unsafe Label Will Trigger School Choice," *Education Week,* October 23, 2002.
71.   Nirvi Shah, "No School in Fla. Expected to Make 'Unsafe' List," *Palm Beach Post,* June 8, 2003.
72.   Duke Helfand, "School Danger Narrowly Defined," *Los Angeles Times,* July 8, 2003.
73.   Erik W. Robelen, "States Report Few Schools as Dangerous," *Education Week,* September 24, 2003.
74.   "States Decide How Dangerous is Too Dangerous, Few Schools Labeled," *School Violence Alert,* September 04, 2003.
75.   Jennifer K. Covino, "Fighting Danger," District Administrator, January 2004.
76.   Anjetta McQueen, "Report Derides Education in Texas," Associated Press, October 24, 2000.
77.   Kate Snow, "Bush Hopes to Bring Texas Education Agenda to National Level," Cable News Network, September 1, 2000.
78.   Sarah Schmidt, "Measuring Up," *National Post* (Canada), November 19, 2002.
79.   Todd Gillman, "Houston Dropout Rate Questions Bedevil Paige," *Dallas Morning News,* September 14, 2003.
80.   Zanto Peabody, Julie Mason, and Alan Bernstein, "Paige's Methods at HISD Reassessed," *Houston Chronicle,* August 3, 2003.
81.   Lou Dubose, "Beyond Belief," *LA Weekly,* September 19, 2003.
82.   Sydney Schanberg, "Bush's New Federal Math Leaves Kids Far Behind." *Village Voice,* September 23, 2003.
83.   Michael Dobbs, "Education 'Miracle' Has a Math Problem," *Washington Post,* November 8, 2003.
84.   Diana Jean Schemo, "For Houston Schools, College Claims Exceed Reality," *New York Times,* August 28, 2003.
85.   Melanie Markley, "Turning a Paige," *Houston Chronicle,* January 19, 2001.
86.   Dobbs, "Education 'Miracle' Has a Math Problem."
87.   Sarah Schmidt, "Measuring Up."
88.   Zanto Peabody, "Tests Show HISD 'Achievement Gap' Back," *Houston Chronicle,* July 24, 2003.
89.   Ibid.
90.   Karen Brandon, "Critics Call into Question Success of Texas Schools," *Chicago Tribune,* March 5, 2001.
91.   Todd J. Gillman, "Houston Dropout Rate Questions Bedevil Paige," *Dallas Morning News,* September 14, 2003.
92.   "National Press Club Luncheon with Education Secretary Rod Paige," Federal News Service, September 24, 2003.
93.   Daniel Golden, "Initiative to Leave No Child Behind Leaves Out Gifted," *Wall Street Journal,* December 29, 2003.
94.   "National Press Club Luncheion with Education Secretary Rod Paige," Federal News Service, September 24, 2003.

95. "Remarks of Secretary Paige before The American Enterprise Institute," Department of
     Education Office of Public Affairs, January 7, 2004.
96. Thernstrom and Thernstrom, *No Excuses,* 13.
97. John Welbes, "Minnesota Worst in U.S. for Black-White Test Gap," *St. Paul Pioneer Press,*
     August 14, 2003.
98. Thernstrom and Thernstrom, *No Excuses,* 14.
99. Stuart Taylor Jr., "Stuck at the Racial Gap," *Legal Times,* October 27, 2003.
100. Thernstrom and Thernstrom, *No Excuses,* 84.
101. Nathan Glazer, "Will Anything Work?," *New Republic,* October 13, 2003.
102. Thernstrom and Thernstrom, *No Excuses,* 126.
103. Ibid., 143.
104. Rona Marech, "Why Do Black Students Lag Behind?" *San Francisco Chronicle,* February
     5, 2001.
105. Courtland Milloy, "A Challenging Analysis of Black America," *Washington Post,* March
     21, 2003.
106. Paul Peterson, "Ticket to Nowhere," *Education Next,* Spring 2003.
107. Ibid.
108. "Bush: Reading the 'New Civil Right,'" United Press International, April 3, 2002.
109. Amy Goldstein, "Bush Outlines education Sequel," *Washington Post,* April 3, 2003.
110. "President Announces Early Childhood Initiative," White House Office of the Press Sec-
     retary, April 2, 2002.
111. Thernstrom and Thernstrom, *No Excuses,* 221.
112. "Address Before a Joint Session of the Congress on the State of the Union," *Public Papers
     of the Presidents,* January 20, 2004.
113. "Remarks to the United States Conference of Mayors," *Public Papers of the Presidents,* Jan-
     uary 23, 2004.
114. Michael A. Fletcher, "Education Law Reaches Milestone Amid Discord," *Washington
     Post,* January 8, 2003.
115. Kirk A. Johnson and Krista Kafer, "Why More Money Will Not Solve America's Educa-
     tion Crisis," Heritage Foundation, June 11, 2001.
116. Stuart Butler, "The Folly of an Education Spending Race," Heritage Foundation, Febru-
     ary 24, 1999.
117. "U.S. Education: Less Bang for Buck," Associated Press, September 16, 2003.
118. Rod Paige, "More Spending Is Not Answer," *USA Today,* January 10, 2003.
119. "No Education Funding Left Behind," *Washington Post,* October 24, 2003.
120. Dan Balz, "House Republicans' Ratings on Education Are Slipping, Pollster Says," *Wash-
     ington Post,* April 22, 2002.
121. Mike Allen, "Bush Touts 9% Rise in Funds for Poor Students," *Washington Post,* January
     5, 2003.
122. Memo from Rep. Deborah Pryce and Rep. John Boehner to members of House Repub-
     lican Conference, Subject: "Education Outreach and Communications," January 27,
     2004.
123. "National Press Club Luncheon with Education Secretary Rod Paige," Federal News Ser-
     vice, September 24, 2003.
124. See, for instance, James S. Coleman and Thomas Hoffer, *Public and Private High Schools*
     (New York: Basic Books, 1987).
125. Isabel Lyman, "Home Schooling and Histrionics," Cato.org, May 31, 2000.
126. Jay Mathews and Rosalind S. Helderman, "Educators Decry Law's Intrusion, Not Its
     Cost," *Washington Post,* February 9, 2004.
127. Diana Jean Schemo, "14 States Ask U.S. to Revise Some Education Law Rules," *New York
     Times,* March 25, 2004.

128. Robert Pear, "Education Chief Calls Union 'Terrorist,' Then Recants," *New York Times,* February 24, 2004.

CHAPTER 6. AMERICORPS AND MORAL REFORMATION

1. "Remarks in a Discussion on Community Service in Philadelphia, Pennsylvania," *Public Papers of the Presidents,* March 12, 2002.
2. "Remarks by President Bush at 2002 'Congress of Tomorrow' Republican Retreat Luncheon," White House Office of the Press Secretary, February 1, 2002.
3. "President Discusses War on Terrorism," White House Office of the Press Secretary, November 8, 2001.
4. James Bovard, *Feeling Your Pain: The Explosion and Abuse of Government Power in the Clinton-Gore Years* (New York: Palgrave, 2000), 7–25.
5. See, for instance, "Remarks at Vandenberg Elementary School in Southfield," *Public Papers of the Presidents,* May 6, 2002, and "Remarks at the Iowa State Fair in Des Moines, Iowa," *Public Papers of the Presidents,* August 14, 2002. During the 1990s, conservative congressmen were furious when Clinton would refer to AmeriCorps members as volunteers.
6. See the comments of Corporation for National and Community Service chief executive officer David Eisner, "Urban Institute Forum: Volunteer Management Capacity," Federal News Service, February 18, 2004.
7. Public Meeting of the Board of Directors of the Corporation for National and Community Service, Washington, D.C., September 9, 1999.
8. Les Lenkowsky, "Sowing the Seeds of Trust," Corporation for National and Community Service, October 26, 2001.
9. "Gun Locks Will be Given Out," *Times-Picayune* (New Orleans), January 19, 2002.
10. Garrett Ordower, "Americorps Volunteers Preserve Farm," *Chicago Daily Herald,* October 27, 2003.
11. "New Highway Name Honors Sacajawea," *Idaho Falls Post Register,* January 31, 2004.
12. Rachel Tuinstra, "Gay Youth Invited to First 'Pink Prom' in Snohomish County," *Seattle Times,* May 1, 2004.
13. John Monahan, "Students Study Super Bowl Sewage Surge," *Telegram & Gazette,* January 18, 2002.
14. Brian Meyer, "Volunteers to Help Undo Winter's Wrath," *Buffalo News,* February 7, 2002.
15. News First Online, KOAA-TV, Colorado Springs/Pueblo, March 2, 2004.
16. Marti Davis, "Program's Aim is to Provide Fresh Vegetables to Needy," *Knoxville News-Sentinel,* February 20, 2002.
17. Editorial, "Give Smoking Survey a Chance," *Wisconsin Rapids Daily Tribune* (Wisconsin Rapids, WI), May 11, 2004.
18. "Communities in Schools making progress in Cabell County," *Herald-Dispatch* (Huntington, W.Va.), November 30, 2003.
19. "Puppet Shows Teach Children Fire Safety," *State Journal-Register* (Springfield, IL), March 6, 2004.
20. Robert C. Gabordi, "Citizen-Times Staff Breaking the Rules to Help Stop Child Abuse," *Asheville Citizen-Times* (North Carolina), March 28, 2004.
21. "AmeriCorps Helps Congress Build America," States News Service, March 26, 2004.
22. Sara Harvey, "AmeriCorps Group Learns Lessons in Ambler Class," *Greenville News* (Greenville, S.C.), March 4, 2004.
23. Angelia Davis, "AmeriCorps Crew Pushes Forward with Mission," *Greenville News,* January 22, 2004 .

24. "Executive Order 13331—National and Community Service Programs," *Public Papers of the Presidents,* February 27, 2004.

25. Fiscal Year 2004 Budget, Performance and Management Assessments, "AmeriCorps," Office of Management and Budget, February 2003. at http://www.whitehouse.gov/omb/budget/fy2004/pma.html.

26. Office of Management and Budget, "Other Independent Agencies Part Assessments," February 2004.

27. General Accounting Office, "National Service Programs: Two AmeriCorps Programs' Funding and Benefits," February 2000.

28. "Remarks in a Discussion on Community Service in Philadelphia, Pennsylvania," *Public Papers of the Presidents,* March 12, 2002.

29. "President Thanks Leaders for Commitment to Service," White House Office of the Press Secretary, December 10, 2002.

30. "Fact Sheet: President Bush Celebrates USA Freedom Corps One-Year Anniversary," White House Office of the Press Secretary, January 30, 2003.

31. "The National Service Trust: Internal Control Weaknesses," Corporation for National and Community Service Office of Inspector General Report 03–007, July 24, 2003.

32. U.S. General Accounting Office, "Preliminary Observations on the National Service Trust and AmeriCorps," April 10, 2003.

33. Editorial, "The AmeriCorps Follies," *Wall Street Journal,* July 30, 2003.

34. David Skinner, "Loving AmeriCorps to Death," *Slate,* June 20, 2003.

35. Ibid.

36. John Bridgeland, "Let Volunteer Corps Help Out Even More," *The Baltimore Sun,* October 30, 2003.

37. Christopher Lee, "$411,655 in Bonuses at AmeriCorps's Parent Agency Decried," *Washington Post,* August 15, 2003.

38. Ibid.

39. "Mr. President: 'Please Be a Citizen, Not a Spectator on AmeriCorps Funding'," PR Newswire, July 25, 2003.

40. Sasha Talcott, "Quality of Life at Stake in AmeriCorps Funding, Mayor Says," *Boston Globe,* July 19, 2003.

41. "Newsweek Guest Essay: Senator John McCain," PR Newswire, September 7, 2003.

42. John McCain, "Putting the 'National' in National Service," *Washington Monthly,* November 2001.

43. E. J. Dionne, "Save AmeriCorps, Mr. President," *Washington Post,* June 27, 2003.

44. Press Release, "Chairman Walsh Statement against Additional FY'03 Funding to Cover AmeriCorps Mismanagement," Office of Rep. James Walsh, July 10, 2003.

45. "President's 2005 Budget Would Engage Record Number of Americans in Service," Corporation for National Service, February 2, 2004.

46. "Executive Order 13331—National and Community Service Programs," *Public Papers of the Presidents,* February 27, 2004.

47. "Address Before a Joint Session of the Congress on the State of the Union," *Public Papers of the Presidents,* January 29, 2002.

48. "Remarks in a Discussion on Community Service in Philadelphia, Pennsylvania," *Public Papers of the Presidents,* March 12, 2002.

49. Dana Milbank, "Should History Record the Unvarnished Bush?" *Washington Post,* April 16, 2002.

50. "Special Supplement: The Full Text of Clinton's FY 1995 Budget Submitted to Congress Feb. 7, 1994. Analytical Perspectives: Generational Accounting," *Daily Report for Executives,* February 10, 1994, d90.

51. Susan J. Ellis, "The Wrong Way to Encourage Volunteerism," *Chronicle of Philanthropy,* February 21, 2002.

52. "A Call to Service," White House, 2002.
53. Editorial, "What Is Operation TIPS?" *Washington Post,* July 14, 2002.
54. Adam Clymer, "Worker Corps to Be Formed To Report Odd Activity," *New York Times,* July 26, 2002
55. "President's Radio Address," White House Office of the Press Secretary, December 20, 2003.
56. "Fact Sheet: USA Freedom Corps Celebrates Two-Year Anniversary," White House Office of the Press Secretary, January 29, 2004.
57. Ian Wilhelm, "Stepping Up to Serve Charity," *Chronicle of Philanthropy,* January 8, 2004.
58. "Volunteering in the United States, 2003 Technical Note," Bureau of Labor Statistics, December 2003.
59. Author interview with BLS analyst Stephanie Borass, May 24, 2004.
60. "Volunteering in the United States, 2003."
61. "Giving and Volunteering," Independent Sector, 2001.
62. Thomas Kostigen, "Volunteerism Rise as Financial Gifts Slip," *CBS MarketWatch,* October 14, 2002 .
63. "A New Definition for Volunteering and Giving Among the 45+ Population Finds Thirty Percent Are More Inclined to Volunteer Since 9/11," American Associated of Retired Persons, November 18, 2003.
64. Siobhan Gorman, "Shaken, Not Stirred," *National Journal,* September 13, 2003.
65. Editorial, "The AmeriCorps Follies," *Wall Street Journal,* July 30, 2003.
66. Editorial, "More AmeriCorps Follies," *Wall Street Journal,* August 7, 2003.

CHAPTER 7. BUSH'S FARM FIASCO

1. Editorial, "Making Hay," *The New Republic,* May 9, 2002.
2. See data on large family farms at http://www.ers.usda.gov/Data/farmfinancialmgmt/typlbal.htm. Most of the "farms" included in the government's official definition are gentleman farmers, hobby farmers, or "tax farmers."
3. Richard E. Cohen and Corine Hegland, "Farm Bill Winners and Losers," *National Journal,* May 11, 2002.
4. David Rogers, "House GOP Plans a Farm-Spending Bill That Would Clean Out Budget Surpluses," *Wall Street Journal,* September 7, 2001.
5. Elizabeth Becker, "White House Criticizes Republican Farm Bill," *New York Times,* October 4, 2001.
6. Elizabeth Becker, "Bush Gives Tight-Fisted Support to Bigger Farm Subsidies," *New York Times,* November 29, 2001.
7. Environmental Working Group. www.ewg.org/farm/findings.php.
8. Editorial, "Prairie Plutocrats," *Wall Street Journal,* February 1, 2002.
9. Mark Arax and Eric Bailey, "Some Farmers Growing Rich on Government Crop Subsidies," *Los Angeles Times,* June 10, 2002.
10. Brian M. Riedl and John E. Frydenlund, "At the Federal Trough: Farm Subsidies for the Rich and Famous," Heritage Foundation, November 26, 2001. (This report was based in part on research by the Environmental Working Group).
11. John Lancaster, "Farm Aid Benefits Lawmakers," *Washington Post,* September 1, 2001.
12. Editorial, "Farm Foolery," *Wall Street Journal,* January 22, 2002.
13. See James Bovard, *The Farm Fiasco* (San Francisco: ICS Press, 1989).
14. Press Release, "Carnahan Urges Farm Bill Conferees to Protect Rice and Cotton Farmers," Office of Sen. Jean Carnhan, February 20, 2002.
15. Press Release, "Ag Talk—House and Senate Farm Bill Negotiations," Office of Rep. Charles Stenholm, March 8, 2002.

16. See I Kings 3:16–27.
17. Press Release, "Excerpts from Sen. Lugar's Floor Statement on the Farm Bill," Office of Sen. Richard Lugar, May 7, 2002.
18. Jeff Flake, "Bloat Watch," *Wall Street Journal,* May 2, 2002.
19. Ibid.
20. Philip Brasher, "Critics Decry Farm Bill Price Tag," Associated Press, May 7, 2002.
21. Richard E. Cohen and Corine Hegland, "Farm Bill Winners and Losers," *National Journal,* May 11, 2002.
22. Mike Allen, "Bush Signs Bill Providing Big Farm Subsidy Increases," *Washington Post,* May 14, 2002.
23. Ibid.
24. Ibid.
25. "Remarks by the President Upon Signing the Farm Bill," Office of the White House Press Secretary, May 13, 2002.
26. Greg Ip, "Federal Reserve Report Shows Rich Dominate 'Investor Class,'" *Wall Street Journal,* January 23, 2003.
27. "Capitol Hill Hearing Testimony, House Agriculture Committee, State of Dairy Industry, Testimony of Constance Tipton of the International Dairy Foods Association," Federal Document Clearing House Congressional Testimony, May 20, 2003.
28. Dan Morgan, "GOP Rejects Move To Alter Farm Bill," *Washington Post,* July 12, 2002.
29. Roger Thurow and Scott Kilman, "U.S. Subsidies Create Cotton Glut That Hurts Foreign Cotton Farms," *Wall Street Journal,* June 26, 2002.
30. "USDA Needs to Better Ensure Protection of Highly Erodible Cropland and Wetlands," General Accounting Office, April 2003.
31. "Remarks at Mount Rushmore National Memorial in Keystone, South Dakota," *Public Papers of the Presidents,* August 15, 2002.
32. Aaron Lukas, "A Sticky State of Affairs," *National Review Online,* February 12, 2004.
33. Ibid.
34. Ibid.
35. "Milk powder supplies flood storage space," Associated Press, June 30, 2002.
36. "Capitol Hill Hearing Testimony, House Agriculture Committee, State of Dairy Industry, Testimony of Constance Tipton of the International Dairy Foods Association," Federal Document Clearing House Congressional Testimony, May 20, 2003.
37. Press Release, "National Dairy Council—3-A-Day of Dairy Battles Calcium Crisis in America," National Dairy Council, February 24, 2003.
38. Michael Doyle, "Dairy Farmers Claim Federal Policy Aggravates Woes," *Modesto Bee,* May 21, 2003.
39. Ibid.
40. "Capitol Hill Hearing Testimony, House Agriculture Committee, State of Dairy Industry, Testimony of Constance Tipton of the International Dairy Foods Association," Federal Document Clearing House Congressional Testimony, May 20, 2003.
41. "2002 Annual Report—The Fruits of Free Trade," Federal Reserve Bank of Dallas, 2002.
42. "Remarks by the President at Milwaukee, Wisconsin Welcome Klotsche Center," Office of the White House Press Secretary, August 14, 2002.
43. See "Congressional Decision Needed on Necessity of Federal Wool Program," General Accounting Office, 1982.
44. James Bovard, "This Farm Program Is Just Plain Nuts," *Wall Street Journal,* August 30, 1995.
45. Dan Morgan, "Subsidies Boosted In Farm Bill Deal," *Washington Post,* April 27, 2002.
46. Roger Thurow and Scott Kilman, "U.S. Subsidies Create Cotton Glut That Hurts Foreign Cotton Farms," *Wall Street Journal,* June 26, 2002.

47.   Amadou Toumani Touré and Blaise Compaoré, "Your Farm Subsidies Are Strangling Us," *New York Times,* July 11, 2003.
48.   Warren Vieth, "U.S. Exports Misery to Africa With Farm Bill," *Los Angeles Times,* May 27, 2002.
49.   Greg Rushford, "What Really Happened in Cancun," *Rushford Report,* October 2003.
50.   Ibid.
51.   "Changes Made to Market Access Program, but Questions Remain on Economic Impact," General Accounting Office, April 1999.
52.   "Fact Sheet: Market Access Program," U.S. Department of Agriculture, June 2003.
53.   Farm Security and Rural Investment Act of 2002, Public Law No. 107–171, May 13, 2002.
54.   "Remarks at the World Pork Expo in Des Moines, Iowa," *Public Papers of the Presidents,* June 7, 2002.
55.   Editorial, *New York Times,* July 21, 1930.

CHAPTER 8. SPENDING AS CARING

1.   Editorial, "Crying Wolfensohn," *Wall Street Journal,* March 6, 2002.
2.   "Remarks on Compassionate Conservatism in San Jose, California," *Public Papers of the Presidents,*" April 30, 2002.
3.   George Gedda, "Rebirth for U.S. Foreign Aid Program," *Seattle Post-Intelligencer,* February 16, 2003.
4.   "75 percent of foreign aid to Bangladesh lost in corruption: study," Agence France Presse, March 29, 2003.
5.   Allan H. Meltzer and Bruce Rich, "World Bank Drain," *Washington Times,* January 13, 2003.
6.   Basildon Peta, "Africa's Leaders 'Stole $140bn'," *Independent* (UK), June 14, 2002.
7.   Marian L. Tupy, "Aiding Is Not Abetting," *National Review* Online (www.nationalreview.com), February 19, 2004.
8.   Laurence Davison, "Kicking Tires around the world," MAR/Hedge October 2003.
9.   Lael Brainard, "Compassionate Conservatism Confronts Global Poverty," *Washington Quarterly,* Spring 2003.
10.   "How to Prevent the Millennium Challenge Account from Becoming Like Traditional Foreign Aid," Heritage Foundation, July 14, 2003.
11.   William Easterly, "The World Bank, the IMF, and the Poor," *Economic Intuition,* Summer 2001.
12.   Aleberto Alesina and Beatrice Weder, "Do Corrupt Governments Receive Less Foreign Aid?," National Bureau of Economic Research Working Paper No. 7108, May 1999.
13.   Alberto Alesina and Beatrice Weder, "Do Corrupt Governments Receive Less Foreign Aid?" *American Economic Review,* 2002.
14.   P. T. Bauer, *Reality and Rhetoric* (Cambridge: Harvard University Press, 1984), p. 104.
15.   Paul Blustein, "Bush Seeks Foreign Aid Boost; Plan Counters Overseas Critics," *Washington Post,* March 15, 2002.
16.   Martha Brant, "West Wing Story: Bush and Bono," *Newsweek* Web Exclusive, March 20, 2002.
17.   Elisabeth Bumiller, "Diplomatic Two-Steps In Latin America Trip," *New York Times,* March 25, 2002.
18.   Ibid.
19.   "Interview With Radio Programas de Peru," *Public Papers of the Presidents,* March 20, 2002.
20.   Elisabeth Bumiller, "Bush, in Monterrey, Speaks of Conditional Global Aid," *New York Times,* March 23, 2002.

21. "Remarks to the United Nations Financing for Development Conference in Monterrey, Mexico," *Public Papers of the Presidents,* March 22, 2002.
22. Ibid.
23. Paul Blustein, "Bush Shift on Foreign Aid Strengthens U.S. Position at Summit," *Washington Post,* March 16, 2002.
24. "Spreading Democracy, Defending Freedom Are Bush's Goals, Rice Says; Outlines Administration Foreign Policy in Lecture at Reagan Library," White House Office of the Press Secretary, February 26, 2004.
25. "Countries Eligible for New U.S. Aid to Be Selected in May; Those Selected May Submit Funding Proposals, State's Larson Says," State Department Office of Public Affairs, March 10, 2004.
26. "Interview with Latin American and American Spanish Language Journalists," *Public Papers of the Presidents,* March 19, 2002.
27. "Interview with African Journalists," *Public Papers of the Presidents,* October 2, 2003 (italics added).
28. "Countries Eligible for New U.S. Aid to Be Selected in May" (italics added).
29. "Chief Israeli Prosecutor Files Recommendation in Sharon Corruption Scandal," Agence France Presse, March 28, 2004.
30. For complaints about Egyptian corruption, see, for instance, Acil Tabbara, "World Bank urges Egypt to Speed Up Reform to Attract Investment," Agence France Presse, December 3, 2003.
31. "Musharraf Asks Foreign Banks to Return Pakistan's 'Looted Wealth,'" Agence France Presse, April 22, 2004.
32. "Remarks at the Inter-American Development Bank," *Public Papers of the Presidents,* March 14, 2002.
33. William Easterly, "The Failure of Development," *Financial Times,* July 4, 2001.
34. William Easterly, "Tired Old Mantras at Monterrey," *Wall Street Journal,* March 18, 2002.
35. Jon Sawyer, "U.S. Wrestles with Notion that Massive Aid Can Stop Terrorism," *St. Louis Post-Dispatch,* December 3, 2001.
36. Harold Brumm, "Aid, Policies, and Growth: Bauer Was Right," *Cato Journal,* Fall 2003.
37. The website for the HUD Office of Inspector General, provides ample evidence of HUD debacles.
38. "Proclamation 7685—National Homeownership Month, 2003," *Public Papers of the Presidents,* June 16, 2003.
39. Richard W. Stevenson, "Bush Visits Pennsylvania to Promote Homeowning," *New York Times,* March 16, 2004.
40. Brian Collins, "HUD Taking Another Look at Downpayment Assistance Programs," *National Mortgage News,* December 2, 2002. Also, Gloria Irwin, "Programs 'gift' down payments," *Akron Beacon Journal,* August 24, 2003.
41. "New Study of Claims on FHA Loans with Down Payment Gifts," *Mortgage Banking,* November 1, 2003.
42. "A Home Of Your Own: Expanding Opportunities for All Americans," White House Office of the Press Secretary, June 17, 2002.
43. Cory Reiss, "House Passes Harris' First Bill," *Sarasota Herald-Tribune,* October 2, 2003.
44. Posting by congressional staffer Norm Singleton, LewRockwell.com Blog, December 16, 2003.
45. "Remarks by the President at Signing of the American Dream Downpayment Act," White House Office of the Press Secretary, December 16, 2003.

46. Ibid.

47. David E. Sanger, "Bush Calls Transformed Area a Model Program for Housing," *New York Times*, June 18, 2002.

48. "Speaker Hastert Touts Law Closing the Homeownership Gap for Minorities," U.S. Newswire, October 1, 2003.

49. Brian Collins, "Homeownership Rate Hits New Record High," *National Mortgage News*, February 9, 2004.

50. "Remarks to the United States Conference of Mayors," *Public Papers of the Presidents*, January 26, 2004.

51. "President Calls on Senate to Pass American Dream Downpayment Act—Remarks by the President on Housing and the Economy," White House Office of the Press Secretary, October 15, 2003 (italics added).

52. Albert R. Karr, "Fed Study Challenges Notion of Bias against Minorities in Mortgage Lending," *Wall Street Journal*, January 26, 1995.

53. Cindy Loose, "Racial Disparity Found in Credit Rating," *Washington Post*, September 21, 1999.

54. "Remarks in a Discussion on Health Care Access," *Public Papers of the Presidents*, March 16, 2004.

55. Julie Kosterlitz, "Home Sweet Home?" *National Journal*, March 6, 2004.

56. "Dismantling the Barriers to Homeownership," White House Office of the Press Secretary, March 26, 2004.

57. Lew Sichelman, "Bush to Offer Zero Down FHA Loan," *Realty Times*, January 20, 2004.

58. Lew Sichelman, "Bush to Offer Zero Down FHAs," *National Mortgage News*, January 26, 2004.

59. Ibid. (italics added).

60. Julie Kosterlitz, "Home Sweet Home?" *National Journal*, March 6, 2004.

61. Daniel Taylor, "Zero Down, Then What?" *Baltimore Sun*, February 22, 2004.

62. D'Vera Cohn, "For Lower-Income Buyers, A Surge in Homeownership," *Washington Post*, December 24, 2002.

63. Lew Sichelman, "Bush to Offer Zero Down FHAs" (italics added).

64. Ibid. (italics added).

65. William Lilley III and Timothy B. Clark, "Federal Programs Spur Abandonment of Housing in Major Cities," *National Journal*, January 1, 1972.

66. *Congressional Record*, April 29, 1975, p. 12267.

67. "Families HUD Abandoned," National Training and Information Center, May 2002.

68. Inez Killingsworth, "FHA, Turning an American Dream into a Neighborhood Nightmare," National Housing Institute, July 2002.

69. Ron Paul, "Compassionate Conservatives' American Dream," LewRockwell.com, October 1, 2003. (Reprint of Paul's statement for the Congressional Record).

70. Julie Kosterlitz, "Home Sweet Home?" *National Journal*, March 6, 2004.

71. http://www.truthandpolitics.org/comp-fed-outlays.php.

72. John F. Dickerson, "Can We Afford All This?" *Time Magazine*, December 8, 2003.

73. "Remarks at the Engelwood Neighborhood Center in Orlando," *Public Papers of the Presidents*, November 13, 2003.

74. Robert Novak, "Hammering Fellow Republicans," *Washington Post*, November 27, 2003.

75. "As GOP Wary of Medicare Number, Frist Unconcerned," National Journal's Congress Daily, January 30, 2004.

76. Robert Pear, "Medicare Law's Costs and Benefits Are Elusive," *New York Times*, December 9, 2003.

77.   Tony Pugh, "Bush Administration Ordered Medicare Plan Cost Estimates Withheld," Knight Ridder Newspapers, March 11, 2004.

78.   Amy Goldstein, "HHS Actuary Feels Bush Aide Put Hold on Medicare Data," *Washington Post,* March 19, 2004.

79.   Sheryl Gay Stolberg and Robert Pear, "Mysterious Fax Adds to Intrigue over the Medicare Bill's Cost," *New York Times,* March 18, 2004.

80.   Sheryl Gay Stolberg, "Senate Democrats Claim Medicare Chief Broke Law," *New York Times,* March 19, 2004.

81.   Vicki Kemper, "Medicare Secrecy Inquiry Is Silenced," *Los Angeles Times,* April 2, 2004.

82.   Tony Pugh, "Report: Medicare Official Defied Court Rulings," *Knight Ridder Newspapers,* May 3, 2004.

83.   Stolberg and Pear, "Mysterious Fax Adds to Intrigue."

84.   "Remarks at the Engelwood Neighborhood Center in Orlando," *Public Papers of the Presidents,* November 13, 2003.

85.   http://www.ncpa.org/pub/ba/ba463/.

86.   "Ron Paul on Medicare Plunder," *Texas Straight Talk,* November 25, 2003.

87.   Jon Frandsen, "Bush, GOP Leaders Work Furiously to Save Medicare Bill," Gannett News Service, November 22, 2003.

88.   Jonathan E. Kaplan, "'Me too, pal,' Says Bush, Hanging Up," *The Hill,* December 3, 2003.

89.   Ibid.

90.   "Remarks Following a Meeting with Congressional Leaders," *Public Papers of the Presidents,* November 17, 2003.

91.   "Remarks on the 38th Anniversary of Medicare," *Public Papers of the Presidents,* July 30, 2003.

91.   Ana M. Aizcorbe, Arthur B. Kennickell, and Kevin B. Moore, "Recent Changes in U.S. Family Finances: Evidence from the 1998 and 2001 Survey of Consumer Finances," *Federal Reserve Bulletin,* January 2003.

93.   Brian M. Riedl and William W. Beach, "New Medicare Drug Entitlement's Huge New Tax on Working Americans," Heritage Foundation, July 30, 2003.

94.   "Remarks on the 38th Anniversary of Medicare."

95.   Robert Pear, "White House's Medicare Videos Are Ruled Illegal," *New York Times,* May 20, 2004.

96.   Ibid.

97.   Amy Goldstein and Helen Dewar, "GOP Still Seeking Afterglow of Vote on Drug Benefits," *Washington Post,* February 29, 2004.

98.   Amy Goldstein, "Dire Report on Medicare Finances," *Washington Post,* March 24, 2004.

99.   Ibid.

100.   Ibid.

101.   Edmund L. Andrews and Robert Pear, "Entitlement Costs Are Expected to Soar," *New York Times,* March 19, 2004.

102.   Deroy Murdock, "Kill the Medicare Drug Law," Scripps Howard News Service, April 3, 2004.

103.   Jennifer Warner, "Support Dwindling for New Medicare Law," WedMD, April 2, 2004.

104.   Goldstein and Dewar, "GOP Still Seeking Afterglow of Vote on Drug Benefits."

105.   Wickard v. Filburn, 317 U.S. 111 (1942).

106.   Mike Allen and Kathy Sawyer, "Return to Moon May Be on Agenda," *Washington Post,* December 5, 2003

107.   "Address of the President to the Joint Session of Congress," White House Office of the Press Secretary, February 27, 2001.

CHAPTER 9. THE POLITICAL PROFITS
OF POINTLESS PUNISHMENT

1.   www.issues2000.org/George_W__Bush_Drugs.htm.
2.   Terry Robinson and Kent Berridge, "Addiction," *Annual Review of Psychology,* January 2003.
3.   "Terror Alert," *PBS NewsHour,* February 7, 2003.
4.   "DEA, USMS Venture Busts Head Shops in Nationwide Sweep," *Marshals Monitor* (U.S. Marshals Service), March 2003.
5.   Ibid.
6.   "Remarks of Attorney General John Ashcroft, 'Operation Pipe Dreams,'" Department of Justice, February 24, 2003
7.   Dean Kuipers, "Tommy Chong's New Joint," *San Diego City Beat,* December 10, 2003.
8.   Editorial, "Reefer Madness; Ridding America of Bongs Shows Wrong Priorities," *Pittsburgh Post-Gazette,* March 5, 2003.
9.   Torsten Ove, "Delay Requested in Chong Term," *Pittsburgh Post-Gazette,* October 16, 2003.
10. "Actor-Comedian Tommy Chong to Stay in Prison While Awaiting Appeal," Associated Press, October 29, 2003.
11. Jacob Sullum, "Tainted by Drugs; The War on Pipes and Dancing," *Reason,* June 2003.
12. Yuval Shavit, "Sales Still High for Ithaca Head Shops," *Cornell Daily Sun,* October 8, 2003.
13. Corey Fram, "DEA Visit to Potsdam Part of Ongoing Probe, 'Fact Finding Mission," *Watertown Daily Times* (New York), October 29, 2003.
14. Ellis Henican, "Limbaugh in the Shadow of His Own Words," *Newsday,* October 3, 2003.
15. Dana Milbank, "Novak Leak Column Has Familiar Sound," *Washington Post,* October 7, 2003.
16. "U.S. Rep. Ron Paul's Comments on the Persecution of Pain Doctors," *DrugSense Weekly,* February 20, 2004.
17. Frank Owen, "The DEA's War on Pain Doctors," *Village Voice,* November 5, 2003.
18. Marc Kaufman, "Worried Pain Doctors Decry Prosecutions," *Washington Post,* December 29, 2003.
19. Owen, "The DEA's War on Pain Doctors."
20. Ronald Fraser, "The DEA's Disastrous War against Pain-Treating Drugs," *Roanoke Times,* November 2, 2003.
21. Kaufman, "Worried Pain Doctors Decry Prosecutions."
22. Cited in Sally Satel, "Limbaugh's Addiction Blurs Benefits of Drug," *York Daily Record* (Penn.), November 16, 2003.
23. Owen, "The DEA's War on Pain Doctors."
24. Jane Spencer, "Crackdown on Drugs Hits Chronic-Pain Patients," *Wall Street Journal,* March 16, 2004.
25. "National D.A.R.E. Day, 2002," *Public Papers of the Presidents,* April 10, 2002.
26. "National D.A.R.E. Day, 2003," *Public Papers of the Presidents,* April 9, 2003.
27. "National D.A.R.E. Day 2004," White House Office of the Press Secretary, April 7, 2004.
28. www.surgeongeneral.gov/library/youthviolence/chapter5/sec4.html.
29. Panel on Juvenile Crime: Prevention, Treatment, and Control, Committee on Law and Justice, and Board on Children, Youth, and Families, National Research Council, and Institute of Medicine, *Juvenile Crime, Juvenile Justice* (Washington: National Academy Press, 2001).

30. Lenny Savino, "D.A.R.E. Program Said Ineffective," *Detroit Free Press,* September 6, 2001.

31. General Accounting Office, "Youth Illicit Drug Use Prevention: DARE Long-Term Evaluations and Federal Efforts to Identify Effective Programs," January 16, 2003.

32. Ibid.

33. "Address before a Joint Session of the Congress on the State of the Union," *Public Papers of the Presidents,* January 20, 2004.

34. Chuck McCutcheon, "At Urging of Drug Czar, Schools Look at Wider Drug Testing—But Cautiously," *Newhouse News Service,* January 14, 2004.

35. Marsha Rosenbaum, "No 'Silver Bullet,'" *AlterNet,* January 28, 2004.

36. "Some Schools Testing Students for Tobacco Use," Join Together Online, October 8, 2002.

37. Dana Milbank and Mike Allen, "Many Gaps in Bush's Guard Records; Released Papers Do Not Document Ala. Service," *Washington Post,* February 14, 2004.

38. Rosenbaum, "No 'Silver Bullet.'"

39. Sylvia A. Smith, "Drug War's Finances Probed," *Journal Gazette* (Fort Wayne, Ind.), February 16, 2003.

40. "U.S. Representative Ernest Istook (R-Okla.) Holds Hearing on Office of National Drug Policy and Youth Anti-Drug Ads," *FDCH Political Transcripts,* June 20, 2002.

41. Damon Chappie, "Move Would Let Drug Czar Campaign," *Roll Call,* May 22, 2003.

42. Ibid.

43. "ONDCP Reauthorization Becomes Lightning Rod for Controversy," *Alcoholism & Drug Abuse Weekly,* June 9, 2003.

44. Peter Wallsten and Phil Long, "Judge: In Rehab, Privacy Laws Apply," *Miami Herald,* October 1, 2002.

45. Doris Bloodsworth and Pedro Ruz Gutierrez, "Judge Shuts Down Investigation of Noelle Bush," *Orlando Sentinel,* October 1, 2002.

46. Wallsten and Long, "Judge: In Rehab, Privacy Laws Apply."

47. Mike Schneider, "Judge: Drug Rehab Center Does Not Have to Cooperate in Case against Jeb Bush's Daughter," Associated Press, October 1, 2002.

48. Wallsten and Long, "Judge: In Rehab, Privacy Laws Apply."

49. Arianna Huffington, "A Crack House Divided," Alternet.Org, September 16, 2002.

50. Michelle Goldberg, "For Noelle Bush, a Different Kind of Justice," *Salon,* September 20, 2002. Goldberg notes that 20,000 people were convicted of drug felonies in Florida in 2000, and a third of them were served time.

51. Mike Schneider, "Noelle Bush to Serve 10 Days in Jail for Drug Program Violations," Associated Press, October 18, 2002.

52. Wallsten and Long, "Judge: In Rehab, Privacy Laws Apply."

53. Stephen Heath, "Unmoved by Tears," *Bradenton Herald* (Florida), May 7, 2002.

54. "Township with Dearth of Jobs, Sewer Lines Eagerly Awaits New Prison," Associated Press, July 3, 2000.

55. The headline was cited in a letter to the editor a few weeks later. See Bill Harper, "Prison Growth Shameful," *Lexington Herald-Leader,* August 11, 2001.

56. Bill Sizemore, "Drugs, Not Violence, Are the Fuel for Prison," *Virginian-Pilot* (Norfolk, Va.), June 6, 2001.

57. Fox Butterfield, "States Easing Stringent Laws on Prison Time," *New York Times,* September 2, 2001.

58. James Bovard, "Pork Barrel Prisons: Who Profits from the War on Drugs?" *Playboy,* February 2002.

59. Nicholas Kulish, "Counted in Census, Convicts Bring Funds to Small Towns," *Wall Street Journal,* August 9, 2001.

60. Frances Robles, "Bolivian Growers Want to Reverse Coca-Eradication," *Miami Herald,* October 29, 2003.
61. Kevin G. Hall, "Bolivian Farmers Use Bombs, Traps to Thwart Anti-Drug Troops," *Sun News* (Myrtle Beach, S.C.), February 9, 2004.
62. Duncan Campbell, "Washington Threatens to Cut Aid If Coca-Growers' Leader Becomes His Country's New President," *Guardian* (U.K.), July 15, 2002.
63. Sebastian Rotella and Natalia Tarnawiecki, "U.S. Role in Peru Plane Downing Adds to Mystery," *Los Angeles Times,* April 22, 2001.
64. James Risen, "Interruption of Effort to Down Drug Planes Is Disclosed," *New York Times,* January 8, 2004.
65. "U.S. Says Mexican Marijuana, Opium Poppy Production Goes Up," Associated Press, April 6, 2004.
66. Christopher Johnson, "Deaths Rise in Thailand's Anti-Drug War," *Japan Today,* March 7, 2003.
67. Alan Sipress, "Thailand's Drug War Leaves Over 1,000 Dead," *Washington Post,* March 9, 2003.
68. Pasuk Phongpaichit and Chris Baker, "Slaughter in the Name of a Drug War," *New York Times,* May 24, 2003.
69. "A U.S. State Dept. Look at the War On Drugs," *The Nation* (Thailand), February 27, 2004.
70. Seth Mydans, "Thais Blame Police for Deadly War on Drugs," *New York Times,* April 8, 2003.
71. Amy Kazmin, "Human Rights Alarm Over Bloody Drugs Crackdown," *Financial Times,* December 27, 2003.
72. Meryam Dabhoiwala, Researcher, Asian Legal Resource Center. Available at www.article2.org/mainfile.php/0203/84/.
73. "Arrest Your Friends, Minister Tells Governors," *Phuket Gazette* (Thailand), March 6, 2003.
74. Ibid.
75. Meryam Dabhoiwala, "A Chronology of Thailand's War on Drugs," Asian Legal Resource Centre.
76. Amy Kazmin and William Barnes, "Thailand Hails Victory in War on Dealers," *Financial Times,* May 1, 2003.
77. Robert Horn and Ban Rai, " The Killing Season," *Time Asia,* March 10, 2003.
78. Meryam Dabhoiwala, ""A Chronology of Thailand's War on Drugs."
79. Vijay Joshi, "Thai Premier Denies Killings in Drug War," Associated Press, May 7, 2003.
80. "Fact Sheet: Major Non-NATO Ally (MNNA) Status for Thailand," U.S. Embassy, Bangkok Thailand, October 2003.
81. "Joint Statement between the United States of America and the Kingdom of Thailand," *Public Papers of the Presidents,* June 11, 2003.
82. Editorial, "PM Thaksin's Politics of Total Supremacy," *The Nation* (Thailand), June 15, 2003.
83. "Thai Government Denies Being Blacklisted by US As Drug State," Xinhau News Agency, September 18, 2003.
84. "Remarks at the Royal Thai Army Headquarters in Bangkok," *Public Papers of the Presidents,* October 27, 2003.
85. Nirmal Ghosh, "Thai Police Launch 'Final' Blitz on Drugs," *Straits Times* (Singapore), November 30, 2003.
86. Nirmal Ghosh, "Thaksin Declares Victory in War on Drug Trade," *Straits Times* (Singapore), December 2, 2003.
87. John Aglionby, "The War on YAA-BAA," *Guardian* (U.K.), December 4, 2003.

88.   "Royal Message: King Wants Drug Toll Explained," *The Nation* (Thailand), December 5, 2003.
89.   "Drug-War Deaths: 'Police Have Dragged Feet,'" *The Nation* (Thailand), December 7, 2003.
90.   Kazmin, "Human Rights Alarm over Bloody Drugs Crackdown."
91.   "Thai Rights Commissioner Concerned over Thousands of Drug-War Arrests," Agence France Presse, December 11, 2003.
92.   Amy Kazmin, "Amnesty Denounces 'Murder Spree' in Thai War on Drugs," *Financial Times,* November 7, 2003.
93.   www.state.gov/g/inl/rls/nrcrpt/2003/vol1/html/29830.htm.
94.   For an analysis of state terrorism, see Bovard, *Terrorism & Tyranny,* pp. 225–240.
95.   "Patterns of Global Terrorism - 2003," State Department Office of the Coordinator for Counterterrorism, April 29, 2004.
96.   Mary Longmore, "Thailand's War on Drugs Pushes Supplies into Cambodia, Laos, India," *The Nation* (Thailand), May 9, 2003.
97.   "Thaksin to Lead New War on Drugs," *Straits Times* (Singapore), February 29, 2004.
98.   "Another Drug War during School Break," *The Nation* (Thailand), February 29, 2004.
99.   "National D.A.R.E. Day 2004," White House Office of the Press Secretary, April 7, 2004.
100. "Press Availability with Asa Hutchinson, Director, Drug Enforcement Agency," Federal News Service, August 20, 2001.

CHAPTER 10. GOVERNMENT BY STEALTH:
THE NEW IRON CURTAIN

1.   "Remarks at Oak Mountain State Park in Birmingham, Alabama," *Public Papers of the Presidents,* June 25, 2001.
2.   Cited in "'Every Thing Secret Degenerates': The FBI's Use of Murderers as Informants," House Government Reform Committee, November 2003.
3.   "Memorandum on the Congressional Subpoena for Executive Branch Documents," *Public Papers of the Presidents,* December 12, 2001 (italics added).
4.   Glen Johnson, "Bush Halts Inquiry of FBI and Stirs Up a Firestorm," *Boston Globe,* December 14, 2001.
5.   Robert Novak, "The Arrogance of Power," *Washington Post,* January 21, 2002.
6.   "Opening Statement of Chairman Dan Burton - Committee on Government Reform" - "The History of Congressional Access to Deliberative Justice Department Documents," Federal News Service, February 6, 2002.
7.   "'Every Thing Secret Degenerates': The FBI's Use of Murderers as Informants," House Government Reform Committee, November 2003.
8.   Fox Butterfield, "Used Killers as Informants, Report Says," *New York Times,* November 21, 2003.
9.   Alexander Bolton, "House GOP Challenges Bush on Records' Gag," *The Hill,* April 24, 2002.
10.   "Remarks of Attorney General John Ashcroft," Justice Department Office of Public Affairs, May 30, 2002.
11.   Editorial, "The Ethics of Deceit," *Las Vegas Review Journal,* December 24, 1997.
12.   Phyllis Schlafly, "Secrecy is a Losing Ploy," Copley News Service, March 13, 2002.
13.   Timothy W. Maier, "Bush Team Thumbs Its Nose at FOIA," *Insight on the News,* April 29, 2002.
14.   Neely Tucker, "Suit Versus Cheney Is Dismissed," *Washington Post,* December 10, 2002.

15. John Heilprin, "Judge Says Bush Administration's View of Executive Privilege is Too Expansive," Associated Press, July 12, 2002.

16. "Cheney's Energy Task Force Is Told to Turn Over Papers," Associated Press, October 17, 2002.

17. Neely Tucker, "Judge Orders White House Papers' Release," *Washington Post*, October 18, 2002.

18. Ibid.

19. "Judges Question Bush Administration's Attempt to Block Lawsuit against Cheney," *San Jose Mercury News*, April 17, 2003.

20. "Supreme Court to Hear Bush Appeal on Energy Secrets," Sierra Club, December 15, 2003.

21. "Statement of Mark Corallo, Director of Public Affairs, Regarding the Supreme Court's Grant of Certiorari in the National Energy Policy Development Group Case," Justice Department Office of Public Affairs, December 15, 2003.

22. Linda Greenhouse, "Administration Says a 'Zone of Autonomy' Justifies Its Secrecy on Energy Task Force," *New York Times*, April 25, 2004.

23. Ibid.

24. Ibid.

25. "Oral Arguments in the Case of Vice President Richard Cheney versus U.S. District Court for the District of Colombia, Re: Vice President Cheney's Energy Task Force Proceedings," Federal News Service, April 27, 2004.

26. David G. Savage, "Justices Appear to Support Cheney Task Force Secrecy," *Los Angeles Times*, April 28, 2004.

27. "Late Night Political Humor," *The Frontrunner*, April 29, 2004.

28. "Prepared Remarks of Attorney General John Ashcroft World Economic Forum at Davos, Switzerland," Justice Department Office of Public Affairs, January 22, 2004.

29. Shelly Strom, "Freedom of Info Attack Directed from the Top," *Business Journal of Portland*, May 10, 2002.

30. http://www.fas.org/sgp/clinton/reno.html

31. http://www.usdoj.gov/oip/annual_report/2001/01foiapg7.htm

32. Attorney General John Ashcroft, "Memorandum on the Freedom of Information Act," Justice Department Office of Public Affairs, October 12, 2001.

33. Christopher Lee, "Agencies Fall Behind on Information Requests," *Washington Post*, September 28, 2002.

34. Ibid.

35. Linda Gasparello, "Survey Finds Mixed Agency Response to Ashcroft and Card Memos," *White House Weekly*, April 15, 2003.

36. "Freedom of Information Act: Agency Views on Changes Resulting from New Administration Policy," General Accounting Office, September 3, 2003.

37. *Detroit Free Press, et al., v. John Ashcroft*, No. 02–1437, 2002 FED App. 0291P, August 26, 2002.

38. Josh Meyer, "U.S. Ordered to Disclose Names of Detainees in Sept. 11 Inquiry," *Los Angeles Times*, August 3, 2002.

39. Charles Lane, "Secrecy Allowed On 9/11 Detention," *Washington Post*, January 13, 2004.

40. Ibid.

41. Ibid.

42. "Summary of Annual FOIA Reports for Fiscal Year 2002," U.S. Department of Justice, September 3, 2003.

43. Chuck McCutcheon, "What's the Problem? Sorry, That's Classified," Newhouse News Service, May 26, 2003.

44. Carl M. Cannon, "For the Record," *National Journal*, January 12, 2002.

45. Jonathan Turley, "An Odious Roadblock to History," *Los Angeles Times*, May 5, 2002.

46. Adam Clymer, "Government Openness at Issue as Bush Holds onto Records," *New York Times,* January 3, 2003.
47. "Press Availability with President Bush," White House Office of the Press Secretary, November 2, 2001.
48. "Press Briefing by Ari Fleischer," White House Office of the Press Secretary, November 1, 2001.
49. Linda Gasparello, "House Moves to Rescind Bush Order on Papers," *White House Weekly,* April 30, 2002.
50. Jonathan Turley, "An Odious Roadblock to History."
51. Cannon, "For the Record."
52. Ibid.
53. Ibid.
54. Charles Lewis, "Freedom of Information Under Attack," Center for Public Integrity, 2002.
55. Adam Clymer, "House Panel Seeks Release of Presidential Papers," *New York Times,* October 10, 2002.
56. "Clinton to Release Papers Years Ahead of Schedule," *American Libraries,* March 1, 2003.
57. Dana Milbank and Mike Allen, "Release of Documents Is Delayed," *Washington Post,* March 26, 2003.
58. Bruce Craig, "NCH Washington Update," National Coalition for History, April 16, 2004.
59. Sheryl Gay Stolberg and Felicia Lee, "Bush Nominee for Archivist Is Criticized for His Secrecy," *New York Times,* April 20, 2004.
60. George Lardner, "Bush Picks Weinstein as Archivist," *Washington Post,* April 20, 2004.
61. http://www.constitution.org/cons/virg1798.htm.
62. "Attorney General Ashcroft Transcript News Conference with FBI Director Mueller Regarding Terrorist Tapes," Justice Department Office of Public Affairs, January 17, 2002.
63. "Remarks to Employees at The Timken Company in Canton, Ohio," *Public Papers of the Presidents,* April 24, 2004.
64. "Text of Bush's Press Conference," Washingtonpost.com, April 13, 2004.
65. Jim Hoagland, "The Limits of Lying," *Washington Post,* March 21, 2002.
66. David Sarasohn, "It's None of Your Business, America," Newhouse News Service, March 11, 2002.

CHAPTER 11. AIRPORT ANTICS: THE TSA ATTITUDE POLICE

1. "TSA Displays Many Deadly Weapons Confiscated At Airports," *Bulletin's Frontrunner,* August 29, 2003. For an extensive discussion of TSA, see James Bovard, *Terrorism and Tyranny* (New York: Palgrave, 2003), 169–206.
2. "Box Cutters Still Bypass Airport Security," ABCNews.com, September 13, 2003.
3. Ibid.
4. "Efforts to Measure Effectiveness and Address Challenges: Statement of Cathleen A. Berrick, Director Homeland Security and Justice Issues," General Accounting Office, November 5, 2003.
5. Chris Strohm, "TSA Falls Short in Evaluating Aviation Security Programs," *Government Executive Magazine,* November 5, 2003.
6. "Uncle Sam Wants You," CBS News, March 4, 2002.
7. "Transportation Security Administration's Checked Baggage Screener Training and Certification: A Letter Report," Department of Homeland Security Office of Inspector General, August 29, 2003.
8. Ibid.

9. Audrey Hudson, "Airport Screeners' Tests Assailed," *Washington Times,* October 10, 2003.

10. "TSA Intelligence Lapses Exposed by 'Box Cutter Kid,'" *Airport Security Report,* November 5, 2003.

11. Sara Kehaulani Goo and David Snyder, "Student Charged in Airport Scheme," *Washington Post,* October 21, 2003.

12. "TSA Intelligence Lapses Exposed by 'Box Cutter Kid.'"

13. Ibid.

14. Ibid.

15. Kehaulani Goo and Snyder, "Student Charged in Airport Scheme."

16. "Mark Hatfield, Transportation Security Administration, Discusses Nathaniel Heatwole's Breaches and Changes Being Made," *Today Show,* NBC News Transcripts, October 21, 2003.

17. "TSA Intelligence Lapses Exposed by 'Box Cutter Kid.'"

18. Julie Hirschfeld Davis, "Box-Cutter 'Sting' Has Admirers on Capitol Hill," *Baltimore Sun,* October 22, 2003.

19. Sara Kehaulani Goo, "TSA to Check Plane Inspections," *Washington Post,* October 22, 2003.

20. Brian Witte, "Charge Reduced for Student Who Hid Box Cutters on Planes," Associated Press, April 13, 2004.

21. "Woman Eludes Security at Midway Airport," Associated Press, August 3, 2003.

22. "Breach Report," *Airport Security Report,* August 12, 2003.

23. "Breach Report," *Airport Security Report,* December 3, 2003.

24. "Breach Report," *Airport Security Report,* January 14, 2004.

25. Ibid.

26. Ibid.

27. "Breach Report," *Airport Security Report,* January 28, 2004.

28. Stacey Stowe, "Knife in Trash Can Leads to Connecticut Airport Evacuation," *New York Times,* January 21, 2004.

29. "Hartford Airport Briefly Evacuated after Discovery of 'Cutting Instrument,'" Associated Press, January 20, 2004.

30. "Suspect X-ray Delays Flights at T.F. Green," *Providence Journal,* January 28, 2004.

31. "Security Breach Spurs Airport Near Capital to Evacuate 200," *Orlando Sentinel,* February 11, 2004.

32. Mitchel Maddux, "False Alarm Clears Terminal at Newark Airport," *The Record* (Bergen County, N.J.), February 20, 2004.

33. "Security Breach Delays Flights," *Orange County Register* (Calif.), March 27, 2004.

34. "Airport Evacuated In Security Breach," *Albuquerque Journal* (New Mex.), April 2, 2004.

35. Jeff Ristine and Joe Hughes, "Rescreenings Hold up Lindbergh Departures," *San Diego Union-Tribune,* April 3, 2004.

36. Stephen Kiehl, "Security Breach at BWI is Probed," *Baltimore Sun,* April 6, 2004.

37. Denver Airport Concourse Sealed Off When FBI Agent Misplaces Gun," TBO.com, October 4, 2003.

38. "Prohibited Weapons Dominate Threats at Airports Worldwide," *Airport Security Report,* January 14, 2004.

39. See, for instance, "Airport Security Screener Charged with Stealing Cash from Bag," Associated Press, July 10, 2003.

40. Roddy Stinson, "Big Wad of Cash Could Trigger 'Seizures' at Airport," *San Antonio Express-News* (Tex.), December 2, 2003.

41. "Prepared Remarks of Attorney General John Ashcroft—Press Briefing with FBI Director Mueller, FBI Headquarters," U.S. Department of Justice, September 27, 2001.

42. James Bovard, *Lost Rights: The Destruction of American Liberty* (New York: St. Martin's, 1994), 10–17.
43. "TSA Takes Heat for Background Check Miscues," *Access Control & Security Systems*, February 11, 2004.
44. Philip Shenon, "Report Faults Lax Controls on Screeners At Airports," *New York Times*, February 6, 2004.
45. "Airport Screener Sentenced for Stealing Jewelry from Baggage," Associated Press, April 13, 2004.
46. "Breach Report," *Airport Security Report*, December 17, 2003.
47. "Security Scare: LAX Terminal Evacuated," CNN.com, April 17, 2004.
48. Dylan Rivera, "Package Concerns Close Airport Checkpoint," *Portland Oregonian*, January 6, 2004.
49. Helen Kennedy, "Airport Security Rubs It In," *Daily News*, January 13, 2004.
50. "Breach Report," *Airport Security Report*, December 3, 2003.
51. "TSA Intelligence Lapses Exposed by 'Box Cutter Kid.'"
52. "Box Cutters Still Bypass Airport Security," ABCNEWS.com, September 13, 2003.
53. Sara Kehaulani Goo, "U.S. Is Slow to Upgrade Airport Security Systems," *Washington Post*, December 8, 2003.
54. Laura Parker, "Weapons in Luggage Will Now Bring Hefty Fines," *USA Today*, February 19, 2004.
55. Mary Lou Pickel, "Silverware Rules Relaxed for Airlines," Cox News Service, September 19, 2003.
56. Federal Register, February 25, 2002, p. 8344. (The regulation was promulgated on February 17, 2002.)
57. "Prohibited Weapons Dominate Threats At Airports Worldwide," *Airport Security Report*, January 14, 2004.
58. Laura Parker, "Weapons in Luggage Will Now Bring Hefty Fines."
59. Joe Sharkey, "Airport Hurdles and the Nonflying Nuns," *New York Times*, March 2, 2004.
60. Keith Alexander, "Expect Airport Security Delays This Summer," *Washington Post*, May 18, 2004.
61. Alan Levin, "Lawmakers Add Pressure to Let Pilots Have Guns," *USA Today*, May 3, 2002.
62. Jonathan D. Salant, "Emergency Number for Air Passengers Considered," *Memphis Commercial Appeal*, May 20, 2002.
63. Mark Murray, "Air Marshals Train to Tackle Terrorism," *National Journal*, June 4, 2002.
64. See Bovard, *Terrorism and Tyranny*, pp. 190–194.
65. Blake Morrison, "Air Marshals' Skills Doubted," *USA Today*, May 24, 2002.
66. See, for instance, Jennifer Ginsberg, "Yeager Screeners Miss Gun; Hand Search Failed to Detect Forgotten Firearm in Carry-on," *Charleston Gazette* (W. Va.), April 14, 2004.
67. Richard Simon and Ricardo Alonso-Zaldivar, "Senate Approves Arming Pilots," *Los Angeles Times*, September 6, 2002.
68. Tracy Price, "Where Are the Armed Pilots?" *Washington Times*, December 12, 2003.
69. Sara Kehaulani Goo, "TSA Faulted for Restricting Information," *Washington Post*, October 10, 2003.
70. Ibid.
71. Jeff Johnson, "TSA's Email Threat 'Last Straw' for Congressman," CNSNews.com, January 26, 2004.
72. Denise Marois, "TSA E-Mail Prompts Ire on Hill Over FFDO Program," *Aviation Daily*, January 29, 2004.
73. Author interview with pilot who wished to remain anonymous, February 4, 2004.
74. Audrey Hudson, "Few Commercial Pilots Apply for Firearm Training," *Washington Times*, February 4, 2004.

75.   Ibid.

76.   Johnson, "TSA's Email Threat 'Last Straw' for Congressman."

77.   Leslie Miller, "Pilots Say Government Regulations Discouraging Them from Carrying Guns in Cockpit," Associated Press, March 12, 2004.

78.   Chris Woodyard and Marilyn Adams," Hot Time for Flying Leads to Security Delays," *USA Today,* June 30, 2003.

79.   "Overtaxed Checkpoints Cause Problems at Major Airports," *The Bulletin's Frontrunner,* June 30, 2003.

80.   "TSA's Performance Fuels Critics of Its Security Role," *Airport Security Report,* July 16, 2003.

81.   Sara Kehaulani Goo, "Air Travelers Should Plan for Long Holiday Lines, TSA Says," *Washington Post,* November 6, 2003.

82.   Eric Gillin, "For Air Travelers, a Happy Thanksgiving," TheStreet.com, December 5, 2003.

83.   Steve Tetreault, "Action on Airport Lines Promised," *Las Vegas Review-Journal,* February 19, 2004.

84.   Chris Jones, "Mess at McCarran: Airport Cures also Have to Wait," *Las Vegas Review-Journal,* February 18, 2004.

85.   Gregory Richards, "Clark Says Comments about TSA Taken the Wrong Way," *Florida Times-Union* (Jacksonville), April 8, 2004.

86.   Todd J. Gillman, "Airports Weigh Private Security; Long Lines Prompt Unhappiness with Government Screening," *Dallas Morning News,* March 26, 2004.

87.   Sara Kehaulani Goo, "Screening Easier for Air Travelers," *Washington Post,* January 15, 2004.

88.   "Aviation Security: Passenger and Baggage Screening; Testimony by: Ms. Cathleen Berrick, Director, Homeland Security and Justice Division, U.S. General Accounting Office," Federal Document Clearing House Congressional Testimony, February 12, 2004.

89.   Ibid.

90.   Sara Kehaulani Goo, "Contractors Complain of TSA Limits," *Washington Post,* November 21, 2003.

91.   Ibid.

92.   "Private Screening Projects Lack Flexibility, Executives Say," *Airport Security Report,* December 3, 2003.

93.   "Efforts to Measure Effectiveness and Address Challenges: Statement of Cathleen A. Berrick, Director Homeland Security and Justice Issues," General Accounting Office, November 5, 2003.

94.   Ken Kaye, "Airports Consider Going Back to Private Screeners," *Sun-Sentinel* (Fort Lauderdale, Fla.), February 15, 2004.

95.   Tom Ramstack, "Federal Screeners May Get the Gate," *Washington Times,* March 25, 2004.

96.   "Airports to Receive Provisions for Private Screening Firms," *Airport Security Report,* May 5, 2004.

97.   "Panel I of a Hearing of the Subcommittee on Aviation of the House Committee on Transportation and Infrastructure; Subject: Airport Screener Privatization Program," Federal News Service, April 22, 2004.

98.   Editorial, "Money Well Spent?" *Washington Post,* May 2, 2004.

99.   "Panel I of a Hearing of the Subcommittee on Aviation."

100. Ibid.

101. "Mark Hatfield Jr. of the Transportation Security Administration Discusses Airport Security," NBC News Transcripts *(Today Show),* April 23, 2004.

102. "Proclamation 7559—National Defense Transportation Day and National Transportation Week, 2002," *Public Papers of the Presidents,* May 10, 2002.

103.   Leslie Miller, "Screener Shortages Troubling Airports," Associated Press, February 12, 2004.

104.   Quoted at his website, http://www.aviationplanning.com/.

CHAPTER 12. JOHN ASHCROFT, KING OF "ORDERED LIBERTY"

1.   "Prepared Remarks of Attorney General Ashcroft at the Federalist Society National Convention," Justice Department Office of Public Affairs, November 15, 2003.

2.   "Justice: From the Ashes of 9/11: Big Bad John," *National Journal,* January 25, 2003.

3.   John Ashcroft, "Welcoming Big Brother," *Washington Times,* August 12, 1997.

4.   "Committee: Senate Judiciary; Headline: War Against Terrorism; Testimony by: John Ashcroft, Attorney General," Federal Document Clearing House Congressional Testimony, March 4, 2003.

5.   Siobhan Gorman, "The Ashcroft Doctrine," *National Journal,* December 21, 2002.

6.   "John Ashcroft; the US Attorney General Talks About His Job and Himself," CBS News Transcripts, June 29, 2003.

7.   "Remarks of Attorney General John Ashcroft on Protecting Life and Liberty—Memphis, Tennessee," Justice Department Office of Public Affairs, September 18, 2003.

8.   Quoted in Federalist Paper #84. See Alexander Hamilton, James Madison, John Jay, *The Federalist Papers* (New York: New American Library, 1961 [originally published in 1787]), p. 512.

9.   Federal News Service, "Senate Judiciary Committee Hearing on War on Terrorism," December 6, 2001 (italics added).

10.   "The September 11 Detainees: A Review of the Treatment of Aliens Held on Immigration Charges in Connection with the Investigation of the September 11 Attacks," Justice Department Office of Inspector General, June 2003.

11.   Richard A. Serrano, "Ashcroft Denies Wide Detainee Abuse," *Los Angeles Times,* October 17, 2001.

12.   Neil A. Lewis, "Detentions After Attacks Pass 1,000, U.S. Says," *New York Times,* October 30, 2001.

13.   "News Conference with Attorney General Ashcroft," Justice Department Office of Public Affairs, November 27, 2001.

14.   Federal News Service, "Senate Judiciary Committee Hearing on War on Terrorism."

15.   *County of Riverside v. McLaughlin,* 500 U.S. 44 (1991).

16.   "The September 11 Detainees: A Review of the Treatment of Aliens Held."

17.   Jess Bravin and Gary Fields, "Report Criticizes U.S. Detentions of Illegal Aliens after Sept. 11," *Wall Street Journal,* June 3, 2003.

18.   Ibid.

19.   "Ashcroft: Detentions Broke No Laws," United Press International, June 5, 2003.

20.   David Sarasohn, "Patriot Act Powers Send Up a Red Flag," *Sunday Oregonian,* July 20, 2003.

21.   "Prepared Remarks of Attorney General Ashcroft—'The Proven Tactics in the Fight against Crime,'" Justice Department Office of Public Affairs, September 15, 2003.

22.   "Supplemental Report on September 11 Detainees' Allegations of Abuse at the Metropolitan Detention Center in Brooklyn, New York," Justice Department Office of Inspector General, December 2003.

23.   Ibid.

24.   Dan Eggen, "Tapes Show Abuse of 9/11 Detainees," *Washington Post,* December 19, 2003.

25. "Statement of Mark Corallo, Director of Public Affairs on the Inspector General's Report," Justice Department Office of Public Affairs, December 18, 2003.

26. Attorney General Ashcroft Speaks about the Patriot Act—Prepared remarks to the American Enterprise Institute," Justice Department Office of Public Affairs, August 19, 2003

27. For a detailed explanation of Carnivore, see James Bovard, *Terrorism & Tyranny,* pp. 133–37.

28. Dan Eggen and Susan Schmidt, "Data Show Different Spy Game Since 9/11," *Washington Post,* May 1, 2004.

29. Ibid.

30. Russell Feingold, "Real Perils in Business Record Subpoenas," *Washington Post,* January 15, 2004.

31. Uniting and Strengthening America by Providing Appropriate Tools Required to Intercept and Obstruct Terrorism (USA Patriot Act) Act of 2001, October 26, 2001, Sec. 213.

32. Walter Shapiro, "Patriot Act Perhaps Not as Popular as Poll Implies," *USA Today,* August 20, 2003.

33. Sullivan, "Amid Criticism."

34. Ibid.

35. Thomas Ginsberg, "Ashcroft: Patriot Act Is Effective," *Philadelphia Inquirer,* August 21, 2003.

36. Jim Ragsdale, "Ashcroft brings Patriot Act defense to Twin Cities," *Saint Paul Pioneer Press,* September 20, 2003.

37. Jon Ward, "Ashcroft Defends Patriot Act in Visit," *Washington Times,* June 18, 2003.

38. Eric Lichtblau, "Ashcroft Criticized for Talks on Terror," *New York Times,* August 22, 2003.

39. Howard Kurtz, "The Scribes of Buzz: They're All Antennae," *Washington Post,* September 15, 2003.

40. Ibid.

41. Darin Oswald, "Ashcroft Defends Patriot Act in Boise," *Idaho Statesman,* August 26, 2003.

42. Howard Altman, "Pretzel Logic," *Philadelphia City Paper,* August 28, 2003.

43. Press Release, "Ashcroft Speeches Should Be More Accessible to the Public and Media," Society of Professional Journalists, September 18, 2003.

44. Carolina Bolado, "FBI Probes Library Goers' Records," *The State* (Columbia, SC), June 29, 2002.

45. "Patriot FOIA: The Government's Response," American Civil Liberties Union, April 2003. At http://www.aclu.org/patriot_foia/foia3.html

46. Carla Hayden, "Ashcroft's Secret Searches Worry Librarians," *Newsday,* September 18, 2003.

47. "Prepared Remarks of Attorney General John Ashcroft," World Economic Forum—Davos, Switzerland," Justice Department Office of Public Affairs, January 22, 2004.

48. Ibid.

49. Press Release, "Three Former Federal Bureau of Prison Guards Sentenced for Violating Inmates' Civil Rights," U.S. Department of Justice, November 21, 2003. (This case involved abuses unrelated to terrorism.)

50. Thomas B. Edsall and Walter Pincus, "FEC Fines Ashcroft's Senate Bid For Breach," *Washington Post,* December 17, 2003.

51. David Goldstein, "Ashcroft Investigated over Violation Allegations," *Kansas City Star,* May 1, 2004.

52. David Shepardson, "Ashcroft Praises Aid from Hmimssa," *Detroit News,* April 18, 2003.

53. David Shepardson, "Ashcroft Sanctioned for Violating Gag Order in Detroit Terror Trial," *Detroit News,* December 16, 2003.

54. David Shepardson, "Ashcroft Got Gag Warning," *Detroit News,* September 19, 2003.
55. David Ashenfelter, "Terror Case Prosecutor Is Probed on Conduct," *Detroit Free Press,* January 17, 2004.
56. Shannon McCaffrey, "Suit Against Ashcroft Claims Department has Bungled War on Terror," Knight Ridder News Service, February 18, 2004.
57. David Ashenfelter, "Cracks Develop in Detroit Terror Case," *Philadelphia Inquirer,* February 1, 2004.
58. Federal News Service, "Senate Judiciary Committee Hearing on War on Terrorism," December 6, 2001.

CHAPTER 13. ANTITERRORISM ABUSES AND FRAUDS

1. Robert Block, Gary Fields, and Jo Wrighton, "U.S. 'Terror' List Still Lacking," *Wall Street Journal,* January 2, 2004.
2. Greta Wodele, "Incomplete Databases Contributed to Terrorism, Panel Says," *National Journal's Technology Daily,* January 26, 2004.
3. "Address Before a Joint Session of the Congress on the State of the Union," *Public Papers of the Presidents,* January 28, 2003.
4. "Letter to Congressional Leaders Transmitting a Report Required by the Enhanced Border Security and Visa Entry Reform Act of 2002," *Public Papers of the Presidents,* March 25, 2003.
5. Dan Eggen, "GAO Criticizes System for Tracking Terrorists," *Washington Post,* April 30, 2003.
6. Mimi Hall, "Terrorist Risk Lists Leave Gap, Even Now," *USA Today,* August 11, 2003.
7. Ibid.
8. "New Terrorist Screening Center Established," Justice Department Office of Public Affairs, September 16, 2003.
9. Ibid.
10. Ibid.
11. Ibid.
12. Block, Fields, and Wrighton, "U.S. 'Terror' List Still Lacking."
13. Ibid.
14. Ibid.
15. Ibid.
16. Shaun Waterman, "U.S. Gets One Terror List at Last," United Press International, March 26, 2004.
17. Michael Isikoff, "Show Me the Money," *Newsweek,* December 1, 2003.
18. Sam Stanton and Emily Bazar, "Patriot Act's Broad Brush," *Sacramento Bee,* December 21, 2003.
19. Ibid.
20. John Solomon, "More Agents Track Castro than Bin Laden," Associated Press, April 29, 2004.
21. Nancy San Martin, "More Focus on Cuba Embargo than Terror Trail Is Questioned," *Miami Herald,* April 30, 2004.
22. Ibid.
23. "Transcript of Pentagon Briefing on Poindexter's 'TIA' Program," Declan McCullagh's Politech, November 24, 2002.
24. Michael Sniffen, "Controversial Terror Research Lives On," Associated Press, February 23, 2004.
25. Michael J. Sniffen, "Privacy Protecting Programs Killed," Associated Press, March 15, 2004.

26.　Eric Wieffering, "New Federal Air Passenger Screening Program Set to Start This Summer," *Minneapolis Star Tribune,* January 25, 2004.

27.　Sara Kehaulani Goo, "Fliers to Be Rated for Risk Level," *Washington Post,* September 9, 2003.

28.　Editorial, "Betraying One's Passengers," *New York Times,* September 23, 2003.

29.　Goo, "Fliers to Be Rated for Risk Level."

30.　Paul Marks, "Screening System Stirs Concerns of Misuse," *Hartford Courant,* January 17, 2004.

31.　Ryan Singel, "JetBlue Data to Fuel CAPPS Test," Wired.com, September 16, 2004.

32.　Anita Ramasastry, "Government Reports Highlight Problems in Airline Safety," CNN.com, March 19, 2004.

33.　"TSA Kicks Off Privacy Education Program," U.S. Newswire, March 8, 2004.

34.　Matthew L. Wald, "Airline Gave Government Information on Passengers," *New York Times,* January 18, 2004.

35.　Harvey Simon, "Deadline Nears for GAO Report on Effectiveness of CAPPS II," *Aviation Week's Homeland Security & Defense,* January 22, 2004.

36.　"Aviation Security: Computer-Assisted Passenger Prescreening System Faces Significant Implementation Challenges," General Accounting Office, February 13, 2004.

37.　Wieffering, "New Federal Air Passenger Screening Program Set to Start."

38.　Jon Hilkevitch, "Travelers Face Extra Scrutiny at Airports," *Chicago Tribune,* January 13, 2004.

39.　"Military Order—Detention, Treatment, and Trial of Certain Non-Citizens in the War Against Terrorism," White House Office of the Press Secretary, November 13, 2001.

40.　Ibid.

41.　Karen Branch-Brioso, "Bush Plan Draws Criticism from Civil Libertarians," *St. Louis Post-Dispatch,* November 18, 2001.

42.　Michael Ratner, "Moving Toward a Police State or Have We Arrived?," HumanRightsNow.org, November 20, 2001.

43.　Jamie Dettmer, "Media MIA in Fight for Civil Liberties," *Insight on the News,* November 23, 2001.

44.　Ibid.

45.　*Ex Parte Milligan,* 71 U.S. (4 Wall.) 2 (1866).

46.　Dan Eggen, "Ashcroft's High Profile, Motives Raise White House Concerns," *Washington Post,* June 17, 2002.

47.　Dan Mihalopoulos, "U.S. Rebuked Over Padilla," *Chicago Tribune,* March 12, 2003.

48.　Neil A. Lewis, "Rules for Terror Tribunals May Deter Some Defense Lawyers," *New York Times,* July 13, 2003.

49.　Ibid.

50.　Neil A. Lewis, "Bush's Power to Plan Trial of Detainees Is Challenged," *New York Times,* January 16, 2004.

51.　Ibid.

52.　"The President's News Conference with Prime Minister Tony Blair of the United Kingdom," *Public Papers of the Presidents,* July 17, 2003.

53.　"Interview with Sir David Frost of BBC Television," *Public Papers of the Presidents,* November 12, 2003. Emphasis added.

54.　"The President's News Conference with Prime Minister Tony Blair."

55.　"Bush Meets Karzai on U.S. Soil," Australian Broadcasting Corporation, January 29, 2002.

56.　Eric Lichtblau, "U.S. Reasserts Right to Declare Citizens to Be Enemy Combatants," *New York Times,* January 8, 2004.

57.　Quoted in Brief of the Cato Institute as Amicus Curiae in support of Petitioners, Yaser Esam Hamdi and Esam Fouad Hamdi v. Donald Rumsfeld, et al., Supreme Court of the United States, February 2004. The brief was written by Timothy Lynch.

58. Ibid.
59. "Oral Arguments in the Case of Yaser Esam Hamdi and Esam Fouad Hamdi versus Donald H. Rumsfeld, Et al.—Re: Detention of American Citizens as 'Enemy Combatants,'" *Federal News Service*, April 28, 2004. Quotes from the Supreme Court case in the following paragraphs are also from this source.
60. Dana Priest and Barton Gellman, "U.S. Decries Abuse but Defends Interrogations," *Washington Post*, December 26, 2002.
61. Ibid.
62. "Oral Arguments in the Case of Donald H. Rumsfeld versus Jose Padilla and Donna R. Newman—Detention of American Citizens as 'Enemy Combatants,'" *Federal News Service*, April 28, 2004. Quotes from the Padilla case in the following paragraphs are from this source.
63. Ibid.
64. Stuart Taylor, "Lawless in the Dungeon," *National Journal*, January 12, 2004.
65. "Remarks on Efforts To Globally Promote Women's Human Rights," *Public Papers of the Presidents*, March 12, 2004.

CHAPTER 14. PROTECTING DEMOCRACY FROM FREEDOM

1. From the oral arguments before the Supreme Court on September 8, 2003: http://www.supremecourtus.gov/oral_arguments/argument_transcripts/02–1674.pdf.
2. Paul Jacob, "The Right to Shut Up and Pay Your Taxes," TownHall.com, December 14, 2003.
3. John Harwood, "In Midterm Election, Money Is Raining on Strange Places," *Wall Street Journal*, November 1, 2002.
4. Fred Hiatt, "Time to Draw the Line," *Washington Post*, May 3, 2004.
5. Congressional Record, February 13, 2002, p. H 351.
6. Ibid., p. H 343.
7. Ibid., p. H 345.
8. Ibid., p. H 347.
9. Ibid., p. H 342.
10. http://www.supremecourtus.gov/opinions/03pdf/02–1674.pdf.
11. "McCain Vows to Keep Campaign Clean," Associated Press, December 22, 1999.
12. Congressional Record, March 23, 2001, p. S 2813.
13. Congressional Record, March 29, 2001, p. S 3113.
14. http://www.supremecourtus.gov/opinions/03pdf/02–1674.pdf.
15. Ibid.
16. Mike Allen and Dana Milbank, "President's Politics of Pragmatism Helped Undermine GOP Opposition," *Washington Post*, February 15, 2002.
17. Ibid.
18. "President Signs Campaign Finance Reform Act—Statement by the President," White House Office of the Press Secretary, March 27, 2002.
19. http://www.supremecourtus.gov/oral_arguments/argument_transcripts/02–1674.pdf
20. http://www.supremecourtus.gov/opinions/03pdf/02–1674.pdf.
21. Jacob, "The Right to Shut Up and Pay Your Taxes."
22. http://www.supremecourtus.gov/opinions/03pdf/02–1674.pdf.
23. http://www.supremecourtus.gov/opinions/03pdf/02–1674.pdf.
24. http://www.supremecourtus.gov/oral_arguments/argument_transcripts/02–1674.pdf.
25. Ibid.
26. Steve Chapman, "Outlawing Political Speech," *Baltimore Sun*, December 16, 2003. (First printed in the *Chicago Tribune*).

27. Nat Hentoff, "Supreme Court's Gag Rule on Us," *Village Voice,* February 3, 2004.
28. Ibid.
29. Luiza Ch. Savage, "Nonprofits Opposing Campaign Law," *New York Sun,* April 14, 2004.
30. Press Release, "Federal Election Commission Action Would Severely Restrict Nonprofit Advocacy, Says National Committee for Responsive Philanthropy," U.S. Newswire, April 14, 2004.
31. Gregory L. Giroux, "Proposed FEC Redefinition of 'Political Committee' Draws Broad Opposition," *Congressional Quarterly Today,* April 9, 2004.
32. Comments of the Drug Policy Alliance, Submitted to the Federal Election Commission, April 5, 2004.
33. "Republican National Committee Letter Requesting that Television Stations Pull Illegal MoveOn.org Ads," U.S. Newswire, March 5, 2004.
34. Liz Sidoti and Sharon Theimer, "Bush Campaign Seeks Probe of Election Ads," Associated Press, March 9, 2004.
35. Ibid.
36. Sharon Theimer, "Bush Campaign Targets Kerry's Soft Money," April 5, 2004.
37. Editorial, "Craven Referee," *New York Times,* May 14, 2004.
38. Sam Dealey, "GOP Mulls Criminal Referrals," *The Hill,* March 25, 2004.
39. Jacob, "The Right to Shut Up and Pay Your Taxes,"
40. "News Alert: Campaign Finance and Lobbying," The Center for Responsive Politics, March 12, 2001.
41. Charles Babington and Dan Morgan, "A Fraying Truce on Ethics Charges," *Washington Post,* March 17, 2004.
42. Ibid.
43. Ibid.
44. http://www.supremecourtus.gov/opinions/03pdf/02–1674.pdf.
45. U.S. Congress, Senate Judiciary Committee, *Reorganization of the Federal Judiciary: Adverse Report from the Senate Committee on the Judiciary Submitted to Accompany S. 1392,* June 7, 1937 (Washington: Government Printing Office, 1937), 8.
46. Quoted in Paul Jacob, "Coburn Shoots Straight," Townhall.com, November 16, 2003. The title of Coburn's memoir, co-authored with John Hart, is *Breach of Trust: How Washington Turns Outsiders into Insiders* (Nashville: Thomas Nelson Books, 2003).
47. Jim Rutenberg, "Campaign Ads Are Under Fire for Inaccuracy," *New York Times,* May 25, 2004.

CHAPTER 15. AFGHAN ABSURDITIES

1. "Address before a Joint Session of the Congress on the State of the Union," *Public Papers of the Presidents,* January 29, 2002.
2. H. Josef Hebert, "Bush Officials Say High Alert May Be Needed for Years with Terrorists Possibly Lurking in U.S.," Associated Press, February 1, 2002.
3. Robert Block and Greg Hitt, "White House Backs Away From Bush '02 Nuclear-Terror Warning," *Wall Street Journal,* February 10, 2004.
4. Matthew Wald, "Nuclear Official Says Bush Erred on Details of Threat to Reactors," *New York Times,* February 10, 2004.
5. Tom Harrison, "Questions Surface over White House Claim in 2002," *Nucleonics Week,* February 12, 2004.
6. "Remarks at a Fundraiser for Gubernatorial Candidate Mike Fisher in Philadelphia, Pennsylvania," *Public Papers of the Presidents,* April 2, 2002.
7. "Remarks at Madison Central High School in Madison, Mississippi," *Public Papers of the Presidents,* August 7, 2002.

8.   "Address to the Nation on Iraq From the U.S.S. Abraham Lincoln," *Public Papers of the Presidents,* May 1, 2003. (Italics added)

9.   Kimberly Sevcik, "What Liberation?" *Mother Jones,* July 2003.

10.   "'Killing You Is a Very Easy Thing for Us': Human Rights Abuses in Southeast Afghanistan," Human Rights Watch, July 2003.

11.   Sevcik, "What Liberation?"

12.   Pamela Constable, "Attacks Beset Afghan Girls' Schools," *Washington Post,* September 8, 2003.

13.   "Afghanistan—Country Reports on Human Rights Practices—2003," U.S. State Department, February 25, 2004.

14.   "Address before a Joint Session of the Congress on the State of the Union," *Public Papers of the Presidents,* January 29, 2002.

15.   Sevcik, "What Liberation?"

16.   "Afghanistan—Country Reports on Human Rights Practices—2003," U.S. State Department.

17.   "Province Bans Female Performers on Airwaves," *Los Angeles Times,* April 18, 2004.

18.   Nicholas Kristof, "Abandoning Afghanistan," *International Herald Tribune,* February 17, 2004.

19.   Kate Allen, "Reality Check," *Guardian* (U.K.), February 25, 2004.

20.   "Afghanistan—Country Reports on Human Rights Practices—2003," U.S. State Department.

21.   Seymour Hersh, "The Other War," *New Yorker,* April 12, 2004.

22.   Ibid.

23.   "Remarks to the Community in Louisville, Kentucky," *Public Papers of the Presidents,* September 5, 2002

24.   Jonathan Stele, "Our Afghan Warlords," *Guardian* (UK), October 6, 2001.

25.   "US 'not to blame' for Afghan raid," BBC News, March 10, 2004.

26.   Afghanistan: Abuses by U.S. Forces," Human Rights Watch, March 8, 2004.

27.   Douglas Jehl and David Rohde, "Afghan Deaths Linked to Unit at Iraq Prison," *New York Times,* May 24, 2004.

28.   "Remarks with President Putin and a Question-and-Answer Session with Crawford High School Students in Crawford," *Public Papers of the Presidents,* November 15, 2001.

29.   Susan Schmidt, "DEA to Bolster Presence Along Mexican Border," *Washington Post,* August 10, 2002.

30.   Ibid.

31.   April Witt, "Afghan Poppies Proliferate," *Washington Post,* July 10, 2003.

32.   Ibid.

33.   "Opium Crop Clouds Afghan Recovery," BBC News, September 22, 2003.

34.   "Afghanistan: Drugs of War," *Guardian* (London), April 8, 2004.

35.   "Remarks at the Marine Corps Air Station in Miramar, California," *Public Papers of the Presidents,* August 14, 2003.

36.   Thomas F. Eagleton, "Kabul Is an Oasis—and a Mirage," *St. Louis Post-Dispatch,* December 4, 2003.

37.   Ann Scott Tyson, "Desertions Deplete Afghan Army," *Christian Science Monitor,* December 17, 2003.

38.   "'Killing You Is a Very Easy Thing For Us': Human Rights Abuses in Southeast Afghanistan," Human Rights Watch, July 2003.

39.   "Remarks to the Troops in Fort Carson, Colorado," *Public Papers of the Presidents,* November 24, 2003.

40.   Pamela Constable, "U.S. Launches New Operation in Afghanistan," *Washington Post,* March 14, 2004.

41. Hamida Ghafour, "Taliban Lurches Back to Power," *Globe and Mail* (Canada), February 28, 2004.
42. Bradley Graham, "NATO Faces Afghan Test, General Warns," *Washington Post,* January 28, 2004.
43. "Afghanistan's Elections Postponed Until September," U.N. Newswire, March 29, 2004.
44. "Statement on Completion of the Kabul-Kandahar Highway," *Public Papers of the Presidents,* December 16, 2003.
45. Kathy Gannon, "Road Rage," *New Yorker,* March 22, 2004.
46. Paul Watson, "Afghanistan Marks a Milepost on Long Road Back to Security," *Los Angeles Times,* December 17, 2003.
47. Pamela Constable, "'A Road to Afghanistan's Future,'" *Washington Post,* December 17, 2003.
48. Matthew Fisher, "Security Tight as New Highway Opens," *Calgary Herald,* December 17, 2003.
49. "Remarks at the Port of Charleston, South Carolina," *Public Papers of the Presidents,* February 5, 2004.
50. "Remarks at a Bush-Cheney Luncheon in New Orleans," *Public Papers of the Presidents,* January 15, 2004.
51. "Letter to the Speaker of the House of Representatives Transmitting a Supplemental Appropriations Request for Ongoing Military and Intelligence Operations in Iraq, Afghanistan, and Elsewhere," *Public Papers of the Presidents,* September 17, 2003.
52. Tim McGirk and Michael Ware, "Remember Afghanistan?" *Time,* February 29, 2004.
53. Amy Waldman, "In Afghanistan, U.S. Envoy Sits In Seat of Power," *New York Times,* April 17, 2004.
54. "Afghanistan—Country Reports on Human Rights Practices—2003," U.S. State Department.
55. Ibid.
56. Ibid.
57. Ibid.
58. Ibid.
59. Ibid.
60. Ibid.
61. "Remarks to the United States Conference of Mayors," *Public Papers of the Presidents,* January 23, 2004.
62. "Remarks in Roswell, New Mexico," *Public Papers of the Presidents,* January 22, 2004.

CHAPTER 16. IRAQ: THE IRON FIST OF FREEDOM

1. "Remarks in Roswell, New Mexico," *Public Papers of the Presidents,* January 26, 2004.
2. Paul Farhi, "Democrats Call Bush's Comedy Skit Tasteless," *Washington Post,* March 26, 2004.
3. "President Says Saddam Hussein Must Leave Iraq Within 48 Hours," White House Office of the Press Secretary, March 17, 2003.
4. Dana Milbank, "U.S. Officials Make It Clear: Exile or War," *Washington Post,* March 17, 2003.
5. Barton Gellman, "Iraq's Arsenal Was Only on Paper," *Washington Post,* January 7, 2004.
6. Dana Milbank, "For Bush, Facts Are Malleable—Presidential Tradition Of Embroidering Key Assertions Continues," *Washington Post,* October 22, 2002.
7. "Transcript of Powell's U.N. Presentation," CNN.com, February 5, 2003.
8. "Remarks Prior to Discussions with President Yoweri Kaguta Museveni of Uganda," *Public Papers of the Presidents,* June 10, 2003.

9.   "Remarks at Northern Virginia Community College in Annandale, Virginia," *Public Papers of the Presidents,* June 17, 2003.
10. "Remarks to the Business Community in Elizabeth, New Jersey," *Public Papers of the Presidents,* June 16, 2003.
11. "The President's Radio Address," *Public Papers of the Presidents,* June 21, 2003.
12. "Remarks at a Reenlistment Ceremony on the 30th Anniversary of the All-Volunteer Force," *Public Papers of the Presidents,* July 1, 2003.
13. "Remarks Announcing the Nomination of Randall Tobias To Be Global AIDS Coordinator and an Exchange With Reporters," *Public Papers of the Presidents,* July 2, 2003.
14. "Interview With CNN International," *Public Papers of the Presidents,* July 3, 2003.
15. Barton Gellman, "Iraq's Arsenal Was Only on Paper," *Washington Post,* January 7, 2004
16. David Rennie, "Critics of US Policy are Racist, Says Rice," *The Telegraph* (U.K.), September 8, 2003.
17. "Remarks to the Greater Manchester Chamber of Commerce in Manchester, New Hampshire," *Public Papers of the Presidents,* October 9, 2003.
18. Gellman, "Iraq's Arsenal Was Only on Paper."
19. "The President's News Conference," *Public Papers of the Presidents,* October 28, 2003.
20. Editorial, "An Unfinished Mission," *Washington Post,* May 4, 2003.
21. "Interview With Sir David Frost of BBC Television," *Public Papers of the Presidents,* November 12, 2003.
22. "CNN Late Edition with Wolf Blitzer," CNN, December 7, 2003.
23. "Excerpts From Interview With President Bush—Part 2," ABC News, December 16, 2003.
24. "Address Before a Joint Session of the Congress on the State of the Union," *Public Papers of the Presidents,* January 20, 2004.
25. Walter Pincus and Dana Priest, "Bush, Aides Ignored CIA Caveats on Iraq," *Washington Post,* February 7, 2004.
26. John Diamond, "Kay: 'We were almost all wrong.'" *USA Today,* January 28,2004.
27. Richard W. Stevenson, "Iraq Illicit Arms Gone Before War, Departing Inspector States," *New York Times,* January 24, 2004.
28. William J. Kole, "Ashcroft: War Justified Even Without WMD," Associated Press, January 26, 2004.
29. David Stout, "Bush Aide Leads White House Offensive on Iraqi Weapons," *New York Times,* January 29, 2004.
30. Dana Priest and Walter Pincus, "Hill Probers Fault Iraq Intelligence," *Washington Post,* January 30, 2004.
31. "Remarks at the Port of Charleston, South Carolina," *Public Papers of the Presidents,* February 5, 2004.
32. Dana Milbank, "President Revises Rationale For War," *Washington Post,* February 8, 2004.
33. "Remarks to Military Personnel at Fort Campbell, Kentucky," *Public Papers of the Presidents,* March 18, 2004.
34. John McCarthy, "Senators Were Told Iraqi Weapons Could Hit U.S.," *Florida Today,* December 15, 2003.
35. Ibid.
36. Dana Priest, "Congressional Oversight of Intelligence Criticized," *Washington Post,* April 27, 2004.
37. "Transcript: Bush Speaks on Iraq Anniversary," Washingtonpost.com, March 19, 2004.
38. "Remarks at a Bush-Cheney Luncheon in Santa Clara, California," *Public Papers of the Presidents,* March 4, 2004.
39. "Poll: Global Distrust Of U.S.," CBS News/Associated Press, March 16, 2004.

NOTES

319

40. Bob Woodward, *Plan of Attack* (New York: Simon and Schuster, 2004), 422–23.
41. "Remarks on the Anniversary of the United States Department of Homeland Security," *Public Papers of the Presidents,* March 2, 2004.
42. "Remarks at a Luncheon for Governor Bob Taft in Columbus," *Public Papers of the Presidents,* May 10, 2002.
43. "Remarks at a Bush-Cheney Reception in Houston, Texas," *Public Papers of the Presidents,* March 8, 2004.
44. "Remarks on the Iraq Threat to America," *Public Papers of the Presidents,* October 7, 2002.
45. "Text of Bush's Press Conference," Washingtonpost.com, April 13, 2004.
46. William Saletan, "Trust, Don't Verify," *Slate,* April 14, 2004.
47. Milbank, "President Revises Rationale For War."
48. Robert Byrd, Congressional Record, March 3, 2004, p. S 2072.
49. "Executive Order 13328—Commission on the Intelligence Capabilities of the United States Regarding Weapons of Mass Destruction," *Public Papers of the Presidents,* February 6, 2004.
50. Sergio Bustos, "McCain Seen as Legitimizing Presence on Panel," *USA Today,* February 6, 2004.
51. Stephen J. Hedges, "Bush Sets Narrow Limits on Inquiry," *Chicago Tribune,* February 8, 2004.
52. "Text of Bush's Press Conference," Washingtonpost.com, April 13, 2004.
53. "Bush Sought 'Way' To Invade Iraq?" CBS News, January 11, 2004.
54. Ibid.
55. Paul Krugman, "Waggy Dog Stories," *New York Times,* May 30, 2003.
56. "Interview With African Print Journalists," *Public Papers of the Presidents,* July 3, 2003.
57. For an extended discussion of sanctions on Iraq, see James Bovard, *Terrorism & Tyranny,* 290–98.
58. Jamie Wilson, "ER, Baghdad-style," *Guardian,* August 11, 2003.
59. "Interview With British Journalists," *Public Papers of the Presidents,* November 14, 2003.
60. "Interview With Abdul Rahman Al-Rashed of Al-Sharq Al-Awsat in London," *Public Papers of the Presidents,* November 19, 2003.
61. "Remarks Announcing the Nomination of Randall Tobias To Be Global AIDS Coordinator and an Exchange With Reporters," *Public Papers of the Presidents,* July 2, 2003.
62. "The President's Radio Address," *Public Papers of the Presidents,* June 21, 2003.
63. "The President's Radio Address," *Public Papers of the Presidents,* September 13, 2003.
64. "The President's Radio Address," *Public Papers of the Presidents,* November 1, 2003.
65. "President's Weekly Radio Address," White House Office of the Press Secretary, April 10, 2004.
66. "Remarks at the Heritage Foundation President's Club Luncheon," *Public Papers of the Presidents,* November 11, 2003.
67. "The President's Radio Address," *Public Papers of the Presidents,* March 6, 2004.
68. Dexter Filkins, "Tough New Tactics by U.S. Tighten Grip on Iraq Towns," *New York Times,* December 7, 2003.
69. Matthew Rosenberg, "U.S. May Study Israel Occupation Tactics," Associated Press, September 18, 2003.
70. Filkins, "Tough New Tactics by U.S."
71. Ibid.
72. Ibid.
73. Ibid.
74. Ibid.
75. Ibid.

76. "Transcript: Bush Speaks on Iraq Anniversary," Washingtonpost.com, March 19, 2004.
77. Jeffrey Gettleman, "As U.S. Detains Iraqis, Families Plead for News," *New York Times,* March 7, 2004.
78. Ibid.
79. Ibid.
80. Ibid.
81. Ibid.
82. "Address to the Nation on Iraq from the U.S.S. Abraham Lincoln," *Public Papers of the Presidents,* May 1, 2003.
83. P. Mitchell Prothero, "Fallujah Quiet as It Awaits U.S. Response," United Press International, April 2, 2004.
84. Juan Cole, "US-Appointed Iraqi Government Close to Collapse?" Antiwar.com, April 10, 2004.
85. Paul Krugman, "Snares and Delusions," *New York Times,* April 13, 2004.
86. Prothero, "Fallujah Quiet as It Awaits U.S. response."
87. Jo Wilding, "US Snipers Shoot Anything that Moves," *Guardian* (UK), April 18, 2004.
88. "U.S. to Insurgents: 'Submit or Die,'" Associated Press, April 11, 2004.
89. Arthur Neslen, "Reality Television," *Guardian* (UK), April 21, 2004.
90. Thomas E. Ricks, "Dissension Grows In Senior Ranks On War Strategy," *Washington Post,* May 9, 2004.
91. Ibid.
92. Quoted in Maureen Dowd, "World of Hurt," New York Times, May 9, 2004. The phrase comes from Rep. Tom Dole (R-Okla.).
93. "Statement on United Nations International Day in Support of Victims of Torture," *Public Papers of the Presidents,* June 26, 2003.
94. William Saletan, "Rape Rooms: A Chronology," *Slate,* May 5, 2004.
95. Ibid.
96. "Seymour M. Hersh, "Torture at Abu Ghraib," *The New Yorker,* April 30, 2004.
97. "President's Radio Address," White House Office of the Press Secretary, May 1, 2004.
98. "President's Radio Address," White House Office of the Press Secretary, May 8, 2004.
99. John Barry, Michael Hirsh and Michael Isikoff, "The Roots of Torture," *Newsweek,* May 24, 2004.
100. Ibid.
101. Douglas Jehl, Steven Lee Myers, and Eric Schmitt, "G.I.'s Prison Abuse More Widespread, Says Army Survey," *New York Times,* May 26, 2004.
102. Barry, et al. "The Roots of Turture."
103. Ibid.
104. "Interview with Alhurra Television," *Public Papers of the Presidents,* May 5, 2004.
105. "Bush's Remarks on Iraq at the Army War College," Washingtonpost.com, May 24, 2004.
106. Miles Moffeit, "Wider Iraqi abuse shown," *Denver Post,* May 26, 2004.
107. Ibid.
108. Todd Richissin, "Soldiers' Warnings Ignored," *Baltimore Sun,* May 9, 2004.
109. Dowd, "World of Hurt."
110. "Senator 'Outraged by Outrage' at Prison Abuse," Reuters News Service, May 11, 2004.
111. Jennifer C. Kerr, "Pentagon to Give Congress Abuse Photos," Associated Press, May 9, 2004.
112. Anne E. Kornblut and Bryan Bender, "Pentagon to Review Photo Ban," *Boston Globe,* April 24, 2004.
113. Jonathan Alter, "Yes, We Can Handle the Truth," *Newsweek,* May 3, 2004.
114. Ibid.
115. Frank Rich, "The Spoils of War Coverage," *New York Times,* April 13, 2003.
116. Maureen Dowd, "Wolfie's Fuzzy Math," *New York Times,* May 2, 2004.

117. Ibid.
118. "Interview with Mouafac Harb of the Middle East Television Network," *Public Papers of the Presidents,* January 29, 2004.
119. "Remarks on Efforts To Globally Promote Women's Human Rights," *Public Papers of the Presidents,* March 12, 2004.
120. Ibid.
121. "Remarks at the 'Churchill and the Great Republic' Exhibit," *Public Papers of the Presidents,* February 4, 2004.
122. "The President's News Conference," *Public Papers of the Presidents,* March 6, 2003.
123. Dana Milbank and Robin Wright, "Off the Mark on Cost of War, Reception by Iraqis," *Washington Post,* March 19, 2004.
124. Ibid.
125. Ibid.
126. Ibid.
127. "Text of Bush's Press Conference," Washingtonpost.com, April 13, 2004.
128. "DoD News: Deputy Secretary Wolfowitz Stakeout Following Operations and Intelligence Brief," Department of Defense, Office of Public Affairs, April 2, 2004.
129. Joseph Stromberg, April 28, 2004 posting at http://blog.lewrockwell.com/lewrw/archives/2004_04.html
130. Arshad Mohammed, "Iraq Sovereignty Handover Seen as Largely Symbolic," Reuters News Service, April 14, 2004.
131. http://www.juancole.com, April 10, 2004.
132. Eric Rosenberg, "Registering Women for Draft is Posed," *Arizona Daily Star* (Tuscon), May 2, 2004.
133. "White House Pressed on Military Draft," Washingtonpost.com, April 23, 2004.
134. Rosenberg, "Registering Women for Draft."
135. "Text of Bush's Press Conference," Washingtonpost.com, April 13, 2004.
136. Ibid.
137. Ibid.
138. See Bovard, *Terrorism & Tyranny,* 257–88.
139. Thomas E. Ricks, "Study Published by Army Criticizes War on Terror's Scope," *Washington Post,* January 12, 2004.
140. Jeffrey Record, "Bounding the Global War on Terrorism," U.S. Army War College, December 2003.
141. Ibid.
142. Ricks, "Study Published by Army."
143. "Remarks in Roswell, New Mexico," *Public Papers of the Presidents,* January 22, 2004.
144. Ibid.
145. "Text of Bush's Press Conference," Washingtonpost.com, April 13, 2004.

CHAPTER 17. CONCLUSION

1. "Remarks at the National Prayer Breakfast," *Public Papers of the Presidents,* February 5, 2004.
2. "Remarks Prior to a Meeting With Virginia Gubernatorial Candidate Mark Earley and an Exchange With Reporters," *Public Papers of the Presidents,* July 26, 2001.
3. Gene Lyons, "For Bush Administration Powers Increasing," *Arkansas Democrat-Gazette,* November 28, 2001.
4. Bob Woodward, *Bush at War* (New York: Simon and Schuster, 2003), p. 145–46.
5. "Remarks at the Dedication of the Oak Cliff Bible Fellowship Youth Education Center in Dallas, Texas," *Public Papers of the Presidents,* October 29, 2003.

6. "Text of Bush's Press Conference," Washingtonpost.com, April 13, 2004.
7. William Hamilton, "Bush Began to Plan War Three Months After 9/11," *Washington Post,* April 17, 2004.
8. Larry Fine, "Rumsfeld Says 'War on Terror' Just Beginning," Reuters News Service, May 29, 2004.]

Index